D1244387

POVERTY, U. S. A.

THE HISTORICAL RECORD

ADVISORY EDITOR: David J. Rothman

Professor of History, Columbia University

THE STANDARD OF LIVING
AMONG WORKINGMEN'S FAMILIES
IN NEW YORK CITY

ROBERT COIT CHAPIN

Arno Press & The New York Times
NEW YORK   1971

Reprint Edition 1971 by Arno Press Inc.

Reprinted from a copy in
The University of Illinois Library

LC# 72—137159
ISBN 0—405—03097—5

POVERTY, U.S.A.: THE HISTORICAL RECORD
ISBN for complete set: 0-405-03090-8

Manufactured in the United States of America

RUSSELL SAGE
FOUNDATION

THE STANDARD OF LIVING AMONG WORKINGMEN'S FAMILIES IN NEW YORK CITY

BY

ROBERT COIT CHAPIN, Ph.D.

HORACE WHITE PROFESSOR OF ECONOMICS AND FINANCE IN BELOIT
COLLEGE, WISCONSIN

NEW YORK
CHARITIES PUBLICATION
COMMITTEE . . MCMIX

PRESS OF
WM. F. FELL COMPANY
PHILADELPHIA

Table of Contents

List of Diagrams

v

List of Tables

vi

LIST OF TABLES

viii

ix

LIST OF TABLES

LIST OF TABLES

Introductory Statement

At the seventh New York State Conference of Charities and Correction, held in Rochester in November, 1906, in accordance with a resolution introduced by Mr. Frank Tucker, of New York, a committee was appointed to report to the Conference the following year the essentials and the cost of a normal standard of living in the cities and towns of the state. This action was the outcome of a spirited discussion of the subject by a committee appointed the previous year.

The Committee as finally constituted consisted of the following persons: Lee K. Frankel, Chairman, New York; Rev. Adolph Guttmann, Syracuse; Edward T. Devine, New York; Cyrus L. Sulzberger, New York; Wm. H. Allen, New York; Abram J. Katz, Rochester; Rt. Rev. David H. Greer, New York; Rev. Wm. J. White, Brooklyn; Homer Folks, New York; Wm. Drescher, Rochester; John J. Fitzgerald, New York; Rt. Rev. Thos. F. Hickey, Rochester; Walter E. Kruesi, New York; Mrs. Wm. Einstein, New York; Wm. Guggenheim, New York; Frank Tucker, New York.

The Committee, at its first meeting, January 21, 1907, elected Robert C. Chapin secretary, and appointed a committee on schedule, consisting of Messrs. Frankel, Tucker, and Chapin. The schedule was prepared, and early in April was ready for distribution among volunteers. Over 400 schedules were put into the hands of volunteers, and a number of extremely valuable schedules were returned by them, but it became evident by the first of June that, in view of the fulness of the schedule and the pressure of many duties upon these willing workers, the number to be expected from such sources would be small. In the end only 57 family reports were received from volunteers. It appeared necessary, therefore, if any considerable number of family reports were to be obtained, to hire visitors who should give their whole time to securing the desired information. The funds at the disposal of the Committee, however, did not suffice for any such

xiii

expenditure. At this juncture, the trustees of the Russell Sage Foundation made a generous appropriation for the prosecution of the investigation, which enabled the Committee to employ a number of visitors, who were at work from the middle of June until the end of August. At the same time an effort was made to enlist the co-operation of the labor unions, and some very interesting schedules were received from them.

Altogether, some 80 different persons were employed, and by the time that the canvass was closed, 642 schedules had been secured from all sources. The compilation of the data thus gathered was carried as far as was practicable before the meeting of the State Conference in Albany, November 12–14, and the results summarized by the Chairman, Dr. Frankel, were presented in a preliminary report at that time. This report is reprinted as Appendix II, page 263, in this volume, and the report of Mr. Frank Tucker, chairman of the committee of the previous year, may be found in Appendix I, page 253.

The original schedules and tables were then re-studied from the beginning by the secretary, and the detailed analysis that follows was prepared. The completed work has been accepted by the Faculty of Political Science in Columbia University in satisfaction of the requirement of a thesis for the degree of doctor of philosophy.

The account of Workingmen's Budgets in Statistical Literature, prepared in connection with the drafting of the schedule, is, at the suggestion of those whose co-operation has made possible the publication of this volume, prefixed to the report of the New York investigation. It is hoped that this sketch of the method used by previous investigators may prove suggestive to those who are engaged in such studies to-day.

To the account of the investigation in New York City is appended a summary of the returns received by the Committee from nine other cities and towns in the State, gathered in the summer of 1907. In 1908 the Committee, with Mr. Frederic Almy of Buffalo as Chairman, organized an investigation in Buffalo, covering one hundred families, under the direction of Mr. John R. Howard, Jr. Mr. Howard's report of the results of this inquiry, which is also included in the present volume

(Appendix V, p. 307), affords an instructive comparison of conditions in Buffalo and in New York.

The secretary desires to make grateful acknowledgment of the assistance and encouragement which he has received from the members of the Committee, from his instructors in Columbia University, and from other friends. To the wise generalship of the Chairman, Dr. Lee K. Frankel, and to the expert skill in schedule-making of Mr. Frank Tucker, are largely due whatever results have been attained. The interest of Miss Lilian Brandt was manifested in very helpful counsel in the initial stages of the investigation, and in the preparation of the diagrams that illustrate its conclusions. The patient ingenuity of Dr. Rasum Brodsky has been devoted to the elaboration of the statistical details.

At every point the undertaking has had the active support of Professor Edward T. Devine, and the secretary desires to express his appreciation, both of the importance of Professor Devine's initiative and advice in all that has been done, and especially of the aid and support that has been so freely given in personal relations.

ROBERT COIT CHAPIN.

BELOIT COLLEGE, January, 1909.

Workingmen's Budgets in Statistical Literature

Workingmen's Budgets in Statistical Literature*

The object of collecting, comparing, and combining working-men's budgets is to get a reliable representation of the standard of living, first, absolutely, for a given time, place and class of laborers; second, relatively, in comparison with the standard of different times, places and classes of men.

Three general methods have been employed to accomplish these objects which, following the historical order of their appearance, are:

I. Estimates, for a family in a given status, of the income, and of the kind, amount and cost of the principal items of expenditure.

II. Reports of the actual income and expenditure, more or less fully itemized, of a single family taken as representing the class in which it is found. These reports are obtained either by the independent testimony of the family, by personal inquiry made by a reporter, or by inducing the members of the family to make out and keep in an account-book a record of the daily expenditures.

III. The combination of reports of individual families obtained by either of the preceding methods. The use of the average has been the expedient most frequently employed in effecting the combinations and comparisons.

During the seventeenth and eighteenth centuries the first method only was employed; in the nineteenth century, the second method was developed by Le Play and the third by Engel. When a single family or a small number of families are studied in great detail the methods may be described as intensive; when a large number of family reports are combined, with little attention to detail, the method is extensive.

I. ESTIMATES.—The earliest recorded instance, perhaps, of an estimate of the laborer's cost of living is to be found in the writings of Sir William Petty (circa 1672). He undertakes such an

---

* In Appendix VIII (page 353) will be found a partial bibliography, containing the full titles of the books mentioned in this essay, and other works on the general subject of workingmen's budgets and the standard of living.

3

estimate both for England and for Ireland. For Ireland he comes to the problem in accounting for the smallness of Ireland's foreign trade. ("Anatomy of Ireland," 1672, Ch. XI.) This trade is small, he says, because the standard of living of the mass of the people is so low. They live in "such cottages as themselves can make in three or four days," and provide their own food and clothing. He estimates the money value of the victuals of a man, wife and three children at 3s. 6d. a week, or 1d. per diem per capita, and "two-sevenths of the expense of the people for food is for tobacco" (*i. e.*, two-sevenths of the cash outlay for food). He estimates the clothing of a man at 30 shillings a year, of children under 16 at 15 shillings on the average. The house is "not worth 5 shillings the building." "Fuel costs nothing but fetching." The whole annual expense of a family of six averages 52 shillings per year.

As to earnings, he calculates that the annual value of all the land of Ireland is about 1,000,000 pounds; the annual value of the labor is three times as much, or 3,000,000 pounds, and this sum is earned by about 750,000 of the 1,100,000 inhabitants. Each therefore earns $\frac{3000000}{750000}$, or 4 pounds a year, if all work, or 8 pounds if half work.

Petty's estimates for England occur in his "Political Arithmetic" (1671–76, Ch. VII), in connection with an argument to show that the country could stand a tax of one-tenth of the whole expense of the people. He proceeds to estimate the yield of such a tax by estimating the average expense of the laborer in the following naïve fashion: The laborer earns, without board, 4s. per week; with board, 2s. per week. The value of his food, therefore, is 4s. minus 2s., which equals 2s. per week, or £5 4s. per year. The expense of clothes cannot be less than the wage of the poorest maid-servant in the country—30s. per year. (The maid is given board and lodging, and must provide clothing out of her wages.) All other necessaries cannot be less than 6s. more, making a total for the year of 7 pounds.* A tax, now, of one-tenth of the

---

* Recapitulation:

	£.	s.	d.
Food per week, 2s.; per year	5	4	0
Clothing	1	10	0
All other		6	0
	7	0	0

annual expense of 10,000,000 subjects would yield 7,000,000 pounds, or enough to pay for 100,000 foot, 20,000 horse and 40,000 men at sea. The people could surely bear this increase. They would only have to work one-twentieth harder, and eat one-twentieth less than before.*

This will suffice for an example of the method of estimating costs of living. Stephan Bauer cites such estimates (Conrad: Handwörterbuch 5: 318) by Vanderlint (about 1735), arguing prices too high; by Massie (1756), arguing against a proposed house-tax; by Cantillon (about 1750, in the lost chapters of his work), giving an estimate of the subsistence-minimum in detail. The method has survived to the present day. Edward Atkinson, for instance, submitted to the Aldrich Committee, in 1892, the following estimate of the expenditures of a laborer's family having an income of $500:

	ANNUAL EXPENDITURE.	PER CENT.
Food	$250	50
Clothing	100	20
Rent	100	20
Other	50	10
	$500	100

Clothing was subdivided as follows: woolen, 45 per cent.; cotton, 35 per cent.; miscellaneous, 20 per cent. (Aldrich Report I; liv, lv.)

The value of estimates depends upon the skill with which they are made. If more exact data are not to be had they are often the only available resource. Estimates like those cited above for a hypothetical family, should be distinguished from estimates made for a given family on the basis of a more or less careful inquiry into particulars. Such an estimate is often the only way in which the second method, the type-study, can be applied.

II. STATEMENTS OF ACTUAL FAMILY RECEIPTS AND EXPENDITURES, UNCOMBINED.—The distressing condition of the laborers of England at the end of the eighteenth century gave rise to much discussion of wages, prices and the poor laws. Two works of this period are notable for their attempts to get at the exact facts by

* Petty anticipates the phrase "standard of living" in the following: The expense of the laborer as he has calculated it, he says, "may well enough stand for the standard of expense of the whole mass of mankind." Economic writings of Sir William Petty. Hull's edition, 1 : 306.

means of reports of actual family budgets. These books are Davies' "Case of the Laborers in Husbandry" (1795), and the better known "State of the Poor," by Sir Frederick Morton Eden (1797).

Davies was a clergyman in Barkham, Berkshire, and the purpose of his book is indicated by its motto: "The labourer is worthy of his hire." Davies collected accounts on his visits to families of his parish in the spring of 1787. Six of them he printed and sent around to friends throughout England, asking them to get similar accounts in their own localities. These friends for the most part were clergymen and country squires. Their returns were printed in full in the appendix, which contains, with Davies' own contributions, accounts from 15 counties in England, 2 in Wales and 3 in Scotland—133 family budgets in all. The method employed was to set down the weekly costs of bread and other items of food expenditure, with candles and thread. This was added together (8s. 11d. for Davies' first family) and multiplied by 52 (£23 4s. 9d.). To this was added a fixed annual sum covering rent, clothing, fuel, expenses occasioned by sickness, deaths and births,— estimated in 1787 at 6 pounds (later 7 pounds) for a family of five.

The earnings per week of father, mother and children were set down and multiplied by 52. In balancing, a deficit appeared in practically every case, even where poor-relief was figured in. It is interesting to note in passing that Davies proposed to have the justices fix a minimum wage (Part III, Section V), and that one of his correspondents complained of the exploitation of the poor by "the harpy claws of pettifogging lawyers," by the short weights of retailers, and by the small loaves of the sellers of bread (p. 163).

Of greater scientific importance is Eden's "State of the Poor."* Besides getting information through clergymen and other friends, he sent out "a competent person" and furnished him with an exhaustive *questionnaire*. His question-sheet included these questions: "Usual diet of labourers"; "Earnings and expenses of labourer's family for a year; distinguishing the number and ages of family; and price and quantity of their articles of consumption." This "faithful and intelligent person" he kept in the field for more than a year, going the round of the English counties. The budgets,

---

* Marx says that Eden is the only disciple of Adam Smith that produced a work of importance. (Capital: English Translation, 2 : 269.)

from whatever source derived, are published, 54 of them collectively, in Appendix XII, Vol. III of Eden's work, and perhaps as many more sandwiched in between the workhouse accounts and the "parochial reports" (Volumes II and III). Engel found 73 of them complete enough to tabulate and average. The method is the same as Davies': a weekly statement of earnings, multiplied by 52; a weekly statement of cost of food, multiplied by 52; an annual statement for other items of expenditure, but figured independently for each family. Fifty-seven of the 73 summarized by Engel reported a deficiency; 19 spent more for food than their total earnings. The method of calculating food-expenditures may explain this result, although food-prices in 1795 were exceptionally high.*

The difficulties of collecting information regarding family expenditures are well stated by Eden. "It must be confessed that the whole annual earnings of the laborer can seldom be ascertained with great precision. Some men are so habitually careless that they are totally unable to give any satisfactory information; others, who could give tolerable answers, think that inquiries concerning them can have no important object in view, and are therefore inaccurate; and a third class (which is by far the most numerous), are so apprehensive that the ultimate object of questioning them is to effect a reduction in wages, or something equally disagreeable, that they are unchangeably mysterious and insincere."†

No marked improvement on Eden's method appears until the second quarter of the nineteenth century. Then we have the remarkable work of Le Play,‡ who carried the intensive study of family accounts to the highest degree of excellence. From 1829 to 1856 he spent a large portion of his vacations (he was professor of metallurgy in Paris), in traveling through the countries

---

* In Vol. III: 711, is a report from Epsom, Surrey, which gives the budget for a gardener, with income 45 to 50 pounds; expenditures £75 1s. 8d. But there was no such deficiency in fact. The writer says that he has tried to make out similar accounts for several other laborers, but found that they always appeared to spend more than they either got or had, and so he "suspected that their statements were inaccurate."

† "State of the Poor." Preface, I : xxvi.

‡ Le Play was born in 1806, and died in 1882. A good account of his work, by Henry Higgs, may be found in the "Quarterly Journal of Economics," IV : 408.

of Europe, studying the condition of workingmen's families. His method was to make in each place careful inquiry of clergy, teachers, and others until he found what was considered to be a really typical family, whether a Sheffield cutler or a Dutch fisherman, and then he would arrange to live with the family for some weeks if necessary, observing their whole manner of living. He would ask questions, make notes of what he saw and heard, and when he had gathered his material, would prepare a family monograph, containing in fifteen or twenty octavo pages a photographic picture of the given family group. In 1855 he published thirty-six of these monographs in three volumes, entitled "Les Ouvriers Européens." He subsequently (1877–1879) added two volumes of monographs and one introductory volume on method. He made studies during the long period of his activity of some 300 families, but carried only fifty-seven of them to the point where he was willing to have them published. The schedule he employed displays the thoroughness of his method. The only criticisms that can fairly be made are: first, that the families are not necessarily typical; second, that the details are carried to an illusive degree of over-refinement. For instance, the festival-clothes of his Dutch family are valued, and one one-hundredth of the value is set down in the annual budget, implying that they will last one hundred years. Some hint of his tact in winning the confidence of the families that he approached may be gained from his statement of the expedients which he used for this purpose. Le Play says* that he always had the good-will, even affection, of families investigated, and thinks that it was due to the method; but he observed the following expedients for gaining the good-will of the families:

"Not to be abrupt in pushing inquiries,—an introduction from a well-chosen source helps in abridging the preliminaries; to secure the confidence and sympathy of the family by explaining the public utility of the inquiry, and the disinterestedness of the observer; to sustain the attention of the people by interesting conversation; to indemnify them in money for time taken by the investigation; to praise with discrimination the good qualities of

* "La Methode Sociale," 1879, pp. 222, 3. (Vol. i of "Les Ouvriers Européens," Edition of 1879.)

8

different members; to make judicious distribution of little gifts to all."*

The work of Le Play was continued by his followers in a serial publication entitled "Les Ouvriers des Deux Mondes." The volumes are made up of family monographs prepared on the same plan as those of Le Play himself. Ninety-one of these monographs are included in the ten volumes of the series published. The last volume, the tenth, appeared in 1899.

III. THE COMBINATION OF REPORTS OF INDIVIDUAL FAMILIES. —The transition to the use of the average in combining workingmen's budgets passed through three stages: First, the Brussels Statistical Congress, in 1853; second, the preliminary inquiry in Belgium under direction of Ducpétiaux, in 1853; third, the elaboration of the data of Ducpétiaux and Le Play by Ernst Engel, in 1857. Of the first and second, Engel gives the following account:†

Fletcher, the secretary of the London Exhibition of 1851, persuaded Visschers, the Belgian Minister, to include workingmen's budgets in the program of the International Statistical Congress to be held in Brussels. Ducpétiaux, the Belgian inspector of prisons and charitable institutions, co-operated, although Fletcher, and also G. R. Porter, of England, died before the Congress met. The Belgian Statistical Bureau, with Quetelet at its head, approved the plan of Ducpétiaux and Visschers for an immediate budget inquiry, so as to have something to lay before the Congress. About one thousand household accounts were collected. Those from two provinces were worked up by the Bureau and laid before the Congress, and final publication was made in 1855. In this inquiry three classes were distinguished:

First, dependent,—income supplemented by public relief.

Second, poor,—self-supporting ordinarily, but saving nothing.

Third, comfortably off,—never receiving public aid, and able to lay up something for old age. "Typical" families were sought; i. e., having 2 parents, and 4 children, ages 16, 12, 6 and 2.‡

Visschers reported to the Congress a scheme for household

* A translation of one of Le Play's monographs may be found in Appendix VII, page 326.

† "Lebenskosten Belgischer Arbeiterfamilien," 16.

‡ Engel remarks on the folly of this limitation to the "typical" family, claiming that it was better to work out the "quets."

reports which was adopted without change. In the debate, in answer to Horace Say, Visschers said that "Laissez-faire, laissez-passer" should not justify "laissez-souffrir, laissez-mourir." The schedule thus adopted was as follows:

I. Income.
 A. Salary and wages of father, mother, children, with record of hours of work, work-days and holidays for each member of the family.
 B. Other sources of income:
  Produce of garden.
  Returns for house or land rented.
  Returns from raising of live stock.
  Share in commercial privileges.
  Pensions—income from investments.
  Miscellaneous income.
  Accidental income.
II. Expenditures (throughout with note of quantity and value or price).
 A. For physical necessaries (Depenses de l'ordre physique et materiel).
  (a) Food (20 specifications, including wine, etc., at home).
  (b) Dwelling (with number of rooms).
  (c) Clothing, for adults and for children.
  (d) Beds.
  (e, f) Heat, Light.
  (g) Washing.
  (h) Care of health.
  (i) Care in disease.
  (k) Dwelling: maintenance and repair; fire insurance.
  (l) Purchase and repair of furniture.
  (m) Taxes.
  (n) Postage, etc.
  (o, p) Expenditure for carrying on of trade (excluding raw materials); for carrying on garden, etc.
 B. For cultural purposes (Depenses de l'ordre religieux, moral et intellectuel).
  (a) Church.
  (b) School-fees.
  (c) Apprenticeship charges.
  (d) Books, pictures, etc.
  (e) Dues to societies for religious, moral and educational purposes.
  (f) Dues to societies for sick-relief, burial-expenses, etc.
  (g) Savings deposits.

10

C. Luxuries and extravagances (Depenses de luxe ou resultant de l'imprevoyance).
   (*a*) Visits to cafés, ale houses, etc.
   (*b*) Tobacco.
   (*c*) Gambling and lotteries.
   (*d*) Ornaments (personal).
   (*e, f*) Theater,—Public festivities.
   (*g*) Interest on loans and pawnbroker's charges.

In the final publication of his returns in 1855 ("Budgets Économiques") Ducpétiaux gives the data gathered in 1853 from 199 families in accordance with the scheme laid before the Congress. He did not combine the returns by averages,* but he did undertake to calculate a minimum by a comparison of his data with the standard allowances for the food of soldiers, sailors and prisoners. He concluded that the laborers were less well-fed than the prisoners, and in general that unless wages rose or the prices of provisions went down, there must be an increase in pauperism and crime, and in the death-rate.

Ernst Engel (1821–1896) had, as a student, accompanied Le Play on some of his excursions, and recalled them in 1895 as red-letter days ("Lichtpunkte meines Lebens"). He was, in 1850, placed at the head of the Saxon Statistical Bureau, and in 1857, in an effort to estimate the balance between production and consumption in the kingdom, made a thorough statistical elaboration of the figures of Ducpétiaux and Le Play.† Taking first the Belgian budgets, he (1) grouped the expenditures under 9 heads, instead of the more extended order of Ducpétiaux; (2) averaged the family total under each of the 9 heads for each of the 3 income-classes, and for all classes combined; (3) calculated the expenditure per capita for each of the 9 headings of expenditure for the Belgian families, and also for the 36 families whose budgets had been published by Le Play; (4) calculated the percentage of total expenditures which was spent for each of the 9 heads, for the Belgian families and for Le Play's; (5) deduced his two laws: First, The smaller the income

* The figures in the budgets are not combined in general averages, save that the local authorities in two or three provinces returned the average for a number of families in place of individual returns. Wages are averaged in the comparison of laborers' and prisoners' fare, but not the details of expenditure.

† From this he argued that the poorer people paid the greater share of the indirect taxes, which fell largely upon articles of food and drink.

the greater the proportionate expenditure for food; second, The proportion expended for food is a sure index of the material prosperity of a people. He then (6) estimated for a family in Saxony in each class, the percentage-expenditure under each of his nine heads; (7) tabulated the per cent. of the income paid for food in a table of incomes rising, by stages of 100 francs, from 200 francs, with 72.96 per cent. for food, to 3000 francs, with 56.90 per cent. for food;* (8) derived from the table for families of the third class, having incomes of 1200 to 1300 francs, a scale for measuring miserliness, parsimony, economy and ex- travagance in the expenditures of a given family; (9) applied his estimate for typical Saxon families (see (6) above) to the 1,894,431 inhabitants of Saxony, reported by the Census of 1849, and thus reached the lump sum of 94,721,500 thalers as the total value of the consumption of all families; (10) estimated from the statistics of occupations the numbers engaged in producing the com- modities in each of his 9 expenditure-groups, and calculated whether the production per individual was equal to the consumption.

The subjoined table shows the percentages as calculated by Engel. It is noteworthy that these Saxon percentages, which are the basis of the deductions familiar under the name of Engel's Law, are based, not on an original collection of Saxon budgets, but on estimates obtained from the study of Ducpétiaux's Belgian budgets.

BELGIUM

	AVERAGE INCOME.			
	565 fr.	796 fr.	1197 fr.	(All Families.) 856.5 fr.
	Per Cent.	Per Cent.	Per Cent.	Per Cent.
Food............................	70.8	67.4	62.0	65.8
Clothing........................	11.7	13.2	14.0	13.2
Shelter.........................	8.7	8.3	9.0	8.7
Heat and light.................	5.6	5.5	5.4	5.5
Utensils........................	0.6	1.2	2.3	1.6
Education.......................	0.4	1.0	1.2	1.0
Public security.................	0.2	0.5	0.9	0.6
Health..........................	1.7	2.8	4.3	3.2
Personal service................	0.2	0.2	0.4	0.3

* Zeitschrift des statistischen Bureaus des königlichen Sächsischen Ministeriums des Innern, 1857: 153 ff.

SAXONY

	AVERAGE INCOME.		
	Under **1200** fr. (Working Class.)	**1200** to **3000** fr. (Middle Class.)	Over **3000** fr. (Well-to-do.)
	Per Cent.	Per Cent.	Per Cent.
Food	62	55	50
Clothing	16	18	18
Shelter	12	12	12
Heat and light	5	5	5
Utensils	2		
Education	2	3.5	5.5
Public security	1	2	3
Health	1	2	3
Personal service	1	2.5	3.5

This shows what can be done by the use of the statistical method. For the sake of showing the further developments in the application of the method, let us pass to the last work of Engel's life, "Die Lebenskosten Belgischer Arbeiterfamilien" (1895), where he works over once more Ducpétiaux's and Le Play's figures of 1855, and also elaborates the returns from a Belgian inquiry of 1891 and compares them with the earlier returns. What is new in this second treatment is:

1. The use of his unit of comparison, the "quet," for families of varying composition (see later).
2. The arrangement, in terms of this unit, of the averages of the 5 income-groups so as to show:
   (1) Value of the unit in marks, in 1853 and 1891.
   (2) Ratios of increase in different items of 1891 over 1853.
   (3) Variations in percentages spent on the separate items in the various groups.
3. Calculations of food-consumption with reference to dietary requirements on the basis of Voit's tables. In this connection occurs a comparison of city and country budgets and a study of Ducpétiaux's estimate, on prisoners'-fare basis, of the minimum.

The results of the comparison of the Belgian investigations of 1853 and 1891 showed an increase of 198 per cent. per "quet" in expenditure for food, and that there was no lessening in the percentage of the total expenditures that was spent for the satisfaction of physical wants. The figures of the comparison are as follows:

| | FRANCS PER QUET. | | PER CENT. | | RATIO OF INCREASE. |
	1853	1891	1853	1891	
Subsistence...........	49.27	97.55	93.80	96.30	1.98
Food................	34.00	16.00	64.90	65.66	1.96
Clothing.............	7.77	14.78	14.80	14.57	1.90
Housing.............	3.96	9.77	7.55	9.64	2.47
Fuel and light........	2.94	5.33	5.60	5.25	1.81
Health..............	0.52	1.24	0.99	1.22	2.38

The most original proposition contained in this final work of Engel's was his solution of the difficulty involved in comparing families differing in the number, age, and sex of their members. Before speaking of Engel's solution it may be well to note some other ways of meeting the difficulty that have been proposed.

The simplest method is to reduce everything to a per capita basis, dividing expenditures for each family by the number of persons in the family. This neglects the differences in consumption that go with differences in age. A second solution is to include in the investigation only families exactly alike as to composition. Ducpétiaux proposed to use only families consisting of father, mother, and 4 children, aged respectively 16, 12, 6 and 2. Col. Carroll D. Wright defined a "normal" family in the reports of the United States Bureau of Labor as one consisting of father, mother, not over 5 children, none over 14, and no other members. The difficulty with Ducpétiaux's method is that it restricts so much the number of families available that it increases greatly the task of gathering the returns. The more flexible limits of the United States Bureau of Labor diminish the difficulty but do not remove it. Of the 25,440 families included in the annual report of 1903, only 11,156, or less than half, were "normal."

A third method, applied by the earlier investigators, is to

apply the rule of thumb, and count 2 children as equal to 1 adult. A fourth method is to calculate the relative consuming-power of persons of different ages and sexes, and evaluate each family in terms of a common unit, usually the demands of 1 adult man. This has been undertaken with reference to food by most of those who have gone into the study of dietetics. The results reached by various authorities may be compared in the following table:

EQUIVALENCE OF DIETARY REQUIREMENTS, STATED IN PER-
CENTAGES OF THE REQUIREMENTS OF AN ADULT MAN

	FOLEY.*	ATWATER.†	U. S. BUREAU OF LABOR.‡	ROWNTREE.§	ENGEL. ‖
Father	100	100	100	100	100
Mother	80 to 60	80	90	80	86
Child 11 to 14 years	60	70 to 80	90	60	70
Child 7 to 10 years	..	50 to 60	75	50	57
Child 4 to 6 years	40	40	40	40	42
Child under 3 years	20	30	30	30	37

Engel's proposition was an elaboration of this fourth method. On the basis of a comparison of the average weight per centimeter of height, for a large number of persons at different ages, he concluded that a man of 25 or over required 3.5 times as much as a child in its first year, and that for each intermediate year between the first and the twenty-fifth, there was an increase of one-tenth over the demands for the first year. That is, a child of 10 would consume twice as much as a child under a year old; a child of 15, 2.5 times as much, and so on. A woman reaches her full measure at 20, when she needs 3 units. These units Engel named, after the famous Quetelet, "quets." The consumption of every family could be reduced to a common denominator by

* In Davies' "Case of the Laborers in Husbandry," 1795, p. 161.

† U. S. Dept. of Agriculture, Farmer's Bulletin No. 142, p. 33.

‡ Eighteenth Annual Report (1903), p. 19.

§ "Poverty," p. 229.

‖ "Lebenskosten Belgischer Arbeiterfamilien," p. 5, the "quets" being reduced for comparison to percentages of the adult's 3.5 quets.

dividing the expenditures in a given case by the number of "quets." *

Engel's methods have been applied on an extensive scale by the American state and national Labor Bureaus. Carroll D. Wright, in the Massachusetts Labor Report for 1875, published the budgets of 397 families and classified the returns according to a large number of categories. His method of gathering returns was to send enumerators supplied with a rather brief schedule to the factory towns to accost the men as they left the factory, and ask one after another until one was found who was willing to furnish the information. The workman was visited in his home, and the schedule was filled out on the basis of his recollections and such written memoranda as he might have.

Substantially this method has been employed in many state compilations, and in those of the United States Labor Bureau, of which Colonel Wright became head in 1888. In 1890, this bureau gathered budgets from 2490 families of men engaged in the

* The following table exhibits the number of quets and the weight in grammes per centimeter, corresponding to the several ages. (Lebenskosten Belgischer Arbeiterfamilien, s, 5.)

AGE.	UNITS (QUETS).	WEIGHT IN GRAMMES PER CENTIMETER.
0	1.0	62.3
1	1.1	132.1
2	1.2	139.8
3	1.3	140.7
4	1.4	149.5
5	1.5	157.7
6	1.6	160.6
7	1.7	168.5
8	1.8	174.2
9	1.9	181.2
10	2.0	187.6
11	2.1	198.8
12	2.2	210.0
13	2.3	233.1
14	2.4	253.2
15	2.5	275.2
16	2.6	304.0
17	2.7	315.5
18	2.8	340.4
19	2.9	....
20	3.0	350.0
21	3.1	....
22	3.2	....
23	3.3	....
24	3.4	....
25	3.5	365.4

coal, iron, and steel industries in the United States, and also of 770 in Europe engaged in the same industries. In 1891, budgets of 5284 families in the textile manufactures and glass-works of the United States were reported on, together with several hundred in Europe. The report of 1903 includes a still greater number; viz., 25,440 in 33 states (including the District of Columbia), most of them gathered during the calendar year 1901.

The report of 1903 may be taken as typical of the method. First, the returns are classified for the whole 25,440; but, second, a selection is made of the 11,156 normal families, (having husband at work, wife, not over 5 children, none over 14, with no dependent boarder, lodger, or servant, and having expenditures reported for food, clothing, rent, fuel and light and sundries.) Third are tabulated the budgets of 2567 families furnishing details as to expenditure for various group-items; and fourth, details for food for the 1043 of these 2567 that were normal.

The returns are summarized and averaged: (1) By states, (2) by nativity, (3) by states and nativity, (4) by number in family, (5) by amount of income.

In marked contrast to the extensive method of the labor bureaus in the United States is the method that has been employed in a few instances in England, Germany and Switzerland. It may be called the account-book method. A selected family is persuaded to keep a daily account of every penny received and spent, and from these accounts the budget is drawn off in due form by the investigator. Landolt, of Basel, published an elaborate exposition of this method in 1894.

In briefer form his account of it appears in the "Bulletin de l'Institut Internationale de Statistique," 1891. In that year he published 10 workingmen's budgets obtained in Basel. His exhaustive schedule includes an inventory of every pin and crust in the house at the beginning and at the end of the year. It includes the suggestive question, "Are there rats or mice in the house? How long have they been there?" This method, essentially, was employed in two well-known English inquiries into conditions of living; Charles Booth's in London, 1889,* and B. S. Rowntree's in York, 1901.†

* "Life and Labor of the People in London."
† "Poverty: A Study of Town Life."

In the first volume of Booth are published 30 family budgets, distributed among 3 income-classes (under 20s. 4d. per week, 6 families; 20s. 4d. to 22s. 8d., 10 families; 22s. 8d. to 32s., 14 families.) Accounts were kept for 5 weeks. Expenses are reduced to a weekly basis, and food values reduced to a uniform man-per-day scale. Mr. Booth was also one of the co-operators in the work of the Economic Club of London, which, in 1896, published the budgets of "Twenty-eight British Households," gathered 1891–1894. These families were scattered over England, and were induced to keep accounts for not less than a month, by the visitors who co-operated in the undertaking. The introduction, signed by Messrs. Booth, Aves and Higgs, says, with great truthfulness: "We cannot, in inquiries of this kind, expect to be able to give the truth, the whole truth, and nothing but the truth. All we can hope to arrive at is the truth, nearly all the truth, and very little but the truth." Possible objections are stated as follows:

1. Absence of any budget of important classes of the community.
2. Incompleteness of analysis and enumeration in many cases.
3. Small number of budgets given.
4. Modifications of accounts due to fact that they are to be inspected; e. g., as to drinks and other indulgences. In answer to the fourth objection it is rejoined; first, that accounts are of respectable families, where such expenditures will be relatively small; second, that the accounts of respectable families are the most representative.

Before Rowntree's study of York was published, Professor W. O. Atwater had, in this country, conducted his investigation into dietary standards. Without going into detail in regard to this investigation it may be said that it consisted of two parts; first, the determination, by the use of his copper chamber for the measuring of wastes given off from the body, of the amount of food required to maintain the physical efficiency of the human body; second, the examination of the dietary of selected workingmen's families to find out whether it included the requisite amount of protein to build up muscular tissue and enough of fats and carbo-hydrates to serve as fuel to supply heat and energy.*

* Farmers' Bulletin No. 142, U. S. Dept. of Agriculture, gives in condensed popular form the results of Professor Atwater's inquiries.

Atwater's standard for the daily consumption of an adult man, at moderate muscular work, is 125 grammes of protein and 3500 calories of heat-energy,—roughly, what is contained in 1½ pounds of lean beef for the protein and in 2½ pounds of bread (10 cents' worth) for the heat-giving food. He worked out also a· scale, to which reference has already been made, for reducing the food demands of other members of a family to aliquot parts of the consumption of the man at moderate muscular work. (See pages 15 and 125.)

In the examination of actual food consumed, the accounts of food expenditures of representative families for 10 days were secured by visitors, and were reduced by the use of the scale to their equivalents in the consumption of an adult man. Then the nutritive value of the articles purchased for the week was estimated by the use of the results of chemical analysis of bread, meat, etc., and the resulting number of grammes of protein and calories of energy, compared on a man-per-day basis with the normal requirements of the standard as previously ascertained. These budgets of food-consumption were gathered in New York in 1895 (21 families) and 1896 (36 families) and subsequently in nine other localities.

It was with these standards of dietary requirements in mind that Rowntree gathered his budgets in York in 1901. He gave note-books to housewives, and published returns for 18 working-class families, having discarded accounts received from 17 more. He also got returns from 6 families of the servant-keeping class. Of the 18 published budgets, 11 covered a period not exceeding 4 weeks (6 were for 3 weeks), 7 were kept for more than 4 weeks, and 3 for 13 weeks. The food-expenditures are compared on the basis of a reduction to a uniform man-per-day equivalent, according to Atwater's scale. The results are presented in striking diagrams, showing a standard for families with incomes under 26 shillings a week much below the requirements of a normal dietary.

An interesting collection of budgets was made by Dr. S. E. Forman in Washington, D. C., and published in United States Labor Bulletin No. 64, May, 1906. Nineteen families are here reported, and the detail of entries in their account-books is published, as well as summaries and averages. The accounts were kept for 3 weeks in August and September, 1905, and 2 weeks in January, 1906. The families were very close to the line of dependence, and the returns are skillfully interpreted to show such particulars as that in the week when the monthly rent was paid the food-expenditure fell. The increased cost of goods purchased in small amounts also appears, one family sending three times a day to purchase tea.

An application of Le Play's method on an extensive scale has been made by Mrs. Louise Bolard More.* Two hundred families living in the Greenwich district in New York City were visited by Mrs. More and her co-workers, and persuaded to keep accounts. Frequent visits were made throughout a period of nearly two years, and the data regarding the family budget gathered by careful and repeated questions, supplemented in 50 cases by accounts kept for periods varying from a week to a year.

In looking back over the various attempts to find out how the laborer spends his earnings, it is interesting to note the occasions that gave rise to the inquiries, and the uses that have been made of their conclusions. Financial exigencies of governments gave rise to the earliest attempts that we have noted. The purpose was to find whether an increase of taxes could be borne by the working population. Another occasion for these inquiries is the economic distress of the people, as seen in high prices for food, lack of employment, increasing demand for poor-relief, unrest and discontent —"les plaies sociales," as Visschers put it. This distress is sometimes acute, as in Eden's day, or at the time of the two Belgian investigations. It may be chronic, like that of London and York that gave rise to the studies of Booth and Rowntree. Scientific interest as well as humanitarian zeal attracted Engel and Le Play to the investigation of the subject, and the necessity of justifying their *raison d'être* has apparently led some of our state labor bureaus to enter the field.

The uses which have been made of the results of inquiries into the cost of living are manifold. Le Play sought to utilize his family monographs in his argument for the maintenance of the monogamic family and paternal authority. Engel connected his studies with generalizations regarding the economic welfare

* "Wage-earner's Budgets." New York, 1907.

of the nation. Eden argued from his reports the need of changes in the poor laws and other remedial legislation. Davies deduced from his data the need of establishing by law a minimum wage. Dietary experts use the figures of expenditure for food to show the need of education in domestic science, and protectionists compare standards of living in the United States and in Europe to justify the protective tariff. Arbitrators appeal to the figures of the family budget in deciding on the reasonableness of a given wage-scale, and charitable organizations want to know how much a dependent family needs in order to live according to a normal standard.

It seems plain from a consideration of the results of the various methods that have been applied, that both the intensive and the extensive methods are valuable, and that they should supplement each other. The intensive study of a single family can be applied to but a limited number of cases, and the assumption that a given case is typical may be mistaken. The extensive method can include a large number of cases, and eliminate, by the use of the average, the exceptional case, but it cannot give the intimate knowledge of detail that the type-study attains. With the extensive method to give breadth and perspective, and the intensive study to give color and definiteness to the outlines obtained by the extensive method, the study of the family budget can best be made to bring out the standard of living.

PART I

The Method of the Investigation

The Method of the Investigation

The origin and purpose of the investigation have been summarized in the introductory statement on page xiii. Before setting forth the results obtained it is in order to give some account of the methods employed, both as an aid in the interpretation of the data secured and as a means of making the lessons of our experience available for other investigators.

1. THE SCHEDULE.—The schedule was prepared, as has been stated, by a sub-committee. After an examination of the schedules used in other inquiries into family budgets, it seemed best to make one that should be detailed and comprehensive. A copy of the form used, and a general interpretation of the meaning of the items included, may be found in Appendix III (page 283). The schedule seemed, to some of those who undertook to work with it, needlessly detailed. But it was necessary to push the questions far enough to include a specification of what was had for the money expended, if much light was to be had on the very important question as to what the families enjoyed in return for their expenditures for food, clothing, amusements, and other purposes. For this reason the dimensions of the rooms were called for, and the enumeration of the forms of recreation, and even an inventory of the furniture in each room. A further reason for elaboration of detail was the fact that in this way fewer expenditures would be likely to be omitted than if only a gross total were asked for. The only way in which a firm or a family can find out exactly what it spends for a given purpose is to add up all the separate items included under the main head. To specify as many as possible of these items in advance, therefore, must conduce to the likelihood of their being included in the returns as rendered. Inasmuch as the schedules were to be worked out by a number of different enumerators, it was all the more desirable to make the questions minute and definite enough to secure uniformity in the arrangement of the data gathered by the various reporters.

25

In the light of experience in the use of the schedule that was adopted, it may be said to have been well adapted to its purpose. Though it appeared somewhat complicated, it was a workable form. Its exhaustiveness was discouraging to volunteer reporters, whether from settlements or from labor unions. But those who persisted with it did secure a pretty full and definite description of the manner of living of the families visited. "You've got our whole story," said one woman, after answering the questions. A few redundancies and ambiguities appeared as it was used, and a few omissions, such as that of macaroni from the food list. Though some of the visitors were inclined to think that considerable facility in the use of the simple processes of arithmetic was demanded, only a very elementary knowledge of bookkeeping was needed to fill out the forms.

The effort to secure information on the basis of a year's expenditure led to some difficulties, especially in regard to the amount expended for food. Here the weekly expenditure for the various food-stuffs was put down in detail and the yearly expenditure was obtained by multiplying each weekly item by 52—or a less number for articles used for less than a year—and adding the sums together. Where a family keeps a careful account, this result can be checked up and verified. But where the weekly expenditure is only an estimate made by the housewife, a total obtained by this process can be only a rough approximation. On the other hand, many careful housewives allow regularly a definite sum per week for the table, and the smaller this sum, the more exactly is the spender likely to know of the detail of its apportionment, and the smaller are the variations likely to be from week to week.

2. THE ENUMERATORS.—Those who filled out the schedules may be grouped into three classes: social workers, without pay, trades-union members, and paid schedule-reporters. Until the appropriation was made from the Russell Sage Foundation, the schedules were entirely in the hands of visitors of the first class. Over 400 schedules were distributed among these volunteers, and 57 were returned, filled out by 43 different persons, including residents of settlements, visitors connected with churches and charitable organizations, and students in Columbia University and in the

School of Philanthropy. These persons had the great advantage of possessing already the confidence of the families interviewed, so that it was easy to secure the information. They also were able to check up the statements made on the basis of a thorough knowledge of the conditions of living in their own neighborhoods. On the other hand, the time required to complete the inquiries of the schedule was more than many of these busy workers could afford; and so, with the best of good-will on their part, the number of schedules that they sent in was comparatively small. These reports, however, as compared with those received from paid visitors, are fuller and richer in minor details that often give an illuminating glimpse of unsuspected family problems. On the other hand, the volunteers, as a whole, had greater difficulty with the mathematical pitfalls of the schedule than those who acquired facility in this respect by frequent repetition.

The co-operation of the trades unions was sought, and at the suggestion of Mr. Herman Robinson, of the American Federation of Labor, schedules were sent to the secretaries of some 300 unions in Greater New York, with the offer to pay for schedules returned at the same rate that was given to the visitors employed by the Committee. Much interest in the investigation was expressed, and 34 reports in all were received from representatives of the unions. Doubtless the complexity of the schedule discouraged many. The reports received were of convincing genuineness and full of instructive detail, although not always entirely satisfactory from the point of view of the accountant. Valuable comments and suggestions as to the work of the Committee were embodied in a letter accompanying one of these trades-union schedules, and the letter is reprinted on page 34.

The paid visitors were employed as soon as funds were available to hire them. Twenty-one different persons were employed for longer or shorter periods in visiting families and filling out schedules, to say nothing of 10 others who registered for service, but for various reasons gave it up without turning in any schedules. Altogether, 551 schedules were received from these paid reporters, 424 coming from the 9 persons who turned in more than 20 apiece. The first members of the paid staff were set to work June 11th, and the greater number of their reports were filled in during

27

the months of July and August. The paid visitors were chiefly persons who either possessed a personal acquaintance with families suitable for the purposes of the inquiry, or who had had experience in similar social work. Of those who brought in 5 or more schedules, 5 were teachers, 5 had been connected with some form of organized charity, 3 were labor-union members, 1 was a physician, 1 an ex-insurance-collector. Ten were women; 13 men. Two of the most successful were married women. Visitors who spoke Italian and Yiddish were sent to the Italian and Jewish families. All of these visitors grew more apt in the work with practice, and some of those who had their first taste of such work in this undertaking developed marked interest and skill. The visitors were paid, some of them $50 a month, the others at the rate of $1.50 for each schedule returned. A comparison of the results of the two methods of payment leads to the conclusion that the time-wage produced the best results. The best visitors did not average more than one schedule a day, by whichever method paid, but the desire to increase earnings tempted some of those on the piece-wage basis to try to double this rate, with the result that many of their reports had to be rejected. On the other hand, the piece-payment made it possible to secure the services of some especially competent persons, who could give only a part of their time to the work. The importance of the work of the visitors was recognized from the outset of the investigation, inasmuch as on their accuracy depended the whole value of the returns. It may be questioned whether a somewhat higher rate of remuneration would not have resulted in securing a larger number of reliable schedules, even though the total number handed in were not so great.

3. THE FAMILIES INTERVIEWED.—The families were selected on the basis of their willingness and ability to give the information that was sought. Dependent families were excluded, and the visitors tried to find families of normal composition and of moderate size, that is, having both parents living and from 2 to 4 children under 16 years of age. As to the amount of income, attention was concentrated on families having an income of from $500 to $1000 a year. An attempt was made to scatter the visitors over the various parts of the city, and among the most important nationalities represented, but beyond this the selection

28

of particular families was left to chance. Visitors naturally began, where possible, with families with which they happened to be acquainted or to which they were introduced by friends, but in nearly half of the cases they canvassed the tenement buildings without introduction, until they found a family whose composition and income were within the prescribed limits, and whose members were willing to give the information that was wanted. It is probable that the families most able to give such information are those of at least average intelligence and thrift, so that the returns are likely to err, if at all, on the side of showing better management and a higher standard than that which prevails among the mass of families having corresponding incomes.

It is, of course, a question how far a few hundred families, selected thus at random, are representative of the million families of New York City, and it is not claimed that what is true of these families is true of all families similarly situated. On the other hand, certain physical necessities must in all families be provided, and must be paid for, in each locality, at a fairly uniform scale of prices. When, therefore, the smallness of the income limits expenditure mainly to these physical necessities, a comparatively small number of cases will be sufficient to indicate the main features in the apportionment of those expenditures which are dictated by circumstances, and also the amount of the variable margin where individual choice has play. On the other hand, the number is large enough, so that averages will eliminate many of the idiosyncrasies of individual divergence from type, although when classified into sub-groups, the numbers are often too small to make the average and percentage of any real significance.

The 391 families whose budgets are discussed in the text of this report have been grouped by nationality, location, income, and occupation, as may be seen in Tables 1–6 A (pages 44–53).

4. THE PROCESS OF GATHERING THE DATA.—It was hoped, when the schedule was first circulated, that those who undertook to fill it out would be able to secure the keeping of cash accounts, for some weeks or months, by the families visited. The ideal method is, of course, to have an exact account kept for a full year, accompanied by an inventory of the family possessions at the beginning and the end of the period. This, however, was im-

possible in the present case, since a preliminary report of the results of the inquiry had to be laid before the State Conference within seven months of the printing of the schedule. It was found very difficult to get housewives to keep accounts for even one month. In a few cases this was done, however, and these reports served as a guide in reviewing the estimates made without account-books. In the majority of cases, however, it was not practicable to secure account-books, and the visitor sat down with the housewife, and ran over the questions of the schedule with her, getting an estimate where exact figures were not available. Often the mother would be able to tell with a good degree of accuracy the principal items of her budget of expenditures. Tactful questioning brought out matters that might have been overlooked, and in case of manifest inconsistencies or exaggerations, a roundabout approach resulted in a revision more nearly correct. All this required time, and the patience of mother and visitor was sometimes exhausted before the end was reached. Several visits were often necessary, although in a few cases the visitor was refused admittance a second time. On the whole, however, visitors were well received, and found it not difficult to present the purpose of the inquiry in such a way that the members of the families were willing to contribute their life-story in furtherance of the end in view.

Among the difficulties encountered was a tendency in some cases to exaggerate in statements of earnings and expenditures, partly from a pardonable pride in making as good a showing as possible, partly from the method of estimating food-expenditures on the basis of a week's outlay. In this case it is natural to reckon a rather more generous bill of fare than the family enjoys week in and week out, representing an ideal rather than the actual state of the table. The opposite tendency to under-estimate appeared in a few cases, prompted apparently by a desire to make out as bad a case as possible. It was usually practicable for the visitor, forewarned, to guard against over-statements by a mild species of cross-examination, but a large number of schedules had to be rejected because of this fault.

Other difficulties arose in the failure to understand the meaning of some of the questions, and in the unwillingness of many to answer certain intimate inquiries, such as the amount of savings, or of expenditures for drink away from home. One visitor relates the following experience regarding the item of expenditure for "drinks away from home": "When the item of 'liquors' (page 7 of the schedule) was touched upon, the wife, who was answering most of the questions, emphatically exclaimed, 'Nothing.' At this the father, sitting silently and letting the wife do the talking, turned his head outside of the window toward the street. However, when I touched again upon the items of beer and whisky, looking straight into the father's face, I emphasized the words 'drinks away from home.' Here the father could no longer restrain himself, and said, 'About 10 to 15 glasses of beer a day and a glass of whisky.' "

Indifference and suspicion were often encountered by the visitors. Many families refused to be interviewed. In some cases the woman answered the questions willingly, but when the visitor called a second time to complete the report, the woman stated that her husband had forbidden her to give the facts. On one occasion a visitor, while interviewing a family, was attacked by an angry landlord, who called in the police to arrest the visitor as a thief. The visitor was able to explain himself to the officer, but sought his next case in another street. The real nature of the landlord's apprehensions may be surmised from the fact that the scene occurred in one of the two or three most densely overcrowded tenement-blocks in the city, and that the visitor found that eleven persons were accustomed to sleep in the three rooms of the apartment. The occurrence of the so-called "wave of crime," widely exploited by the newspapers in July and August of 1907, increased the suspicion with which the visitors were met. One of them, inquiring his way of a child on the landing, was assailed with violent language by the child's mother, and only his quickness of wit saved him from a mob attack. These were exceptional instances, however, and in general the visitors met with a friendly reception.

It cannot be claimed that every account is exact down to the last cent, or even the last dollar. But it is believed that the reports present an approximation to the facts sufficiently accurate to give a correct general impression of the way in which the income is apportioned in families like those under consideration.

31

5. THE PROBABLE ACCURACY OF THE RETURNS.—It would be absurd to claim for these family reports the exactness of a bank statement. But although only approximations, they were carefully prepared. They show abundant evidence of good faith, as a rule, on the part of visitors and the members of the families themselves, and the majority of them are fairly consistent, whether taken each by itself or compared one with another. Some sources of error have already been suggested. In addition to indifference and suspiciousness on the part of those interviewed, ignorance, misunderstanding of the meaning of questions asked, forgetfulness, and impatience gave rise to inaccuracies. Enumerators at the outset were inexperienced; they and those whom they questioned became weary before the end of the schedule was reached, and gave less attention to some of its later pages. No doubt the total income was often misstated through failure to make an exact allowance for days of unemployment. The calculation of the food-expenditures for the year on the basis of weekly expenditures opened the way, as has already been stated, to considerable divergences from the exact sum of the expenditures for the fifty-two weeks.

Some of the dangers could be foreseen and guarded against by the visitors. Some of these inaccuracies would counterbalance one another, and be eliminated by the process of averaging. Thus the tendency to exaggeration would be offset by the tendency to concealment. It would not be safe to suppose that all errors would disappear by any such magic process, however, especially with no more cases than in the present instance.

The errors due to the causes mentioned probably entered very slightly into statements regarding the kinds of things used, but affected, to a greater degree, statements as to quantity and price of what was bought. A comparison of the estimates as to food-expenditure with the account-book returns from a few families comparable with the others, suggests the tentative estimate of 10 per cent. as the probable margin of error in the food-statements, the error most frequently occurring in the form of over-statement. The constantly recurring elements in the food-budget are so large a proportion of the whole, and the seasonal fluctuations of prices are in so far compensatory, that it does not seem unreasonable that an estimate, prepared as were those of the schedules, should come within 10 per cent. of the amount actually expended. This is the more probable if the schedule as a whole is made out with due regard to keeping the proper balance between income and outgo. In the selection of the schedules for tabulation, none were admitted showing an excess of total expenditure over total income of more than 5 per cent., save in cases where a wider divergence was accounted for by circumstances explained in the body of the schedule. It is believed, therefore, that a tentative estimate of the cost of living may be deduced from the data procured, subject to correction in the light of further investigations based upon a larger number of families. The experience gained in the conduct of the present inquiry may, perhaps, do something toward making the next investigation more exact and comprehensive.

6. COST OF THE INVESTIGATION.—The following statement shows the cost of the investigation, including the printing of the preliminary report:

Postage	$39.57
Printing and Stationery	451.03
Professional services of food expert	200.00
Services of secretary for three months	300.00
Services of visiting schedule-reporters	939.17
Clerical service; stenographers, tabulators, etc.	490.82
Miscellaneous	59.94
	$2480.53

To this amount should be added the expenditures for clerical assistance in the more detailed elaboration of the data for the final report, making the total cost as follows:

Expenditures enumerated above	$2480.53
Clerical service, etc., for final report	495.17
	$2975.70

The whole of this expense, as has already been stated, was borne by the Russell Sage Foundation. The secretary received remuneration only during the three months when his entire time was given to the investigation.

NOTE.—The following letter, referred to on a previous page, was received by the Committee on Standard of Living, with a schedule filled out by the writer:

Gentlemen: I have spoken to quite a number of men in our trade about your family report. They are not as a rule interested enough to ask their wives how, much it costs. Their usual answer is, "All I can earn." Put specific questions to them and they could not make a good guess. Now if the committee find this to be the rule I would suggest that something be gotten up where a woman will only have to mark down what she has laid out, such as I have sketched in the book, and that for a specified time. Women as a rule have so much to do in the house, particularly

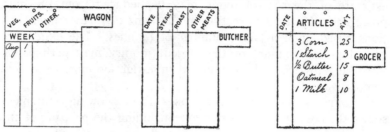

where there are five children that they can give no time to family reports. I am very much interested in this as I think it is something every man should know. Hand up $20 on Saturday night week after week and then come home and see your son 12 or 13 years old, after coming out of a sham battle, waist all gone, overalls about gone, undershirt about spent. Grab him, bring him before his mother and ask her, are those the only clothes he has. And at this time of the year particularly (it's vacation) your liable to be answered yes—then you begin to think of your 20 a week and ask where it goes and your liable to be sued for divorce. Good luck to the committee, keep it up, its what working men and women want and until they know it they are groping in the dark.

After giving your report all the consideration possible and diving into accounts that could be found around I concluded to do some figuring. The enclosed figures are conservative although they run in the grand total a few hundred dollars more than my income. But when it is understood that considerable overtime is made in our trade that will even accounts. I have endeavored to interest several men in your report but when I explained how essential it was to have facts and not guess work they refused to attempt to fill one. But I think if the committee will adopt some plan where the future accounts could be easily enumerated, working men who want to know how much it costs to live would be pleased to assist their wives in keeping those correctly. And in so doing would be educating themselves and their children along with acquiring a knowledge of one of the most essential things in a home, co-operation in economy and that with pleasure instead of friction and many times trouble for the lack of knowledge where all of one's money goes to.

I believe that if the committee will have a report similar to this one sent to the men in the city that work for a living, arranged so that when his wife runs out to a wagon in the street and spends 25 or 50 cents that she will only have to go to the report and where it says wagon mark what she spent and so on with all expenditures. For example a number of pages strung together like this sketch or something equally as good. As to the past no one can or will attempt to fill out report accurate, it can not be done. and be correct, look to future not to the Past.

From one of them,

A. J. F.

PART II
Analysis of the Returns Received

I. Material Used and Method of Treatment

The number of schedules received from Greater New York was 642, as follows:

From volunteers............................ 57
From trades unions......................... 34
From paid agents........................... 551

Total............................... 642

Of these, 251 were rejected, as follows:

Incomplete................................ 14
Palpably inaccurate........................ 107
Of abnormal families....................... 18
Of house-owning families.................. 6
Of families having less than 4 or more than
6 members.............................. 106

Total............................... 251

There remained, accordingly, reports from 391 families, each consisting of 4, 5, or 6 persons. The number of persons in the standard family being assumed as 5, families containing 1 more and 1 less than this number were included as being fairly comparable with families of 5 persons in mass groupings where excess and deficiency would tend to offset one another. In cases where this method appears to bias the results, attention will be called to the difficulty. The number of persons to a family is shown in Table 6 A* (page 53).

* That 5 persons per family is a sufficiently large allowance appears from the following tabulation of the size of the 319,000 families, comprising 1,402,897 persons, reported as living in tenements in New York in 1900, as given by the New York Tenement House Department. (Tenement House Department of the City of New York. First Report, 1902–1903, vol. ii, pp. 152–153.)

Families of 1 comprise 4.01 per cent. of all families
"   2   "   16.67 "   "   "   "
"   3   "   18.65 "   "   "   "
"   4   "   18.06 "   "   "   "
"   5   "   15.10 "   "   "   "
"   6   "   11.26 "   "   "   "
"   7   "   7.42   "   "   "   "
"   8   "   4.51   "   "   "   "
"   9   "   2.40   "   "   "   "
"   10   "   1.14   "   "   "   "
" over 10   "   0.78   "   "   "   "

37

As will be seen from the tables which follow, 318 of the 391 families report incomes between $600 and $1100. The 25 below $600 and the 48 above $1100 are included for the sake of indicating tendencies, but the main attention is given to the 318 families within the narrower range. Among the different boroughs (Table 2, page 45), the families are distributed as follows:

BOROUGH.	INCOMES BETWEEN $600 AND $1100.	ALL INCOMES.
Manhattan	243	291
Bronx	15	17
Brooklyn	52	64
Queens	8	9
	318	391

DIAGRAM 1.—Distribution of the 391 families according to nationality.

The distribution by nationalities, determined according to the nationality of the father (his birthplace, save in case of colored persons), is as follows:

38

MATERIAL USED AND METHOD OF TREATMENT

NATIONALITY.	INCOMES BETWEEN $600 AND $1100.	ALL INCOMES.
United States*....................	67	88
Teutonic nations†...............	39	46
Irish...........................	24	26
Colored.........................	28	29
Bohemian.......................	14	14
Russian.........................	57	78
Austro-Hungarian, etc.‡..........	32	39
Italian.........................	57	69
Others.........................		2
	318	391

* The nativity of the fathers of the natives of the United States is as follows:

	INCOMES $600 TO $1100.	ALL INCOMES.
United States	24	34
Great Britain	4	5
German Empire	19	25
Ireland	18	22
Bohemia	1	1
Holland	1	1
	67	88

† Including the following, by nativity of father:

	INCOMES $600 TO $1100.	ALL INCOMES.
Great Britain	8	10
German Empire	24	29
Holland	1	1
Norway and Sweden	5	5
Switzerland	1	1
	39	46

‡ Including the following, by nativity of father:

	INCOMES $600 TO $1100.	ALL INCOMES.
Austria	10	14
Hungary	15	16
Galicia	6	7
Roumania	1	2
	32	39

39

By incomes, the grouping of families may be summarized as follows:

$400 to $599............................ 25
600 to 699............................ 72
700 to 799............................ 79
800 to 899............................ 73
900 to 999............................ 63
1000 to 1099............................ 31
1100 and over............................ 48
                                          ———
                                          391

The occupations represented are principally those of the less skilled employments, in which the wage is from $2.00 to $3.00

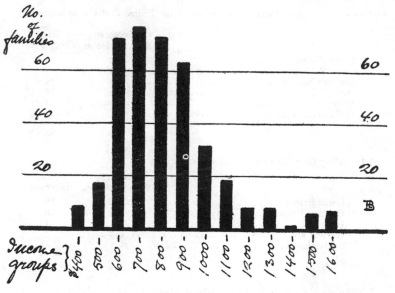

DIAGRAM 2.—Number of families in each income-group. (See Table 1, page 44.)

a day. The classification employed follows that of the Twelfth Census of the United States, and in every case the occupation specified is that of the father. Of the 391 men included in the tables, laborers (38), teamsters (30), and garment-workers (66), make up one-third. The following table shows the apportionment among the main groups of the Census Bureau's classification:

Professional service........................... 6
Domestic and personal service................. 96
Trade... 47
Transportation................................ 53
Manufactures and mechanical trades...........189
                                             ———
                                             391

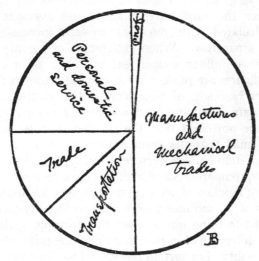

DIAGRAM 3.—Distribution of the 391 families according to the occupation of the head of the family.

In the tables which follow, the families are classified by occupation of the father and by income. In Tables 3 and 6 (pages 46, 49), the classification is on the basis of the total income of the family; in Table 4 (page 47), on the basis of the earnings of the father. It must not be supposed that the range of annual earnings in the lower paid occupations is as great as in the range of incomes of the families of the men thus employed, because it is especially these low incomes from fathers' earnings that need to be supplemented by rent from lodgers and the earnings of mother and children.

The number of persons per family ranges from 4 to 6; 142 of the 318 families consist of 5 persons, 80 of 4, 96 of 6. The average number is 5, and the average for each income-group is either 5, 4.9, or 5.1. (Table 6A, page 53.)

In the statistical treatment of the material discussed, the object has been, first, to bring out as fully as practicable the facts, considered collectively; and, in the second place, to compare the results in such a way as to find out, if possible, on what income a family may meet the demands of a normal standard. With these ends in view, general averages of the returns for all families have been for the most part avoided, and averages and percentages calculated with reference to each income-group and nationality separately. Where differences of locality were important in their influence upon expenditures, as in the matter of rent, the figures are presented for Manhattan apart from those for the other boroughs of New York. This method brings together the data that are most completely comparable. It is subject to the objection that the number of cases in any one group is so small that the main advantage of the average—the elimination of individual departures from type—is lost. To meet this difficulty, comparisons and averages have been regularly made by combining families of all nationalities in each income-group, and families of all incomes within each nationality-group. This method ought to bring out at least the principal variations due primarily to difference of income and those due primarily to difference of nationality. For certain purposes it has seemed safe to combine adjacent income-groups; *i. e.*, to compare all cases in income-groups between $600 and $800 with all cases in income-groups between $900 and $1100. Also, for many purposes, the families of American, Teutonic and Irish parentage may advantageously be combined for the purpose of contrasting them with families of the stocks predominating in recent immigration—the Russian, Austro-Hungarian, and Italian.

When the average has been employed it has in every case been obtained by dividing the sum of the items by the number of cases. This amounts, in cases where combination is made of different groups (*e. g.*, of the 291 Manhattan cases and the 100 non-Manhattan cases), to adding together all the items in all groups and dividing the sum by the total number of cases (by 391 in the instance cited). In other words, in all such cases the weighted average has been applied.

More useful than the average, sometimes, has been found the grouping of items into classes, and the enumeration of the number of cases falling in each class; e. g., the number of families paying less than $10 monthly rent and the number paying over $15. This method has been applied to the study of wages in Professor Dewey's special report in the Twelfth Census. For the modest purpose of the present report it has not been thought necessary to calculate the cumulative percentage as Professor Dewey has done, but the ordinary percentage calculations have been made. Again, it should be remembered that all percentages diminish in significance as the number of cases grows small. For this reason, the number of cases should always be kept in mind, and therefore these numbers, wherever practicable, are printed in connection with the percentages.

TABLE 1.—ENUMERATION OF FAMILIES.—BY INCOME AND NATIONALITY OF FATHER.

NATIONALITY OF FATHER.	$400 TO $499	$500 TO $599	$600 TO $699	$700 TO $799	$800 TO $899	$900 TO $999	$1000 TO $1099	$1100 TO $1199	$1200 TO $1299	$1300 TO $1399	$1400 TO $1499	$1500 TO $1599	$1600 AND OVER	TOTAL
United States	2	2	11	19	13	16	8	6	2	5	..	3	1	88
Teutonic	..	..	4	7	9	11	8	2	3	1	..	1	..	46
Irish	..	..	4	7	7	5	1	..	..	..	..	1	1	26
Colored	..	1	11	6	8	2	1	..	..	..	..	..	..	25
Bohemian	..	..	4	3	3	4	..	..	..	..	..	..	..	14
Russian	3	6	16	14	12	9	6	5	2	..	..	..	4	78
Austrian, etc.	1	3	6	9	9	7	1	2	..	1	1	..	..	39
Italian	1	4	16	14	12	9	6	3	1	1	..	1	1	69
Others	1	1	..	..	..	..	..	..	..	..	..	..	..	2
Total	8	17	72	79	73	63	31	18	8	8	1	6	7	391

44

TABLE 2.—ENUMERATION OF FAMILIES.—BY BOROUGH, INCOME AND NATIONALITY OF FATHER.

Nationality of Father	$400 to $499 Man.	$400 to $499 Bklyn.	$500 to $599 Man.	$500 to $599 Bklyn.	$600 to $699 Man.	$600 to $699 Bronx	$600 to $699 Bklyn.	$700 to $799 Man.	$700 to $799 Bronx	$700 to $799 Bklyn.	$800 to $899 Man.	$800 to $899 Bronx	$800 to $899 Bklyn.	$800 to $899 Queens	$900 to $999 Man.	$900 to $999 Bronx	$900 to $999 Bklyn.	$900 to $999 Queens	$1000 to $1099 Man.	$1000 to $1099 Bronx	$1000 to $1099 Bklyn.	$1000 to $1099 Queens	$1100 to $1199 Man.	$1100 to $1199 Bronx	$1100 to $1199 Bklyn.	$1200 to $1299 Man.	$1200 to $1299 Bklyn.	$1300 to $1399 Man.	$1300 to $1399 Bklyn.	$1300 to $1399 Queens	$1400 to $1499 Bklyn.	$1500 to $1599 Man.	$1500 to $1599 Bklyn.	$1600 to $1699 Man.	$1600 to $1699 Bklyn.	$1700 to $1799 Man.	$2000 to $2099 Man.	$2100 to $2299 Man.	Total Man.	Total Bronx	Total Bklyn.	Total Queens	Total All Boroughs
United States	2				6	2	3	14	1	4	8	1	4		11		2	3	5	1	2		3	1	2	2		3	1	1		3		1					60	6	18	4	88
Teutonic					2		2	7			8	1			4	2	3	2	6		1	1	2			3		1					1						33	3	7	3	46
Irish					3		1	5		2	5	1	1		3		1	1	1													1			1				18	1	6	1	26
Colored			1		11			6			8				2				1																				29				29
Bohemian					4			3			3				4																								14				14
Russian		3	3	3	7	2	7	8		6	8		4		6		3		5		1		1		4	1	1				1			1		1	1	1	43	2	33		78
Austrian, etc.		1	2	1	5		1	8		1	9				7				1				1		1	1													33		6		39
Italian	1		3		14	1		12	1	2	9	2		1	8		1		6				2	1				1	1			1				1			59	5	4	1	69
Other	1		1																																				2				2
Total	4	4	12	5	52	5	14	63	2	15	58	5	9	1	45	2	10	6	25	1	4	1	9	2	7	7	1	5	2	1	1	5	1	2	1	2	1	1	291	17	74	9	391

45

TABLE 3.—OCCUPATIONS.—BY TOTAL FAMILY INCOME.

Occupations.	$400 to $499	$500 to $599	$600 to $699	$700 to $799	$800 to $899	$900 to $999	$1000 to $1099	$1100 to $1199	$1200 to $1299	$1300 to $1399	$1400 to $1499	$1500 to $1599	$1600 and Over	Total.
Professional service	..	..	2	..	..	..	..	1	..	1	..	1	1	6
Personal and domestic service:														
Bartenders, cooks, waiters, etc.	..	..	6	3	3	4	1	..	..	..	..	..	..	17
Janitors, porters, etc.	..	2	3	6	6	1	1	..	..	..	..	..	..	19
Longshoremen	..	..	2	3	4	..	1	..	..	..	..	..	..	10
Laborers	2	1	8	7	6	2	2	..	..	..	..	..	..	28
Public service employees	..	..	..	4	2	3	..	..	..	2	..	..	..	11
Others	..	..	3	1	1	2	1	1	1	..	..	..	1	11
Trade:														
Agents, clerks, salesmen	..	..	5	6	3	..	..	3	..	..	..	2	1	20
Merchants and dealers	1	2	6	7	3	2	2	2	1	..	..	..	1	27
Transportation:														
City railway employees	..	..	..	..	2	6	1	..	..	..	..	..	..	9
Teamsters, drivers, etc.	..	1	8	9	4	3	1	2	..	2	..	..	..	30
Others	..	..	..	4	2	3	..	1	1	1	..	2	..	14
Manufactures and Mechanical Trades:														
Building trades	..	2	5	2	9	9	5	1	..	2	1	..	1	37
Food and food products	..	1	1	4	2	2	3	..	..	..	..	..	..	13
Leather	..	4	..	1	1	1	..	1	1	..	..	..	..	9
Lumber	..	..	..	1	3	..	3	1	1	..	..	..	..	9
Metal	1	..	..	2	4	3	1	..	1	..	..	..	1	13
Printing	..	..	1	3	1	2	1	..	..	..	..	1	1	10
Textiles	2	4	13	13	11	12	6	3	3	..	..	..	..	67
Others	2	1	6	4	6	8	2	2	..	..	..	..	..	31
Total	8	17	72	79	73	63	31	18	8	8	1	6	7	391

46

TABLE 4.—OCCUPATIONS.—BY EARNINGS OF FATHER.

Occupations	Total	$1600 and over	$1500 to $1599	$1400 to $1499	$1300 to $1399	$1200 to $1299	$1100 to $1199	$1000 to $1099	$900 to $999	$800 to $899	$700 to $799	$600 to $699	$500 to $599	$400 to $499	$300 to $399	$200 to $299	$100 to $199
Professional service	6	1			1		1	1				1	1				
Personal and domestic service:																	
Bartenders, cooks, waiters, etc.	17							1	2	1	2	9	1	1			
Janitors, porters, etc.	19								1	1	4	7	4	2			
Longshoremen	10										5	5					
Laborers	28				1				1	1	8	8	5		2	1	1
Public service	11				1				1	1	6	1		1			
Others	11						1		2	1	1	3	2		1		
Trade:																	
Agents, clerks, salesmen, etc.	20		2				2		1	2	7	5	1		1		
Merchants and dealers	27		1			1	2	1	2	2	7	6	3	2			
Transportation:																	
City railway employees	9								7	1	1						
Teamsters, drivers, etc.	30								2	4	6	14	3		1		
Others	14							1	2	1	5	3	2				
Manufactures and Mechanical Trades:																	
Building trades	37			1	2		1	1	5	6	5	8	6	2			
Food and food products	13						1	1	2	2	2	2	1	1	1		
Leather	9								1	1		3	3				1
Lumber	9								2	2	1	3		1			
Metal	13					1		1	3	2	2	2	1				1
Printing	10		1			1			1	2	3	2					
Textiles	67						2	2	8	7	13	15	10	7	2		1
Others	31						1	1	4	1	7	7	6	4			
Total	391	1	4	1	5	4	8	13	47	38	85	99	53	24	6	1	2

47

TABLE 5.—OCCUPATIONS.—BY NATIONALITY.

OCCUPATIONS.	UNITED STATES.	TEUTONIC.	IRISH.	COLORED.	BOHEMIAN.	RUSSIAN.	AUSTRO-HUNGARIAN.	ITALIAN.	OTHERS.	TOTAL.
Professional service	1	..	..	..	..	2	..	3	..	6
Personal and domestic service:										
Bartenders, cooks, waiters, etc.	2	6	1	5	1	..	1	1	..	17
Janitors, porters, etc.	3	3	4	6	1	..	..	2	..	19
Longshoremen	1	1	3	4	..	..	..	1	..	10
Laborers	1	3	5	2	..	2	2	12	1[a]	28
Public service	4	1	1	4	..	..	..	1	..	11
Others	..	..	..	..	..	3	1	7	..	11
Trade:										
Agents, clerks, salesmen, etc.	10	4	3	..	..	1	1	1	..	20
Merchants and dealers	3	1	..	..	..	7	3	13	..	27
Transportation:										
City railway employees	4	2	3	..	..	..	..	..	..	9
Teamsters, drivers, etc.	13	6	..	2	1	3	1	4	..	30
Others	7	2	3	1	..	..	1	..	..	14
Manufactures and Mechanical Trades:										
Building trades	9	5	1	2	2	8	6	4	..	37
Food and food products	..	6	..	..	1	2	1	3	..	13
Leather	2	1	..	..	..	2	1	3	..	9
Lumber	2	1	..	..	1	1	2	2	..	9
Metal	6	2	1	..	..	..	3	1	..	13
Printing	6	1	..	..	..	..	..	3	..	10
Textiles	3	..	..	..	..	45	13	6	..	67
Others	11	1	1	3	7	2	3	2	1[b]	31
Total	88	46	26	29	14	78	39	69	2	391

a Syrian. b Cuban.

48

TABLE 6.—OCCUPATIONS IN DETAIL.—BY TOTAL FAMILY INCOME.

OCCUPATIONS.	$400 TO $499	$500 TO $599	$600 TO $699	$700 TO $799	$800 TO $899	$900 TO $999	$1000 TO $1099	$1100 TO $1199	$1200 TO $1299	$1300 TO $1399	$1400 TO $1499	$1500 TO $1599	$1600 AND OVER	TOTAL.
Professional service:														
Clergyman													1	1
Dentist												1		1
Fashion artist			1							1				2
Journalist			1											1
Teacher								1						1
Personal and domestic service:														
Barber—Proprietor				1										1
" —Employee			2	2				1	1				1	7
Bartender		1	3			3								7
Bootblack						1	1							2
Cook					1	1	1							3
Elevatorman			3											3
Janitor				1										1
Office-cleaner		1												1
Watchman				2		1								3
Laundry worker			1											1
Porter			3	3	5									11
Waiter			2	2	3									7
Laborers:														
Casual	1	1												2
Coal heaver					4									4
Longshoreman			1	3	4	2								10
Laborer (unspecified)	1	1	6	6	6	2								22
Public service:														
Park employee						1								1
Policeman						1				1				2
P. O. employee						1								1
Street cleaner				3	1	1								5
Turnkey										1				1
Civil service					1									1

TABLE 6.—OCCUPATIONS IN DETAIL.—(Continued.)

OCCUPATIONS.	$400 TO $499	$500 TO $599	$600 TO $699	$700 TO $799	$800 TO $899	$900 TO $999	$1000 TO $1099	$1100 TO $1199	$1200 TO $1299	$1300 TO $1399	$1400 TO $1499	$1500 TO $1599	$1600 AND OVER	TOTAL
Trade:														
Agent				1	1									2
Clerk			2	4	2			2				1		11
Peddler	1		2	1	1	1	1	1						7
Salesman			1	1				1				1	1	5
Merchants and dealers:														
Candy				1										1
Coal and wood			2	4	1		1	1						9
Groceries			1											1
Ice man			1	1										2
Newsdealer									1					1
Packer			1	1										2
Produce and provisions					1					2				3
Shoes					1									1
Storekeeper (unspecified)		1											1	2
Transportation:														
Boatman				1						1				2
Carriage and hack driver		1												1
Drayman, teamster, etc.			8	9	4	3	1	2						30
Hostler, stableman			1	2	1	2		1						7
R. R. Inspector						1				1				2
R. R. Laborer				1										1
Street R. R. Laborer		1				1								2
" " Conductor					2	1								3
" " Motorman						4								4
" " Inspector								1						1
Telegrapher												1		1
Manufactures and Mechanical Trades:														
Building Trades:														
Carpenter				1	3	2	1			1		1		10
Mason		1	1		2	1					1			6
Painter, varnisher		1	3		3	3	3				1			13
Plumber					1	1		1		1			1	5

TABLE 6.—Occupations in Detail.—(Continued.)

OCCUPATIONS.	$400 TO $499	$500 TO $599	$600 TO $699	$700 TO $799	$800 TO $899	$900 TO $999	$1000 TO $1099	$1100 TO $1199	$1200 TO $1299	$1300 TO $1399	$1400 TO $1499	$1500 TO $1599	$1600 AND OVER	TOTAL.
Roofer						1								1
Whitewasher						1		1						2
Food and food products:														
Baker				2	1	1	2	1						7
Butcher				1	1	1								3
Confectioner			1	1			1							3
Leather:														
Boot and shoe maker		3	1		1		2							7
Currier and tanner		1					1							2
Lumber, wood, etc.:														
Basket maker						1								1
Cabinet maker					1	1		1						3
Piano varnisher			1						1					2
Picture framer					1									1
Upholsterer				1									1	2
Metal:														
Iron and steel:														
Blacksmith					1	1								2
Iron worker													1	1
Machinist				1										1
Pattern maker						1								1
Sawsmith									1					1
Auto repairer						1								1
Badge maker						1								1
Brass worker				1	1									1
Gold and silver worker					1	1								1
Lead worker	1													1
Tinplate maker									1			1		2
Printing, etc.:														
Bookbinder			1			1								2
Electrotyper														1
Lithographer				1						1				2
Pressman					1		1							2
Printer				2	1									3

TABLE 6.—OCCUPATIONS IN DETAIL.—(Continued.)

OCCUPATIONS.	$400 TO $499	$500 TO $599	$600 TO $699	$700 TO $799	$800 TO $899	$900 TO $999	$1000 TO $1099	$1100 TO $1199	$1200 TO $1299	$1300 TO $1399	$1400 TO $1499	$1500 TO $1599	$1600 AND OVER	TOTAL
Manufactures and Mechanical Trades:														
Textiles:														
Buttonhole maker	1			1	1									3
Cloak maker			1	1	1									3
Clothing carrier								1						1
Cutter			1	1		1			1					4
Clothing sorter			1	1										2
Dyer		1				1								1
Garment worker (unspecified)	1	1	4	4	3	3		2						18
Hat and cap maker		1	1											2
Lining cutter		1							1					1
Pants maker		1												1
Presser	1	1	1	1		1	1							5
Tailor	1		4	5	6	6	4							26
Miscellaneous:														
Bottle labeller	1													1
" washer														1
Brewer														1
Brick maker					1	2								1
Button maker						1								1
Carpet layer				1	3									2
Cigar maker	1		3	2	1	5								5
Cigarette maker		1	1			2	1	1						2
Electrical worker						1								1
Engineer						2	2							5
Factory hand (unspecified)			3			1	1	1						5
Fireman			1			1	1							3
Pipe layer				1	1									1
Photographer														1
Rag picker														1
Total	8	17	72	79	73	63	31	18	8	8	1	6	7	391

TABLE 6A.—NUMBER OF PERSONS PER FAMILY.—BY INCOME AND NATIONALITY.

NATIONALITY.	$600 TO $699				$700 TO $799				$800 TO $899			
	Average Number of Persons per Family.	Four Persons.	Five Persons.	Six Persons.	Average Number of Persons per Family.	Four Persons.	Five Persons.	Six Persons.	Average Number of Persons per Family.	Four Persons.	Five Persons.	Six Persons.
United States..	5.0	3	6	2	5.3	1	13	5	5.0	4	5	4
Teutonic......	4.7	1	3	..	5.0	3	1	3	5.1	3	2	4
Irish..........	6.0	..	..	4	5.3	..	5	2	4.9	2	4	1
Colored.......	5.4	..	7	4	5.5	..	3	3	5.2	1	4	3
Bohemian.....	4.5	1	3	..	6.0	..	..	3	5.7	..	1	2
Russian.......	5.1	3	8	5	5.1	3	5	6	5.4	2	2	8
Austrian, etc...	4.3	3	2	1	4.8	3	4	2	5.0	3	4	2
Italian........	4.6	11	3	2	4.6	7	6	1	4.5	8	2	2
Total.........	4.9	22	32	18	5.1	17	37	25	5.0	23	24	26

NATIONALITY.	$900 TO $999				$1000 TO $1099				TOTAL.			
	Average Number of Persons per Family.	Four Persons.	Five Persons.	Six Persons.	Average Number of Persons per Family.	Four Persons.	Five Persons.	Six Persons.	Average Number of Persons per Family.	Four Persons.	Five Persons.	Six Persons.
United States..	5.2	2	8	6	5.4	1	3	4	5.2	11	35	21
Teutonic.......	5.1	3	5	3	5.0	1	5	2	5.0	11	16	12
Irish..........	5.4	..	3	2	5.0	..	1	..	5.3	2	13	9
Colored.......	5.5	..	1	1	5.0	..	1	..	5.4	1	16	11
Bohemian.....	5.2	..	3	1	..	..	..	..	5.3	1	7	6
Russian.......	5.0	3	3	3	4.8	2	3	1	5.1	13	21	23
Austrian, etc...	4.9	2	4	1	6.0	..	..	1	4.8	11	14	7
Italian........	5.1	1	6	2	4.5	3	3	..	4.6	30	20	7
Total.........	5.1	11	33	19	5.0	7	16	8	5.0	80	142	96

$400 to 599; av., 5.2 persons per f'ly; 5 families of 4 persons; 11 of 5; 9 of 6
$1100 and over; " 5.0 " " 16 " " 18 " 14 "

53

II. Sources of Income

An examination of the sources of income of the families included in this report shows that, while the earnings of the father are the main dependence, the importance of additions from the earnings of others, and from lodgers, increases with the higher incomes.

Tables 7 to 14 (pages 61–67) show the sources of income for the families included in the tabulations of the report. Two methods of analyzing the sources of income are followed in the tables The first method proceeds on the basis of the average amount in dollars and cents received from each source, and the percentage of the average total income for each group of families, by income and nationality, which the average from each source represents. The other method proceeds by counting in each group the number of families that receive income from each source, and calculating the corresponding percentage of the total number of families in each group.

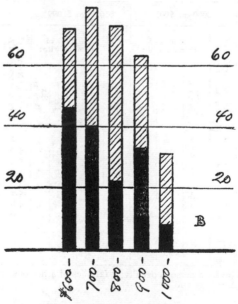

DIAGRAM 4.—Total number of families, and number supported entirely by the father, in the principal income-groups.

The most significant item is the earnings of the father. These constitute 97 per cent. of the whole income for the families with incomes of between $400 and $500, 94 per cent. for families in the next two groups ($500 to $599 and $600 to $699), 89 per cent. for families with a total income of from $700 to $800, 84 per cent. for families in the $800 group, 85 per cent. for the $900 families, 82 per cent. for the $1000 group. If we count the families supported wholly by the father's earnings in each income-group the same decrease in the higher income-groups appears, while the fact is also brought out that in a large number of families the additions to the income from sources outside the main wages form a small proportion of the whole. The number and percentage of families supported entirely by the father in the successive income-groups are as follows:

INCOME.	TOTAL NUMBER OF FAMILIES.	FAMILIES SUPPORTED ENTIRELY BY FATHER: NUMBER.	PER CENT.
$600 to $699	72	46	63.9
700 to 799	79	40	50.6
800 to 899	73	22	30.1
900 to 999	63	33	54.0
1000 to 1099	31	8	25.8
	318	149	46.8

That is to say, less than half of these 318 families are able or willing to get along with what the father's wages bring in. The table of averages shows that it must be, for the most part, a small amount that is added in the lower income-grades. The fact that the proportion of families not supported by father alone, and the average amount of the additions from other sources both increase in the higher income-groups, shows that, for the particular families that our visitors have reached, an income of above $700 or $800 is obtainable as a rule only by taking lodgers or by putting mother and children to work. It will be noticed from Table 9 (page 63) that the average earnings of the father do not reach $900 in any of the income-groups until a total income of $1100 to $1200 is reached.

A glance at the tables of occupations (pages 44–52) explains why

55

the father's earnings are so inadequate. The occupations pre-dominating (*e. g.*, laborers, garment-workers, teamsters) are those in which it is seldom possible for the father to earn more than from $600 to $800 a year. If his family is to enjoy comforts beyond what this sum will provide, someone else must earn, or a lodger or two be taken in, to help out in the rent. It will be

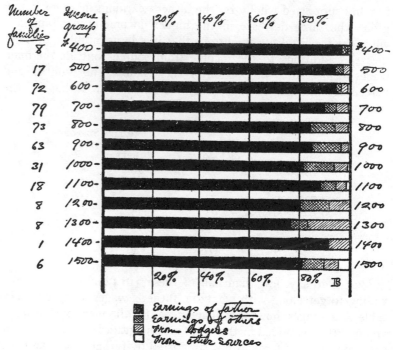

DIAGRAM 5.—Percentage of income from each source in each income-group.

found, further, as comparisons are made at specific points, that the families with composite income do not live as well, on the same amount, as do the families supported entirely by the father.

The principal resources for additions to what the father earns are the earnings of wife and children, and the income from lodgers. In Table 11 (page 64) will be found the data regarding the number of families dependent on these means of support, and in Tables 7–9 (pages 61–63) the average amount and per cent. of average total income yielded by these sources. In 86 of the 318 families with incomes between $600 and $1100, or 27 per cent., there are wage-earners besides the father; 93 families, or 29 per cent., have lodgers. By incomes, the proportion of other wage-earners is least in the $600 income-group (12.5 per cent.), and greatest in the $800 group (41 per cent.). It is notably high, however, in the $900 and $1000 groups, the percentage for these groups combined being 34, as compared with 16 per cent. for the combined $600 and $700 groups. The average earnings of these other members of the family increase likewise, with increase of income, being $14.62, or 2.3 per cent., for the $600 families; $81.93, or 9.7 per cent., for the $800 group, and $121.36, or 11.6 per cent., for the $1000 group.

Who these other wage-earners are may be seen in Tables 13–14 (pages 66–67). In the 318 families with incomes between $600 and $1100 there are reported 103 wage-earners, besides the father, belonging to 86 different families. Sixteen families have 2 supplementary wage-earners; 1 family (Bohemian) reports 3. Of these 103 persons, 58 are the mothers. Twenty-seven of these women receive pay for janitor service, in many cases in the tenement buildings in which they live. In the majority of cases where the woman is janitress of a tenement building she is given in payment the use of an apartment rent free. In 31 cases the woman earns money in some other way. The cases where the mother is a wage-earner occur most frequently in the $800 income-group, where 24 of the 58 cases occur. No more than 12 are found in any other income-group.

Forty-five children are reported at work for wages, 20 boys and 25 girls. The children are reported more frequently in the higher income-groups than in the lower, as will be seen from the following table:

INCOME.	TOTAL NUMBER OF FAMILIES.	NUMBER WITH CHILDREN EARNING WAGES
$600 to $699	72	3
700 to 799	79	7
800 to 899	73	9
900 to 999	63	15
1000 to 1099	31	11
1100 and over	48	15

57

These figures, taken in connection with the occupations most largely represented, would corroborate the impression that, where the father's earnings are low, say under $800, the children have to go to work as soon as the law allows,—sometimes earlier,—if the standard of living is not to be lowered in the effort to make the same income meet the wants of children who, as they grow, must have continually more to eat and to wear.

The different nationalities show some differences in regard to the supplementary wage-earners. Among the Bohemians the largest proportion of mothers at work is reported; viz., in 7 out of 14 families. The Russians report only 4 women as wage-earners out of 57 families, and these are all janitresses. The women are reported as wage-earners in 1 family out of 7 among the Americans, in 1 out of 6 among the Irish, in 1 out of 4 among the Teutonic families, in 1 out of 5 families among the Austrians, and in 1 out of 8 among the Italians.

Families with more than one supplementary wage-earner are more frequent among the families in our second nationality-group, 12 out of the 16 cases being found among the Bohemians, Russians, Austrians and Italians. In regard to children at work there is no apparent difference among the different nationalities, the number reported at work bearing, practically, the same ratio to the total number of families in the case of each nationality.

The families dependent on lodgers for part of their support are more evenly distributed among the income-groups than are the families with supplementary wage-earners. Twenty-four per cent. of the $600 families report lodgers, and 39 per cent. of the $1000 families, but the fluctuations in the returns for the intermediate groups do not show any regular increase. The number reporting lodgers in the $600 and $700 groups combined is 28.5 per cent. of the whole; in the $900 and $1000 groups it is 26.6 per cent. of the whole. The amount contributed by lodgers averages $18.26 for the $600 families (2.8 per cent. of the whole income), and $60.94 (5.8 per cent.) for the $1000 families. The small average for the lower income-group is due in part to the small number of families reporting income from lodgers. The average amount received by each of the 17 families in this group that report lodgers is $77.33, or 12 per cent. of the average total income of the families in this group. The average per family taking lodgers among the $1000 families is $157.43, or 15 per cent. of the average total income of this group. The relation between lodgers and over-crowding is discussed in another connection (page 83).

An examination of Tables 10 and 12 (pages 63 and 65) shows that, so far as our families are concerned, those resident in Brooklyn depend less upon lodgers for supplementary income than those in Manhattan. All of the families in the Bronx that report lodgers are in two income-groups ($800 to $899 and $1100 to $1199), and in these cases the lodgers pay as large a share of the total income as in Manhattan. The number of families in the Bronx is altogether too small, however, to warrant any general conclusions, and the same observation holds in less degree regarding the 52 Brooklyn families, as compared with the 243 in Manhattan.

A comparison of the different nationalities with reference to the sources of income shows that the greatest dependence on other resources than the father's wages is found among the Bohemians, Austrians and Russians. If to these there be added the Italians, making 160 families, we find that only 60 families, or 37.5 per cent., report no additional sources of income. Among the 158 families of the other four nationalities (Americans, Teutonic peoples, Irish, colored), 89, or 56.3 per cent., are supported by the father alone. The Italians, however, with 51 per cent. of families supported entirely by the father, rank above the colored, with 43 per cent. (Table 11, page 64).

As to the secondary sources of income, dependence on the earnings of others than the father is found to be more general among all nationalities than is reliance upon lodgers. The proportion with women or children at work varies from 16 per cent. among the Russians to 64 per cent. among the Bohemians. Dividing the families into two groups as before, according to nationality, 45, or 28.5 per cent., of the families in the first group have other wage-earners than the father, as compared with 41, or 25.6 per cent., of the families in the second group. As regards lodgers, however, only 26 families, or 16.5 per cent., of the first group report income from this source, while 67 families, or 41.9 per cent. of the second group, report taking lodgers.

The "income from other sources" than those already discussed, for which space is assigned in the tables, includes gifts of money, loans and other occasional windfalls. This is so inconsiderable a factor, however, amounting to from 0.5 to 0.9 per cent. in the averages of the income-groups, that further mention of it seems not to be necessary.

In regard to the whole subject of the proportion between families with and without income from supplementary sources, a concluding word may be in place. It is not claimed that three-fifths of all the families in New York that spend from $800 to $1100 a year are obliged to eke out the earnings of the father by taking lodgers or sending mother and children out to work. The fact here shown is only that three-fifths of the 167 families selected at random within the range of incomes mentioned did thus fall back on supplementary sources of income. But this fact, taken in connection with the reports of what that income was spent for, raises the question whether an income of less than $800 is sufficient to maintain a family of five up to the time when the children are really old enough to be set to work.

TABLE 7.—SOURCES OF INCOME. AVERAGES.—BY INCOME AND NATIONALITY.

NATIONALITY.	$600 TO $699					$700 TO $799					$800 TO $899				
	Number of Families.	Earnings of Father.	Earnings of Others.	From Lodgers.	From Other Sources.	Number of Families.	Earnings of Father.	Earnings of Others.	From Lodgers.	From Other Sources.	Number of Families.	Earnings of Father.	Earnings of Others.	From Lodgers.	From Other Sources.
United States	11	650.92	..	..	..	19	701.27	10.03	34.48	6.05	13	705.43	49.69	25.55	6.15
Teutonic	4	606.50	6.82	..	..	7	615.86	89.85	66.86	..	9	815.11	34.67	1.56	3.55
Irish	4	650.00	47.75	..	..	7	705.71	19.72	..	7.04	7	762.57	31.89	37.15	11.43
Colored	11	614.73	14.18	5.91	..	6	672.99	73.50	21.67	..	8	649.65	147.25	35.75	..
Bohemian	4	569.00	30.00	45.50	..	3	654.33	58.33	34.67	..	3	511.33	334.67	..	..
Russian	16	597.53	10.66	23.75	15.62	14	672.86	26.57	37.99	..	12	678.17	61.58	100.33	19.55
Austrian, etc.	6	577.22	..	79.93	..	4	603.56	51.33	93.22	..	9	626.00	106.56	91.33	..
Italian	16	604.00	19.00	19.75	10.94	14	680.86	29.71	23.14	10.00	12	731.00	76.67	40.00	..
Total	72	611.39	14.62	18.26	5.90	79	670.38	35.96	38.63	3.86	73	712.74	81.93	46.55	5.04

NATIONALITY.	$900 TO $999					$1000 TO $1099				
	Number of Families.	Earnings of Father.	Earnings of Others.	From Lodgers.	From Other Sources.	Number of Families.	Earnings of Father.	Earnings of Others.	From Lodgers.	From Other Sources.
United States	16	846.87	76.25	19.50	1.94	8	958.25	26.00	52.00	16.87
Teutonic	11	828.56	111.28	..	..	8	875.87	94.75	55.99	14.38
Irish	5	930.00	..	..	..	1	624.00	416.00	182.00	..
Colored	4	741.06	138.00	32.50	..	1	624.00	260.00	..	..
Bohemian	4	551.75	436.37	..	..	..	..	..	..	..
Russian	9	772.53	52.50	111.00	..	6	820.17	80.00	134.66	..
Austrian, etc.	7	669.57	214.00	28.00	37.14	1	498.00	584.00	6.00	8.33
Italian	9	867.55	34.67	31.78	..	6	838.92	176.00	..	..
Total	63	881.00	107.11	29.49	4.62	31	852.50	121.36	60.94	9.68

TABLE 8.—SOURCES OF INCOME. PERCENTAGES.—BY INCOME AND NATIONALITY.

Nationality.	$600 TO $699					$700 TO $799					$800 TO $899				
	Number of Families.	Earnings of Father Only.	Earnings of Others.	From Lodgers.	From Other Sources.	Number of Families.	Earnings of Father.	Earnings of Others.	From Lodgers.	From Other Sources.	Number of Families.	Earnings of Father.	Earnings of Others.	From Lodgers.	From Other Sources.
United States	11	91.1	8.9	..	..	19	93.1	1.5	4.6	0.8	13	90.5	5.8	3.0	0.7
Teutonic	4	92.7	7.3	..	..	7	79.7	11.7	8.6	..	9	95.3	4.1	0.2	0.4
Irish	4	100.0	..	..	..	7	95.3	2.7	..	1.0	7	90.5	3.8	4.4	1.3
Colored	11	96.9	2.2	0.9	..	6	87.6	9.6	2.8	..	8	78.0	17.7	4.3	..
Bohemian	4	87.0	6.0	7.0	2.7	3	87.6	7.8	4.6	..	3	60.4	39.6	..	..
Russian	16	92.3	1.6	3.7	..	14	91.3	3.6	5.1	..	12	80.7	7.3	12.0	..
Austrian, etc.	6	87.8	..	12.2	1.7	9	80.7	6.9	12.4	..	9	74.2	12.7	10.8	..
Italian	16	92.4	2.9	3.0	..	14	91.6	4.0	3.1	1.3	12	86.2	9.1	4.7	2.3
Total	72	94.0	2.3	2.8	0.9	79	89.5	4.8	5.2	0.5	73	84.2	9.7	5.5	0.6

Nationality.	$900 TO $999					$1000 TO $1099				
	Number of Families.	Earnings of Father.	Earnings of Others.	From Lodgers.	From Other Sources.	Number of Families.	Earnings of Father.	Earnings of Others.	From Lodgers.	From Other Sources.
United States	16	89.6	8.1	2.1	0.2	8	91.0	2.5	4.9	1.6
Teutonic	11	88.2	11.8	..	..	8	84.1	9.1	5.4	1.4
Irish	5	100.0	..	..	..	1	60.0	40.0	..	..
Colored	2	81.3	15.1	3.6	..	1	58.5	24.4	17.1	..
Bohemian	4	55.8	44.2	..	..	..	..	..	..	..
Russian	9	82.5	5.6	11.9	..	6	79.4	7.7	..	..
Austrian, etc.	7	70.5	22.6	3.0	3.9	1	46.0	54.0	12.9	..
Italian	9	92.9	3.7	3.4	..	6	81.5	17.1	0.6	0.8
Total	63	85.0	11.4	3.1	0.5	31	81.7	11.6	5.8	0.9

TABLE 9.—SOURCES OF INCOME. AVERAGES AND PERCENTAGES.—BY INCOME.

Income.	No. of Families.	Total Income.	Earnings of Father.		Earnings of Others.		From Lodgers.		From Other Sources.	
			Amount.	Per Cent.	Amount.	Per Cent.	Amount.	Per Cent.	Amount.	Per Cent.
$400– 499.....	8	$452.38	$437.91	96.8	$9.97	2.2	$4.50	1.0	..	..
$500– 599.....	17	544.11	509.41	93.6	17.47	3.2	17.23	3.2	..	..
$600– 699.....	72	650.17	611.39	94.0	14.62	2.3	18.26	2.8	$5.90	0.9
$700– 799.....	79	748.33	670.38	89.5	35.96	4.8	38.63	5.2	3.86	0.5
$800– 899.....	73	846.26	712.74	84.2	81.93	9.7	46.55	5.5	5.04	0.6
$900– 999.....	63	942.03	881.00	85.0	107.11	11.4	29.49	3.1	4.62	0.5
$1000–1099.....	31	1044.48	852.50	81.7	121.36	11.6	60.94	5.8	9.68	0.9
$1100–1199.....	18	1137.42	1003.95	88.3	69.69	6.1	48.50	4.3	15.28	1.3
$1200–1299.....	8	1256.25	1012.75	80.6	139.50	11.1	104.00	8.3	..	..
$1300–1399.....	8	1344.12	1028.25	76.5	93.12	7.0	222.75	16.5	..	..
$1400–1409.....	1	1425.00	1300.00	91.2	8.80	..	125.00	..	..	..
$1500–1599.....	6	1518.47	1236.67	81.4	120.00	7.9	93.47	6.2	68.33	4.5

TABLE 10.—SOURCES OF INCOME. PERCENTAGES.—BY BOROUGH AND INCOME.

Income.	Earnings of Father, Per Cent.			Earnings of Others, Per Cent.			From Lodgers, Per Cent.			From Other Sources, Per Cent.		
	Manhattan.	Bronx.	Brooklyn.	Manhattan.	Bronx.	Brooklyn.	Manhattan.	Bronx.	Brooklyn.	Manhattan.	Bronx.	Brooklyn.
$400– 499 ..	93.8	..	100.0	4.3	..	..	1.9	..	..	..	..	..
$500– 599 ..	91.8	..	98.1	3.8	..	1.9	4.4	..	0.5	1.2	..	..
$600– 699 ..	92.2	97.7	99.5	2.9	2.3	..	3.7	..	0.5	..	..	..
$700– 799 ..	87.9	100.0	95.6	5.8	..	1.0	5.8	..	2.9	0.5	..	0.5
$800– 899 ..	82.1	90.1	96.3	11.1	4.9	1.3	16.1	5.0	2.4	0.7	..	..
$900– 999 ..	81.0	100.0	91.2	14.4	..	6.7	3.9	..	2.1	0.7	..	..
$1000–1099 ..	80.8	100.0	79.1	12.8	..	8.3	5.3	..	12.6	1.1	..	..
$1100–1199 ..	82.7	82.2	97.5	8.7	8.9	1.9	6.0	8.9	0.6	2.6	..	..
$1200–1299 ..	84.0	..	57.1	8.3	..	30.6	7.7	..	12.3	..	..	..
$1300–1399 ..	69.3	..	82.4	11.1	..	..	19.6	..	17.6	..	..	..
$1500–1599 ..	77.7	..	100.0	9.5	..	..	7.4	..	..	5.4	..	..

TABLE 11.—SOURCES OF INCOME. NUMBER OF FAMILIES REPORTING INCOME FROM GIVEN SOURCES.— BY INCOME AND NATIONALITY.

NATIONALITY.	$600 TO $699.				$700 TO $799.				$800 TO $899.			
	Number of Families.	Earnings of Father Only.	Earnings of Others.	From Lodgers.	Number of Families.	Earnings of Father Only.	Earnings of Others.	From Lodgers.	Number of Families.	Earnings of Father Only.	Earnings of Others.	From Lodgers.
United States.....	11	10	1	..	19	11	2	5	13	7	4	3
Teutonic	4	2	2	..	7	2	3	3	9	5	2	1
Irish............	4	4	..	..	7	5	1	..	7	3	3	1
Colored.........	11	9	1	1	6	3	3	1	8	..	6	3
Bohemian........	4	1	1	2	3	2	1	1	3	..	3	..
Russian	16	11	1	5	14	6	1	8	12	2	4	8
Austrian, etc......	6	1	..	5	9	2	3	5	9	1	3	5
Italian..........	16	8	3	4	14	9	1	3	12	4	5	4
Total...........	72	46	9	17	79	40	15	26	73	22	30	25

NATIONALITY.	$900 TO $999.				$1000 TO $1099.				TOTAL.					
	Number of Families.	Earnings of Father Only.	Earnings of Others.	From Lodgers.	Number of Families.	Earnings of Father Only.	Earnings of Others.	From Lodgers.	Number of Families.	Earnings of Father Only.		Earnings of Others.		From Lodgers.
										Number.	Per Cent.	Number.	Per Cent.	Number. Per Cent.
United States	16	9	5	2	8	3	2	2	67	40	61.2	14	20.9	12	17.9
Teutonic	11	8	3	..	8	3	3	2	39	20	51.2	13	33.3	6	15.4
Irish	5	5	..	..	1	..	1	..	24	17	70.8	5	20.8	1	4.1
Colored	2	..	2	1	1	..	1	1	28	12	42.9	13	46.4	7	25.0
Bohemian ...	4	..	4	..	..	..	..	..	14	3	21.4	9	64.1	3	21.4
Russian	9	2	2	6	6	..	1	6	57	21	36.9	9	15.8	33	57.9
Austrian, etc.	7	3	3	2	1	..	1	..	32	7	21.9	10	34.4	17	53.1
Italian	9	6	1	2	6	2	3	1	57	29	50.8	13	22.8	14	24.5
Total.......	63	33	20	13	31	8	12	12	318	149	46.8	86	27.0	93	29.2

TABLE 12.—SOURCES OF INCOME. NUMBER OF FAMILIES RE-PORTING INCOME FROM LODGERS: MANHATTAN.—BY INCOME AND NATIONALITY.

NATIONALITY.	TOTAL NUMBER OF FAMILIES.	FAMILIES RECEIVING INCOME FROM LODGERS: MANHATTAN.						
		$600 to $699	$700 to $799	$800 to $899	$900 to $999	$1000 to $1099	Total.	Per Cent. of All Families.
United States............	44	..	5	3	2	1	11	25.0
Teutonic................	27	..	3	1	..	2	6	22.2
Irish....................	17	..	..	1	..	..	1	5.8
Colored................	28	1	1	3	1	1	7	25.0
Bohemian..............	14	2	1	..	..	..	3	21.4
Russian................	34	4	7	6	5	5	27	79.4
Austrian, etc...........	30	5	4	5	2	..	16	53.3
Italian.................	49	3	3	3	2	1	12	24.5
Total.................	..	15	24	22	12	10	83	..
Total number of families...	..	52	63	58	45	25	243	..
Per cent. with lodgers......	..	28.8	38.1	37.9	26.6	45.0	..	34.1

TABLE 13.—SOURCES OF INCOME. NUMBER OF FAMILIES REPORTING WAGE-EARNERS OTHER THAN FATHER.—BY NATIONALITY AND INCOME.

$600 to $699

Nationality	Number of Families	Mother — Janitress	Mother — Other	Boys	Girls	Two Wage-earners	Total
United States	11	1	.	.	.	.	1
Teutonic	4	.	2	.	.	.	2
Irish	4	.	.	.	.	.	.
Colored	11	.	1	.	.	.	1
Bohemian	4	1	.	.	.	.	1
Russian	16	.	.	.	.	.	.
Austrian, etc.	6	.	.	.	2	.	2
Italian	16	.	2	1	.	1	3
Total	72	2	5	1	2	1	10

$700 to $799

Nationality	Number of Families	Mother — Janitress	Mother — Other	Boys	Girls	Two Wage-earners	Total
United States	19	1	.	.	1	1	2
Teutonic	7	2	.	1	.	1	3
Irish	7	1	2	.	.	.	3
Colored	6	1	.	.	1	.	2
Bohemian	3	1	1	.	.	.	2
Russian	14	.	.	.	1	.	1
Austrian, etc.	9	1	1	1	1	1	3
Italian	14	.	1	1	.	1	3
Total	79	7	5	3	4	4	19

$800 to $899

Nationality	Number of Families	Mother — Janitress	Mother — Other	Boys	Girls	Two Wage-earners	Total
United States	13	1	2	2	1	.	6
Teutonic	9	1	.	.	.	1	1
Irish	7	5	.	.	.	1	5
Colored	8	.	3	.	.	.	3
Bohemian	3	.	2	.	1	1	3
Russian	12	4	.	1	1	.	6
Austrian, etc.	9	1	2	1	.	1	5
Italian	12	1	2	1	1	.	4
Total	73	13	11	5	4	4	33

$900 to $999

Nationality	Number of Families	Mother — Janitress	Mother — Other	Boys	Girls	Two Wage-earners	Total
United States	16	2	1	2	.	.	5
Teutonic	11	2	1	.	.	.	3
Irish	5	1	.	1	.	.	1
Colored	2	.	.	.	2	.	1
Bohemian	4	.	3	2	3	2*	7
Russian	9	.	.	.	3	1	3
Austrian, etc.	7	.	1	.	4	2	5
Italian	9	.	1	.	1	.	1
Total	63	5	7	5	10	5	27

$1000 to $1099

Nationality	Number of Families	Mother — Janitress	Mother — Other	Boys	Girls	Two Wage-earners	Total
United States	8	.	1	.	1	.	2
Teutonic	8	.	1	1	2	.	3
Irish	1	.	.	1	.	.	1
Colored	1	.	1	.	.	.	1
Bohemian	.	.	.	.	.	.	.
Russian	6	.	.	1	1	1	2
Austrian, etc.	1	.	.	1	.	.	1
Italian	6	.	.	2	1	1	4
Total	31	.	3	6	5	2	14

TOTAL.

Nationality [¶]	Number of Families	Mother — Janitress	Mother — Other	Boys	Girls	Two Wage-earners	Total
United States	67	5	4	4	3	2	16
Teutonic	39	4	6	2	2	1	14
Irish	24	2	2	1	1	1	6
Colored	28	7	4	1	1	1	13
Bohemian	14	2	5	3	2	2*	12
Russian	57	4	.	1	6	4	13
Austrian, etc.	32	2	4	3	3	4	14
Italian	57	1	6	5	7	2	15
Total	318	27	31	20	25	16	103

* One case, 2 wage-earners; 1 case, 3 wage-earners.

TABLE 14.—SOURCES OF INCOME. NUMBER OF FAMILIES REPORTING WAGE-EARNERS OTHER THAN FATHER.—BY INCOME.

INCOME.	NUMBER OF FAMILIES.	NUMBER WITH OTHER WAGE-EARNERS.	WAGE-EARNER BESIDES FATHER.				
			MOTHER.		Boys.	Girls.	Two Wage-Earners.
			Janitress.	Other.			
$400 to $499	8	2	..	2	..	..	..
$500 to $599	17	3	..	3	..	..	..
$600 to $699	72	9	2	5	1	2	1
$700 to $799	79	15	7	5	3	4	4
$800 to $899	73	29	13	11	5	4	4
$900 to $999	63	21	5	7	5	10	5
$1000 to $1099	31	12	..	3	6	5	2
$1100 to $1199	18	6	1	1	4	..	..
$1200 to $1299	8	3	..	1	1	2	1
$1300 to $1399	8	3	1	1	3	..	2
$1400 and over	14	4	..	1	4	1	2
Total	391	107	29	40	32	28	21
$400 to $599	25	5	..	5	..	..	..
$600 to $799	151	24	9	10	4	6	5
$800 to $899	73	29	13	11	5	4	4
$900 to $1099	94	33	5	10	11	15	7
$1100 and over	48	16	2	4	12	3	5

III. Objects of Expenditure

A. Apportionment (Averages and Percentages) Between Different Heads of Expenditure

The relative expenditure for different purposes is shown in Tables 15 and 16 (pages 70–74). The percentages show which are the elastic elements. Housing demands a decreasing proportion of income as income increases; food remains nearly constant; clothing claims a larger proportion of the higher incomes than of the lower. The expenditures for sundries, including furnishings, society and church dues, amusements and miscellanies, show a rapid increase in percentage with increasing income. Further

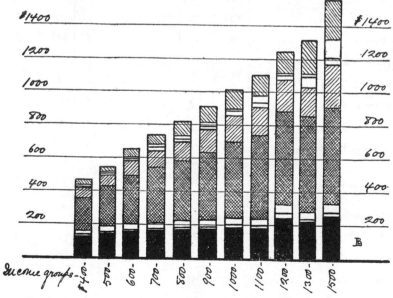

DIAGRAM 6.—Total average expenditure for each income group, and average amounts expended for various purposes.

The items are arranged in each column in the following order, beginning at the bottom: rent; car-fare; fuel and light; food; clothing; insurance; health; sundries.

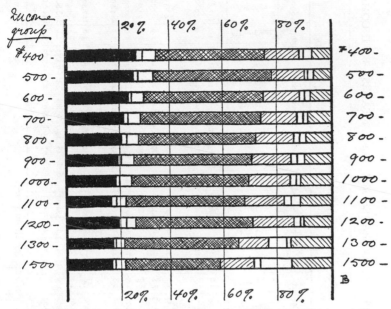

DIAGRAM 7.—Percentage of expenditure for each item. The items are arranged in the same order as in Diagram 6. Beginning at the left: rent; car-fare; fuel and light; food; clothing; insurance; health; sundries.

discussion of the variations of amount and percentage of the expenditures under the different heads for the several income-groups and nationalities will be taken up in the consideration of the successive items. The heading "Units, Average" in the fourth column (Table 15) refers to the food-requirements of the families, stated in multiples of the requirement of an adult man as a unit. The method of reckoning these equivalents is described in another connection, on page 125.

TABLE 15.—EXPENDITURES FOR GIVEN OBJECTS. AVERAGES AND PERCENTAGES.—BY INCOME.

Description				Income.	Expenditures.															
Income-group.	Number of Families.	Number of Persons, Average.	Units, Average.	Total Average.	Total Average.	Rent.		Car-fare.		Fuel and Light.		Food.		Clothing.		Insurance.		Health.		Sundries.	
						Average.	*Per Cent.	Average.	*Per Cent.	Average.	*Per Cent.	Average.	*Per Cent.	Average.	*Per Cent.	Average.	*Per Cent.	Average.	*Per Cent.	Average.	*Per Cent.
$400– 499 ..	8	5.4	3.3	$452.38	$463.98	$124.50	26.8	$11.94	2.6	$25.97	5.6	$189.30	40.8	$60.65	13.0	$5.57	1.2	$14.18	3.1	$31.87	6.9
$500– 599 ..	17	5.0	3.2	544.11	547.30	141.53	25.9	9.80	1.8	32.55	5.9	243.32	44.4	67.95	12.4	7.00	1.3	10.31	1.9	34.84	6.4
$600– 699 ..	72	4.9	3.27	650.17	650.57	153.59	23.6	11.31	1.7	37.71	5.8	290.10	44.6	83.48	12.9	13.05	2.0	13.78	2.1	47.55	7.3
$700– 799 ..	79	5.1	3.46	748.83	735.98	161.36	21.9	10.53	1.5	36.94	5.0	335.82	45.6	98.79	13.4	18.24	2.5	14.02	1.9	66.28	8.2
$800– 899 ..	73	5.2	3.51	846.26	811.88	168.24	20.7	15.86	2.0	41.04	5.0	359.26	44.3	113.59	14.0	17.62	2.2	22.19	2.7	74.08	9.1
$900– 999 ..	63	5.1	3.61	942.03	906.70	171.67	19.0	13.79	1.5	46.70	5.1	405.19	44.7	132.34	14.6	23.71	2.6	23.30	2.6	90.00	9.9
$1000–1099 ..	31	5.0	3.75	1044.48	1009.57	183.12	18.1	18.46	1.8	46.11	4.5	451.46	44.7	155.57	15.5	25.46	2.5	14.80	1.5	114.59	11.4
$1100–1199 ..	18	5.0	3.2	1137.42	1103.30	178.33	16.2	20.74	1.9	42.53	3.8	502.73	45.6	163.80	14.9	27.69	2.5	40.18	3.6	127.30	11.5
$1200–1299 ..	8	5.4	4.3	1256.25	1249.00	248.25	19.8	27.61	2.2	47.68	3.8	562.02	45.0	189.57	15.2	27.50	2.2	16.03	1.3	130.34	10.5
$1300–1399 ..	8	4.9	3.96	1344.12	1312.37	220.50	16.8	14.72	1.1	47.64	3.6	572.04	43.6	180.48	13.7	63.88	4.9	14.31	1.1	198.80	15.2
$1500–1599 ..	6	4.7	3.5	1518.47	1556.28	254.00	16.3	18.27	1.2	64.57	4.1	572.32	36.8	266.97	16.8	36.50	2.3	115.62	7.4	234.03	15.1

*Per cent. of expenditure for all purposes.

70

TABLE 15A.—EXPENDITURES FOR GIVEN OBJECTS. AVERAGES AND PERCENTAGES.—BY INCOME AND NATIONALITY.

Income-group	Nationality	Number of Families	Number of Persons, Average	Units, Average	Total Average (Income)	Total Average (Expend.)	Rent Average	Rent Per Cent.	Car-fare Average	Car-fare Per Cent.	Fuel and Light Average	Fuel and Light Per Cent.	Food Average	Food Per Cent.	Clothing Average	Clothing Per Cent.	Insurance Average	Insurance Per Cent.	Health Average	Health Per Cent.	Sundries Average	Sundries Per Cent.
$600- 699	U. S.	11	5.0	3.2	657.74	665.20	146.47	22.0	7.23	1.1	40.17	6.2	292.74	44.0	86.87	13.0	25.26	3.8	11.09	1.6	55.37	8.4
" "	Teut.	4	4.7	3.1	654.25	660.69	153.00	22.9	29.30	4.4	27.43	4.1	283.35	42.3	94.08	14.0	31.02	4.6	15.33	2.3	36.18	5.3
" "	Irish	4	6.0	4.0	650.00	662.97	133.50	20.1	22.52	3.4	27.14	4.1	292.83	44.2	90.87	13.7	36.00	5.4	17.05	2.6	43.06	6.5
" "	Col.	11	5.4	3.3	634.82	647.11	175.64	27.1	18.53	2.9	44.10	6.8	263.06	40.6	85.46	13.1	19.59	3.3	7.95	1.2	32.78	5.0
" "	Boh.	4	4.5	3.4	633.50	694.16	133.50	19.2	7.80	1.1	59.93	8.6	315.51	45.5	110.92	16.0	6.73	1.0	9.50	1.4	50.27	7.2
" "	Rus.	16	5.1	3.4	647.56	627.79	157.50	25.1	6.69	1.1	33.28	5.3	273.31	43.5	85.77	13.6	4.83	0.8	14.38	2.3	52.03	8.3
" "	Aus.	6	4.3	3.3	657.15	604.96	173.50	28.7	14.17	2.3	30.07	5.0	258.92	42.8	62.48	10.4	3.33	0.5	14.15	2.3	48.34	8.0
" "	Ital.	16	4.6	3.1	653.68	663.99	142.12	21.4	6.27	0.9	38.59	5.8	330.00	49.7	74.02	11.2	3.38	0.5	18.75	2.8	50.86	7.7
$700- 799	U. S.	19	5.3	3.5	752.75	763.13	157.31	20.6	12.98	1.7	43.10	5.6	348.44	45.7	112.95	14.8	26.73	3.5	10.26	1.4	51.36	6.7
" "	Teut.	7	5.0	3.7	772.57	759.29	177.43	23.3	12.35	1.6	35.88	4.7	358.90	47.3	85.65	11.3	36.67	4.9	7.51	1.0	44.00	5.9
" "	Irish.	7	5.3	3.4	732.57	766.32	137.14	17.9	9.23	1.2	33.73	4.4	366.40	47.8	119.08	15.6	24.18	3.1	20.16	2.6	56.40	7.4
" "	Col.	6	5.5	3.4	768.16	783.04	207.00	26.5	12.41	1.6	53.72	6.9	321.40	41.0	114.07	14.6	27.02	3.4	5.02	0.6	42.40	5.4
" "	Boh.	3	6.0	4.1	747.33	736.92	118.00	16.0	2.17	0.3	45.32	6.2	363.89	49.3	111.67	15.2	19.03	2.6	12.53	1.7	64.31	8.7
" "	Rus.	14	5.1	3.5	737.41	698.88	167.96	24.0	9.31	1.3	33.54	4.8	299.34	42.8	84.28	12.1	3.28	0.5	26.52	3.8	74.65	10.7
" "	Aus.	9	4.8	3.6	748.11	710.51	163.72	23.1	8.04	1.1	35.54	5.0	321.97	45.3	86.43	12.2	15.67	2.2	15.63	2.2	63.51	8.9
" "	Ital.	14	4.6	3.0	743.71	705.40	152.57	21.6	10.74	1.5	26.03	3.7	337.39	47.8	89.14	12.7	7.24	1.0	9.93	1.4	72.36	10.3
$800- 899	U. S.	13	5.0	3.5	856.82	867.89	167.54	19.3	13.75	1.6	42.61	4.9	409.88	47.2	127.06	14.6	24.86	2.9	8.53	1.0	73.65	8.5
" "	Teut.	9	5.1	3.2	854.91	873.28	158.67	18.2	25.81	2.9	40.61	4.6	347.06	39.8	143.14	16.4	25.33	2.9	30.30	3.5	102.36	11.7
" "	Irish.	7	4.9	3.3	843.04	812.82	164.57	22.2	16.20	2.0	38.26	4.7	357.09	43.9	124.26	15.3	23.37	2.9	19.41	2.4	69.66	8.6
" "	Col.	8	5.2	3.3	832.65	788.93	212.25	26.9	16.10	2.0	52.61	6.7	297.22	37.7	115.34	14.6	23.31	3.0	15.91	2.0	56.19	7.1

71

TABLE 15A (*Continued*).—EXPENDITURES FOR GIVEN OBJECTS. AVERAGES AND PERCENTAGES.—BY INCOME AND NATIONALITY.

Income-group	Nationality	Number of Families	Number of Persons, Average	Units, Average	Income Total Average	Total Average	Rent Average	Rent Per Cent.	Car-fare Average	Car-fare Per Cent.	Fuel and Light Average	Fuel and Light Per Cent.	Food Average	Food Per Cent.	Clothing Average	Clothing Per Cent.	Insurance Average	Insurance Per Cent.	Health Average	Health Per Cent.	Sundries Average	Sundries Per Cent.
$800–$900	Boh.	3	5.7	3.7	846.00	840.16	130.00	15.5	20.80	2.5	37.44	4.4	408.87	48.7	138.75	16.5	17.97	2.1	18.40	2.2	67.93	8.1
" "	Rus.	12	5.4	3.9	840.08	770.56	165.34	21.5	14.91	1.9	40.83	5.3	348.44	45.2	94.16	12.2	6.99	.9	27.18	3.5	72.71	9.5
" "	Aus.	9	5.0	3.6	843.44	821.87	174.17	21.2	12.74	1.5	46.58	5.7	318.69	38.8	108.68	13.2	24.42	3	49.41	6.0	87.18	10.6
" "	Ital.	12	4.5	3.2	847.67	746.66	157.00	21.0	12.37	1.7	30.52	4.1	385.03	51.6	86.28	11.5	2.31	.3	12.23	1.6	60.92	8.2
$900–999	U. S.	16	5.2	3.5	944.56	949.23	172.50	18.2	16.49	1.7	40.10	4.2	425.75	44.8	143.26	15.0	38.24	4.2	23.08	2.5	88.91	9.4
" "	Teut.	11	5.1	3.4	939.84	917.90	164.84	18.0	17.07	1.9	51.69	5.6	395.44	43.1	135.85	14.8	31.52	3.4	22.02	2.4	99.47	10.8
" "	Irish	5	5.4	3.5	930.00	911.56	160.80	17.6	7.68	.9	42.07	4.6	404.87	44.3	149.17	16.4	41.83	4.6	9.53	1.0	95.61	10.5
" "	Col.	2	5.5	3.7	911.56	843.89	156.00	18.5	18.70	2.2	50.67	6.0	341.53	40.5	146.54	17.4	25.06	2.9	13.25	1.6	92.14	10.9
" "	Boh.	4	5.2	4.0	988.12	983.26	144.00	14.6	16.35	1.7	69.96	7.1	416.18	42.4	181.79	18.5	28.40	2.9	37.41	3.8	89.17	9.0
" "	Rus.	9	5.0	4.2	936.03	892.51	206.67	22.7	18.11	2.3	41.28	4.6	372.39	41.7	113.16	12.6	5.92	0.6	27.21	3.0	111.77	12.5
" "	Aus.	7	4.9	3.4	948.71	905.20	166.15	18.3	7.06	0.8	43.39	4.8	419.54	46.4	130.87	14.4	14.50	1.6	38.02	4.2	85.67	9.5
" "	Ital.	9	5.1	3.5	934.00	810.04	173.69	21.5	7.04	0.9	51.67	6.4	411.65	50.8	94.43	11.6	0.87	0.1	11.95	1.5	58.74	7.2
$1000–1099	U. S.	8	5.4	3.7	1053.12	1072.83	174.95	16.3	19.23	1.8	42.52	4.0	497.29	46.3	165.18	15.4	40.72	3.8	13.55	1.3	119.39	11.1
" "	Teut.	8	5.0	3.7	1040.00	1035.50	191.87	18.5	23.08	2.2	54.29	5.2	421.40	40.7	183.36	17.7	43.97	4.3	7.72	0.7	109.81	10.6
" "	Irish	1	5.0	4.0	1040.00	915.86	210.00	22.9	..	..	69.68	7.6	492.33	53.7	67.63	7.5	..	..	21.00	2.3	55.22	6.0
" "	Col.	1	5.0	4.0	1066.00	886.73	180.00	20.3	31.20	3.5	54.60	6.2	302.44	34.1	107.74	12.2	20.80	2.3	1.00	0.1	188.95	21.3
" "	Rus.	6	4.8	4.0	1043.88	1046.75	197.00	18.8	10.18	1.0	47.80	4.6	469.36	44.8	139.46	13.3	8.17	0.8	32.92	3.1	141.86	13.6
" "	Aus.	1	6.0	5.1	1082.00	978.79	168.00	17.1	68.00	6.9	42.90	4.4	451.91	46.2	177.30	18.1	8.20	0.9	..	..	62.48	6.4
" "	Ital.	6	4.5	3.4	1029.25	894.71	107.00	18.7	12.25	1.4	33.51	3.7	430.48	48.1	140.84	15.7	5.64	0.6	11.53	1.3	93.46	10.5

TABLE 16.—EXPENDITURES FOR GIVEN OBJECTS. AVERAGES AND PERCENTAGES.—BY OCCUPATION.

GARMENT-WORKERS.

Description	Income				Expenditures																
Income	Number of Families	Number of Persons, Average	Number of Units, Average	Total, Average	Total, Average	Rent Average	Rent Per Cent	Car-fare Average	Car-fare Per Cent	Fuel and Light Average	Fuel and Light Per Cent	Food Average	Food Per Cent	Clothing Average	Clothing Per Cent	Insurance Average	Insurance Per Cent	Health Average	Health Per Cent	Sundries Average	Sundries Per Cent
$400– 499	2	4.5	2.8	$437.50	$420.52	$120.00	28.5	$15.50	3.7	$30.90	7.4	$179.48	42.7	$42.30	10.1	..	..	$13.75	3.2	$18.60	4.4
$500– 599	3	5.0	2.8	542.00	550.23	126.00	22.9	17.33	3.1	32.49	5.9	250.06	45.5	56.77	10.3	$1.67	0.3	20.00	3.6	45.90	8.4
$600– 699	13	5.0	3.4	658.69	637.54	170.08	26.7	7.97	1.2	33.50	5.3	272.51	42.8	80.85	12.7	4.73	0.7	14.10	2.2	53.80	8.4
$700– 799	12	4.6	3.3	751.90	721.45	176.38	24.4	6.60	0.9	34.24	4.7	310.63	43.0	82.90	11.6	10.36	1.4	18.96	2.7	81.36	11.3
$800– 899	10	5.1	3.7	839.70	794.47	159.00	20.0	10.52	1.3	47.93	6.0	373.59	47.1	92.73	11.7	7.34	0.9	23.39	2.9	79.97	10.1
$900– 999	10	4.9	3.9	934.95	860.57	170.13	19.8	7.86	0.9	44.75	5.2	422.68	49.2	95.59	11.1	9.82	1.1	17.10	2.0	92.65	10.7
$1000–1099	5	4.8	4.0	1052.60	1084.38	200.40	18.5	6.22	0.6	50.05	4.6	494.04	45.6	144.53	13.3	8.90	0.8	29.10	2.7	151.14	13.9
$1100–1199	3	5.0	3.2	1140.33	1087.14	212.00	19.5	14.07	1.3	50.95	4.6	490.71	45.2	158.05	14.6	3.80	0.4	27.53	2.5	130.03	11.9
$1200–1299	1	6.0	4.0	1280.00	1104.61	260.00	23.5	..	..	42.29	3.8	409.08	36.1	137.26	12.4	4.00	0.4	10.00	0.9	141.98	12.9

73

TABLE 16.—(Continued.)—EXPENDITURES FOR GIVEN OBJECTS. AVERAGES AND PERCENTAGES.—BY OCCUPATION.

Income.	Number of Families.	Number of Persons, Average.	Number of Units, Average.	Total, Average.	Total Average.	Rent. Average.	Rent. Per Cent.	Car-fare. Average.	Car-fare. Per Cent.	Fuel and Light. Average.	Fuel and Light. Per Cent.	Food. Average.	Food. Per Cent.	Clothing. Average.	Clothing. Per Cent.	Insurance. Average.	Insurance. Per Cent.	Health. Average.	Health. Per Cent.	Sundries. Average.	Sundries. Per Cent.
LABORERS.																					
$400– 499	1	6.0	3.5	$450.00	$500.95	$126.00	25.2	31.00	6.2	29.50	5.9	$202.50	40.4	$68.70	13.7	..	..	$9.00	1.8	$48.15	6.8
$600– 699	10	5.2	3.4	639.60	630.20	142.80	22.7	15.78	2.5	36.96	5.8	291.02	46.2	76.67	12.1	13.68	2.1	10.65	1.8	42.64	6.8
$700– 799	10	5.3	3.7	745.14	751.58	168.00	22.4	10.02	1.3	37.29	5.0	352.13	46.8	105.57	14.1	25.52	3.3	4.61	0.6	48.44	6.5
$800– 899	12	4.8	3.3	832.20	745.07	177.60	23.8	12.86	1.7	33.99	4.6	327.97	44.0	96.94	13.0	15.60	2.1	15.46	2.1	64.62	8.7
$900– 999	2	5.5	4.2	960.00	787.92	141.00	17.9	..	..	32.52	4.1	413.40	52.4	125.36	15.9	13.00	1.7	2.85	0.4	59.80	7.6
$1000–1099	3	5.0	4.0	1043.33	944.76	180.00	19.1	..	..	45.86	4.9	509.86	54.0	94.15	9.9	10.38	1.1	12.43	1.3	92.08	9.7
TEAMSTERS.																					
$600– 699	9	5.1	3.1	641.44	644.93	166.66	25.9	7.63	1.2	36.89	5.7	260.51	40.3	79.42	12.3	20.66	3.2	21.79	3.4	51.36	8.0
$700– 700	9	5.6	3.8	751.44	727.72	146.31	20.1	0.25	..	39.74	5.5	357.25	49.1	97.09	13.4	22.49	3.1	7.12	1.0	57.46	7.8
$800– 899	4	4.3	2.7	870.00	863.26	174.00	20.1	24.80	2.9	34.27	3.9	339.52	39.5	126.76	14.7	4.46	0.7	37.19	4.3	120.25	13.9
$900– 999	3	5.3	3.7	939.33	900.67	152.00	28.0	18.93	2.2	46.39	5.1	387.35	43.0	65.48	7.2	59.83	6.6	27.15	3.1	43.55	4.8
$1000–1099	1	5.0	3.0	1003.53	975.04	180.00	18.4	31.20	3.2	40.91	4.2	351.06	36.0	169.01	17.3	10.40	1.1	24.20	2.5	169.10	17.3
$1100–1199	2	5.5	3.2	1147.50	1170.37	180.00	15.3	31.20	2.6	49.83	4.2	605.85	51.7	146.43	12.5	40.50	3.4	11.35	0.9	110.21	9.4
$1300–1399	2	4.5	4.2	1322.50	1336.74	210.00	15.7	16.10	1.1	47.92	3.6	647.97	48.4	145.69	11.0	50.20	3.7	0.60	0.1	218.26	16.4

B. Discussion of Separate Heads of Expenditure.

1. HOUSING.

1. Rent as a Factor in the Budget.—As the table of averages shows (Table 15, pages 70–72), the amount paid for rent increases with increase of income, while the percentage of all expenditures paid for rent tends to diminish as the income increases. Twenty-seven per cent. of all expenditures is paid for housing, on the average, by the 8 families with incomes between $400 and $500, and 26 per cent. by the 17 families with incomes between $500 and $600. The 63 families with incomes between $900 and $1000 average only 19 per cent., although paying $171 on an average, as compared with $124, the average of the rent of families in the $400 income-group.

A study of the rent payments (Tables 20 and 21, page 88) shows the same tendency. Of the 243 Manhattan families with incomes between $600 and $1100, 74 families, or 30 per cent., pay from $12 to $14 a month for rent; and 157 families, or 60 per cent., pay $14 and under. But in the $600 income-group 73 per cent. of the families pay not more than $14; in the $700 group, 67 per cent.; in the $800 group, 62 per cent.; while in the $900 group, 49 per cent., and in the $1000 group, 36 per cent. are in this category. Or, drawing the line in another way, as in Table 23, the percentage of families in the different income-groups spending $14 or more monthly for rent is:

$600 to $699 . . . . 36.5 per cent.
700 to 799 . . . . 44.5   "
800 to 899 . . . . 51.7   "
900 to 999 . . . . 66.7   "
1000 to 1099 . . . . 72.0   "

When it is remembered that in most quarters of the city an apartment of 4 rooms costs more than $14 a month, it will be seen that no very high standard, in the matter of housing, is assured on an income of less than $900.

2. Comparison of Rent-charges According to Locality and Nationality.—The tables of averages (Tables 18 and 19, pages 86–87) show that families living in Manhattan spend somewhat

75

more for rent than those living in Brooklyn. The average yearly expenditure for this purpose in Manhattan ranges from $157.33 to $185.72 as the income rises from $600 to $1100, or 24 and 18.1 per cent., respectively, of all expenditures. In Brooklyn the averages range from $144.21 to $171.40, or 22.3 and 17.9 per cent. respectively, of all expenditures. The number of families in the Bronx and Queens is too small to justify citation of averages, but in the cases from these boroughs the figures run somewhat lower than in Brooklyn.

For the purpose of comparing rents in different parts of Manhattan, arbitrary lines were drawn on the map, dividing the boroughs into five districts: North, all territory north of 96th street; East, east of Broadway, between 14th and 96th streets; South-east, east of Broadway, south of 14th street; South-west, west of Broadway, south of 14th street; West, west of Broadway, between 14th and 96th streets. The tables on pages 90–91 show the apportionment of the Manhattan families among these districts, both by income and nationality. Table 26 (page 91) shows that the lowest rents are paid in the South-west, where only 2 families out of 24 pay more than $15 a month. Between the other districts, the differences are not so marked. However, 40 per cent. of the families north of 96th street pay more than $15 a month, as compared with 25 per cent. in the western section, 33 per cent. in the east, and 36 per cent. in the lower east side.

A comparison of the housing expenditure of different nationalities shows that the highest average and the highest percentage of all expenditures is reported by the colored people, the lowest by the Bohemians. It was reported that higher charges were made to the former than to whites. Arranging the nationalities in descending scale according to expenditure for housing, the order seems to be: Colored, Teutonic peoples, Russian, Austrian, American, Irish, Italian, Bohemian. In some instances the number of cases is too small to warrant very confident assertions on this point. (See Table 17, page 85.)

3. CHARACTER OF HOUSING ACCOMMODATIONS.—Indications on this point may be found in the number of rooms, the number of rooms without direct access to outside light and air, the presence or absence of bath-room and toilet in the apartment, and the

ratio of number of rooms to number of persons occupying them at night. The measurement of each room was also asked for in the schedule, and the number of cubic feet per occupant was calculated. But the measurements were in so many cases in-exact that this item has not been included in the tables.

The average number of rooms per family increases with income regularly, being for Manhattan, 3.1 for families with incomes of between $600 and $700, and 3.8 for families between $1000 and $1100. For the other boroughs the figures rise correspond-ingly from 3.7 to 4.2. (See Tables 27 and 34, pages 91 and 98.)

The number of families reported as occupying tenements of 2 rooms, 3 rooms, etc., is exhibited in Tables 28–33 (pages 92–97). It appears from the final summary that out of 115 Manhattan families with incomes between $600 and $800, 71 per cent. have no more than 3 rooms; of the 58 families in the $800 group, 48 per cent. have not more than 3 rooms, and of the 70 families with incomes between $900 and $1100, 39 per cent. live in 3 rooms or less. The percentage of families having not more than 3 rooms is as follows:

INCOME.	TOTAL NUMBER OF FAMILIES.		PER CENT. LIVING IN THREE ROOMS.	
	Manhattan.	Other Boroughs.	Manhattan.	Other Boroughs.
$600 to $799..........	115	36	71	31
$800 to $899..........	58	15	48	27
$900 to $1099..........	70	24	39	17

A comparison of nationalities with respect to number of rooms shows a range for Manhattan of an average for the American fam-ilies of from 3.2 ($700) to 4.3 ($800); for the Teutonic nations from 3.4 ($800) to 4.3 ($1000); colored, from 3.4 ($600) to 4 ($900); Bohemians, 3 ($700) to 3.25 ($900); Russian, 3.1 ($600) to 3.8 ($1000). Austrians average 3 rooms for the $1000 group, 3.6 for the $600 group. The Irish range from 3 ($600) to 3.7 ($900), with a single case of 5 rooms on an income of over $1000. The Italian reports show the lowest average, 2.6 at $600 and 3.9 at $900. Considered by count of families, the same relation ex-ists. Three-quarters of the Italian families reported from Manhattan were living in 2 and 3 rooms, one-quarter of them in 2 rooms. Sixty per cent. of the Manhattan Russians were in 2 and 3 rooms, and the same proportion was true of the Austrians. Only 2 of the 14 Bohemian families reported as many as 4 rooms. Combining the Americans, Teutons and Irish, 36 out of 88 families in Manhattan, or 40 per cent., had no more than 3 rooms.

Fifty-three per cent. of all the 391 families report dark rooms; *i. e.*, rooms without direct access to outside air and light. (See Tables 34–38, pages 98–102.) Sixty per cent. of the Manhattan families report dark rooms, and 32 per cent. of the families in the outlying boroughs. The frequency of dark rooms seems from the table of averages (Table 34, page 98) to be as great with high incomes as with lower. The count of cases, however, yields more favorable indications, as appears in the following table giving the percentage of families reporting one or more dark rooms:

INCOME.	ALL BOROUGHS. PER CENT.	MANHATTAN. PER CENT.	OTHER BOROUGHS. PER CENT.
$400 to $599	64	81	33
600 to 799	54	64	19
800 to 899	64	67	53
900 to 1099	49	54	33
1100 and over	38	38	38
All incomes	53	60	32

DIAGRAM 8.—Percentage of families reporting one or more dark rooms.
The black part of the bar represents the proportion of families who had at least one dark room; the shaded part, the proportion who had none.

78

The extent to which bath-rooms and toilets are included within the apartments appears from the following summary of the number and percentage of families reporting them:

INCOME.	TOTAL NUMBER OF FAMILIES.	REPORTING BATH-ROOM.		REPORTING TOILET.	
		No.	Per Cent.	No.	Per Cent.
$400 to $599	25	1	4	8	32
$600 to $799	151	21	14	40	26
$800 to $899	73	12	16	18	24
$900 to $1099	94	23	24	29	31
$1100 and over	48	23	48	25	40

In other words, not more than a quarter of the families possess these conveniences on any income below $1100. To more than three-fourths of the families with incomes under this amount, bath-tubs and separate toilets for each family are luxuries in the sense in which Professor Patten uses the term; i. e., they have not yet been included in the standard of living. As between different localities, about one family in 7 of the Manhattan group have bath-rooms, and about 2 out of 7 in the other boroughs. A private toilet is reported by 22 per cent. of the families in Manhattan, and by 43 per cent. of those outside. These figures in every case are for the 318 families with incomes between $600 and $1100, 243 being in Manhattan and 75 outside. Taking the same families by nationality, the colored and Russian families make the best showing, one family in every three reporting bath-rooms and about the same proportion reporting private toilets. This may be due in part to the selection of families among the negroes, the whole number being only 28, and to the fact that the Russians are more largely housed in the new-law tenements of the East Side than the families of the other races. Of the American families 1 in 7 reports bath-room, 1 in 3, private toilet. The Teutons and Irish report both fewer bath-rooms and private toilets, in proportion, than the Italians. The Austrian families show 1 bath-room for every 5 families, and a private toilet in 2 cases out of every 7.

79

4. RELATION BETWEEN NUMBER OF ROOMS AND NUMBER OF PERSONS.—For the purpose of judging of the degree of over-crowding in the cases embraced in this report the number of families having less than 4 rooms is tabulated in Tables 39–45 (pages 103–108) and also the number of families where the number of rooms is less than 1 to every 1½ persons. Since none of the families includes less than 4 persons and the greater number consist of 5 or 6,

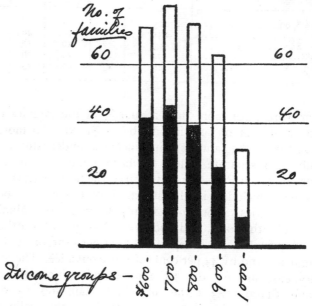

DIAGRAM 9.—Number of over-crowded families in each of the principal income-groups.

The black part of the column represents the over-crowded families.

an allowance of 4 rooms would not seem to exceed, as a rule, the demands of decency. To make allowance for variations in the number of persons using the family apartment, a standard of 1½ persons to a room has been applied. That is, more than 6 persons to 4 rooms, and more than 4 persons to 3 rooms, are considered to constitute over-crowding. Lodgers are included in the number of persons occupying the rooms, since the most serious difficulty regarding fresh air is found at night, when the lodgers are in their quarters. A count of families on this basis shows that of the 391 families 171, or 44 per cent., have less than 3 rooms, while 187, or 48 per cent., have more than 1½ persons per room. In the lower income-groups over-crowding is the rule. Sixty-one per cent. of the families with incomes between $600 and $800 have less than 4 rooms; 58 per cent., more than 1½ persons per room. In the $800 group 36 per cent. of the families have less than 4 rooms, but 53 per cent. have more than 1½ persons per room. This means that while more space is rented, lodgers are called in to help pay for it. Thirty-five per cent. of the $900 and $1000 families have less than 4 rooms, and practically the same proportion exceed the standard ratio of persons to rooms. The relief when the income exceeds $1100 is apparent. Of the 48 families in this income-group only 2 report less than 4 rooms, and 10 report a ratio of more than 1½ persons per room.

As is to be expected, the congestion in Manhattan exceeds that reported in Brooklyn, Bronx and Queens. In the outlying boroughs the percentage of over-crowded families, measured by the 4-room standard, is 23 as compared with 51 per cent. in Manhattan. As for the persons-per-room standard, 29 per cent. of the families in the outside boroughs fall below it, as against 55 per cent. in Manhattan. As regards nationalities, the following table shows the proportion of families out of the 318, with incomes between $600 and $1100, reporting more than 1½ persons per room:

NATIONALITY.	TOTAL NUMBER OF FAMILIES.	NUMBER REPORTING MORE THAN 1½ PERSONS PER ROOM.	PER CENT.
United States	67	20	30
Teutonic nations	39	8	21
Irish	24	12	50
Colored	28	16	57
Bohemian	14	11	79
Russian	57	35	61
Austrian, etc.	32	21	66
Italian	57	37	65
	318	160	50

Our figures indicate that the over-crowding is most frequent in the families with incomes less than $800 and among immigrants from southern Europe. Further light may be thrown on the subject by noticing the apportionment of the over-crowded families among those having surplus, deficit, or even balance at the end of the year. Grouped on this basis of classification, as in Tables 44 and 45 (page 108), we find that 34 per cent. of the over-crowded families come out even, 44 per cent. report a surplus and only 22 per cent. report a deficit. When this is compared with the percentage for all families; viz., 36 per cent. even balance, 36 per cent. surplus, 28 per cent. deficiency (Table 119, page 235), it seems not improbable that the over-crowded families are able to come out on the right side in the larger number of instances

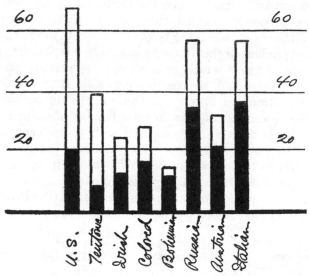

DIAGRAM 10.—Number of over-crowded families in each of the nationality-groups.

by reason of their living according to a low standard in the matter of housing. This is suggested especially by a comparison of families reporting surplus, by income-groups:

Income.	Percentage of all Families Reporting Surplus.	Percentage of Over-crowded Families Reporting Surplus.
$600 to $699	28	30
700 to 799	33	43
800 to 899	48	56
900 to 999	35	48
1000 to 1099	42	44

The analysis of over-crowded families according to sources of income shows that over-crowding is more frequent among families where the father is not the sole bread-winner (Table 43, page 107). Forty-seven per cent. of all the 318 families are supported by the father alone, while only 41 per cent. of the over-crowded families are thus supported. This disparity is most striking in the families with incomes between $900 and $1000. Fifty-four per cent. of all families in this group are supported entirely by the father, as against 36 per cent. of the over-crowded families in this group. In the other income-groups the ratio corresponds more nearly to that prevailing among the families as a whole.

5. OVER-CROWDING AND LODGERS.—An analysis of over-crowded families with reference to sources of income brings out the relation of lodgers to the housing problem. In the first place, the function of the lodger as a rent-paying necessity appears in the large proportion of lodgers in high-priced tenements. It will be seen in Table 46 (page 109) that lodgers are reported by 20 per cent. of the Manhattan families which pay $10 or less a month for rent, by 23 per cent. of those paying from $10 to $14, by 50 per cent. of those paying from $14 to $16, and by 62 per cent. of the families paying over $16. An inspection of the same table will show also that many families with incomes under $900 pay $175 and more annually for housing, but that in almost all of these cases, lodgers are taken to eke out the income.*

Coming now to the over-crowded families (Table 48, page 110), it appears that lodgers are more frequent among them than among the remaining families reported. Twenty-nine per cent. of the 318 families with incomes between $600 and $1100 have lodgers, while 41 per cent. of the 160 over-crowded families have lodgers. Further, of the 93 families reporting lodgers, 65 families, or 70 per cent., are over-crowded.

6. INCREASE OF RENT SINCE 1905.—The burden of high rentals was increased up to the middle of the year 1907 by the general ten-

---

* One man who filled out a schedule for his own family writes: "I think it would be just as well to include in the report the letting of one room at the rate of $5.00 per week, 50 weeks per year. That is the general thing we have done, but I dislike to have roomers and had decided to do without them, but figuring up the expense without them, guess will have to try it again soon." The writer was paying $360 a year for a steam-heated apartment on a total income of $1500.

dency of rents to rise. In answer to the questions in regard to increase of rent it was reported by the 243 Manhattan families that 45 of them had been in their present quarters less than one year. Of the 198 who had been a year or more in the same tenement, 102, or a trifle more than half, reported increase of rent. The amount of increase varied from 50 cents to $5 a month,* but in the majority of cases was $1.00, $1.50, or $2.00. As between the different parts of the island, divided into the regions already designated, an increase was reported in 60 per cent. of the cases in the central East, in 57 per cent. of the cases in the central West, in 53 per cent. of the cases in the Southeast, 43 per cent. for the South-west, and 17 per cent. (3 cases out of 18) for the North. As between the different amounts paid for rent, the increase seems to vary arbitrarily. The details may be found in Tables 49 and 50 (page 110).

* One family on Essex Street has been in its present tenement for 10 years. It now pays $23.00 a month for 4 rooms, with toilet in apartment. Two years before the rent was $18.00.

TABLE 17.—RENT PER ANNUM: ALL BOROUGHS. AVERAGE AMOUNT, AND PER CENT. OF TOTAL EXPENDITURE.—BY INCOME AND NATIONALITY.

NATIONALITY.	$600 to $699			$700 to $799			$800 to $899			$900 to $999			$1000 to $1099		
	Number of Families.	Average Amount.	*Per Cent.	Number of Families.	Average Amount.	*Per Cent.	Number of Families.	Average Amount.	*Per Cent.	Number of Families.	Average Amount.	*Per Cent.	Number of Families.	Average Amount.	*Per Cent.
United States.	11	$146.47	22.0	19	$157.31	20.6	13	$167.54	19.3	16	$172.50	18.2	8	$174.95	16.3
Teutonic.....	4	153.00	22.9	7	177.43	23.3	9	158.67	18.2	11	164.84	18.0	8	191.87	18.5
Irish.........	4	133.50	20.1	7	137.14	17.9	7	164.57	20.2	5	160.80	17.6	1	210.00	22.9
Colored......	11	175.64	27.1	6	207.00	26.5	8	212.25	26.9	2	156.00	18.5	1	180.00	20.3
Bohemian.....	4	133.50	19.2	3	118.00	16.0	3	130.00	15.5	4	144.00	14.6	..	......	....
Russian......	16	157.50	25.1	14	167.96	24.0	12	165.34	21.5	9	206.67	22.7	6	197.00	18.8
Austrian, etc.	6	173.50	28.7	9	163.72	23.1	9	174.17	21.2	7	166.15	18.3	1	168.00	17.1
Italian.......	16	142.12	21.4	14	152.57	21.6	12	157.00	21.0	9	173.69	21.5	6	167.00	18.7
Total........	72	153.59	23.6	79	161.36	21.9	73	168.24	20.7	63	171.67	19.0	31	183.12	18.1

* Per cent. of expenditure for all purposes.

85

TABLE 18.—RENT PER ANNUM: MANHATTAN. AVERAGE AMOUNT, AND PER CENT. OF TOTAL EXPENDITURE.—BY INCOME AND NATIONALITY.

NATIONALITY.	$600 TO $699			$700 TO 799			$800 TO $899			$900 TO $999			$1000 TO $1099		
	Number of Families.	Average Amount.	*Per Cent.	Number of Families.	Average Amount.	*Per Cent.	Number of Families.	Average Amount.	*Per Cent.	Number of Families.	Average Amount.	*Per Cent.	Number of Families.	Average Amount.	*Per Cent.
United States	6	$143.00	21.3	14	$151.14	20.1	8	$180.00	20.2	11	$190.91	20.1	5	$174.00	15.9
Teutonic	2	156.00	25.1	7	177.43	23.3	8	154.50	17.4	4	181.50	20.1	6	201.83	19.3
Irish	3	138.00	21.0	5	139.20	18.2	5	159.00	20.7	3	164.00	18.2	1	195.00	19.4
Colored	11	175.64	27.1	6	207.06	26.5	8	212.25	26.9	2	156.00	18.5	1	180.00	20.3
Bohemian	4	133.50	19.2	3	118.00	16.0	3	130.00	15.5	4	144.00	14.6	..	......	....
Russian	7	176.57	27.4	8	185.81	25.1	8	177.75	22.9	6	206.00	22.8	5	240.00	18.5
Austrian,etc	5	179.40	29.8	8	166.19	23.3	9	174.17	21.2	7	166.15	18.3	1	168.00	17.1
Italian	14	142.72	21.3	12	162.00	22.6	9	160.00	21.1	8	178.91	22.4	6	167.00	18.7
Total	52	157.33	24.0	63	165.24	22.3	58	172.27	21.0	45	178.58	19.8	25	185.72	18.1

* Per cent. of expenditure for all purposes.

TABLE 19.—RENT PER ANNUM: BRONX, BROOKLYN, QUEENS. AVERAGE AMOUNT AND PER CENT. OF TOTAL EXPENDITURE.—BY INCOME AND NATIONALITY.

NATIONALITY.	$600 TO $699			$700 TO $799			$800 TO $899			$900 TO $999			$1000 TO $1099		
	Number of Families.	Average Amount.	* Per Cent.	Number of Families.	Average Amount.	* Per Cent.	Number of Families.	Average Amount.	* Per Cent.	Number of Families.	Average Amount.	* Per Cent.	Number of Families.	Average Amount.	* Per Cent.
BRONX.															
United States	2	$153.00	23.9	1	$192.00	22.3	1	$174.00	19.5	..	..	..	1	$192.00	17.1
Teutonic	..	..	..	..	..	..	1	192.00	24.4	2	192.00	20.9	..	..	..
Irish	..	..	..	..	..	..	1	186.00	21.6	..	..	..	..	..	..
Russian	2	144.00	23.2	..	..	..	..	..	..	..	..	..	..	..	..
Italian	1	120.00	21.0	1	72.00	12.8	2	150.00	22.2	..	..	..	..	..	..
Total	5	142.80	23.0	2	132.00	18.6	5	170.40	21.8	2	192.00	20.9	1	192.00	17.1
BROOKLYN.															
United States	3	149.07	22.2	4	170.20	21.7	4	141.00	17.3	2	162.00	17.1	2	168.80	17.0
Teutonic	2	150.00	20.9	..	..	..	..	..	..	3	178.40	19.2	1	168.00	17.1
Irish	1	120.00	17.7	2	132.00	17.1	1	168.00	17.5	1	168.00	17.7	..	..	..
Russian	7	142.29	23.2	6	144.17	22.4	4	140.50	20.2	3	196.00	22.4	1	180.00	21.0
Austrian, etc.	1	144.00	23.1	1	144.00	20.8	..	..	..	..	..	..	..	..	..
Italian	1	156.00	24.0	1	120.00	16.4	..	..	..	1	132.00	14.5	..	..	..
Total	15	144.21	22.3	14	148.13	20.8	9	143.78	18.5	10	174.72	19.1	4	171.40	17.9
QUEENS.															
United States	..	..	..	..	..	..	..	..	..	..	..	..	..	..	..
Teutonic	..	..	..	..	..	..	..	..	..	3	112.00	11.8	..	..	..
Irish	..	..	..	..	..	..	..	..	..	2	84.00	9.1	1	156.00	15.5
Italian	..	..	..	..	..	..	1	144.00	18.1	1	144.00	16.1	..	..	..
Total	..	..	..	..	..	..	1	144.00	18.1	6	108.00	11.6	1	156.00	15.5

* Per cent. of expenditure for all purposes.

TABLE 20.—RENT PER MONTH: MANHATTAN. NUMBER OF FAMILIES PAYING GIVEN AMOUNTS.—BY INCOME.

RENT PER MONTH.	INCOME.								
	$400 to $599.	$600 to $699.	$700 to $799.	$800 to $899.	$900 to $999.	$1000 to $1099.	$1100 and Over.	Total, Incomes $600 to $1099.	Total, All Incomes.
$10 and under.	4	10	12	6	3	..	1	31	36
$10 to $12.....	5	8	17	9	6	2	1	42	48
$12 to $14.....	5	20	13	21	13	7	4	74	83
$14 to $16.....	1	8	6	8	9	7	3	38	42
$16 to $18.....	1	5	8	3	7	6	3	29	33
Over $18......	..	1	7	11	7	3	20	29	49
Total.........	16	52	63	58	45	25	32	243	291

TABLE 21.—RENT PER MONTH: MANHATTAN. NUMBER AND PER CENT. OF FAMILIES PAYING GIVEN AMOUNTS.—BY NATIONALITY.

NATIONALITY.	NUMBER OF FAMILIES.	$10 Per Month and Under.		Over $10 to $12 Per Month.		Over $12 to $14 Per Month.		Over $14 to $16 Per Month.		Over $16 to $18 Per Month.		Over $18 Per Month.	
		Number.	Per Cent.	Number.	Per Cent.	Number.	Per Cent.	Number.	Per Cent.	Number.	Per Cent.	Number.	Per Cent.
United States..	44	7	16	8	18	13	29	6	14	4	9	6	14
Teutonic......	27	3	11	7	26	6	22	2	8	3	11	6	22
Irish..........	17	3	18	6	35	3	18	3	18	2	11	..	..
Colored.......	28	1	4	1	4	9	32	6	21	4	14	7	25
Bohemian.....	14	6	42	6	42	1	8	1	8	..	..	..	..
Russian.......	34	1	3	1	3	9	26	9	26	12	36	2	6
Austrian, etc...	30	1	3	5	17	13	43	5	17	5	17	1	3
Italian........	49	9	19	8	16	20	41	6	12	3	6	3	6
Total.........	243	31	13	42	17	74	30	38	16	33	12	25	12

TABLE 22.—RENT PER MONTH: MANHATTAN. NUMBER AND PER CENT. OF FAMILIES PAYING GIVEN AMOUNTS.—BY INCOME.

INCOME.	NUMBER OF FAMILIES.	$10 and under.		$10 to $12.		$12 to $14.		$14 to $16.		$16 to $18.		Over $18.	
		Number.	Per Cent.	Number.	Per Cent.	Number.	Per Cent.	Number.	Per Cent.	Number.	Per Cent.	Number.	Per Cent.
$600 to $699	52	10	19	8	15	20	39	8	15	4	8	2	4
$700 to $799	63	11	18	17	27	13	21	6	10	8	13	7	11
$800 to $899	58	6	10	9	16	21	36	8	14	3	5	11	19
$900 to $999	45	3	7	6	13	13	28	9	20	7	16	7	16
$1000 to $1099	25	..	..	2	8	7	28	7	28	6	24	3	12
$600 to $799	115	21	18	25	22	33	29	14	12	12	11	9	8
$800 to $899	58	6	10	9	16	21	36	8	14	3	5	11	19
$900 to $1099	70	3	4	8	11	20	29	16	23	13	19	10	14

TABLE 23.—RENT PER MONTH: MANHATTAN. NUMBER AND PER CENT. OF ALL FAMILIES PAYING GIVEN AMOUNTS.—BY CUMULATIVE GROUPING.

INCOME.	NUMBER OF FAMILIES.	BELOW $10 PER MONTH.		$10 PER MONTH AND BELOW.		$12.50 PER MONTH AND BELOW.		$14 PER MONTH AND ABOVE.		$15 PER MONTH AND ABOVE.		$17 PER MONTH AND ABOVE.		$19 PER MONTH AND ABOVE.		$20 PER MONTH AND ABOVE.	
		Number.	Per Cent.	Number.	Per Cent.	Number.	Per Cent.	Number.	Per Cent.	Number.	Per Cent.	Number.	Per Cent.	Number.	Per Cent.	Number.	Per Cent.
$600 to $699	52	5	9.6	10	19.2	22	42.3	19	36.5	12	23.1	4	7.7	1	1.9	..	..
$700 to $799	63	7	11.1	12	19.0	30	47.6	28	44.5	21	33.4	12	19.0	7	11.1	6	9.5
$800 to $899	58	1	1.7	6	10.3	17	29.3	30	51.7	22	38.0	14	24.1	10	17.3	5	8.6
$900 to $999	45	3	6.6	3	6.7	10	22.2	30	66.7	21	46.7	13	28.9	7	15.6	6	13.3
$1000 to $1099	25	..	..	..	..	3	12.0	18	72.0	15	60.0	9	36.0	3	12.0	1	4.0

89

TABLE 24.—RENT PER MONTH: BROOKLYN AND BRONX. NUMBER OF FAMILIES PAYING GIVEN AMOUNTS.—BY INCOME.

RENT PER MONTH.	NUMBER OF FAMILIES.	BROOKLYN. Income.					BRONX. Income.
		$600 to $699.	$700 to $799.	$800 to $899.	$900 to $999.	$1000 to $1099.	All Incomes
$10 and under....	9	3	4	2	..	..	3
$10 to $12........	20	7	5	4	..	..	2
$12 to $14........	10	3	2	2	3	1	2
$14 to $16........	11	2	3	1	3	2	6
$16 to $18........	1	..	..	..	1	..	1
Over $18.........	1	..	..	..	1	..	1
Total............	52	15	14	9	10	4	15

TABLE 25.—DISTRIBUTION INTO DISTRICTS OF 243 MANHATTAN FAMILIES.—BY RENT, INCOME AND NATIONALITY.

(A) BY MONTHLY RENT.

MONTHLY RENT.	N.	E.	S. E.	S. W.	W.	TOTAL.
$10 and under........	5	9	6	5	6	31
$10.50 to $12.50.....	8	9	21	6	8	52
$13.00 to $15.00.....	5	15	27	11	28	86
$15.50 to $17.50.....	4	6	16	1	9	36
$18.00 and over......	8	10	14	1	5	38
Total................	30	49	84	24	56	243

(B) BY INCOME.

INCOME.	N.	E.	S. E.	S. W.	W.	TOTAL.
$600 to $699.........	7	9	15	6	15	52
$700 to $799.........	10	8	25	6	14	63
$800 to $899.........	7	15	19	4	13	58
$900 to $999.........	2	12	17	4	10	45
$1000 to $1099.......	4	5	8	4	4	25
Total................	30	49	84	24	56	243

(C) BY NATIONALITY.

NATIONALITY.	N.	E.	S. E.	S. W.	W.	TOTAL.
United States........	2	14	8	6	14	44
Teutonic.............	2	5	7	3	10	27
Irish................	4	..	..	5	8	17
Colored..............	10	1	..	..	17	28
Bohemian.............	..	14	..	..	..	14
Russian..............	2	3	29	..	..	34
Austrian, etc.	..	8	21	..	1	30
Italian..............	10	4	19	10	6	49
Total................	30	49	84	24	56	243

TABLE 26.—RENT PER MONTH: MANHATTAN. NUMBER AND
PER CENT. OF FAMILIES PAYING RENT OF GIVEN
AMOUNTS.—BY DISTRICT.

DISTRICT.	TOTAL NUMBER OF FAMILIES.	FAMILIES PAYING MONTHLY RENTAL OF:									
		$10.00 and under.		$10.50 to $12.50		$13.00 to $15.00		$15.50 to $17.50		$18.00 and over.	
		Number.	Per Cent.	Number.	Per Cent.	Number.	Per Cent.	Number.	Per Cent.	Number.	Per Cent.
North........	30	5	16.7	8	26.7	5	16.7	4	13.3	8	26.7
East.........	49	9	18.4	9	18.4	15	30.6	6	12.2	10	20.4
South-east. ..	84	6	7.1	21	25.0	27	32.1	16	19.0	14	16.7
South-west...	24	5	20.8	6	25.0	11	45.8	1	4.2	1	4.2
West.........	56	6	10.7	8	14.3	28	50.0	9	16.1	5	8.9
Total........	243	31	12.7	52	21.4	86	35.4	36	14.8	38	15.6

TABLE 27.—NUMBER OF ROOMS PER FAMILY: MANHATTAN.
AVERAGES.—BY INCOME AND NATIONALITY.

NATIONALITY.	NUMBER OF FAMILIES.	INCOME.				
		$600 to $699	$700 to $799	$800 to $899	$900 to $999	$1000 to $1099
United States.............	44	3.3	3.2	4.25	4.1	3.8
Teutonic.................	27	3.5	3.7	3.4	4.25	4.3
Irish....................	17	3.0	3.4	3.4	3.7	5.0
Colored.................	28	3.45	4.3	3.9	4.0	4.0
Bohemian................	14	3.25	3.0	3.0	3.25	..
Russian.................	34	3.1	3.25	3.25	3.7	3.8
Austrian, etc.............	30	3.6	3.1	3.55	3.0	3.0
Italian..................	49	2.6	2.8	3.2	3.9	3.2
Total...................	243	3.1	3.3	3.5	3.7	3.8

TABLE 28.—NUMBER OF ROOMS PER FAMILY.—BY INCOME, BOROUGH AND NATIONALITY.

NATIONALITY.		$600 TO $699						$700 TO $799						$800 TO $899					
		Number of Families.	Two Rooms.	Three Rooms.	Four Rooms.	Five Rooms.	Six Rooms.	Number of Families.	Two Rooms.	Three Rooms.	Four Rooms.	Five Rooms.	Six Rooms.	Number of Families.	Two Rooms.	Three Rooms.	Four Rooms.	Five Rooms.	Six Rooms.
United States	Manhattan*	6	..	5	..	1	..	14	3	5	6	..	..	8	..	..	6	2	..
	Other†	5	..	1	3	1	..	5	..	1	3	1	..	5	1	..	2	2	..
Teutonic	Manhattan	2	..	1	1	..	..	7	..	2	5	..	..	8	..	5	3	..	..
	Other	2	..	1	1	..	..	..	..	..	..	..	..	1	..	..	1	..	..
Irish	Manhattan	3	..	3	..	..	..	5	..	3	2	..	..	5	..	3	2	..	..
	Other	1	..	1	..	..	..	2	..	1	1	..	..	2	..	..	..	1	1
Colored	Manhattan	11	..	7	3	1	..	6	..	4	..	..	2*	8	..	1	7	..	..
	Other	..	..	..	..	..	..	..	..	..	..	..	..	..	..	..	..	..	..
Bohemian	Manhattan	4	..	3	1	..	..	3	..	3	..	..	..	3	..	3	..	..	..
	Other	..	..	..	..	..	..	..	..	..	..	..	..	..	..	..	..	..	..
Russian	Manhattan	7	1	4	2	..	..	8	..	6	2	..	..	8	..	6	2	..	..
	Other	9	1	1	6	1	..	6	..	1	3	1	..	4	..	2	2	..	..
Austrian, etc.	Manhattan	5	..	2	3	..	..	8	..	5	2	..	..	9	..	4	5	..	..
	Other	1	..	..	1	..	..	1	1	..	1	..	..	..	..	..	..	..	..
Italian	Manhattan	14	6	8	..	..	..	12	5	5	1	1	..	9	2	4	2	..	..
	Other	2	..	..	2	..	..	2	..	2	..	..	..	3	1	..	1	1	1
Total	Manhattan	52	7	33	10	2	..	63	9	33	18	1	2*	58	2	26	27	3	..
	Other	20	1	4	13	2	..	16	1	5	8	2	..	15	2	2	6	3	2

* Seven rooms. † Other boroughs combined.

92

TABLE 28 (Continued).—NUMBER OF ROOMS PER FAMILY.—BY INCOME, BOROUGH AND NATIONALITY.

Nationality		$900 to $999						$1000 to $1099						Total					
		Number of Families	Two Rooms	Three Rooms	Four Rooms	Five Rooms	Six Rooms	Number of Families	Two Rooms	Three Rooms	Four Rooms	Five Rooms	Six Rooms	Number of Families	Two Rooms	Three Rooms	Four Rooms	Five Rooms	Six Rooms
United States	Manhattan	11	..	3	5	2	1	5	1	1	2	..	1	44	4	14	19	5	2
	Other	5	..	..	3	1	1	3	..	1	1	1	..	23	1	3	12	6	1
Teutonic	Manhattan	4	..	..	3	2	1	6	..	..	5	..	1	27	..	8	17	1	1
	Other	7	..	2	4	1	1	2	..	..	1	..	1	12	..	3	7	1	1
Irish	Manhattan	3	..	1	2	..	..	1	..	..	..	1	..	17	..	10	6	1	..
	Other	2	..	..	1	1	..	..	..	..	..	..	..	7	..	2	2	2	1
Colored	Manhattan	2	..	..	2	..	..	1	..	..	1	..	..	28	..	12	13	1	2*
	Other	..	..	..	..	1	..	..	..	..	..	..	..	..	..	..	..	..	..
Bohemian	Manhattan	4	..	3	1	..	..	..	..	..	..	..	..	14	..	12	2	..	..
	Other	..	..	..	..	..	..	..	..	..	..	..	..	..	..	..	..	..	..
Russian	Manhattan	6	..	2	4	..	..	5	..	2	2	1	..	34	..	20	12	..	..
	Other	3	..	1	1	1	..	1	..	..	..	1	..	23	2	5	12	4	..
Austrian, etc.	Manhattan	7	2	4	..	1	..	1	..	1	..	..	..	30	3	16	10	1	..
	Other	..	..	..	..	..	..	..	..	..	..	..	..	2	..	..	2	..	..
Italian	Manhattan	8	2	2	5	1	..	6	..	5	1	1	..	49	13	24	9	3	..
	Other	1	..	..	1	1	..	..	..	..	..	1	..	8	1	2	4	..	1
Total	Manhattan	45	2	15	22	5	1	25	1	9	11	2	2	243	21	116	88	13	5
	Other	18	..	3	10	4	1	6	..	1	2	2	1	75	4	15	39	13	4

* Seven rooms.

TABLE 29.—NUMBER OF ROOMS PER FAMILY.—BY BOROUGH AND INCOME.

INCOME.	MANHATTAN.						BRONX, BROOKLYN, AND QUEENS.					
	Number of Families.	Two Rooms.	Three Rooms.	Four Rooms.	Five Rooms.	Six Rooms	Number of Families.	Two Rooms.	Three Rooms.	Four Rooms.	Five Rooms.	Six Rooms.
$400 to $499.....	4	1	2	1	..	..	4	..	2	2	..	..
$500 to $599.....	12	3	7	2	..	..	5	..	3	2	..	..
$600 to $699.....	52	7	33	10	2	..	20	1	4	13	2	..
$700 to $799.....	63	9	33	18	1	2	16	1	5	8	2	..
$800 to $899.....	58	2	26	27	3	..	15	2	2	6	3	2
$900 to $999.....	45	2	15	22	5	1	18	..	3	10	4	1
$1000 to $1099.....	25	1	9	11	2	2	6	..	1	2	2	1
$1100 to $1199.....	9	1	2	5	1	..	9	..	..	2	6	1
$1200 to $1299.....	7	..	..	3	1	3	1	..	..	..	1	..
$1300 to $1399.....	5	..	..	3	2	..	3	..	1	..	2	..
$1400 and over.....	11	..	1	4	4	2	3	..	1	2	..	..
Total...............	291	26	128	106	21	10	100	4	22	47	22	5
$400 to $599.....	16	4	9	3	..	..	9	..	5	4	..	..
$600 to $799.....	115	16	66	28	3	2	36	2	9	21	4	..
$800 to $899.....	58	2	26	27	3	..	15	2	2	6	3	2
$900 to $1099.....	70	3	24	33	7	3	24	..	4	12	6	2
$1100 and over....	32	1	3	15	8	5	16	..	2	4	9	1

94

TABLE 30.—NUMBER OF ROOMS PER FAMILY: ALL BOROUGHS COMBINED.—BY INCOME AND NATIONALITY.

NATIONALITY.	$600 TO $699						$700 TO $799						$800 TO $899					
	Number of Families.	Two Rooms.	Three Rooms.	Four Rooms.	Five Rooms.	Six Rooms.	Number of Families.	Two Rooms.	Three Rooms.	Four Rooms.	Five Rooms.	Six Rooms.	Number of Families.	Two Rooms.	Three Rooms.	Four Rooms.	Five Rooms.	Six Rooms.
United States	11	..	6	3	2	..	19	3	6	9	1	..	13	1	..	8	4	..
Teutonic	4	..	2	2	-	..	7	..	2	5	..	..	9	..	5	4	..	..
Irish	4	..	4	.	.	..	7	..	4	3	..	..	7	..	3	2	1	1
Colored	11	..	7	3	1	..	6	..	4	..	..	2*	8	..	1	7	..	..
Bohemian	4	..	3	.	.	..	3	1	3	.	.	..	3	.	3	.	.	..
Russian	16	2	5	8	1	..	14	1	7	5	1	..	12	.	8	4	.	..
Austrian, etc.	16	.	2	4	.	..	9	1	5	3	.	..	9	.	4	5	.	.
Italian	16	6	8	2	.	..	14	5	7	1	1	..	12	3	4	3	.	1
Total	72	8	37	23	4	..	79	10	38	26	3	2	73	4	28	33	6	2

NATIONALITY.	$900 TO $999						$1000 TO $1099						TOTAL.					
	Number of Families.	Two Rooms.	Three Rooms.	Four Rooms.	Five Rooms.	Six Rooms.	Number of Families.	Two Rooms.	Three Rooms.	Four Rooms.	Five Rooms.	Six Rooms.	Number of Families.	Two Rooms.	Three Rooms.	Four Rooms.	Five Rooms.	Six Rooms.
United States	16	..	3	8	3	2	8	1	2	3	1	1	67	5	17	31	11	3
Teutonic	11	..	2	7	3	..	8	..	..	6	..	2	39	..	11	24	2	2
Irish	5	..	1	3	2	..	1	..	..	.	1	..	24	..	12	8	3	1
Colored	2	.	.	2	.	..	1	.	.	1	.	..	28	.	12	13	1	2*
Bohemian	4	.	3	1	.	.	.	.	.	.	2	.	14	.	12	3	2	.
Russian	9	.	3	5	1	.	6	.	2	2	.	.	57	3	25	24	5	.
Austrian, etc.	7	2	4	.	1	.	.	.	1	2	.	.	32	3	16	12	1	.
Italian	9	.	2	6	1	.	6	.	5	1	.	.	57	14	26	13	3	1
Total	63	2	18	32	9	2	31	1	10	13	4	3	318	25	131	127	26	9

* Seven rooms.

95

TABLE 31.—NUMBER OF ROOMS PER FAMILY: ALL BOROUGHS
COMBINED.—BY INCOME.

INCOME.	NUM-BER OF FAM-ILIES.	TWO ROOMS.	THREE ROOMS.	FOUR ROOMS.	FIVE ROOMS.	SIX ROOMS.
$400 to $499	8	1	4	3	..	..
$500 to $599	17	3	10	4	..	..
$600 to $699	72	8	37	23	4	..
$700 to $799	79	10	38	26	3	2
$800 to $899	73	4	28	33	6	2
$900 to $999	63	2	18	32	9	2
$1000 to $1099	31	1	10	13	4	3
$1100 to $1199	18	1	2	7	7	1
$1200 to $1299	8	..	..	3	2	3
$1300 to $1399	8	..	1	3	4	..
$1400 and over	14	..	2	6	4	2
Total	391	30	150	153	43	15
$400 to $599	25	4	14	7	..	..
$600 to $799	151	18	75	49	7	2
$800 to $899	73	4	28	33	6	2
$900 to $1099	94	3	28	45	13	5
$1100 and over	48	1	5	19	17	6

TABLE 32.—NUMBER OF ROOMS PER FAMILY. PERCENTAGES. —BY INCOME AND BOROUGH.

Income.	Manhattan.						Bronx, Brooklyn and Queens.					
	Number of Families.	Two Rooms, Per cent.	Three Rooms, Per cent.	Four Rooms, Per cent.	Five Rooms, Per cent.	Six Rooms, Per cent.	Number of Families.	Two Rooms, Per cent.	Three Rooms, Per cent.	Four Rooms, Per cent.	Five Rooms, Per cent.	Six Rooms, Per cent.
$600 to $699	52	14	63	19	4	..	20	5	20	65	10	..
$700 to $799	63	14	52	29	2	3	16	6	31	50	13	..
$800 to $899	58	3	45	47	5	..	15	13	14	40	20	13
$900 to $999	45	5	33	49	11	2	18	..	16	56	22	6
$1000 to $1099	25	4	36	44	8	8	6	..	17	33	33	17
$400 to $599	16	25	56	19	..	..	9	..	56	44	..	..
$600 to $799	115	14	57	24	3	2	36	6	25	58	11	..
$800 to $899	58	3	45	47	5	..	15	13	14	40	20	13
$900 to $1099	70	5	34	47	10	4	24	..	17	50	25	8
$1100 and over	32	3	9	47	25	16	16	..	13	25	56	6
Total (all incomes)	291	9	45	36	7	3	100	4	22	47	22	5

TABLE 33.—NUMBER OF ROOMS PER FAMILY: ALL BOROUGHS COMBINED. PERCENTAGES.—BY INCOME.

Income.	Number of Families.	Two Rooms, Per cent.	Three Rooms, Per cent.	Four Rooms, Per cent.	Five Rooms, Per cent.	Six Rooms, Per cent.
$600 to $699	72	11	51	32	6	..
$700 to $799	79	13	48	33	4	2
$800 to $899	73	6	38	45	8	3
$900 to $999	63	3	29	51	14	3
$1000 to $1099	31	3	32	42	13	10
$400 to $599	25	16	56	28	..	..
$600 to $799	151	12	50	32	5	1
$800 to $899	73	6	38	45	8	3
$900 to $1099	94	3	30	48	14	5
$1100 and over	48	2	10	40	35	13
Total (all incomes)	391	8	38	39	11	4

TABLE 34.—NUMBER OF ROOMS, DARK ROOMS, BATH ROOMS PRIVATE TOILETS, PER FAMILY. AVERAGES.—BY INCOME AND BOROUGH.

INCOME.	Number of Families.	MANHATTAN.				Number of Families.	BROOKLYN, BRONX, AND QUEENS.			
		AVERAGE NUMBER PER FAMILY.					AVERAGE NUMBER PER FAMILY.			
		Rooms.	Dark Rooms.	Bathrooms.	Private Toilets.		Rooms.	Dark Rooms.	Bathrooms.	Private Toilets.
$400 to $499....	4	3.0	1.0	..	..	4	3.5	0.2	..	0.7
$500 to $599....	12	2.9	1.2	0.08	..	5	3.4	0.4	0.2	0.4
$600 to $699....	52	3.1	1.1	0.10	0.17	20	3.7	0.2	0.4	0.7
$700 to $799....	63	3.3	0.97	0.08	0.19	16	3.7	0.2	0.3	0.5
$800 to $899....	58	3.5	1.3	0.17	0.24	15	3.9	1.5	0.1	..
$900 to $999....	45	3.7	1.1	0.18	0.27	18	3.9	0.4	0.4	0.8
$1000 to $1099....	25	3.8	1.4	0.24	0.24	6	4.25	0.75	0.5	0.75
$1100 to $1199....	9	3.7	0.3	0.11	0.33	9	4.9	0.2	0.7	0.6
$1200 to $1299....	7	5.0	1.0	0.7	0.7	1	5.0	3.0	1.0	1.0
$1300 to $1399....	5	4.4	0.4	0.2	0.2	3	4.3	1.7	0.3	0.7
$1400 and over....	11	5.0	1.4	0.8	0.8	3	4.0	1.0	1.0	1.0
Total families......	291	..	..	..	..	100	..	..	..	..
$400 to $599....	16	2.9	1.2	0.06	..	9	3.4	0.3	0.1	0.5
$600 to $799....	115	3.2	1.3	0.09	0.18	36	3.7	0.2	0.4	0.6
$800 to $899....	58	3.5	1.3	0.17	0.24	15	3.9	1.5	0.1	..
$900 to $1099....	70	3.7	1.2	0.19	.026	24	4.0	0.5	0.4	0.6
$1100 and over....	32	4.5	0.85	0.49	0.55	16	4.6	0.8	0.7	0.7

TABLE 35.—DARK ROOMS, BATH-ROOMS, ETC.: ALL BOROUGHS. NUMBER OF FAMILIES REPORTING.—BY INCOME AND NATIONALITY.

NATIONALITY.	$600 TO $699				$700 TO $799				$800 TO $899				$900 TO $999				$1000 TO $1099				TOTAL.			
	Number of Families.	One or more Dark Rooms.	Bath-rooms.	Private Toilet.	Number of Families.	One or more Dark Rooms.	Bath-rooms.	Private Toilet.	Number of Families.	One or more Dark Rooms.	Bath-rooms.	Private Toilet.	Number of Families.	One or more Dark Rooms.	Bath-rooms.	Private Toilet.	Number of Families.	One or more Dark Rooms.	Bath-rooms.	Private Toilet.	Number of Families.	One or more Dark Rooms.	Bath-rooms.	Private Toilet.
United States	11	6	..	3	19	15	2	6	13	9	3	4	16	13	1	4	8	5	3	3	67	48	9	20
Teutonic	4	3	..	..	7	5	..	..	9	5	1	1	11	1	2	4	8	4	2	2	39	18	5	7
Irish	4	2	..	..	7	2	..	..	7	6	1	3	5	3	..	..	1	1	..	..	24	14	1	3
Colored	11	10	1	1	6	3	2	2	8	6	4	4	2	2	1	1	1	1	..	..	28	22	8	8
Bohemian	4	3	..	..	3	3	..	..	3	3	..	..	4	3	1	1	..	..	..	..	14	12	1	1
Russian	16	3	5	7	14	2	3	5	12	6	1	1	9	3	4	5	6	3	3	2	57	17	16	20
Austrian, etc.	6	2	3	3	9	4	1	2	9	7	1	3	7	..	1	1	1	1	..	..	32	14	6	9
Italian	16	10	2	6	14	8	2	5	12	5	1	2	9	4	3	5	6	2	1	1	57	29	9	19
Total	72	39	11	20	79	42	10	20	73	47	12	18	63	29	13	21	31	17	9	8	318	174	55	87

99

TABLE 36.—DARK ROOMS, BATH-ROOMS, ETC. NUMBER OF FAMILIES REPORTING.—BY BOROUGH, INCOME, AND NATIONALITY.

Nationality.	Boroughs.	$600 to $699				$700 to $799				$800 to $899				$900 to $999				$1000 to $1099				Total			
		Number of Families.	One or more Dark Rooms.	Bath-rooms.	Private Toilet.	Number of Families.	One or more Dark Rooms.	Bath-rooms.	Private Toilet.	Number of Families.	One or more Dark Rooms.	Bath-rooms.	Private Toilet.	Number of Families.	One or more Dark Rooms.	Bath-rooms.	Private Toilet.	Number of Families.	One or more Dark Rooms.	Bath-rooms.	Private Toilet.	Number of Families.	One or more Dark Rooms.	Bath-rooms.	Private Toilet.
United States {	Manhattan	6	4	·	·	14	13	1	4	8	6	2	3	11	9	1	3	5	4	1	1	44	36	5	11
	Other	5	2	·	3	5	2	1	2	5	3	1	1	5	4	·	1	3	1	2	2	23	12	4	9
Teutonic {	Manhattan	2	2	·	·	7	5	·	·	8	5	1	1	4	1	·	1	6	3	2	2	27	16	3	3
	Other	2	1	·	·	·	·	·	·	1	·	·	·	7	·	2	·	2	1	·	·	12	2	2	4
Irish {	Manhattan	3	2	·	·	5	2	·	·	5	4	·	1	3	1	1	1	1	1	·	·	17	10	·	1
	Other	1	·	·	·	2	·	·	·	2	2	1	2	2	2	·	2	·	·	·	·	7	4	1	2
Colored {	Manhattan	11	10	1	1	6	3	2	2	8	6	4	4	2	2	1	·	1	1	·	·	28	22	8	8
	Other	·	·	·	·	·	·	·	·	·	·	·	·	·	·	·	·	·	·	·	·	·	·	·	·
Bohemian {	Manhattan	4	3	1	·	3	3	·	·	3	3	·	·	4	3	1	1	·	·	·	·	14	12	·	1
	Other	·	·	·	·	·	·	·	·	·	·	·	·	·	·	·	·	·	·	·	·	·	·	·	·
Russian {	Manhattan	7	2	1	1	8	1	·	·	8	4	1	1	6	3	1	1	5	3	2	1	34	13	5	5
	Other	9	1	4	6	6	1	3	5	4	2	·	·	3	·	3	3	1	·	1	1	23	4	11	15
Austrian, etc. {	Manhattan	5	2	2	2	8	4	·	1	9	7	1	3	7	·	1	·	1	1	·	1	30	14	4	7
	Other	1	·	2	1	1	·	1	1	·	·	·	·	·	·	·	·	·	·	·	·	2	·	2	2
Italian {	Manhattan	14	10	1	5	12	8	2	5	9	4	1	2	8	4	3	5	6	2	1	1	49	28	8	18
	Other	2	·	1	1	2	·	·	·	3	1	·	·	1	·	·	·	·	·	·	·	8	1	1	1
Total {	Manhattan	52	35	5	9	63	39	5	12	58	39	10	15	45	23	8	13	25	15	6	5	243	151	34	54
	Other	20	4	6	11	16	3	5	8	15	8	2	3	18	6	5	8	6	2	3	3	75	23	21	33

100

TABLE 37.—DARK ROOMS, BATH-ROOMS, ETC. NUMBER OF FAMILIES REPORTING.—BY BOROUGHS, (COMBINED AND SEPARATE) AND INCOME.

INCOME.	ALL BOROUGHS.				MANHATTAN.				BRONX, BROOKLYN, AND QUEENS.			
	Number of Families.	One or more Dark Rooms.	Bath-rooms.	Private Toilet.	Number of Families.	One or more Dark Rooms.	Bath-rooms.	Private Toilet.	Number of Families.	One or more Dark Rooms.	Bath-rooms.	Private Toilet.
$400 to $499	8	4	..	3	4	3	..	..	4	1	..	3
$500 to $599	17	12	1	5	12	10	1	3	5	2	1	2
$600 to $699	72	39	11	20	52	35	5	9	20	4	6	11
$700 to $799	79	42	10	20	63	39	5	12	16	3	5	8
$800 to $899	73	47	12	18	58	39	10	15	15	8	2	3
$900 to $999	63	29	14	21	45	23	8	13	18	6	5	8
$1000 to $1099	31	17	9	8	25	15	6	5	6	2	3	3
$1100 to $1199	18	4	7	8	9	3	1	3	9	1	6	5
$1200 to $1299	8	4	6	6	7	3	5	5	1	1	1	1
$1300 to $1300	8	4	1	2	5	2	1	1	3	2	..	1
$1400 and over	14	6	9	9	11	4	7	7	3	2	2	2
Total	391	208	80	120	291	176	49	73	100	32	31	47
$400 to $599	25	16	1	8	16	13	1	3	9	3	1	5
$600 to $799	151	81	21	40	115	74	10	21	36	7	11	19
$800 to $899	73	47	12	18	58	39	10	15	15	8	2	3
$900 to $1099	94	46	23	29	70	38	14	18	24	8	8	11
$1100 and over	48	18	23	25	32	12	14	16	16	6	9	9

TABLE 38.—DARK ROOMS, BATH-ROOMS, ETC. NUMBER OF FAMILIES REPORTING. PERCENTAGES.—BY BOROUGHS (COMBINED AND SEPARATE) AND INCOME.

INCOME.	ALL BOROUGHS.				MANHATTAN.				BROOKLYN, BRONX, AND QUEENS.			
	Number of Families.	One or More Dark Rooms, Per Cent.	Bath-rooms, Per Cent.	Private Toilet, Per Cent.	Number of Families.	One or More Dark Rooms, Per Cent.	Bath-rooms, Per Cent.	Private Toilet, Per Cent.	Number of Families.	One or More Dark Rooms, Per Cent.	Bath-rooms, Per Cent.	Private Toilet, Per Cent.
$600 to $699	72	54	15	28	52	67	10	17	20	4	30	55
$700 to $799	79	53	8	16	63	56	8	19	16	17	31	50
$800 to $899	73	64	16	25	58	67	17	26	15	53	13	20
$900 to $999	63	46	21	33	45	51	18	29	18	33	28	44
$1000 to $1099	31	55	34	26	25	60	24	20	6	33	50	50
$400 to $599	25	64	4	32	16	81	8	19	9	33	11	55
$600 to $799	151	54	14	26	115	64	9	18	36	19	31	53
$800 to $899	73	64	16	24	58	67	17	26	15	53	13	20
$900 to $1099	94	49	24	31	70	54	20	26	24	33	33	46
$1100 and over	48	38	48	40	32	38	43	50	16	38	56	56
Total (all incomes)	391	53	20	31	291	60	17	25	100	32	31	47

TABLE 39.—OVER-CROWDED FAMILIES. NUMBER OF FAMILIES REPORTING LESS THAN FOUR ROOMS AND MORE THAN 1½ PERSONS PER ROOM.—BY NATIONALITY AND INCOME.

NATIONALITY.	$600 to $699						$700 to $799						$800 to $899					
	Manhattan.			Other Boroughs.			Manhattan.			Other Boroughs.			Manhattan.			Other Boroughs.		
	Total.	Less than Four Rooms.	More than 1½ Persons per Room.	Total.	Less than Four Rooms.	More than 1½ Persons per Room.	Total.	Less than Four Rooms.	More than 1½ Persons per Room.	Total.	Less than Four Rooms.	More than 1½ Persons per Room.	Total.	Less than Four Rooms.	More than 1½ Persons per Room.	Total.	Less than Four Rooms.	More than 1½ Persons per Room.
United States	6	5	3	5	1	1	14	8	7	5	1	1	8	..	..	5	1	1
Teutonic	2	1	1	2	1	1	7	2	1	..	..	..	8	5	3	1	..	..
Irish	3	3	3	1	1	1	5	3	3	2	1	1	5	1	3	2	..	..
Colored	11	7	7	..	..	..	6	4	4	..	..	..	8	2	3	..	..	..
Bohemian	4	3	2	..	..	..	3	3	3	..	..	..	3	3	3	..	..	..
Russian	7	5	6	9	2	1	8	5	6	6	1	3	8	3	8	4	..	4
Austrian, etc.	5	2	3	1	..	..	8	6	6	1	..	..	9	4	5	..	..	..
Italian	14	14	11	2	1	1	12	10	11	2	2	..	9	6	7	3	1	2
Total	52	40	36	20	6	5	63	41	41	16	5	5	58	24	32	15	2	7

TABLE 39 (*Continued*).—OVER-CROWDED FAMILIES. NUMBER OF FAMILIES REPORTING LESS THAN FOUR ROOMS AND MORE THAN 1¼ PERSONS PER ROOM.—BY NATIONALITY AND INCOME.

NATIONALITY.	$900 to $999 Manhattan Total.	Less than Four Rooms.	More than 1¼ Persons per Room.	Other Boroughs Total.	Less than Four Rooms.	More than 1¼ Persons per Room.	$1000 to $1099 Manhattan Total.	Less than Four Rooms.	More than 1¼ Persons per Room.	Other Boroughs Total.	Less than Four Rooms.	More than 1¼ Persons per Room.	TOTAL Manhattan Total.	Less than Four Rooms.	More than 1¼ Persons per Room.	Other Boroughs Total.	Less than Four Rooms.	More than 1¼ Persons per Room.
United States	11	3	4	5	...	...	5	2	2	3	1	1	44	18	16	23	4	4
Teutonic	4	...	4	7	2	2	6	...	...	2	...	...	27	8	5	12	3	3
Irish	3	1	1	2	...	...	1	...	...	...	...	...	17	8	10	7	2	2
Colored	2	1	1	...	...	...	1	1	1	...	...	...	28	15	16	...	...	...
Bohemian	4	3	3	3	...	...	...	...	...	...	...	...	14	12	11	...	...	...
Russian	6	3	4	...	...	1	5	2	2	...	...	...	34	18	26	23	3	9
Austrian, etc.	7	6	6	...	...	...	1	1	1	1	...	...	30	19	21	2	...	...
Italian	8	2	3	1	...	...	6	5	2	...	...	...	49	37	34	8	4	3
Total	45	19	22	18	2	3	25	11	8	6	1	1	243	135	139	75	16	21

TABLE 40.—OVER-CROWDED FAMILIES. NUMBER OF FAMILIES REPORTING MORE THAN 1½ PERSONS PER ROOM. PERCENTAGES.—BY NATIONALITY AND INCOME.

NATIONALITY.	$600 to $699			$700 to $799			$800 to $899		
	MANHAT-TAN, Per Cent.	BROOKLYN, BRONX, AND QUEENS, Per Cent.	ALL BOR-OUGHS, Per Cent.	MANHAT-TAN, Per Cent.	BROOKLYN, BRONX, AND QUEENS, Per Cent.	ALL BOR-OUGHS, Per Cent.	MANHAT-TAN, Per Cent.	BROOKLYN, BRONX, AND QUEENS, Per Cent.	ALL BOR-OUGHS, Per Cent.
United States	50	20	37	50	20	42		20	8
Teutonic	50	50	50	14		14	38		33
Irish	100	100	100	60	50	57	60		42
Colored	64		64	67		67	38		38
Bohemian	50		50	100		100	100		100
Russian	86	11	44	75	50	64	100	100	100
Austrian, etc.	60		50	75		67	55		56
Italian	79	50	75	93		79	78	75	75
Total	69	25	57	65	31	58	55	47	53

NATIONALITY.	$900 to $999			$1000 to $1099			TOTAL.		
	MANHAT-TAN, Per Cent.	BROOKLYN, BRONX, AND QUEENS, Per Cent.	ALL BOR-OUGHS, Per Cent.	MANHAT-TAN, Per Cent.	BROOKLYN, BRONX, AND QUEENS, Per Cent.	ALL BOR-OUGHS, Per Cent.	MANHAT-TAN, Per Cent.	BROOKLYN, BRONX, AND QUEENS, Per Cent.	ALL BOR-OUGHS, Per Cent.
United States	36		25	40	33	38	36	17	30
Teutonic		29	18				19	25	21
Irish	33		20	100*		100*	59	29	50
Colored	50		50				57		57
Bohemian	75		75				79		79
Russian	67		56			33	76	39	60
Austrian, etc.	86	33	86	40		100*	70		66
Italian	37		33	100*		33	71	38	65
Total	49	17	41	32	17	29	58	28	50

* 1 case.

TABLE 41.—OVER-CROWDED FAMILIES. NUMBER OF FAMILIES REPORTING LESS THAN FOUR ROOMS AND OVER 1½ PERSONS PER ROOM.—BY INCOME AND BOROUGHS (COMBINED AND SEPARATE).

INCOME.	ALL BOROUGHS.					MANHATTAN.					BROOKLYN, BRONX, AND QUEENS.				
	Total Number of Families.	Having less than Four Rooms.		Over 1½ Persons per Room.		Total Number of Families.	Having less than Four Rooms.		Over 1½ Persons per Room.		Total Number of Families.	Having less than Four Rooms.		Over 1½ Persons per Room.	
		Number.	Per Cent.	Number.	Per Cent.		Number.	Per Cent.	Number.	Per Cent.		Number.	Per Cent.	Number.	Per Cent.
$400 to $499	8	5	63	5	63	4	3	75	3	75	4	2	50	2	50
$500 to $599	17	13	76	12	71	12	10	83	9	75	5	3	60	3	60
$600 to $699	72	46	64	41	57	52	40	77	36	69	20	6	30	5	25
$700 to $799	79	46	58	46	58	63	41	65	41	65	16	5	31	5	31
$800 to $899	73	26	36	39	53	58	24	41	32	55	15	2	13	7	47
$900 to $999	63	21	33	25	40	45	19	42	22	49	18	2	11	3	17
$1000 to $1099	31	12	39	9	29	25	11	44	8	32	6	1	17	1	17
$1100 to $1199	18	1	6	3	17	9	..	..	3	33	9	1	11	..	..
$1200 to $1299	8	..	..	..	..	7	..	..	..	..	1	..	..	..	..
$1300 to $1399	8	..	..	4	50	5	..	..	2	40	3	..	..	2	67
$1400 and over	14	1	7	3	21	10	..	..	2	20	4	1	25	1	25
Total.........	391	171	44	187	48	290	148	51	158	55	101	23	23	29	29
$400 to $599	25	18	72	17	68	16	13	81	12	80	9	5	55	5	55
$600 to $799	151	92	61	87	58	115	81	70	77	67	36	11	31	10	30
$800 to $899	73	26	36	39	53	58	24	41	32	55	15	2	13	7	47
$900 to $1099	94	33	35	34	36	70	30	43	30	43	24	3	13	4	17
$1100 and over	48	2	42	10	21	31	..	..	7	23	17	2	12	3	18

TABLE 42.—OVER-CROWDED FAMILIES. NUMBER OF FAMILIES HAVING MORE THAN 1½ PERSONS PER ROOM.— BY NATIONALITY AND INCOME.

NATIONALITY.	TOTAL NUMBER OF FAMILIES.	OVER-CROWDED—NUMBER OF FAMILIES.					
		$600 to $699.	$700 to $799.	$800 to $899.	$900 to $999.	$1000 to $1099.	TOTAL.
United States..............	67	4	8	1	4	3	20
Teutonic..................	39	2	1	3	2	..	8
Irish.....................	24	4	4	3	1	..	12
Colored..................	28	7	4	3	1	1	16
Bohemian................	14	2	3	3	3	..	11
Russian..................	57	7	9	12	5	2	35
Austrian, etc.	32	3	6	5	6	1	21
Italian...................	57	12	11	9	3	2	37
Total....................	318	41	46	39	25	9	160

106

TABLE 43.—OVER-CROWDED FAMILIES.—BY SOURCE OF INCOME AND NATIONALITY.

Nationality	$600 to $699 Number of Families	Number Over-crowded	Father Only	Other Sources	Lodgers	$700 to $799 Number of Families	Number Over-crowded	Father Only	Other Sources	Lodgers	$800 to $899 Number of Families	Number Over-crowded	Father Only	Other Sources	Lodgers
United States	11	4	4	·	·	19	8	3	5	3	13	1	1	·	·
Teutonic	4	2	1	1	·	7	1	·	·	·	9	3	3	·	·
Irish	4	4	4	·	·	7	4	3	1	·	7	3	1	2	·
Colored	11	7	6	·	1	6	4	2	2	·	8	3	1	2	2
Bohemian	4	2	·	2	2	3	3	1	2	2	3	3	·	3	·
Russian	16	7	3	4	4	14	9	2	7	7	12	12	2	10	8
Austrian, etc.	6	3	·	3	3	9	6	1	5	4	9	5	1	4	3
Italian	16	12	6	6	4	14	11	7	4	4	12	9	2	7	3
Total	72	41	24	17	14	79	46	20	26	20	73	39	11	28	16

Nationality	$900 to $999 Number of Families	Number Over-crowded	Father Only	Other Sources	Lodgers	$1000 to $1099 Number of Families	Number Over-crowded	Father Only	Other Sources	Lodgers
United States	16	4	2	2	·	8	3	2	1	1
Teutonic	11	2	2	·	·	8	1	·	·	·
Irish	5	1	1	·	·	1	·	·	·	·
Colored	2	1	·	1	1	1	1	·	1	1
Bohemian	4	3	·	3	·	·	·	·	·	·
Russian	9	5	3	5	4	6	2	·	2	2
Austrian, etc.	7	6	1	3	2	1	1	·	1	·
Italian	9	3	1	2	2	6	2	·	2	2
Total	63	25	9	16	9	31	9	2	7	6

TOTAL.

Nationality	Total Number of Families	Total Over-crowded	Father Only Number	Father Only Per Cent	Other Sources Number	Other Sources Per Cent	Lodgers Number	Lodgers Per Cent
United States	67	20	12	60	8	40	4	20
Teutonic	39	8	7	88	1	13	·	·
Irish	24	12	9	75	3	25	·	·
Colored	28	16	9	56	7	44	5	31
Bohemian	14	11	1	9	10	91	5	36
Russian	57	35	7	20	28	80	25	71
Austrian, etc.	32	21	5	24	16	76	12	57
Italian	57	37	16	43	21	56	15	40
Total	318	160	66	41	94	59	65	41

TABLE 44.—OVER-CROWDED FAMILIES. NUMBER AND PER CENT. REPORTING SURPLUS AND DEFICIT.—BY INCOME.

INCOME.	Number of Families.	Number of Over-crowded.	Reporting: Balance within $25.00.		Surplus.		Deficit.	
			Number.	Per Cent.	Number.	Per Cent.	Number.	Per Cent.
$600 to $699	72	41	15	36	12	30	14	34
$700 to $799	79	46	17	37	20	43	9	20
$800 to $899	73	39	10	26	22	56	7	18
$900 to $999	63	25	10	40	12	48	3	12
$1000 to $1099	31	9	2	22	4	44	3	10
Total	318	160	54	34	70	44	36	22
$600 to $799	151	87	32	37	32	37	23	26
$800 to $899	73	39	10	26	22	56	7	18
$900 to $1099	94	34	12	35	16	47	6	18

TABLE 45.—OVER-CROWDED FAMILIES. NUMBER REPORTING SURPLUS AND DEFICIT.—BY NATIONALITY AND INCOME.

NATIONALITY.	$600 TO $699				$700 TO $799				$800 TO $899			
	Total Number of Families.	Balance within $25.00.	Surplus.	Deficit.	Number of Families.	Balance within $25.00.	Surplus.	Deficit.	Number of Families.	Balance within $25.00.	Surplus.	Deficit.
United States	4	3	..	1	8	3	2	3	1	1	..	..
Teutonic	2	1	..	1	1	..	1	..	3	1	..	2
Irish	4	2	1	1	4	1	1	2	3	..	3	..
Colored	7	3	1	3	4	3	..	1	3	..	..	3
Bohemian	2	1	..	1	3	3	..	..	3	3	..	..
Russian	7	2	2	3	9	2	7	..	12	1	10	1
Austrian, etc.	3	1	2	..	6	3	3	..	5	3	2	..
Italian	12	2	6	4	11	2	6	3	9	1	7	1
Total	41	15	12	14	46	17	20	9	39	10	22	7

NATIONALITY.	$900 TO $999				$1000 TO $1099				TOTAL.						
	Number of Families.	Balance within $25.00.	Surplus.	Deficit.	Number of Families.	Balance within $25.00.	Surplus.	Deficit.	Total Number of Families.	Balance. Number.	Balance. Per Cent.	Surplus. Number.	Surplus. Per Cent.	Deficit. Number.	Deficit. Per Cent.
United States	4	2	1	1	3	2	..	1	20	11	55	3	15	6	30
Teutonic	2	..	1	1	..	..	..	..	8	2	25	2	25	4	50
Irish	1	..	1	..	..	..	..	..	12	3	25	6	50	3	25
Colored	1	..	1	..	1	..	1	..	16	6	38	3	19	7	43
Bohemian	3	3	..	..	..	..	..	..	11	10	91	..	..	1	9
Russian	5	1	3	1	2	..	..	2	35	6	17	22	63	7	20
Austrian, etc.	6	3	3	..	1	..	1	..	21	10	48	11	52	..	..
Italian	3	1	2	..	2	..	2	..	37	6	17	23	63	8	21
Total	25	10	12	3	9	2	4	3	160	54	34	70	44	36	22

TABLE 46.—RENT IN RELATION TO LODGERS: MANHATTAN.— BY INCOME.

RENT PER MONTH.	$600 TO $699 Number of Families.		$700 TO $799 Number of Families.		$800 TO $899 Number of Families.		$900 TO $999 Number of Families.		$1000 TO $1099 Number of Families.		TOTAL. Number of Families.		
	Total.	With Lodgers.	Total.	With Lodgers.	Total.	With Lodgers.	Total.	With Lodgers.	Total.	With Lodgers.	Total.	With Lodgers.	Per Cent.
$10 and under..........	10	2	12	4	6	..	3	..	..	..	31	6	19.5
$10 to $12..............	8	2	17	4	9	2	6	1	2	1	42	10	23.8
$12 to $14..............	20	4	13	5	21	6	13	1	7	1	74	17	23.0
$14 to $16..............	8	3	6	2	8	2	9	2	7	5	28	14	50.0
$16 to $18..............	5	4	8	5	3	2	7	5	6	2	29	18	62.1
Over $18..............	1	..	7	4	11	10	7	3	3	1	29	18	62.1
Total..................	52	15	63	24	58	22	45	12	25	10	243	83	34.0

TABLE 47.—RENT IN RELATION TO LODGERS: MANHATTAN. PERCENTAGES*.—BY INCOME.

RENT PER MONTH.	$600 TO $699		$700 TO $799		$800 TO $899		$900 TO $999		$1000 TO $1099	
	All Families, Per Cent.	Families without Lodgers, Per Cent.	All Families, Per Cent.	Families without Lodgers, Per Cent.	All Families, Per Cent.	Families without Lodgers, Per Cent.	All Families, Per Cent.	Families without Lodgers, Per Cent.	All Families, Per Cent.	Families without Lodgers, Per Cent.
Below $10........	9.6	9.6	11.1	7.9	1.7	1.7	6.6	4.4	..	..
$10 and below	19.2	15.4	19.0	12.7	10.3	10.3	6.7	6.7	..	..
$12 and below	34.6	26.9	46.0	33.3	25.9	22.4	20.0	17.8	8.0	4.0
$14 and above	36.5	21.1	44.5	22.2	51.7	22.4	66.7	44.5	72.0	40.0
$15 and above	23.1	11.5	33.4	15.9	38.0	13.8	46.6	26.7	60.0	32.0
$16 and above	19.2	7.7	28.6	12.7	29.3	5.2	35.6	15.5	40.0	24.0
$18 and above	1.9	1.9	12.7	6.3	21.2	1.7	24.4	11.1	24.0	12.0
$20 and above	1.9	1.9	9.5	3.2	8.6	1.7	13.3	6.7	4.0	4.0

*Percentages are reckoned in each income-group on the basis of the total number of families in that group.

109

TABLE 48.—LODGERS IN RELATION TO OVER-CROWDING. NUMBER AND PER CENT. OF FAMILIES.—BY INCOME.

INCOME.	NUMBER OF FAMILIES.				PERCENTAGES.		
	Total Number of Families.	Over-crowded.	Having Lodgers.	Over-crowded Having Lodgers.	Having Lodgers. Per Cent. of all Families.	Over-crowded. Having Lodgers. Per Cent. of All Over-crowded Families.	Per Cent. of All Families Having Lodgers.
$600 to $699	72	41	17	14	24	34	82
$700 to $799	79	46	26	20	33	43	77
$800 to $899	73	39	25	16	34	41	64
$900 to $999	63	25	13	9	21	36	70
$1000 to $1099	31	9	12	6	39	67	50
Total	318	160	93	65	29	41	70
$600 to $799	151	87	43	34	28	39	79
$800 to $899	73	39	25	16	34	41	64
$900 to $1099	94	34	25	15	27	74	60

TABLE 49.—INCREASE OF RENT: MANHATTAN.—BY DISTRICTS.

DISTRICTS OF MANHATTAN.	Total Number of Families.	Number Having Moved Within One Year.	Number Not Having Moved.	REPORTED INCREASE.			AMOUNT OF INCREASE REPORTED.						
				Number of Families.	Per Cent. of Total.	Per Cent. of Those Not Having Moved.	$0.50	$1.00	$1.50	$2.00	$2.50	$3.00	Over $3.00
North	30	12	18	3	10	17	..	3	..	..	..	..	..
East	49	7	42	25	51	60	3	8	4	9	1	..	..
South-east	84	16	68	36	43	53	4	16*	3	6	1	2	4‡
South-west	24	3	21	9	38	43	..	5	1	2	1	..	..
West	56	7	49	29	52	57	3	4	5	10	1	3	3†
Total	243	45	198	102	42	52	10	36	13	27	4	5	7

* Including one case at $1.25.   † One case at $3.50; two cases at $4.00.
‡ Three cases at $4.00; one case at $5.00.

TABLE 50.—INCREASE OF RENT: MANHATTAN.—BY MONTHLY RENTAL.

RENT PER MONTH.	Total Number of Families.	Number Having Moved Within One Year.	Number Not Having Moved.	RELATIVE INCREASE.			AMOUNT OF INCREASE REPORTED.						
				Number of Families.	Per Cent. of Total.	Per Cent. of Those Not Having Moved.	$0.50	$1.00	$1.50	$2.00	$2.50	$3.00	Over $3.00
$10 and under	31	2	29	13	42	44	2	6	..	4	1	..	..
$10 to $12	42	9	33	24	57	73	2	10*	6	6	..	..	..
$12 to $14	74	8	66	31	42	47	5	12	2	6	..	4	2‡
$14 to $16	38	6	32	19	50	59	..	..	4	9	3	1	2‡
$16 to $18	29	11	18	6	21	33	1	2	1	1	..	..	1†
Over $18	29	9	20	9	31	45	..	6	..	1	..	..	2§
Total	243	45	198	102	42	53	10	36	13	27	4	5	7

* Including one at $1.25.   † $3.50.   ‡ $4.00.   § One case $4.00; one case $5.00.

2. CAR-FARE.

Closely allied to expenditure for rent is expenditure for car-fare. The general averages for this item give little information because the amount of car-fare paid in a given case depends upon the distance of the dwelling from the wage-earner's place of work, rather than upon income or nationality or even occupation. It is to be expected, therefore, that car-fares will bulk larger, absolutely and relatively, in Brooklyn and the Bronx than in Manhattan. Tables 51–53 (pages 113–114) show that 67 per cent. of our families outside of Manhattan, and only 52 per cent. of the families residing in Manhattan, report expenditure for car-fare.

In the elaboration of the returns, car-fares for visiting, recreation, etc., have been taken out of the car-fare account and charged to recreation. Such car-fares are not considered in the discussion of this section. As to the amount paid, families paying $30 or more constitute 23 per cent. of the total number of families in Manhattan, and 36 per cent. of the families in the other boroughs. Those paying $20 and over constitute 31 per cent. of the families in Manhattan, and 39 per cent. of the families in the other boroughs. It is to be noted, however, that a large number of families report no expenditure for car-fare; namely, 48 per cent. of all in Manhattan, and 33 per cent. of all in the other boroughs. This means that a large proportion even of the workers who reside in Brooklyn and the Bronx are employed within walking distance of their homes. An examination of the returns regarding car-fare from the different sections of Manhattan (page 114) shows that families living north of 14th street pay more in car-fare than families in other regions, while those residing in the South-east, paying the highest rents, have the smallest expenditure for car-fare. Or, by number of families: Of 30 families in the North, 60 per cent. pay car-fare; of 49 in the East, 72 per cent.; of 84 in the South-east, 35 per cent.; of 24 in the South-west, 46 per cent.; and of 56 families in the West, 61 per cent. pay car-fare.

Of the 243 Manhattan families, 76 report an expenditure of $20 and over for car-fares. This indicates that the father usually rides to his work. Of these 76 families, 17 were in our North section, making 57 per cent. of all the families there; 22 were in the East, or 45 per cent. of all families in that section. In the South-east were only 14 of these cases, comprising 17 per cent. of all families in that region. The same percentage prevailed in the South-west, while in the West 19, or 34 per cent. of all families, paid over $20 in car-fare. That is to say, the people who live in the Southern end of the island save in car-fare a part of what they have to pay out in rent. A comparison of expenditures for car-fare in different income-groups and nationalities yields no significant results. It is to be observed that of the 25 families with incomes under $600, 13 report payments for car-fare, and 13 of the 48 families with incomes of $1100 and above report no expenditure for this purpose. Table 51 shows the variation in car-fare with variations in rent. So far as it is possible to make any generalization from it, it seems to show that expenditure for car-fare does not fall off as rent increases. If the line is drawn at a $15 rental, of 138 families paying from $10.50 to $15.00 a month, 76 families, or 55 per cent., report car-fare, as against 51 per cent. of the 74 families paying a rent of $15.50 to $18.00 a month.

TABLE 51.—CAR-FARE: MANHATTAN AND BROOKLYN. NUMBER OF FAMILIES REPORTING GIVEN AMOUNTS.—BY MONTHLY RENTAL.

EXPENDITURE FOR CAR-FARE.	$10 and Under.		$10.50 to $12.50		$13 to $15		$15.50 to $17.50		Over $17.50		TOTAL NUMBER OF FAMILIES.		PER CENT. OF ALL FAMILIES.	
	Manhattan.	Brooklyn.	Manhattan.	Brooklyn.	Manhattan.	Brooklyn.	Manhattan.	Brooklyn.	Manhattan.	Brooklyn.	Manhattan.	Brooklyn.	Manhattan.	Brooklyn.
Under $10......	5	1	10	3	10	3	4	..	9	..	38	7	15.6	13.5
$10 to $20......	2	2	3	2	7	2	1	..	..	1	13	7	5.3	13.5
$20 to $30......	..	..	5	1	8	1	2	..	5	..	20	2	8.2	3.8
$30 to $40......	3	1	9	3	20	4	6	2	9	..	47	10	19.3	19.2
Over $40.......	3	2	1	3	3	2	1	2	1	..	9	9	3.7	17.5
Total reporting car-fare.......	13	6	28	12	48	12	14	4	24	1	127	35	..	..
Total number of families.......	31	9	52	20	86	17	36	5	38	1	243	52	..	..

TABLE 52.—CAR-FARE. NUMBER OF FAMILIES REPORTING GIVEN AMOUNTS.—BY BOROUGH.

BOROUGH.	TOTAL NUMBER OF FAMILIES.	NUMBER REPORTING CAR-FARE OF:					Total.	
		Under $10.	$10 to $20.	$20 to $30.	$30 to $40.	Over $40.	Number.	Per Cent. of All Families.
Manhattan...........	243	38	13	20	47	9	127	52
Bronx...............	15	3	..	..	4	..	7	47
Brooklyn............	52	7	7	2	10	9	35	67
Queens..............	8	1	3	..	2	2	8	100

8   113

TABLE 53.—CAR-FARE: MANHATTAN. FAMILIES REPORTING EXPENDITURES FOR CAR-FARE.—BY DISTRICT AND AMOUNT OF RENT.

RENT PER MONTH.	NORTH.			EAST.			SOUTH-EAST.			SOUTH-WEST.			WEST.			TOTAL.		
	Total Number of Families.	Number Reporting Car-fare.	Per Cent. Reporting Car-fare.	Total Number of Families.	Number Reporting Car-fare.	Per Cent. Reporting Car-fare.	Number of Families.	Number Reporting Car-fare.	Per Cent. Reporting Car-fare.	Number of Families.	Number Reporting Car-fare.	Per Cent. Reporting Car-fare.	Number of Families.	Number Reporting Car-fare.	Per Cent. Reporting Car-fare.	Total Number of Families.	Number Reporting Car-fare.	Per Cent. Reporting Car-fare.
$10 and under............	5	..	..	9	7	77.8	6	..	..	5	1	20.0	6	5	83.4	31	13	42
$10.50 to $12.50.........	8	7	87.6	9	4	44.4	21	8	38.1	6	2	33.3	8	7	87.5	52	28	54
$13.00 to $15.00.........	5	4	80.0	15	13	86.6	27	8	29.6	11	7	63.6	28	16	59.1	86	48	56
$15.50 to $17.50.........	4	3	75.0	6	3	50.0	16	5	31.2	1	1	100.0	9	2	22.2	36	14	40
$18 and over.............	8	4	50.0	10	8	80.0	14	8	57.0	1	..	..	5	4	80.0	38	24	63
Total................	30	18	60	49	35	72	84	29	35	24	11	46	56	34	61	243	127	52

3. FUEL AND LIGHT.

The expenditures for fuel and light as shown in the tables of averages (Table 54, page 118, and Table 15, page 70) vary less with differences of income and nationality than most of the other items of the budget. The average for families with $600 incomes is $37.71, and for families with $1000 incomes $46.11; and in no case does the average reach $50.00 with incomes below $1500 a year. Among different nationalities the expenditure varies more widely, owing, in some instances, to the small number of cases. The Bohemians and the colored people show the highest range of expenditure for fuel; the Italians, except in the $600 income-group, the lowest. Expenditure for fuel and light forms a constantly decreasing per cent. of the total expenditures, being 5.8 per cent. for incomes between $600 and $700, and 3.8 per cent. for incomes between $1100 and $1200. (Table 15, page 70.)

An indication of the low standard of living is found in the gathering of fuel, for the most part wood, on the streets and elsewhere free of cost (Table 55, page 119). One hundred and nineteen of the 318 families, with incomes between $600 and $1100, report the gathering of fuel in this way. These cases are most frequent in families of the lower income-groups as will be seen in Table 55 A. Fifty-one per cent. of the families in the $600 group gather wood free, 35 per cent. in the $700 group, 42 per cent. in the $800 group, and 24 and 26 per cent. of the families in the $900 and $1000 groups respectively. By nationalities, 64 per cent. of the Bohemian families, 54 per cent. of the Irish, 50 per cent. of the colored, 49 per cent. of the Italians (including 9 cases where the man is a fuel-dealer), and 46 per cent. of the American families gather free fuel. Only 11 per cent. of the Russians and 16 per cent. of the Austrian group report free fuel. In most cases the wood gathered consists of boxes thrown out by the merchants, or waste material from building operations. One family reports picking up coal in the neighborhood of a coal-yard, and the employees of wood-working establishments sometimes bring home more or less fuel. Considered by locality, the proportion of wood-gatherers is exactly the same in Manhattan and in Brooklyn, or 35 per cent. Sixteen out of the 23 families reported from Bronx and Queens gathered wood free.

What is provided in return for the outlay for fuel and light varies much more widely between the individual families than the group-average would indicate. There is a difference in the amount of fuel required, according to the number and size of the rooms occupied and according to the character of the building. Families living in the Yorkville district reported larger expenditures for fuel than those living in the more compactly built tenement-houses of the lower East Side. Individual economy and extravagance also appear in the variation of the expenditures for fuel and light, as well as differences of taste and habit as to the amount of heat and light required. A comparison of the books is the basis of the following estimate of the requirements for a family occupying a four-room tenement:

Three tons coal at $6.50.....................$21.00
Wood and matches........................ 3.00
Gas, $2.00 a month in summer and $1.00 in
  winter................................. 18.00
                                         _____
                                         $42.00

Coal is bought, in a few cases, by the ton or half-ton, but usually in small quantities—by the bag of 100 pounds for 35 or 40 cents, by the bushel of 75 pounds at 25 cents, or by the pail of 25 pounds for 10 cents. If the 6000 pounds (3 tons) of coal in the estimate given above were bought by the bag at 40 cents, or by the pail at 10 cents, it would cost $24.00.*

* One report of coal for a family with income of $600, occupying 4 rooms is as follows:

2 months in winter, 3 bushels a week .... 24 bu.
4 months in winter, 2 bushels a week .... 32 "
6 months in summer .... 6 "
                                                    _____
                                                    62 bu.

Another family with income of $650, occupying 3 rooms, shows coal used about 5 months:

300 lbs. at 35 cents for 1 week in very cold weather.
200 lbs. at 35 cents for 1 week in moderately cold weather.
In summer bought by 100 pounds for 6 weeks, just for
  washday, ... $1.75

The report for another family, with an income of $792, occupying 4 rooms is:

For 17 weeks in winter 3 bags a week, at 35 cents....... $17.85
For 35 weeks in summer 2 pails a week at 11 cents...... 7.70
                                                       _____
                                                       $25.55

In regard to the kind of lighting provided, gas is the main reliance (Tables 56–58, pages 120–122). In no case was electricity used. Seventy-five out of the grand total of 391 families reported no use of gas. Gas is more largely used in Manhattan than in the outlying boroughs, 15 per cent. of the Manhattan families reporting no gas, as against 29 per cent. of families in the other boroughs. The families in Manhattan that did not use gas are almost all in the income-groups below $900. The use of gas for cooking is somewhat less general than its use for lighting. Two hundred and ninety-one of the whole 391 families use gas for cooking and 307 of them use gas for lighting. The use of kerosene is reported by 133 families of the grand total. In many cases, of course, its use is auxiliary to the use of gas, but the larger number of cases are reported by the poorer families. Out of the 99 Manhattan families, for instance, which report the use of kerosene, 42 are families with incomes under $800 and only 15 are families with incomes above $1000. Only 8 families with incomes over $900 report no gas. Where kerosene is used the average amount is about a gallon a week, costing from 12 to 14 cents a gallon and from $6 to $8 for the year. Expenditure for gas is eliminated in cases where kerosene is the only illuminant. The cases where gas is used for cooking and not for light are extremely rare. The gas bills reported range from $1 to $2 a month, for the most part, according to season. There is little variation among the families of different nationalities in regard to fuel and light, a common necessity being imposed upon them all. The Italian families use wood in larger proportion than most of the others, even in cases where it has to be bought.

TABLE 54.—FUEL AND LIGHT. AVERAGE AMOUNT AND PER CENT. EXPENDED.—BY NATIONALITY AND INCOME.

Nationality.	$600 to $699			$700 to $799			$800 to $899			$900 to $999			$1000 to $1099		
	Number of Families.	Average Amount.	Per Cent.*	Number of Families.	Average Amount.	Per Cent.*	Number of Families.	Average Amount.	Per Cent.*	Number of Families.	Average Amount.	Per Cent.*	Number of Families.	Average Amount.	Per Cent.*
United States	11	$40.17	6.2	19	$43.10	5.6	13	$42.61	4.9	16	$40.10	4.2	8	$42.52	4.0
Teutonic	4	27.43	4.1	7	35.88	4.7	9	40.61	4.6	11	51.69	5.6	8	54.29	5.2
Irish	4	27.14	4.1	7	33.73	4.4	7	38.26	4.7	5	42.07	4.6	1	69.68	7.6
Colored	11	44.10	6.8	6	53.72	6.9	8	52.61	6.7	2	50.67	6.0	1	54.60	6.2
Bohemian	4	59.93	8.6	3	45.32	6.2	3	37.44	4.4	4	69.96	7.1	..	..	..
Russian	16	33.28	5.3	14	33.54	4.8	12	40.83	5.3	9	41.28	4.6	6	47.80	4.6
Austrian, etc.	6	30.07	5.0	9	35.54	5.0	9	46.58	5.7	7	43.39	4.8	1	42.90	4.4
Italian	16	38.59	5.8	14	26.03	3.7	12	30.52	4.1	9	51.67	6.4	6	33.51	3.7
Total	72	37.71	5.8	79	36.94	5.0	73	41.04	5.0	63	46.70	5.1	31	46.11	4.5

* Per cent. of expenditure for all purposes.

TABLE 55.—FUEL GATHERED FREE. NUMBER OF FAMILIES RE-
PORTING AND PERCENTAGES.—BY INCOME AND NATIONALITY.

| NATIONALITY. | FAMILIES GATHERING SOME FUEL FREE. | | | | | | | | | | | |
| | $600 to $699 | | $700 to $799 | | $800 to $899 | | $900 to $999 | | $1000 to $1099 | | TOTAL. | | |
	Total Number.	Number Gathering Fuel Free.	Total Number.	Number Gathering Fuel Free.	Total Number.	Number Gathering Fuel Free.	Total Number.	Number Gathering Fuel Free.	Total Number.	Number Gathering Fuel Free.	Total Number of Families.	Total Number Gathering Fuel Free.	Per Cent.
United States........	11	8	19	8	13	7	16	5	8	3	67	31	46.3
Teutonic............	4	1	7	3	9	2	11	5	8	2	39	13	33.3
Irish...............	4	3	7	3	7	5	5	1	1	1	24	13	54.1
Colored............	11	8	6	2	8	4	2	..	1	..	28	14	50.0
Bohemian..........	4	2	3	2	3	3	4	2	..	..	14	9	64.1
Russian............	16	5	14	..	12	..	9	1	6	..	57	6	10.5
Austrian, etc........	6	2	9	2	9	1	7	..	1	..	32	5	15.6
Italian.............	16	8*	14	8†	12	9‡	9	1	6	2	57	28	49.1
Total..............	72	37	79	28	73	31	63	15	31	8	318	119	37.4

*2 cases, fuel dealers.   †4 cases, fuel dealers.   ‡1 case, fuel dealer.

TABLE 55A.—FUEL GATHERED FREE. SUMMARY OF TABLE 55.—
BY INCOME.

INCOME.	TOTAL NUMBER OF FAMILIES.	TOTAL NUMBER GATHERING FUEL FREE.	PER CENT.
$400 to $599.....................	25	11	44
$600 to $699.....................	72	37	51
$700 to $799.....................	79	28	35
$800 to $899.....................	73	31	42
$900 to $999.....................	63	15	24
$1000 to $1099.....................	31	8	26
$1100 and over.....................	48	10	21
Total.............................	391	140	36

119

TABLE 56.—FUEL AND LIGHT. USE OF GAS AND KEROSENE: MANHATTAN.—BY NATIONALITY AND INCOME.

NATIONALITY.	$600 TO $699					$700 TO $799					$800 TO $899				
	Number of Families.	Gas for Cooking.	Gas for Light.	Kerosene.	No Gas.	Number of Families.	Gas for Cooking.	Gas for Light.	Kerosene.	No Gas.	Number of Families.	Gas for Cooking.	Gas for Light.	Kerosene.	No Gas.
United States	6	5	5	1	1	14	9	11	4	3	8	5	6	2	2
Teutonic	2	2	1	1	..	7	3	6	1	1	8	7	7	4	..
Irish	3	2	1	2	1	5	4	4	3	1	5	3	3	..	2
Colored	11	2	2	11	8	6	2	3	5	3	8	1	5	6	3
Bohemian	4	4	4	3	..	3	3	2	2	..	3	1	3	1	..
Russian	7	7	6	1	..	8	8	8	1	..	8	8	8	2	..
Austrian, etc.	5	4	4	1	1	8	8	8	1	..	9	8	9	3	..
Italian	14	9	9	4	5	12	10	11	2	1	9	8	8	2	1
Total	52	35	32	24	16	63	47	53	19	9	58	41	49	20	8

NATIONALITY.	$900 TO $999					$1000 TO $1099					TOTAL.				
	Number of Families.	Gas for Cooking.	Gas for Light.	Kerosene.	No Gas.	Number of Families.	Gas for Cooking.	Gas for Light.	Kerosene.	No Gas.	Number of Families.	Gas for Cooking.	Gas for Light.	Kerosene.	No Gas.
United States	11	9	9	4	2	5	4	4	3	..	44	32	35	14	8
Teutonic	4	3	3	1	..	6	5	5	2	..	27	20	22	9	1
Irish	3	3	3	1	..	1	..	1	..	..	17	12	12	6	4
Colored	2	1	1	1	1	1	1	1	..	..	28	7	12	23	15
Bohemian	4	4	4	1	..	..	..	..	..	..	14	12	13	7	..
Russian	6	6	6	1	..	5	5	5	1	..	34	34	33	6	..
Austrian, etc.	7	7	7	3	..	1	1	1	..	..	30	28	29	8	1
Italian	8	8	8	..	..	6	5	5	1	1	49	40	41	9	8
Total	45	41	41	12	3	25	21	22	7	1	243	185	197	82	37

TABLE 57.—FUEL AND LIGHT. USE OF GAS AND KEROSENE BRONX, BROOKLYN, AND QUEENS.—BY NATIONALITY AND INCOME.

NATIONALITY.	$600 TO $699					$700 TO $799					$800 TO $899				
	Number of Families.	Gas for Cooking.	Gas for Light.	Kerosene.	No Gas.	Number of Families.	Gas for Cooking.	Gas for Light.	Kerosene.	No Gas.	Number of Families.	Gas for Cooking.	Gas for Light.	Kerosene.	No Gas.
United States	5	3	3	2	2	5	4	4	2	1	5	..	1	5	5
Teutonic	2	..	..	2	2	..	..	..	..	..	1	..	1	..	..
Irish	1	..	..	1	1	2	..	..	2	2	2	2	2	..	..
Colored	..	..	..	..	..	..	..	..	..	..	..	..	..	..	..
Bohemian	..	..	..	..	..	..	..	..	..	..	..	..	..	..	..
Russian	9	6	6	3	3	6	6	6	..	..	4	4	4	..	..
Austrian, etc.	1	1	1	..	..	1	1	1	..	..	..	..	..	..	..
Italian	2	1	1	1	..	2	1	1	2	1	3	1	..	2	2
Total	20	11	11	9	8	16	12	12	6	4	15	7	8	7	7

NATIONALITY.	$900 TO $999					$1000 TO $1099					TOTAL.				
	Number of Families.	Gas for Cooking.	Gas for Light.	Kerosene.	No Gas.	Number of Families.	Gas for Cooking.	Gas for Light.	Kerosene.	No Gas.	Number of Families.	Gas for Cooking.	Gas for Light.	Kerosene.	No Gas.
United States	5	1	2	3	3	3	2	2	1	1	23	10	12	13	12
Teutonic	7	5	5	2	2	3	2	2	1	..	12	7	8	5	4
Irish	2	..	..	2	2	..	..	..	..	..	7	2	2	5	5
Colored	..	..	..	..	..	..	..	..	..	..	..	..	..	..	..
Bohemian	..	..	..	..	..	..	..	..	..	..	..	..	..	..	..
Russian	3	3	3	..	..	1	1	1	..	..	23	20	20	3	3
Austrian, etc.	..	..	..	..	..	..	..	..	..	..	2	2	2	..	..
Italian	1	..	..	1	1	..	..	..	..	..	8	3	2	6	4
Total	18	9	10	8	8	6	5	5	2	1	75	44	46	32	28

TABLE 58.—FUEL AND LIGHT.   USE OF GAS AND KEROSENE.—BY BOROUGHS (COMBINED AND SEPARATE) AND INCOME.

INCOME.	ALL BOROUGHS.					MANHATTAN.					BROOKLYN, BRONX, AND QUEENS.				
	Number of Families.	Gas for Cooking.	Gas for Light.	Kerosene.	No Gas.	Number of Families.	Gas for Cooking.	Gas for Light.	Kerosene.	No Gas.	Number of Families.	Gas for Cooking.	Gas for Light.	Kerosene.	No Gas.
$400 to $499	8	6	6	2	2	4	2	2	2	2	4	4	4	:	:
$500 to $599	17	13	14	7	3	12	8	9	7	3	5	5	5	:	:
$600 to $699	72	46	43	33	24	52	35	32	24	16	20	11	11	9	8
$700 to $799	79	59	65	25	13	63	47	53	19	9	16	12	12	6	4
$800 to $899	73	48	57	27	15	58	41	49	20	8	15	7	8	7	7
$900 to $999	63	50	51	20	11	45	41	41	12	3	18	9	10	8	8
$1000 to $1099	31	26	27	9	3	25	21	22	7	1	6	5	5	2	1
$1100 to $1199	18	15	15	3	3	9	7	7	2	2	9	8	8	1	1
$1200 to $1299	8	9	10	2	.	7	7	7	2	.	1	2	3	.	.
$1300 to $1399	8	4	4	2	2	5	3	3	2	2	3	1	1	:	:
$1400 and over	14	15	15	3	.	11	11	11	2	.	3	4	4	1	.
Total	391	291	307	133	75	291	223	236	99	46	100	68	71	34	29
$400 to $599	25	19	20	9	5	16	10	11	9	5	9	9	9	:	:
$600 to $799	151	105	108	58	37	115	82	85	43	25	36	23	23	15	12
$800 to $899	73	48	57	27	15	58	41	49	20	8	15	7	8	7	7
$900 to $1099	94	76	78	29	13	70	62	63	19	4	24	14	15	10	9
$1100 and over	48	43	44	10	5	32	28	28	8	4	16	15	16	2	1

4. FOOD.

1. Food as a Factor in the Budget.—Food is much the largest item in the family budget, comprising nearly half of the total outlay. (See Table 59, page 137, and Table 15, page 70.) The average amount spent for food rises from $290.10 per annum for the $600 families to $451.46 for the $1000 group. But, although the average amount increases by about $50 with each $100 added income, the percentage of total expenditures remains almost constant at about 45 per cent. When a wider range of income is included, the percentage variations are greater. Thus, the 8 families with average income of $452.38 spend only 40.8 per cent. of it for food; the 17 families with incomes between $500 and $600 spend 44.4 per cent. of their money for food. Among the larger incomes, the percentage remains close to 45 for the $1100 and $1200 groups, and begins to fall only with the families whose income is $1300, where it is 42.6. For the 6 families with incomes of $1500 the percentage is 36.8. These figures would seem to indicate that not until the family is able to spend well beyond $1000 does it satisfy its wants for food upon a smaller proportion of its total income than when it had only $600 or $700 for all purposes. Whether this is due to insufficient nutrition on lower incomes, or to indulgence of more expensive tastes as resources increase, we may be able at a later point to suggest. Certainly, the point of diminishing percentage of expenditure for food is placed much higher in the income scale than in the cases on which Engel based his well-known generalizations.

A comparison of nationalities suggests that the families which spend the largest proportion of their income for food are those which pay the smallest share of it for rent. The Italians and Bohemians, whose rent-expense is relatively low, expend in the various income-groups from 45 to 50 per cent. of their total outlay upon food; while for the colored people and the Russians, who pay heavy rents, the percentage range is between 40 and 45 per cent., rising to 45.2 per cent. for the Russians with incomes of $800, and falling to 37.7 per cent. for colored families in the same income-group.

The expenditures for different classes of food have been arranged by income-groups and nationalities, and the percentage of total expenditures for food-materials calculated (Tables 60 and 61, pages 138–140). The percentage calculation is on the basis of the sum only of the items mentioned, excluding meals away from home and ice. The summary by incomes shows a tendency to spend in increasing proportion for meats as income rises, and to diminish relative expenditure for bread and other cereal foods. For eggs and dairy products and for alcoholic drinks the percentage fluctuations seem erratic. For meats and fish the percentage is 29.4 for $600 incomes, and 32.1 for incomes in the $1000 group. For cereals the results are 21 per cent. for the $600 families, and 17.3 per cent. for $1000 families. For eggs and dairy products the percentages vary from 19.8 ($700 incomes) to 23.3 ($900 incomes). For sugar, tea, and coffee the percentage remains not far from constant at 8 per cent. In fruits and vegetables there is a slight increase, from 13.8 per cent. among the $600 families to 14.2 per cent. among those with incomes of $1000 to $1100. For alcoholic drinks, the percentage ranges between 6 and 7.4 per cent.

The varieties of national custom in regard to diet are reflected only slightly in these tables of averages. It appears that the Russian and Austrian Jews report the largest percentage expenditure for meat, and the Italians the smallest. In the matter of cereals and vegetables the tables are reversed, the Italians showing the greatest percentage and the Russians and Austrians the least. This corresponds with the Italians' well known dependence on macaroni and dried beans. For the 16 American families with incomes between $900 and $1000, the averages and the percentages are as follows:

	AVERAGE EXPENDITURE.	PERCENTAGE OF ALL EXPENDITURES FOR FOOD PROPER.
Meats and fish	$127.56	32.5
Eggs, butter, milk, etc.	83.43	21.2
Cereals	72.45	18.5
Vegetables and fruit	65.49	16.7
Sugar, tea, coffee, etc.	31.63	8.0
Alcoholic drinks at home	12.01	3.1
	392.57	100.0

The constituents of the family dietary are more clearly exhibited in summaries of the reports from typical families which may be found at the end of the present section (page 154).

2. INADEQUACY IN KIND AND AMOUNT OF FOOD.—In order to judge how far the food provided is sufficient for the needs of a family, the food-stuffs consumed should be analyzed and the amount of nutritive value contained in the various constituents should be calculated and compared with the established standards of what is needed to maintain physical efficiency. In order to compare families composed of persons of varying age and sex, tables have been worked out showing the proportionate amount to be assigned to each person, as compared with the requirements for an adult man. The scale adopted by the United States Department of Agriculture is as follows:*

An adult woman requires.....	.8	as much as an adult man
A boy of 15 to 16	.9	" " " "
A boy of 13 to 14	.8	" " " "
A boy of 12	.7	" " " "
A boy of 10 to 11	.6	" " " "
A girl of 15 to 16	.8	" " " "
A girl of 13 to 14	.7	" " " "
A girl of 10 to 12	.6	" " " "
A child from 6 to 9	.5	" " " "
A child from 2 to 5	.4	" " " "
A child under 2.............	.3	" " " "

By the application of this scale the equivalent of each family in "units" of an adult man has been figured out and applied under the head "number of units" in the comprehensive tables of averages (Tables 15 and 16, pages 70–74, and in Table 62, page 140).

In order to secure evidence as to the nutritive value of the food reported by the families interviewed, 100 schedules selected so as to represent all nationalities and income-groups were sent for examination to Dr. Frank P. Underhill, assistant professor of Physiological Chemistry in Yale University. While the returns were not stated with scientific exactness as to the amount of each article consumed, and no allowance could be made for

* U. S. Department of Agriculture. Farmer's Bulletin, No. 142, p. 33.

wastes, a rough approximation to the nutritive value of the dietary
was calculated, which is not without value. Professor Underhill's report may be found in Appendix VI (page 319). On
the basis of the prices prevailing in the summer of 1907, Dr. Underhill found that the families which spent at the rate of less than
22 cents per man per day were not receiving enough food to
maintain physical efficiency*; that is, for less than this amount
the family did not purchase materials sufficient to provide a
minimum allowance of 100 to 125 grams of protein and 2500
to 3000 calories of fuel for the tissues.†

The detailed figures for two schedules analyzed by Dr. Underhill may be found on page 323. For all the families included
in the report a calculation was made of the expenditure reduced
to terms of "cents per man per day."

This method of calculation may be easily illustrated by an
example: A certain family consists of father, mother, a girl of
4 years, a boy of 3 and a baby under 2. The father buys lunch
6 days in the week. The calculation therefore runs, applying the
equivalents given on page 125:

```
1 man     15 meals per week .........................................................15.0
1 woman   21 meals, equivalent for man to 21 × 0.8 meals per week .......16.8
1 boy     21   "        "        "   "  " 21 × 0.4   "    "    "   ...... 8.4
1 girl    21   "        "        "   "  " 21 × 0.4   "    "    "   ...... 8.4
1 child   21   "        "        "   "  " 21 × 0.3   "    "    "   ...... 6.3
```
    Total number of meals, on basis of consumption of adult man............54.9

This total is equivalent, counting 3 meals per day, to meals for 1
man for 18 days. The weekly expenditure for food foots up $4.24;
that is, to meet a demand for food equivalent to the needs of one
man for 18 days, this family spends $4.24, or, dividing $4.24 by 18,
spends 23.6 cents per man per day. This calculation makes it

* Dr. Atwater, from data gathered 1896–7, estimated the cost at 23–25 cents per
man per day. (U. S. Dept. of Agriculture. Bulletin of Experiment Stations No.
116, pp. 74, 75.) Of 63 families, tabulated by Dr. Underhill as adequately nourished,
two spent 22 cents per man per day; two less than 22 cents. Of 37 tabulated
by him as under-nourished, 6 spent 22 cents per man per day, 7 over 22 cents.

† The non-technical reader may be reminded that one calorie is the amount of
heat necessary to raise one kilogram of water one degree centigrade (1.8 degrees Fah-
renheit) in temperature. Into the disputed questions as to the minimum allowance of protein for tissue-building and of fats and carbo-hydrates for fuel, it is not
the purpose of this report to enter. But the amounts as given will be recognized
as conservative as compared with the standard set by most dietary experts.

possible to compare families without regard to differences in number and age of their members, and to apply a uniform standard to them all. The tabulation of the average expenditure per man per day is given in Table 64 (page 141).

Applying the minimum suggested by Dr. Underhill, 22 cents per man per day, we have the result shown in Table 63 (page 141). The showing by income-groups is as follows:

INCOME.	TOTAL NUMBER OF FAMILIES.	UNDER-FED FAMILIES. (22 cents per man per day and under.)	
		NUMBER.	PER CENT.
$400 to $599.............	25	19	76
600 to 799.............	151	48	32
800 to 899.............	73	16	22
900 to 1099.............	94	8	9
1100 and over.............	48	0	0
	391	91	23.2

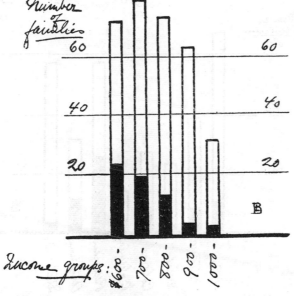

DIAGRAM 11.—Number of under-fed families in each of the principal income-groups.

127

This means that with less than $600 to spend for all purposes, an adequate food-supply is not provided, and that on from $600 to $800 incomes 1 family in 3 is under-fed, while less than 1 in 10 of the families having $900 and $1000 to spend fell short of the minimum for food. Of the nationalities represented, the proportion of under-fed was greatest among the Russians, where more than half of the families with incomes between $600 and $800, spent less than the minimum for food. For the 318 families with incomes between $600 and $1100 the figures are as follows:

NATIONALITY.	NUMBER OF FAMILIES.	UNDER-FED FAMILIES.	
		NUMBER.	PER CENT.
United States............	67	10	14.9
Teutonic................	39	8	20.5
Irish....................	24	2	8.3
Colored.................	28	8	28.6
Bohemian...............	14	4	28.6
Russian.................	57	26	45.5
Austrian, etc............	32	11	34.5
Italian.................	57	3	5.3
	318	72	22.7

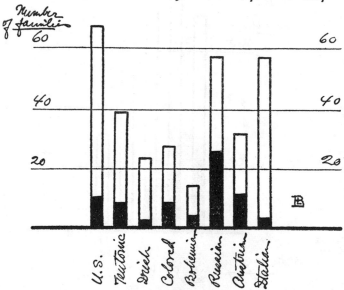

DIAGRAM 12.—Number of under-fed families in each of the nationality-groups.

The small proportion among the Italians is due in part to the fact that the Italian families reported on consist, very many of them, of parents and two young children. The large proportion of income devoted to buying food by the Italians has already been pointed out (page 123).

By occupations, the three groups selected for comparison show a larger proportion of under-fed families than the whole mass. The figures, for incomes between $600 and $1100, are as follows:

OCCUPATION.	TOTAL NUMBER OF FAMILIES.	UNDER-FED FAMILIES: NUMBER.	PER CENT.
Garment-workers	45	16	33.3
Laborers	35	11	31.4
Teamsters, etc.	26	8	30.7
	106	35	33

The same distribution of these under-fed families among the income-groups is found that appears in regard to the families as a whole. Ten of the 16 under-fed among the garment-workers have less than $800 income; 9 of the 11 under-fed laborers' families, and all of the 8 under-fed among the teamsters, have incomes under $800.

The analysis of all under-fed families with reference to sources of income (Table 65, page 142) shows that the scanty provision of food is more frequent among families with composite incomes than among families supported by the father alone. Of the 149 families (out of 318) which are supported by father alone, 30 families, or 20 per cent., are under-fed, as against 42 under-fed families out of the 169 with composite incomes, or 24.8 per cent. That the scant provision of food is often a necessity, if expenditures are to be brought within income, appears from noting the relation of under-fed families to the families at large in the matter of surplus or deficiency in the annual budget (Tables 66 and 67, pages 143–144). Of all the 318 families, 116 families, or 36.5 per cent., report a surplus (Table 120, page 236). Of the 72 under-fed families, 36 families, or 50 per cent., report a surplus. Eighty-six families, or 27 per cent. of the total 318 families, report a deficit, and 116 report an even balance, within $25. Of the 72 under-fed, only 9 families, or 12.5 per cent., report a deficit, and 27 families, or 37.5 per cent., report an even balance.

One other point that should be considered with reference to these under-fed families is the relation of deficiency of nutrition to the size of the family. In regard to this point, the following data are available. As appears from Table 62 (page 140), the number of "units" in the average of all the 318 families is 3.5. By number of units is meant, as already explained, the number of full-grown men whose food-requirements would be equal to those of the given family. The average number of "units" of the 62 under-fed families is 3.85, as compared with the average of 3.5 for all families. Comparing income-groups and sources of income with reference to this point, the results are even more suggestive, as will be seen from the following table:

NUMBER OF FAMILIES.	AVERAGE NUMBER OF UNITS.					
	$600 to $699	$700 to $799	$800 to $899	$900 to $999	$1000 to $1099	ALL IN-COMES.
26 (Families supported by father alone.)	3.5	3.6	3.7	4.0	...	3.6
36 (Families with composite income) ..	3.8	4.2	4.0	5.4	4.1	4.1
62 (All under-fed families)............	3.6	4.0	3.9	5.1	4.1	3.85
318 (All families)	3.3	3.5	3.5	3.6	3.7	3.5

By income:

INCOME.	TOTAL NUMBER OF FAMILIES.	NUMBER UNDER-FED.	AVERAGE NUMBER OF UNITS.	
			All Families.	Under-fed Families.
$600– $799 ...	151	42	3.4	3.8
$800– $899 ...	73	13	3.5	3.9
$900–$1099 ...	94	7	3.7	4.7

For this comparison the 10 families with expenditure of exactly 22 cents per man per day are omitted, leaving 62 families spending 21 cents and under. These figures indicate that the increase of expenditure for food does not keep pace with the increase of demand for it as children grow older, even though the income be pieced out by additions from lodgers and by the earnings of mother and children. It is significant that although few under-fed families are found in the higher income-groups, the cases that do occur show the need of an exceptionally large amount of food.*

Reviewing the causes for insufficient provision of food as suggested by the statistics of the comparisons, we have discovered that four circumstances frequently attend the families that are under-fed. These circumstances are, first, a larger number of mouths to be fed, or rather, a larger food-necessity to be supplied; second, a larger dependence on other resources than the wages of the father; third, a desire to save money even at cost of inadequate nutrition; fourth, a low family income. It will readily be seen that the last mentioned cause, low income, is in a sense inclusive of most of the others. Excluded from this enumeration is the lack of economy in management, and of wisdom in the purchase of food, but even with the best economy the other causes do not cease to operate. In a few of the cases classified as under-fed there is evidence of exceptional expenditure for drink, but the number of these cases is too small to overshadow the causes already mentioned.

3. ITEMS OF DETAIL.—Some interesting side-lights are thrown on the subject by the returns regarding certain more or less significant items of detail in the food-budget. Frequency in food purchases, meals away from home, the use of alcoholic drinks,

---

* Pursuing the same analysis on the basis of nationality, the following results appear:

NATIONALITY.	INCOME $600 TO $699.			
	Number Families.		Average Number Units.	
	Total.	Under-fed.	All.	Under-fed.
U. S., Teutonic, Irish...............	52	12	3.4	3.3
Russian, Austrian and Bohemian.....	52	24	3.5	3.9
	INCOME $900 to $1099.			
U. S., Teutonic, Irish...............	49	1	3.6	4.3
Russian, Austrian and Bohemian.....	27	4	4.0	5.1

the kind of milk used, the use of ice and refrigerators, dependence upon the baker for bread, are the matters included under this head.

Dependence on Baker.—Taking the last item first, it is sufficient in a word to say that New York families such as those under consideration universally buy bread. Only 26 families out of 318 reported making bread at home for the whole or a part of the year. Eight of these were Italian families, 6 Russian and 5 colored. Among the Italian families the custom prevails of mixing the bread at home and taking it to a bakery to be baked at a charge of 10 cents a week. The contrast in this regard with families outside of New York City is striking. Out of 19 families in Syracuse, with incomes between $500 and $1650, 17 reported making bread at home. Seven out of 10 in Richfield Springs made bread at home.

Frequency of Food Purchase.—In regard to the frequency of the purchase of food, the questions of the schedule did not bring out answers as definite as were desired. Most families buy their supplies from day to day in very small quantities, partly from the lack of facility for storing and keeping food, and partly from the lack of money enough at one time to enable them to buy any large amount. Many families reported buying staple articles, like flour and sugar, once a week; but mention is equally frequent of purchasing butter by the quarter-pound, potatoes by the pound, and other supplies by the nickel's-worth. The nature of the material did not seem to warrant the effort to make statistical tables of these data.

Meals Away from Home.—Tables 68-70 (pages 145-146) show that 136 of the 318 families reported expenditure for meals away from home. Expenditure for this purpose is more frequent in the case of families having children at work. Only 38 per cent. of the 149 families where the father's earnings constitute the whole income, report meals away from home, while 50 per cent. of the 86 families where other members are wage-earners report expenditure for this purpose. Of the various nationalities, the expenditure for lunches is most frequent among the American families, 54 per cent. of whom spend money for this purpose. Only 21 per cent. of the colored families and 32 per cent. of the Italian families report such expenditure. In the three occupations classified separately, 38 per cent. of the laborers, 50 per cent. of the teamsters and 53 per cent. of the garment-makers bought lunches. In certain occupations one or more meals are furnished free to employees. Fourteen such cases were counted among the 318 families, 8 being bartenders, cooks and waiters, and 3 drivers of provision-wagons. Location of families with reference to place of work is, of course, a determining factor in regard to the purchase of meals, but the classification by boroughs does not bring out this relation. Forty-four per cent. of the Manhattan families and 40 per cent. of the families in other boroughs report expenditure for meals away from home.

In the matter of income there is a noticeable increase in the amount paid for lunches as the income increases. This appears in the following table:

INCOME.	TOTAL NUMBER OF FAMILIES.	NUMBER OF FAMILIES REPORTING MEALS AWAY FROM HOME.	AVERAGE EXPENDITURE.
$500 to $699 72		22	$34.48
700 to 799 79		42	41.87
800 to 899 73		31	42.87
900 to 999 63		28	51.08
1000 to 1099 31		13	65.06
	318	136	

Fifteen of 25 families, with incomes between $400 and $600, spend on the average $29.29 for lunch, and 26 of 48 families, with incomes of $1100 and over, report spending $71.36 each on the average for this purpose. In Tables 69 and 70 (page 146) the increase in the amount expended for lunches with increase of income, and also its relation to the composition of the family income, is shown under groups according to the daily expenditure per family.

Alcoholic Drinks.—The expenditure for drinks was divided in the schedule. The cost of alcoholic liquors drunk at home was included under the specification of food; the cost of drinks away from home was put with the miscellaneous expenditures. The result was that a fairly complete report regarding liquors drunk at home was received, inasmuch as the families regarded this item as a matter of course, and felt no more reticence about it than about any other detail. What was drunk away from home, on the other hand, was considered as a more personal matter, and the information was not as readily secured. When the mother answered the questions she often knew only that she was in the habit of giving her husband perhaps $1 a week for spending money, and that out of it he paid for what he drank, along with other incidentals. It may safely be assumed that the expenditure for drinks away from home, as reported, did not exceed the actual amount.

In regard to the use of alcoholic drinks at home there is a marked difference, among the nationalities represented, in the proportion of families reporting expenditure. Table 71 (page 147) shows that all of the Bohemian families, and 98 per cent. of the Italian families report some expenditure for alcoholic drinks; only the American families report this expenditure in the case of less than two-thirds of the families, the percentage of the American families being 46.3. The amounts expended are in many of these cases small, as will be seen in Tables 71–73 (pages 147–149). Ninety of the 243 families expending money for drinks, spend less than $20 a year. More than half of the Russian families spend less than $20. On the other hand, 11 out of 14 Bohemian families, 19 out of 28 Teutonic families and 9 out of 17 Irish families that expend for this purpose, spend more than $30 a year.

Table 74 (page 149) shows the increase in expenditure for drink with increase of income. The actual amount (average expenditure of the families using alcoholic drinks) increases from $23.23 in the $600 income-group to $37.03 in the $1000 income-group. If to the expenditure reported for drinks at home the expenditure for alcoholic drinks away from home be added, and the totals in each income-group divided by the number of families using alcoholic drinks, the average total expenditure by income-groups is as follows, together with the percentage of the average total income which goes for this purpose:

134

INCOME.	AVERAGE EXPENDITURE FOR ALCOHOLIC DRINKS.	PER CENT. OF INCOME.
$400 to $599	$18.47	2.7
600 to 699	27.25	4.2
700 to 799	32.52	4.4
800 to 899	37.65	4.4
900 to 999	36.36	3.9
1000 to 1099	50.67	4.9
1100 to 1199	59.96	5.2

This table suggests that a rise in the standard of living to certain families means, among other things, an increased indulgence in intoxicants.

Milk.—Some indication of the quality of the milk used may be found in the price paid for it. Ordinary "loose" milk at the grocery and provision stores was sold for 5 and 6 cents a quart during the summer of 1907. The bottled milk, complying with the sanitary requirements, was sold for 8 cents a quart bottle. Condensed milk at 10 cents a can was not infrequently used, in a few cases to the exclusion of fresh milk. The classification of families by nationalities and income with reference to the price paid for milk will be found in Tables 75 and 76 (pages 150–151). Seventeen families, 9 of them under-fed, reported 4-cent milk, the quality of which may be inferred from the price. One hundred and sixty-six families, or 52 per cent., reported 5-cent milk; 41, or 13 per cent., reported 6-cent milk; 78, or 24.5 per cent., reported 8-cent milk; 13, condensed milk only. Three families reported no milk used. Eleven of the 4-cent cases were in families with incomes under $800. We should expect to find 5-cent milk less frequent and 8-cent milk more frequent as the income increases, but the figures show no such tendency. About one-quarter of the families in each income-group use the bottled milk, and about two-thirds use the loose milk at 5 and 6 cents a quart. An extraordinary proportion of the Italian families (33 out of 57) report the use of bottled milk, while only 4 out of 57 Russian families use it. Eight of the 13 families depending on condensed milk are American.

Ice and Refrigerators.—(See Tables 77 and 78, pages 152–153.) Only 41 of the 318 families report no expenditure for ice, so that its use may be considered a part of the accepted standard for New York City. The amount expended increases on the average from $4.64 for the $600 families to $7.80 for the $1000 families, or to $9.21 for the families with incomes of $1100 and over. Classified on the basis of the amount expended, 64 per cent. of the $600 families pay not more than $5.00 a year for ice. Forty-eight per cent. of the $800 families and 70 per cent. of the $1000 families pay for ice $5.00 a year or more. An expenditure of less than $1.00 is reported by 21 families, 15 of them having incomes of less than $800. Twenty-five of the 41 families without ice have incomes under $800.

Refrigerators are found in more than four-fifths of the families, or in 81 per cent. of the families with incomes between $600 and $800, and in 90 per cent. of the families with higher incomes. In some cases it is reported that the ice is kept in a tub; in some cases an ice-box is reported, which is often hardly better than the tub; but in the majority of cases the refrigerator serves as a place for keeping perishable food as well as for keeping the ice itself.

TABLE 59.—FOOD. AVERAGE ANNUAL EXPENDITURE AND PER CENT. OF TOTAL EXPENDITURE.—BY NATIONALITY AND INCOME.

NATIONALITY.	$600 to $699			$700 to $799			$800 to $899			$900 to $999			$1000 to $1099		
	Number of Families.	Average Amount.	Per Cent.*	Number of Families.	Average Amount.	Per Cent.*	Number of Families.	Average Amount.	Per Cent.*	Number of Families.	Average Amount.	Per Cent.*	Number of Families.	Average Amount.	Per Cent.*
United States	11	$292.74	44.0	19	$348.44	45.7	13	$409.88	47.2	16	$425.75	44.8	8	$497.29	46.3
Teutonic	4	283.35	42.3	7	358.90	47.3	9	347.06	39.8	11	395.44	43.1	8	421.40	40.7
Irish	4	292.83	44.2	7	366.40	47.8	7	357.09	43.9	5	404.87	44.3	1	492.33	53.7
Colored	11	263.06	40.6	6	321.40	41.0	8	297.22	37.7	2	341.53	40.5	1	302.44	34.1
Bohemian	4	315.51	45.5	3	363.89	49.3	3	408.87	48.7	4	416.18	42.4	..	..	..
Russian	16	273.31	43.5	14	299.34	42.8	12	348.44	45.2	9	372.39	41.7	6	469.36	44.8
Austrian, etc.	6	258.92	42.8	9	321.97	45.3	9	318.69	38.8	7	419.54	46.4	1	451.91	46.2
Italian	16	330.00	49.7	14	337.39	47.8	12	385.03	51.6	9	411.65	50.8	6	430.48	48.1
Total	72	290.10	44.6	79	335.82	45.6	73	359.26	44.3	63	405.19	44.7	31	451.46	44.7

* Per cent. of expenditure for all purposes.

137

TABLE 60.—FOOD. AVERAGE AMOUNT AND PER CENT. OF EXPENDITURE FOR FOOD-MATERIAL OF VARIOUS KINDS.—BY NATIONALITY AND INCOME.

Expenditure for Meat and Fish.

	$600 TO $699	PER CENT.	$700 TO $799	PER CENT.	$800 TO $899	PER CENT.	$900 TO $999	PER CENT.	$1000 TO $1099	PER CENT.
United States	$82.97	29.6	$104.74	33.5	$122.08	33.5	$127.56	32.5	$146.63	32.7
Teutonic	80.53	29.3	103.35	30.6	92.67	28.8	117.54	30.6	132.54	33.5
Irish	69.04	27.0	95.08	27.6	99.89	33.5	114.83	29.1	123.37	28.7
Colored	71.81	28.3	103.90	34.2	97.70	34.1	88.28	28.0	81.12	27.0
Bohemian	71.29	23.6	80.49	23.2	96.76	24.7	114.83	31.4	..	..
Russian	82.21	32.2	93.17	35.4	113.03	35.2	118.57	34.3	157.96	37.1
Austrian, etc.	90.07	36.6	94.78	31.5	90.22	29.8	123.72	32.9	131.98	36.5
Italian	85.03	26.8	89.57	28.3	110.82	30.5	91.15	23.9	102.05	25.2

Expenditure for Eggs, Butter, Milk and Cheese.

	$600 TO $699	PER CENT.	$700 TO $799	PER CENT.	$800 TO $899	PER CENT.	$900 TO $999	PER CENT.	$1000 TO $1099	PER CENT.
United States	$63.68	22.7	$61.54	19.7	$71.66	19.7	$83.43	21.2	$98.95	22.1
Teutonic	64.04	23.3	66.18	19.6	76.99	23.9	100.91	26.3	77.15	19.5
Irish	67.60	26.5	73.54	21.3	74.27	25.0	96.30	24.4	73.32	17.0
Colored	48.50	19.1	55.38	18.2	59.82	20.8	63.72	20.1	92.56	30.8
Bohemian	66.69	22.1	64.29	18.5	66.56	17.0	71.10	19.4	..	..
Russian	59.93	23.5	52.45	19.9	65.11	20.3	83.79	24.3	83.85	19.6
Austrian, etc.	55.66	22.6	65.86	21.9	58.23	19.3	87.60	23.2	80.08	22.1
Italian	59.60	18.7	59.21	18.7	66.63	18.3	90.99	23.8	93.58	23.1

Expenditure for Cereals.

	$600 TO $699	PER CENT.	$700 TO $799	PER CENT.	$800 TO $899	PER CENT.	$900 TO $999	PER CENT.	$1000 TO $1099	PER CENT.
United States	$61.64	21.9	$65.84	21.0	$76.88	21.1	$72.45	18.5	$86.13	19.2
Teutonic	62.66	22.8	60.98	18.0	49.74	15.4	63.11	16.4	60.64	15.3
Irish	53.42	20.9	72.26	21.0	45.67	15.3	70.33	17.8	83.20	19.3
Colored	55.40	21.8	57.07	18.8	54.05	18.8	75.46	23.9	33.80	11.3
Bohemian	65.78	21.8	80.28	23.2	99.93	25.5	63.83	17.4	..	..
Russian	49.62	19.5	45.68	17.3	63.47	19.8	56.51	16.4	74.93	17.6
Austrian, etc.	39.55	16.1	56.84	18.9	57.98	19.2	58.95	15.7	45.76	12.7
Italian	69.87	22.0	65.22	20.6	69.65	19.2	72.40	19.0	73.44	18.2

TABLE 60 (*Continued*).—FOOD. AVERAGE AMOUNT AND PER CENT. OF EXPENDITURE FOR FOOD-MATERIAL OF VARIOUS KINDS.—BY NATIONALITY AND INCOME.

EXPENDITURE FOR VEGETABLES AND FRUIT.

	$600 TO $699	PER CENT.	$700 TO $799	PER CENT.	$800 TO $899	PER CENT.	$900 TO $999	PER CENT.	$1000 TO $1099	PER CENT.
United States	$39.04	13.9	$41.99	13.4	$48.69	13.4	$65.49	16.7	$66.24	14.7
Teutonic	30.76	11.3	50.68	15.0	39.53	12.3	49.21	12.8	59.68	15.1
Irish	30.69	12.0	45.18	13.1	31.50	10.5	54.86	14.0	93.20	21.7
Colored	42.22	16.6	49.97	16.5	33.16	11.6	46.87	14.8	43.16	14.4
Bohemian	33.23	11.0	52.83	15.2	52.08	13.2	51.08	14.0	..	..
Russian	31.16	12.2	32.36	12.3	38.16	11.9	40.87	11.8	39.59	9.3
Austrian, etc.	26.91	10.9	38.29	12.8	39.71	13.1	48.29	12.8	48.36	13.4
Italian	50.47	15.9	48.61	15.3	64.88	17.8	59.84	15.6	65.27	16.1

EXPENDITURE FOR SUGAR, TEA, COFFEE AND CONDIMENTS.

	$600 TO $699	PER CENT.	$700 TO $799	PER CENT.	$800 TO $899	PER CENT.	$900 TO $999	PER CENT.	$1000 TO $1099	PER CENT.
United States	$25.86	9.2	$28.47	9.1	$30.95	8.5	$31.63	8.0	$36.56	8.2
Teutonic	23.46	8.6	35.09	10.4	31.76	9.9	33.59	8.8	37.60	9.5
Irish	22.88	9.0	35.62	10.3	28.62	9.6	38.22	9.7	20.54	4.8
Colored	24.12	9.5	29.75	9.8	28.61	10.0	32.50	10.3	33.80	11.3
Bohemian	27.20	9.0	22.13	6.4	28.34	7.2	30.80	8.4	..	..
Russian	20.06	7.9	22.50	8.6	24.04	7.4	25.12	7.3	33.33	7.8
Austrian, etc.	18.47	7.5	22.90	7.6	26.36	8.7	24.57	6.5	31.92	8.8
Italian	18.66	5.9	17.01	5.4	20.53	5.6	28.05	7.2	25.35	6.3

EXPENDITURE FOR ALCOHOLIC DRINKS AT HOME.

	$600 TO $699	PER CENT.	$700 TO $799	PER CENT.	$800 TO $899	PER CENT.	$900 TO $999	PER CENT.	$1000 TO $1099	PER CENT.
United States	$7.65	2.7	$10.49	3.3	$13.69	3.8	$12.01	3.1	$14.11	3.1
Teutonic	13.00	4.7	21.54	6.4	31.36	9.7	19.59	5.1	28.17	7.1
Irish	11.70	4.6	23.07	6.7	18.11	6.1	19.76	5.0	36.40	8.5
Colored	12.09	4.7	7.67	2.5	13.48	4.7	9.10	2.9	15.60	5.2
Bohemian	37.95	12.5	46.93	13.5	48.87	12.4	34.36	9.4	..	..
Russian	12.02	4.7	17.15	6.5	17.44	5.4	20.41	5.9	36.68	8.6
Austrian, etc.	15.39	6.3	21.86	7.3	30.54	9.9	33.70	8.9	23.70	6.5
Italian	34.26	10.7	37.00	11.7	31.30	8.6	40.21	10.5	44.78	11.1

TABLE 61.—FOOD.   AVERAGE ANNUAL EXPENDITURE AND PER CENT. OF TOTAL EXPENDITURE FOR FOOD-MATERIAL OF VARIOUS KINDS.—BY INCOME.

INCOME.	NUMBER OF FAMILIES.	MEATS AND FISH.		EGGS, MILK, ETC.		CEREALS.		VEGETABLES AND FRUITS.		SUGAR, ETC.		ALCOHOL.		TOTAL.
		Average.	Per Cent.	Average.	Per Cent.	Average.	Per Cent.	Average.	Per Cent.	Average.	Per Cent.	Average.	Per Cent.	
$600 to $699	72	$80.59	29.4	$59.35	21.6	$57.83	21.0	$38.05	13.8	$21.87	8.0	$18.06	6.5	$274.72
$700 to $799	79	96.90	31.4	61.12	19.8	61.15	19.9	43.11	13.9	25.82	8.3	20.93	6.7	308.95
$800 to $899	73	105.35	31.6	67.51	20.2	63.27	18.9	44.17	13.2	28.42	8.5	24.68	7.4	336.98
$900 to $999	63	115.77	30.8	87.69	23.3	66.42	17.7	54.06	14.4	30.24	8.0	22.91	6.0	376.02
$1000 to $1099	31	132.78	32.1	87.35	21.1	71.37	17.3	58.50	14.2	33.17	8.0	29.62	7.2	413.09

TABLE 62.—AVERAGE NUMBER OF UNITS PER FAMILY.—BY INCOME AND NATIONALITY.

NATIONALITY.	$600 to $699		$700 to $799		$800 to $899		$900 to $999		$1000 to $1099		TOTAL.	
	Number of Families.	Average Number of Units.	Number of Families.	Average Number of Units.	Number of Families.	Average Number of Units.	Number of Families.	Average Number of Units.	Number of Families.	Average Number of Units.	Number of Families.	Average Number of Units.
United States	11	3.2	19	3.5	13	3.5	16	3.5	8	3.7	67	3.5
Teutonic	4	3.1	7	3.7	9	3.2	11	3.4	8	3.7	39	3.4
Irish	4	3.6	7	3.4	7	3.7	5	3.5	1	4.0	24	3.6
Colored	11	3.3	6	3.4	8	3.3	2	3.7	1	4.0	28	3.4
Bohemian	4	3.4	3	4.1	3	3.7	4	4.0	..	..	14	3.8
Russian	16	3.4	14	3.5	12	3.9	9	4.2	6	4.0	57	3.7
Austrian, etc.	6	3.3	9	3.6	9	3.6	7	3.4	1	5.1	32	3.6
Italian	16	3.1	14	3.0	12	3.2	9	3.5	6	3.4	57	3.2
Total	72	3.3	79	3.5	73	3.5	63	3.6	31	3.7	318	3.5

TABLE 63.—UNDER-FED FAMILIES.   NUMBER REPORTING EXPEN-
DITURE OF 22 CENTS PER MAN PER DAY AND UNDER FOR
FOOD.—BY NATIONALITY AND INCOME.

NATIONALITY.	TOTAL NUMBER OF FAMILIES.	UNDER-FED—NUMBER OF FAMILIES.										
		$600 to $699		$700 to $799		$800 to $899		$900 to $999		$1000 to $1099		TOTAL.	
		Under 22c.	22c.	Under 22c.	22c.	Under 22c.	22c.	Under 22c.	22c.	Under 22c.	22c.	Under 22c.	22c.
United States	67	3	1	4	1	1	..	..	..	..	..	8	2
Teutonic	39	1	..	2	3	1	..	..	..	1	..	5	3
Irish	24	2	..	..	..	..	..	..	..	..	..	2	..
Colored	28	3	..	1	1	2	..	..	..	1	..	7	1
Bohemian	14	1	..	1	..	..	1	1	..	..	..	3	1
Russian	57	9	..	7	..	5	1	2	1	1	..	24	2
Austrian, etc.	32	2	..	4	..	4	1	..	..	..	..	10	1
Italian	57	2	..	..	..	..	..	1	..	..	..	3	..
Total	318	23	1	19	5	13	3	4	1	3	..	62	10

TABLE 64.—FOOD EXPENDITURES REDUCED TO NUMBER OF
CENTS PER MAN PER DAY.   AVERAGES.*—BY INCOME
AND NATIONALITY.

NATIONALITY.	INCOME.				
	$600 to $699	$700 to $799	$800 to $899	$900 to $999	$1000 to $1099
United States	23.9	26.0	32.4	33.8	38.1
Teutonic	25.3	26.4	29.5	31.6	31.9
Irish	20.8	30.0	26.5	31.4	32.0
Colored	23.5	25.7	24.5	25.0	21.0
Bohemian	25.5	24.3	30.2	28.5	..
Russian	23.1	23.6	24.0	25.5	29.7
Austrian, etc.	24.0	25.1	23.8	31.1	23.0
Italian	31.1	31.2	33.9	31.5	34.3
Total	25.3	26.7	25.6	30.8	32.9

* See footnote, Appendix V (p. 312).

TABLE 65.—UNDER-FED FAMILIES. SOURCES OF INCOME.—BY INCOME AND NATIONALITY.

NATIONALITY.	$600 TO $699				$700 TO $799				$800 TO $899			
	Total Number of Families.	Total Under-fed.	Income from: Father Only.	Other Sources.	Total Number of Families.	Total Under-fed.	Income from: Father Only.	Other Sources.	Total Number of Families.	Total Under-fed.	Income from: Father Only.	Other Sources.
United States	11	4	4	..	19	5	5	..	13	1	..	1
Teutonic	4	1	..	1	7	5	1	4	9	1	1	..
Irish	4	2	2	..	7	..	..	..	7	..	..	..
Colored	11	3	2	1	6	2	1	1	8	2	..	2
Bohemian	4	1	..	1	3	1	1	..	3	1	..	1
Russian	16	9	6	3	14	7	2	5	12	6	2	4
Austrian, etc.	6	2	..	2	9	4	1	3	9	5	..	5
Italian	16	2	1	1	14	..	..	..	12	..	..	..
Total	72	24	15	9	79	24	11	13	73	16	3	13

NATIONALITY.	$900 TO $999				$1000 TO $1099				TOTAL.					
	Total Number of Families.	Total Under-fed.	Income from: Father Only.	Other Sources.	Total Number of Families.	Total Under-fed.	Income from: Father Only.	Other Sources.	Total Number of Families.	Total Under-fed.	Father Only. Number.	Per cent.	Other Sources. Number.	Per cent.
United States	16	..	..	..	8	..	..	..	67	10	9	90	1	10
Teutonic	11	..	..	..	8	1	..	1	39	8	2	25	6	75
Irish	5	..	..	..	1	..	..	..	24	2	2	100	..	..
Colored	2	..	..	..	1	1	..	1	28	8	3	37	5	63
Bohemian	4	1	..	1	..	..	..	..	14	4	1	25	3	75
Russian	9	3	..	3	6	1	..	1	57	26	10	39	16	61
Austrian, etc.	7	..	..	..	1	..	..	..	32	11	1	9	10	91
Italian	9	1	1	..	6	..	..	..	57	3	2	67	1	33
Total	63	5	1	4	31	3	..	3	318	72	30	42	42	58

TABLE 66.—UNDER-FED FAMILIES. NUMBER REPORTING SURPLUS AND DEFICIT.—BY NATIONALITY AND INCOME.

NATIONALITY.	$600 to $699				$700 to $799				$800 to $899			
	Number of Families Under-fed.	Number Reporting:			Number of Families Under-fed.	Number Reporting:			Number of Families Under-fed.	Number Reporting:		
		Balance within $25.	Surplus.	Deficit.		Balance within $25.	Surplus.	Deficit.		Balance within $25.	Surplus.	Deficit.
United States	4	2	1	1	5	3	1	1	1	1	..	..
Teutonic	1	1	..	..	5	2	2	1	1	1	..	1
Irish	2	1	1	..	..	..	..	..	..	..	..	..
Colored	3	2	..	1	2	2	..	..	2	..	1	1
Bohemian	1	1	..	..	1	1	..	..	1	1	..	..
Russian	9	2	5	2	7	1	6	..	6	..	6	..
Austrian, etc	2	..	2	..	4	1	3	..	5	4	1	..
Italian	2	..	2	..	..	..	..	..	..	..	..	..
Total	24	9	11	4	24	10	12	2	16	6	8	2

NATIONALITY.	$900 to $999				$1000 to $1099				TOTAL.						
	Number of Families Under-fed.	Number Reporting:			Number of Families Under-fed.	Number Reporting:			Total Number of Families Under-fed.	Families Reporting:					
		Balance within $25.	Surplus.	Deficit.		Balance within $25.	Surplus.	Deficit.		Balance within $25.		Surplus.		Deficit.	
										Number.	Per cent.	Number.	Per cent.	Number.	Per cent.
United States	..	..	..	..	..	..	..	..	10	6	60.0	2	20.0	2	20
Teutonic	..	..	..	..	1	..	1	..	8	3	37.5	3	37.5	2	25
Irish	..	..	..	..	..	..	..	..	2	1	50.0	1	50.0	..	..
Colored	..	..	..	..	1	..	1	..	8	4	50.0	2	25.0	2	25
Bohemian	1	1	..	..	..	..	..	..	4	4	100.0	..	......	..	..
Russian	3	1	1	1	1	..	1	..	26	4	15.0	19	73.0	3	12
Austrian, etc	..	..	1	..	..	..	..	..	11	5	45.0	6	55.0	..	..
Italian	1	..	1	..	..	..	..	..	3	..	......	3	100.0	..	..
Total	5	2	2	1	3	..	3	..	72	27	37	36	50	9	13

143

TABLE 67.—UNDER-FED FAMILIES. NUMBER REPORTING SURPLUS AND DEFICIT.—BY INCOME.

Income.	Total Number of Families.	Number Under-fed.	Reporting: Balance within $25.		Reporting: Surplus.		Reporting: Deficit.	
			Number.	Per cent.	Number.	Per cent.	Number.	Per cent.
$600 to $699.................	72	24	9	38	11	46	4	16
$700 to $799.................	79	24	10	42	12	50	2	8
$800 to $899.................	73	16	6	37	8	50	2	13
$900 to $999.................	63	5	2	40	2	40	1	20
$1000 to $1099.................	31	3	..	..	3	100	..	..
Total.................	318	72	27	38	36	50	9	12
$600 to $799.................	151	48	19	40	23	48	6	12
$800 to $899.................	73	16	6	38	8	50	2	12
$900 to $1099.................	94	8	2	25	5	63	1	12

TABLE 68.—MEALS AWAY FROM HOME. NUMBER OF FAMILIES REPORTING.—BY NATIONALITY, INCOME, BOROUGH, SOURCES OF INCOME, AND OCCUPATION.

BY NATIONALITY.

Nationality.	Total Number of Families.	Reporting Expenditure for Meals Away. Number.	Reporting Expenditure for Meals Away. Per Cent.	Average Amount for Families Spending.
United States	67	36	54	$53.68
Teutonic	39	13	33	40.98
Irish	24	12	50	36.55
Colored	28	6	21	36.40
Bohemian	14	7	50	46.16
Russian	57	28	50	45.61
Austrian, etc.	32	15	50	38.44
Italian	57	18	32	38.68
Total	318	136	42	$44.82

BY INCOME.

Income.	Total Number of Families.	Reporting Expenditure for Meals Away. Number.	Reporting Expenditure for Meals Away. Per Cent.	Average Amount for Families Spending.
$600 to $699	72	22	31	$34.48
$700 to $799	79	42	53	41.87
$800 to $899	73	31	42	42.08
$900 to $999	63	28	44	51.01
$1000 to $1099	31	13	42	65.06
Total	318	136	42	44.82
$400 to $599	25	15	52	29.29
$600 to $1099	318	136	42	44.82
$1100 and over	48	26	54	71.36

BY BOROUGH.

Borough.	Number of Families.	Reporting Expenditure for Meals Away. Number.	Reporting Expenditure for Meals Away. Per Cent.	Average Amount for Families Spending.
Manhattan	243	106	44	$46.26
Brooklyn, Bronx, and Queens	75	30	40	39.71
Total	318	136	42	$44.82

BY SOURCES OF INCOME.

Sources of Income.	Number of Families.	Reporting Expenditure for Meals Away. Number.	Reporting Expenditure for Meals Away. Per Cent.	Average Amount for Families Spending.
Father's earnings only	149	57	38	$43.60
Other wage-earners	86	43	50	47.85

BY OCCUPATION.

Occupation.	Number of Families.	Reporting Expenditure for Meals Away. Number.	Reporting Expenditure for Meals Away. Per Cent.	Average Amount for Families Spending.
Laborers	37	14	38	$40.53
Garment workers	59	31	53	47.15
Teamsters	30	15	50	66.75

TABLE 69.—MEALS AWAY FROM HOME. NUMBER OF FAMILIES REPORTING EXPENDITURE OF GIVEN AMOUNTS.—BY SOURCE OF INCOME.

Income.	Number of Cases Spending Daily 5c. and Below.		Number of Cases Spending Daily 10c.		Number of Cases Spending Daily 15c.		Number of Cases Spending Daily 20c.		Number of Cases Spending Daily 25c.		Number of Cases Spending Daily 30c.		Number of Cases Spending Daily over 30c.		Total.	
	Income from Earnings of Father Only.	Composite Income.	Income from Earnings of Father Only.	Composite Income.	Income from Earnings of Father Only.	Composite Income.	Income from Earnings of Father Only.	Composite Income.	Income from Earnings of Father Only.	Composite Income.	Income from Earnings of Father Only.	Composite Income.	Income from Earnings of Father Only.	Composite Income.	Income from Earnings of Father Only.	Composite Income.
$600 to $799...	4	3	15	7	9	1	3	1	1	1	..	..	1	..	33	13
$900 to $1099...	..	1	3	4	4	4	1	5	3	3	1	..	..	4	12	21

TABLE 70.—MEALS AWAY FROM HOME. NUMBER OF FAMILIES AND THEIR EXPENDITURES.—BY INCOME, IN CUMULATIVE FORM.

Income.	Number of Cases Spending Daily 5c. and Below.		Number of Cases Spending Daily 10c. and Above.		Number of Cases Spending Daily 15c. and Above.		Number of Cases Spending Daily 20c. and Above.		Number of Cases Spending Daily 25c. and Above.		Number of Cases Spending Daily 30c. and Above.		Number of Cases Spending Daily Above 30c.	
	Income from Earnings of Father Only.	Composite Income.	Income from Earnings of Father Only.	Composite Income.	Income from Earnings of Father Only.	Composite Income.	Income from Earnings of Father Only.	Composite Income.	Income from Earnings of Father Only.	Composite Income.	Income from Earnings of Father Only.	Composite Income.	Income from Earnings of Father Only.	Composite Income.
$600 to $799...	..	1	12	20	8	15	5	12	4	7	2	4	..	4
$900 to $1099...	4	3	29	10	14	3	5	2	2	1	1	..	1	..

TABLE 71.—ALCOHOLIC DRINKS AT HOME. NUMBER AND PER CENT. OF FAMILIES REPORTING EXPENDITURE.—BY NATIONALITY AND SPECIFIED AMOUNTS.

NATIONALITY.	TOTAL NUMBER OF FAMILIES.	FAMILIES WITH EXPENDITURE FOR DRINK.		REPORTING EXPENDITURE OF:					
				Under $20.		$20 to $30.		Over $30.	
		Number.	Per Cent.	Number.	Per Cent.	Number.	Per Cent.	Number.	Per Cent.
United States.	67	31	46.3	12	17.9	4	6.0	15	22.4
Teutonic.	39	28	71.7	8	20.5	1	2.5	19	48.7
Irish.	24	17	70.8	6	25.0	2	8.3	9	37.5
Colored	28	19	67.9	14	50.0	2	7.2	3	10.7
Bohemian.	14	14	100.0	1	7.5	2	13.9	11	78.6
Russian.	57	51	89.4	32	56.1	6	10.5	13	22.8
Austrian, etc.	32	27	84.4	9	28.1	7	21.9	11	34.4
Italian.	57	56	98.2	8	14.0	4	7.0	44	77.2
Total.	318	243	76.4	90	28.3	28	8.8	125	39.3

147

TABLE 72.—ALCOHOLIC DRINKS AT HOME. NUMBER OF FAMILIES REPORTING EXPENDITURE OF GIVEN AMOUNTS.—BY NATIONALITY AND INCOME.

$600 to $699

Nationality.	Total.	With Expenditure for Drink.	Number of Families Reporting Expenditure of: Under $10	$10 to $30	$30 to $50	Over $50
United States	11	6	3	2	1	..
Teutonic	4	1	..	..	1	..
Irish	4	2	..	1	1	..
Colored	11	9	3	5	1	..
Bohemian	4	4	..	1	2	1
Russian	16	14	6	5	3	..
Austrian, etc.	6	5	1	5	..	..
Italian	16	15	..	3	6	3
Total	72	56	13	22	15	4

$700 to $799

Nationality.	Total.	With Expenditure for Drink.	Number of Families Reporting Expenditure of: Under $10	$10 to $30	$30 to $50	Over $50
United States	19	7	1	1	5	..
Teutonic	7	4	..	..	4	..
Irish	7	6	1	2	3	..
Colored	6	2	1	..	1	..
Bohemian	3	3	1	1	1	..
Russian	14	14	3	10	1	..
Austrian, etc.	9	8	2	3	2	1
Italian	14	14	2	2	6	4
Total	79	58	10	19	23	6

$800 to $899

Nationality.	Total.	With Expenditure for Drink.	Number of Families Reporting Expenditure of: Under $10	$10 to $30	$30 to $50	Over $50
United States	13	7	1	3	3	..
Teutonic	9	9	1	1	7	..
Irish	7	4	1	1	1	1
Colored	8	6	1	5	..	..
Bohemian	3	3	..	..	3	..
Russian	12	10	..	4	5	1
Austrian, etc.	9	8	2	2	2	1
Italian	12	12	2	3	6	3
Total	73	59	8	19	25	7

$900 to $999

Nationality.	Total.	With Expenditure for Drink.	Number of Families Reporting Expenditure of: Under $10	$10 to $30	$30 to $50	Over $50
United States	16	8	2	2	4	..
Teutonic	11	8	..	4	4	..
Irish	5	4	..	2	2	..
Colored	2	1	..	..	..	..
Bohemian	4	4	..	1	3	..
Russian	9	7	2	3	1	1
Austrian, etc.	7	5	1	..	2	2
Italian	9	9	..	..	5	4

$1000 to $1099

Nationality.	Total.	With Expenditure for Drink.	Number of Families Reporting Expenditure of: Under $10	$10 to $30	$30 to $50	Over $50
United States	8	3	..	1	2	..
Teutonic	8	6	..	3	1	2
Irish	1	1	..	..	1	..
Colored	1	1	..	..	..	..
Bohemian	..	..	..	..	..	..
Russian	6	6	2	..	..	2
Austrian, etc.	1	1	1	1	..	..
Italian	6	6	1	..	3	2

Total

Nationality.	Total.	With Expenditure for Drink.	Number of Families Reporting Expenditure of: Under $10	$10 to $30	$30 to $50	Over $50
United States	67	31	7	9	15	..
Teutonic	39	28	1	8	16	2
Irish	24	17	2	6	8	3
Colored	28	19	4	12	3	1
Bohemian	14	14	..	3	8	..
Russian	57	51	16	22	9	3
Austrian, etc.	32	27	5	11	7	4
Italian	57	56	4	8	8	4

TABLE 73.—ALCOHOLIC DRINKS AT HOME. NUMBER AND PER
CENT. OF FAMILIES REPORTING EXPENDITURE
OF GIVEN AMOUNTS.—BY INCOME.

INCOME.	TOTAL NUMBER OF FAMILIES.	FAMILIES WITH EXPENDITURE FOR DRINK.		FAMILIES REPORTING EXPENDITURE OF.							
				Under $10.		$10 to $30.		$30 to $50.		Over $50.	
		Number.	Per Cent.	Number.	Per Cent.	Number.	Per Cent.	Number.	Per Cent.	Number.	Per Cent.
$600 to $699......	72	56	78	13	18	22	31	15	21	6	8
$700 to $799......	79	58	73	10	13	19	24	23	29	6	7
$800 to $899......	73	59	81	8	11	19	26	25	34	7	10
$900 to $999......	63	46	73	5	8	13	21	21	33	7	11
$1000 to $1099......	31	24	77	3	10	6	19	9	29	6	19
Total..............	318	243	76	39	12	79	25	93	29	32	10
$400 to $599......	25	20	80	7	28	8	32	5	20	..	..
$600 to $799......	151	114	75	23	15	41	27	38	25	12	8
$800 to $899......	73	59	81	8	11	19	26	25	34	7	10
$900 to $1099......	94	70	74	8	8	19	20	30	32	13	14
$1100 and over......	48	37	77	4	8	7	15	10	21	16	33

TABLE 74.—ALCOHOLIC DRINKS AWAY FROM HOME AND AT HOME.
AVERAGE ANNUAL EXPENDITURE AND NUMBER
OF FAMILIES REPORTING.—BY INCOME.

INCOME.	TOTAL NUMBER OF FAMILIES.	AVERAGE INCOME (TOTAL).	AVERAGE EXPENDITURE FOR ALCOHOLIC DRINKS AT HOME.	REPORTING ALCOHOLIC DRINKS AT HOME.		AVERAGE EXPENDITURE FOR ALCOHOLIC DRINKS AT HOME AND AWAY.	
				Number of Families.	Average Expenditure of Families Reporting.	Average Amount.	Per cent. of Average Total Income.
$400 to $599......	25	$503.03	$14.13	20	$17.67	$18.47	2.7
$600 to $699......	72	650.17	18.06	56	23.23	27.25	4.2
$700 to $799......	79	748.83	20.93	58	28.51	32.52	4.4
$800 to $899......	73	846.26	24.68	59	30.53	37.65	4.4
$900 to $999......	63	942.03	22.91	46	31.38	36.56	3.9
$1000 to $1099......	31	1044.48	28.67	24	37.03	50.67	4.9
$1100 to $1199......	18	1137.42	39.63	14	50.95	59.96	5.2

TABLE 75.—MILK. NUMBER OF FAMILIES REPORTING GIVEN PRICES.—BY NATIONALITY AND INCOME.

$600 TO $699

Nationality	Number of Families	Number Paying for Milk per qt.: 4c.	5c.	6c.	8c.	10c.*
United States	11	..	6	3	1	1
Teutonic	4	1	1	..	2	..
Irish	4	1	1	1	1	..
Colored	10	..	8	..	2	..
Bohemian	4	1	3	..	..	..
Russian	16	2	8	3	3	..
Austrian, etc.	6	1	2	2	1	..
Italian	16	..	5	1	10	..
Total	71	6	34	10	20	1

$700 TO $799

Nationality	Number of Families	Number Paying for Milk per qt.: 4c.	5c.	6c.	8c.	10c.*
United States	19	1	7	2	6	3
Teutonic	7	1	5	..	..	1
Irish	7	..	5	1	1	..
Colored	5	..	2	1	2	..
Bohemian	3	1	2	..	..	..
Russian	14	2	8	4	..	..
Austrian, etc.	8	..	6	2	..	..
Italian	14	..	7	1	6	..
Total	77	5	42	11	15	4

$800 TO $899

Nationality	Number of Families	Number Paying for Milk per qt.: 4c.	5c.	6c.	8c.	10c.*
United States	13	..	8	..	3	2
Teutonic	9	1	5	2	1	..
Irish	7	..	2	2	3	..
Colored	8	..	2	..	4	2
Bohemian	3	1	2	..	..	..
Russian	12	..	12	..	..	..
Austrian, etc.	9	2	6	1	..	..
Italian	12	..	3	..	7	2
Total	73	4	40	5	18	6

$900 TO $999

Nationality	Number of Families	Number Paying for Milk per qt.: 4c.	5c.	6c.	8c.	10c.*
United States	16	..	8	3	3	2
Teutonic	11	..	3	3	5	..
Irish	5	..	4	..	1	..
Colored	2	..	..	1	1	..
Bohemian	4	1	3	..	..	..
Russian	9	..	6	2	1	..
Austrian, etc.	7	1	4	1	1	..
Italian	9	..	4	..	5	..
Total	63	2	32	10	17	2

$1000 TO $1099

Nationality	Number of Families	Number Paying for Milk per qt.: 4c.	5c.	6c.	8c.	10c.*
United States	8	..	3	4	1	..
Teutonic	8	..	7	..	1	..
Irish	1	..	1	..	..	..
Colored	1	..	..	..	1	..
Bohemian	..	..	..	..	..	..
Russian	6	..	5	1	..	..
Austrian, etc.	1	..	1	..	..	..
Italian	6	..	1	..	5	..
Total	31	..	18	5	8	..

TOTAL

Nationality	Number of Families	Number Paying for Milk per qt.: 4c.	5c.	6c.	8c.	10c.*
United States	67	1	32	12	14	8
Teutonic	39	3	21	5	9	1
Irish	24	1	13	4	6	..
Colored	26	..	12	2	10	2
Bohemian	14	4	10	..	..	..
Russian	57	4	39	10	4	..
Austrian, etc.	31	4	19	6	2	..
Italian	57	..	20	2	33	2
Total	315	17	166	41	78	13

* Condensed milk.

TABLE 76.—MILK. NUMBER OF FAMILIES REPORTING GIVEN PRICES.—BY INCOME.

INCOME.	NUMBER OF FAMILIES.	FAMILIES PAYING FOR MILK PER QUART.			
		5c. and 6c.		8c.	
		Number.	Per cent.	Number.	Per cent.
$600 to $699............	72	44	61	20	28
$700 to $799............	79	53	67	15	19
$800 to $899............	73	45	62	18	25
$900 to $999............	63	42	67	17	24
$1000 to $1099..........	31	23	74	8	26
$600 to $799............	151	97	64	35	23
$800 to $899............	73	45	62	18	25
$900 to $1099...........	94	63	69	25	27

TABLE 77.—ICE. NUMBER OF FAMILIES REPORTING EXPENDITURE OF GIVEN AMOUNTS AND AVERAGE AMOUNT EXPENDED.—BY NATIONALITY AND INCOME.

NATIONALITY.	$600 TO $699							$700 TO $799							$800 TO $899						
	Number of Families.	None.	Under $1.00.	$1.00 to $5.00.	$5.00 and over.	Having Refrigerator.	Average Expenditure.	Number of Families.	None.	Under $1.00.	$1.00 to $5.00.	$5.00 and over.	Having Refrigerator.	Average Expenditure.	Number of Families.	None.	Under $1.00.	$1.00 to $5.00.	$5.00 and over.	Having Refrigerator.	Average Expenditure.
United States	11	1	..	5	5	9	$4.80	19	4	..	7	8	12	$4.60	13	2	..	3	7	11	$4.93
Teutonic	4	..	2	1	1	3	2.45	7	1	1	1	4	6	4.74	9	..	1	6	3	9	5.25
Irish	4	..	1	2	..	3	2.40	7	1	..	5	1	6	3.73	7	1	..	4	2	7	3.84
Colored	11	1	1	5	3	10	3.24	6	..	..	3	3	5	4.67	8	..	..	4	3	6	4.55
Bohemian	4	..	..	1	3	3	5.57	3	1	1	1	..	2	1.33	3	1	1	2	..	3	2.20
Russian	16	4	2	6	4	11	3.04	14	1	3	2	7	12	5.26	12	..	1	3	8	11	6.23
Austrian, etc.	6	2	1	..	3	5	3.69	9	2	1	1	5	7	4.46	9	1	..	1	8	9	6.12
Italian	16	2	1	6	7	14	5.15	14	3	..	7	4	13	3.99	12	1	..	7	4	11	5.35
Total	72	11	9	26	26	59	3.93	79	14	6	27	32	63	4.42	73	5	3	30	35	67	5.14

NATIONALITY.	$900 TO $999							$1000 TO $1099							TOTAL.						
	Number of Families.	None.	Under $1.00.	$1.00 to $5.00.	$5.00 and over.	Having Refrigerator.	Average Expenditure.	Number of Families.	None.	Under $1.00.	$1.00 to $5.00.	$5.00 and over.	Having Refrigerator.	Average Expenditure.	Total Number of Families.	None.	Under $1.00.	$1.00 to $5.00.	$5.00 and over.	Having Refrigerator.	Average Expenditure.
United States	16	2	..	5	9	13	$5.79	8	1	..	1	6	8	$6.13	67	10	1	21	35	53	$6.07
Teutonic	11	2	1	4	4	9	4.35	8	..	..	1	7	7	9.32	39	3	4	13	19	35	6.00
Irish	5	1	..	3	4	4	4.40	1	..	..	..	..	..	..	24	5	1	14	14	20	4.43
Colored	2	..	..	1	2	2	4.20	1	1	..	1	..	..	2.40	28	1	3	14	10	23	4.10
Bohemian	4	1	..	1	2	4	4.50	..	..	..	..	..	..	..	14	2	1	5	5	12	4.24
Russian	9	..	2	..	7	8	7.80	6	..	..	..	6	6	8.68	57	7	7	11	32	48	6.39
Austrian, etc.	7	..	..	3	4	7	4.71	1	..	..	..	1	1	9.10	32	4	1	5	21	29	5.70
Italian	9	2	..	3	4	9	4.50	6	1	..	3	2	6	5.19	57	9	1	26	21	53	5.71
Total	63	8	3	20	32	56	5.27	31	3	..	6	22	28	7.05	318	41	21	109	147	273	5.63

TABLE 78.—ICE. NUMBER AND PER CENT. OF FAMILIES REPORTING EXPENDITURE OF GIVEN AMOUNTS AND AVERAGE AMOUNT EXPENDED.—BY INCOME.

INCOME.	TOTAL NUMBER OF FAMILIES.	EXPENDITURE REPORTED.								HAVING REFRIGERATORS.		AVERAGE AMOUNT EXPENDED BY FAMILIES SPENDING
		None.		Under $1.00.		$1.00 to $5.00.		Over $5.00.				
		Number.	Per Cent.	Number.	Per Cent.	Number.	Per Cent.	Number.	Per Cent.	Number.	Per Cent.	
$600 to $699............	72	11	15	9	13	26	36	26	36	59	82	$4.64
$700 to $799............	79	14	17	6	8	27	34	32	41	63	80	5.37
$800 to $899............	73	5	7	3	4	30	41	35	48	67	92	5.52
$900 to $999............	63	8	13	3	5	20	31	32	51	56	89	6.04
$1000 to $1099.........	31	3	10	..	..	6	20	22	70	28	90	7.80
Total............	318	41	13	21	7	109	34	147	46	273	81	5.63
$400 to $599...........	25	9	36	3	12	9	36	4	16	16	64	3.66
$600 to $799...........	151	25	17	15	10	53	34	58	38	122	81	5.02
$800 to $899...........	78	5	7	3	4	30	41	35	48	67	92	5.52
$900 to $1099.........	94	11	12	3	3	26	28	54	57	84	90	6.63
$1100 and over........	48	7	14	1	2	8	17	32	67	36	75	9.21*

* Average for thirty-two families buying ice, having incomes from $1100 to $1599.

153

NOTE ON DETAILS OF FOOD-BUDGETS

To illustrate the items of detail in expenditures for food, six fairly representative schedules are presented in detail; 2 American, 1 Russian, 1 Austrian and 2 Italian. Three are chosen from families having an income between $600 and $700, and 3 from families, comparable in nationality, with incomes of about $900. This selection makes possible a comparison of the diet of a family somewhat below the normal standard of living, with that of one not far above the normal.

1. The first family is that of an American truck-driver, living in Harlem. The father earns $12 a week, $600 a year. The family consists of the man and his wife and 3 children, aged 2, 4 and 8 years. The nutrition demanded weekly for this family is the equivalent of that required for an adult man for 22 days. The dietary analysis made by Dr. F. P. Underhill (see Appendix VI, page 319) showed a total of 102 grams of protein and fuel-values to the amount of 2504 calories, both reckoned per man per day. The average expenditure, on the same basis, was 21.6 cents per man per day. The details of the weekly food-budget are as follows:

Meats and fish: WEEKLY EXPENDITURE.
    4 lbs. fresh beef..................$0.48
    4 lbs. salt beef................... .28
    1 lb. ham.......................... .16
    1 lb. chicken (4 lbs. once a month).. .14
    1 lb. fish (4 lbs. once a month)...... .05 $1.11

Eggs, dairy products, etc.:
    1 lb. butter....................... .27
    14 eggs............................ .25
    7 qts. milk........................ .70
    1 can condensed milk............... .10   1.32

Cereals:
    12 loaves bread.................... .60
    3½ doz. rolls...................... .35
    1 package crackers................. .10
    1 package breakfast-food........... .10
    Flour.............................. .05   1.20

                    Carried forward $3.63

	Brought forward		$3.63

Vegetables and fruits:

2 qts. potatoes	.16	
Turnips, onions, etc	.10	
½ lb. dried peas	.05	
1 can tomatoes	.08	
Fresh fruit	.05	.44

Sugar, tea, etc.:

½ lb. tea	.18	
3½ lbs. sugar	.17	
Molasses (1 pt. monthly)	.03	
1 bottle pickles	.10	.48

Alcoholic drinks:

2 pints beer	.20	.20

	Total		$4.75

2. The following is the food-budget for an American family living on East 80th street. The father drives an express-wagon; the family consists of the parents, 3 girls, aged 14, 10, and 2, and 1 boy 9 years old. The father's earnings amount to $816, supplemented by $144 from other members of the family. The dietary equivalents per week amount to what would be needed by 1 man for 26 days. The dietary analysis shows a total of 129 grams of protein and 3483 calories per man per day, and the average expenditure per man per day is 27 cents. The weekly expenditures are reported as follows:

Meats and fish: WEEKLY EXPENDITURE.

5 lbs. beef	$0.68	
½ lb. beef	.03	
2½ lbs. pork	.40	
2 lbs. ham	.19	
1 lb. mutton (4 lbs. once a month)	.18	
½ lb. chicken (goose at Christmas $2.00; chicken once in 3 months, 85 cts.)	.10	
1½ lbs. fresh fish	.20	
½ can salmon	.07	$1.85

	Carried forward		$1.85

Brought forward		$1.85
Eggs, dairy products, etc.:		
1 lb. butter	.30	
½ lb. cheese	.15	
15 eggs	.25	
21 qts. milk	1.05	1.75
Cereals:		
21 loaves (stale) bread	.53	
1 dozen rolls	.10	
Cake twice a week	.20	
Rice (1 lb. a month)	.02	
Flour (3½ lbs. twice a month)	.06	
Oatmeal	.05	
Grapenuts, etc.	.13	1.09
Vegetables, fruits, etc.:		
6 qts. potatoes (8 to 12 cents)	.60	
Turnips or carrots	.03	
2 lbs. onions	.09	
Fresh vegetables	.70	
Dried beans and peas	.03	
1 can tomatoes	.10	
1 can corn monthly, per week	.03	
Jelly (6 glasses a year at 10 cents)	.01	
Fresh fruit	.25	
Dried prunes (1 lb. a month)	.03	1.87
Sugar, tea, coffee, etc.:		
1½ lbs. coffee	.30	
1¾ lbs. sugar	.09	
Syrup, 10-cent can twice a year	.01	
Pickles and spices	.05	
Alcoholic drinks:		
Beer, 10 cents in 2 months	.01	.46
Total		$7.02

3. The following is the food report for a Russian family in Brooklyn (Brownsville). The father is a carpenter (non-union) with wages of $15 a week, but, on account of unemployment, earning only $600 a year, which is the entire income of the family. Besides the parents there are 4 boys, aged 6, 4, and 2 years and 6 months, respectively, making a food equivalent of 3.3 units, the

weekly requirement being that of 1 man for 22 days. The food-values amount to 115 grams of protein and 2710 calories per man per day. The expenditure amounts to 21 cents per man per day.

		WEEKLY EXPENDITURE.
Meats and fish:		
7 lbs. beef................	$0.84	
1 lb. mutton.............	.16	
2 lbs. fish...............	.20	
2 cans salmon...........	.28	$1.48
Eggs, dairy products, etc.:		
2 lbs. butter............	.64	
2 packages cheese........	.08	
1 dozen eggs.............	.24	
6 qts. milk (at Straus depot)........	.20	
3 cans condensed milk........	.30	1.46
Cereals:		
7 loaves of bread........	.56	
24 rolls.................	.20	
3½ lbs. flour............	.10	
¼ lb. cereal.............	.02	.88
Vegetables and fruits:		
6 lbs. potatoes..........	.09	
2 lbs. onions............	.06	
Fresh vegetables.........	.10	
1 lb. dried beans........	.08	
1 lb. dried peas.........	.04	
Fresh fruit..............	.15	
½ lb. dried prunes.......	.06	.58
Sugar, tea, etc.:		
⅛ lb. tea...............	.05	
¼ lb. coffee............	.05	
3½ lb. sugar............	.20	
¼ lb. spice.............	.02	.32
Alcoholic drinks:		
(Wine on holidays, $1.50 a year)....	.03	.03
Total		$4.75

4. The report which follows is for an Austrian family on East 82nd street. The father is a shipping-clerk, earning $760 a year, to which is added $104 from a lodger. There is a boy of 12 and a girl of 3. The weekly food requirements of the family are equivalent to those of an adult man for 20 days. The dietary computations show a total of 150 grams of protein per man per day and 3685 calories, at a cost of 35 cents per man per day.

		WEEKLY EXPENDITURE.
Meats and fish:		
4 lbs. beef	$0.72	
½ lb. corned beef (cooked)	.15	
2 lbs. mutton	.36	
4 lbs. chicken	.75	
2 lbs. fish	.25	
1 can salmon	.10	$2.33
Eggs, dairy products, etc.:		
1 lb. butter	.10	
1 lb. cheese	.32	
16 eggs weekly (in summer)	.25	
21 qts. milk (4 cents)	.84	1.51
Cereals:		
7 loaves bread	.35	
49 rolls (7 for 5 cents daily)	.35	
2 boxes crackers	.10	
3½ lbs. flour	.10	
1 box breakfast-food	.14	1.04
Vegetables, fruits, etc.:		
4 qts. potatoes	.20	
1½ lbs. onions	.06	
Carrots	.05	
Fresh vegetables	.24	
½ qt. dried beans	.06	
½ qt. dried peas	.06	
Cucumbers (10 cents weekly in summer)	.05	
Jelly (12 cents weekly in winter)	.06	
Oranges and bananas	.25	
½ lb. nuts in winter	.08	1.11
	Carried forward	$5.99

	Brought forward		$5.99

Sugar, tea, etc.:

⅛ lb. tea	.05	
½ lb. coffee	.10	
1 box cocoa	.10	
3½ lbs. sugar	.18	
Spices	.04	.47

Alcoholic drinks:

1 pint bottle whiskey	.50	
Wine	.08	.58

	Total		$7.04

5. An Italian family living on West Houston Street makes the report of food-expenditures that follows. The father is a long-shoreman, earning $14 a week, or allowing for unemployment, $672 a year. The family consists of the parents, the woman's father, a girl of 13, a boy of 9 and a boy of 14 months. The nutriment required amounts to 4.2 in terms of an adult man, and the weekly requirement is the equivalent of food for 1 man for 29 days. The dietary analysis shows 106 grams of protein and 3888 calories per man per day, at a cost of 24 cents per man per day, or of 20 cents for everything except beer.

WEEKLY EXPENDITURE.

Meats and fish:

11 lbs. beef	$0.90	
3 lbs. fish	$0.30	$1.20

Eggs, dairy products, etc.:

7 lbs. lard	.50	
½ lb. cheese	.15	
8 eggs	.20	
7 qts. milk	.35	1.20

Cereals:

21 loaves bread	1.05	
4 lbs. flour	.14	
14 lbs. macaroni (American)	.98	2.17

	Carried forward		$4.57

	Brought forward	$4.57
Vegetables, fruit, etc.:		
3 qts. potatoes......................	.15	
Onions.............................	.05	
Fresh vegetables.....................	.10	
2 lbs. dried beans	.15	
Fresh fruits.........................	.10	.55
Sugar, tea, etc.:		
1 lb. coffee.........................	.35	
3 lbs. sugar.........................	.18	
1 qt. olive oil.......................	.20	.73
Alcoholic liquors:		
14 pints beer........................	1.40	1.40
Total		$7.25

6. Another Italian family, that of a printer, living on Oliver
Street, is comprised of father, mother, a boy of 9 years and
a girl of 7. The man earns $884 a year, which is the sole
income of the family. The nutriment required for the family is
2.8 times the requirements of an adult man, and the weekly requirement is equivalent to that for one man for 20 days, The
food-analysis shows 176 grams of protein, and 4390 calories per
man per day at a cost of 33 cents per man per day. The weekly
expenditures for food are reported as follows:

Meats and fish:	WEEKLY EXPENDITURE.	
8 lbs. beef	$1.28	
¼ lb. bologna sausage................	.10	
9 lbs. fish............................	.54	
5 lbs. salt fish	.35	$2.27
Eggs, dairy products, etc.:		
2 lbs. lard..........................	.25	
½ lb. Roman cheese..................	.11	
1 doz. eggs..........................	.25	
7 qts. milk..........................	.56	1.17
	Carried forward	$3.44

	Brought forward		$3.44
Cereals:			
14 loaves bread	.70		
9 lbs. flour	.27		
5 lbs. macaroni (imported)	.35	1.32	
Vegetables and fruits:			
5 qts. potatoes	.25		
Turnips	.05		
Onions	.15		
Carrots	.10		
Fresh vegetables	.40		
4 lbs. dried beans	.40		
2 lbs. dried peas	.15		
Fresh fruit	.20		
Dried fruits	.15	1.85	
Sugar, tea, etc.:			
½ lb. coffee	.12		
2 lbs. sugar	.12		
1 qt. olive oil	.50	.74	
Alcoholic drinks:			
7 pints beer	.70	.70	
Total		$8.05	

A comparison of these selected budgets shows some features that are typical of the classes that they represent. The Italian schedules show a dependence on vegetable food for a larger part of the protein provided than do those of the other nationalities. Olive oil and lard take the place of butter; macaroni and dried beans and dried peas furnish their share of protein. The poorer families throughout buy cheaper kinds of food,—more bread and less meat, for instance, and cheaper qualities of the same kind of food. Of the $600 families, none provides the standard amount of both protein and fuel-food, and the expenditure in each case is under the 22-cent minimum suggested by Dr. Underhill. In the 3 schedules for higher incomes, the standard amount of protein and fuel-value is provided, but the cost ranges from 27 to 35 cents per man per day. The Italian family gets more of both protein and fuel-values for 33 cents, than the Austrian family for 35 cents.

5. CLOTHING.

1. AMOUNT AND PERCENTAGE OF EXPENDITURE FOR CLOTHING.—
The expenditure for clothing increases steadily with increase
of income, as shown in the table of averages (Table 79, page 172),
and the percentage of expenditures devoted to this purpose also
increases, as may be seen in the following summary, taken from
Table 79:

INCOME.	NUMBER OF FAMILIES.	AVERAGE EXPENDITURE FOR CLOTHING.	PER CENT. OF TOTAL EXPENDITURE.
$600 to $699	72	$83.48	12.9
700 to 799	79	98.79	13.4
800 to 899	73	113.59	14.0
900 to 999	63	132.34	14.6
1000 to 1099	31	155.59	15.5

Of the nationalities represented, the Italians report the smallest expenditure for clothing, the Austrians and Russians next. The
highest averages and percentages are found among the Bohemians,
and the American, Teutonic and Irish families are above the
average in almost every income-group. Considered by occupations
(Table 16, page 73) the laborers report clothing-expenditures somewhat below the average for all families of the corresponding
income-groups, the teamsters are close to the general average,
and the garment-workers are distinctly below the average. The
following table shows the figures for all the income-groups where
more than 3 families are represented:

INCOME.	ALL FAMILIES.		LABORERS.		TEAMSTERS.		GARMENT-WORKERS.	
	Ave.	Per Cent.	Ave.	Per Cent.	Ave.	Per Cent.	Ave.	Per Cent.
$600–$699	$83.48	12.9	$76.67	12.1	$79.42	12.3	$80.85	12.7
$700–$799	98.79	13.4	105.57	14.1	97.09	13.4	82.90	11.6
$800–$899	113.59	14.0	96.94	13.0	126.76	14.7	92.73	11.7
$900–$999	132.34	14.6	..	..	..	..	95.59	11.1
$1000–$1099	155.59	15.5	..	..	..	..	144.53	13.3

A certain offset in the case of the garment-workers is to be
found in their greater opportunities for making their own clothes.

In the slack season of the garment-trades the men are often found, when materials are procurable, making clothing for the members of the family.

Inquiry was made as to gifts of clothing received by the families interviewed. While the answers bring out no very exact data as to the value of the gifts received, they do show that a large proportion of the families on the lower incomes depend upon gifts to keep up such standard in regard to dress as they maintain. The figures may be found in Table 80 (page 173), from which it appears that 87 of the 318 families with incomes between $600 and $1100, or 27 per cent., report gifts of clothing. Separating the American, Teutonic, Irish and colored families from the others, we find that in 71 of the 158 cases of these nationalities, or 45 per cent., gifts of clothing are reported, as against only 16, or 10 per cent., among the 160 families of Bohemians, Russians, Austrians and Italians. The tabulation by income-groups shows that until the $900 level is reached, more than one-quarter of all families, or more than 40 per cent. of those included in the four nationalities first named above, report gifts of clothing. Inasmuch as these four nationalities also report a higher average expenditure than the South-European families, it seems a safe inference that a higher standard prevails, in the matter of dress, among the American and North-European families of our group than among the Russians, Austro-Hungarians and Italians.

The apportionment of expenditure for clothing among the different members of the family is a subject of some interest. In Table 81 (page 174) may be found the average amount, by income-groups, and the percentage of the total outlay for clothing that is expended for each member of the family. In the case of the children, the average is obtained by adding the amount for each boy or each girl reported, and dividing by the number of families reporting expenditure for boys or for girls. The amount for each child as included in the addition above described, is the amount reported for each boy or girl where one is reported in the family; when more than 1 boy or more than 1 girl is reported, the amount entered is the average amount expended per boy, or per girl, in the given family. Table 81 I-III shows the averages and percentages, first, for all the 318 families; second, for the 231 families which report no gifts; third, for the 87 families reporting gifts. The amount expended for each member of the family increases with each rise in the income-scale in almost every instance. In the case of the families receiving gifts, however, the movement is quite erratic, perhaps because the amount of gifts received bears no necessary relation to income. The father's clothing takes about one-third of the clothing-allowance, the mother's about one-fifth; each child from one-eighth to one-sixth. It appears in the table that the father's clothing costs more than that of any other member of the family, and also that the percentage, but not the actual amount, diminishes as income increases. In the case of families without gifts,—perhaps the most significant for this comparison,—the father spends, on the average, 35.6 per cent. of all that is spent for clothing, in the case of families with incomes of between $600 and $700, as against 29.3 per cent. in the case of families with incomes of from $1000 to $1100. The mother's percentage remains nearly constant, but is lowest in the $1000 income-group, where it is 20.3 per cent. The mother, that is, spends much less on her clothing than the father. Even in the families with incomes of over $1100, hardly a case was reported in which the woman spent as much for clothing as the man. The boys and girls stand nearly on an even footing as regards expenditure for clothing. The average for each boy is, however, a trifle above that for each girl, in each income-group. The children's clothing consumes a larger proportion of all that is spent for clothing in the case of higher incomes than in the lower. In the $600 group, 12.5 per cent. of the total goes for each boy, 12.2 per cent. for each girl; in the $1000 income-group the percentages are 15.7 and 16.1 respectively. This increase may be in part referred to the fact that a larger proportion of the children among the families with higher incomes are wage-earners (see page 57), and that these children are likely to need relatively large expenditure for clothing, by reason both of age and of occupation.*

* The money-value of the assistance received in the way of gifts may be inferred from a comparison of the averages for the families "without gifts" and "with gifts." This is an uncertain reliance, however, since several families "with gifts" report a larger clothing-bill than other families of the same income and nationality "without gifts." It may be noted, however, for what it is worth, that the average

Table 82 (page 175) shows, for the incomes above $1100 and below $600, the data regarding expenditure for clothing. The tendency of clothing to claim a larger part of the income as income increases appears also in these scattering cases, as well as the tendency for the father's dress to claim a diminishing proportion of the whole expenditure for clothing. In the averages of the 6 families with $1500 incomes the mother's amount ($54.34) and percentage (21) approach more nearly to the father's ($66.47, or 25.5 per cent.) than on the lower incomes. But the number of families is too few to warrant anything more than the suggestion that it is only in families with a relatively high standard of living that the woman is able to spend more on dress than her husband.

In Table 83 (page 176) is given the average expenditure for clothing for each member of the family, by nationalities, of the families without gifts of clothing in two representative income-groups ($700–799 and $900–999). These tables are given to permit a comparison of nationalities in regard to the point before us. The general tendencies already noticed appear in most cases. In every case save the Austrians the father's percentage is less on the higher income than on the lower. The Irish, Bohemian, Russian and Italian mothers spend a larger percentage of the total on the higher income than on the lower. The proportion expended for Italian children is exceptionally low, but this is accounted for in part by the low average age of the children reported in the Italian schedules.

2. ESTIMATE OF THE CLOTHING NECESSARY FOR A NORMAL FAMILY AND ITS COST.—On the basis of the averages of expenditures and the details given in typical schedules, the following estimate is made of the articles of clothing needed annually by a normal family, consisting of father, mother, and 3 children; for instance, a girl of 10, a boy of 6 and a boy of 4:

total expenditure for clothing is less by $6.39 in the $600 income-group for families with gifts than for those without, and in the $1000 income-group is less by $30.63. The figures are as follows:

INCOME.	FAMILIES WITHOUT GIFTS.	FAMILIES WITH GIFTS.	DIFFERENCE.
$600 to $699	$85.70	$79.31	$6.39
700 to 799	102.79	86.99	15.80
800 to 899	113.63	113.49	0.14
900 to 999	135.67	122.06	13.61
1000 to 1099	162.49	131.86	30.63

For the Man.

2 hats or caps..........	$2.00
1 overcoat*............	5.00
1 suit.................	10.00
1 pair pantaloons.......	2.00
2 pair overalls..........	1.50
3 working shirts........	1.00
2 white shirts..........	1.00
6 collars...............	.60
4 ties.................	.50
4 handkerchiefs........	.30
Summer underwear.....	1.00
Winter underwear......	1.50
6 pair hose..............	.60
2 pair shoes............	4.00
Repair of shoes.........	1.50
Gloves or mittens.......	.50
	$33.00

For the Woman.

1 hat.................	$1.50
1 cloak†..............	2.50
2 dresses of wash goods	2.50
1 woolen dress........	5.00
3 waists...............	1.50
1 petticoat............	.50
Linen, etc.............	.70
Summer underwear.....	.50
Winter underwear......	1.00
6 handkerchiefs........	.45
Gloves or mittens......	.50
3 aprons..............	.50
6 pair stockings........	.60
2 pair shoes............	3.00
Repair of shoes........	1.25
Sundries..............	1.00
	$23.00

For Each Boy.

2 hats.................	$0.50
1 overcoat............	2.50
1 suit.................	2.50
1 pair trousers........	.50
2 waists...............	.50
Summer underwear.....	.50
Winter underwear......	1.00
6 pair stockings.........	.50
2 pair shoes............	2.00
Repair of shoes........	1.25
Mittens................	.25
	$12.00

For the Girl.

2 hats.................	$1.25
1 cloak................	2.00
4 dresses of wash goods	2.00
1 woolen dress..........	1.50
4 waists...............	1.00
2 petticoats............	.50
Summer underwear.....	.50
Winter underwear......	1.00
Ribbons, etc...........	.50
6 handkerchiefs........	.25
Gloves or mittens......	.25
6 pair stockings........	.50
2 pair shoes............	2.50
Repair of shoes........	1.25
	$15.00

For Washing.

Soap, etc. (15 cts. a week)	$7.50
Laundry (5 cts. a week)	2.50
	$10.00

Summary.

For the man..........	$33.00
For the woman........	23.00
For 2 boys, each $12.00..	24.00
For 1 girl..............	15.00
For washing..........	10.00
	$105.00

* Costs $10 to $15, lasts 2 or 3 years.   † Costs $5, lasts 2 years.

Such an estimate presupposes, on the part of the mother, a high grade of efficiency in mending and remaking. It makes a meager allowance for outside garments, and one quite insufficent for men in certain occupations. It seems within bounds to assume that less than $100 will not suffice to provide decent clothing for a normal family of five.*

Assuming, then, that less than $100 marks a standard in

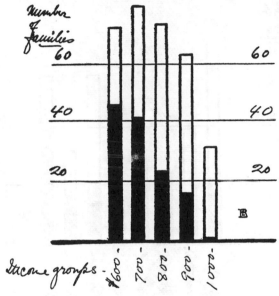

DIAGRAM 13.—Number of under-clad families in each of the principal income-groups. (See Table 84, page 177.)

clothing below the normal, the families reporting less than this amount have been counted and designated "under-clothed." An exception has been made in the case of garment-workers, and $80 has been assumed as the minimum expenditure indispensable for the families of those in this occupation (page 162). Tables 84–87 (pages 177–179) show the results of this analysis.

* The writer is not prepared to affirm the converse statement that $100 will suffice to provide decent clothing for the ordinary family of five.

Of the 318 families with incomes between $600 and $1100, 126, or 40 per cent., report less than $100 spent for clothing.* By incomes, 57 per cent. of the families with incomes of between $600 and $800 are under-clad, 32 per cent. of those with incomes of $800 to $900, and 18 per cent. of those with incomes between $900 and $1100. Of those with incomes below $600 we find that three-quarters are under-clothed, while only 1 in 12 of the families

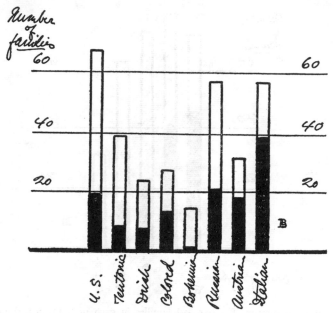

DIAGRAM 14.—Number of under-clad families in each of the nationality-groups.

with over $1100 to spend falls in this category. By nationalities, the under-clad families are most frequent in the group comprising Russians, Austrians, Italians, and Bohemians, where they comprise 79 out of 160 families, or 49 per cent. Of the other nationalities (American, Teutonic, Irish, colored), the under-clad number 47 out of 158 families, or 30 per cent. Thirteen, however, of the

* Of the garment-workers, only those reporting less than $80 are included in the 126 enumerated as under-clad. Twelve garment-workers' families reported between $80 and $100 for clothing.

28 colored families are under-clad. Considered with reference
to sources of income, we find (Table 85, page 177, and Table 125,
page 241), that with the exception of families having incomes
between $600 and $700, the under-clad are less frequent, relatively, among families supported by the father alone than among
all families. In tabular form this will readily be seen:*

	UNDER-CLAD FAMILIES.	
INCOME.	PER CENT. OF ALL FAMILIES.	PER CENT. OF UNDER-CLOTHED FAMILIES.
$600 to $699	63.9	76
700 to 799	50.6	46
800 to 899	30.1	22
900 to 999	54.0	31
1000 to 1099	25.8	..

Considered with reference to the reporting of surplus or deficit
at the end of the year, the under-clad families make the same sort of
showing as the under-fed and over-crowded. Table 86 (page 178)
shows that the under-clothed are the families that, as a rule, oftener
come within their income than all the families taken at large. Of
the whole 318 families, 36.5 per cent. report an even balance
(within $25.00) between income and expenditure, 36.5 per cent.
report a surplus, and 27 per cent. a deficit (Table 119, page 235).
Of the under-clothed families 32 per cent. report an even balance,
65 per cent. a surplus, and only 17 per cent. a deficit. The percentage reporting a deficit by income-groups, is as follows:

	FAMILIES REPORTING DEFICIT.	
INCOME.	PER CENT. OF ALL FAMILIES.	PER CENT. OF UNDER-CLOTHED FAMILIES.
$600 to $699	29	25
700 to 799	25	15
800 to 899	30	13
900 to 999	22	6
1000 to 1099	29	..

An examination of Table 86 shows that the Americans, the
Teutons, and the colored have a larger proportion of families

* In the above enumeration, families receiving gifts and reporting a clothing
expenditure under $100 are counted as under-clothed, because so far as their
own resources are concerned they are not able to maintain the standard.

reporting deficit among their under-clothed than have the families representing the other nationalities. Only 2 of the 21 under-clothed Russian families report a deficit, and these are both in the $600 income-group.

3. WASHING.—Following the example of Le Play, expenditures for washing are included under the head of clothing, as pertaining to the up-keep of that part of the family equipment. In almost all of the families under consideration, the washing is done at home, involving an outlay of money only for soap and minor washing-materials. This is usually reported at from 10 to 15 cents a week. In some cases,—most frequent in our schedules among the Bohemian families, where the mother goes out to work, —some one outside the family is paid to do the washing. The same arrangement is reported for one or two families with an invalid mother. Table 88 (page 179) shows the average expenditure for washing, by income, and the number and per cent. of families spending (1) under $10, (2) from $10 to $20, and (3) over $20 for washing. The average expenditure increases with each increase of income, from $8.36 for the $600 families to $13.53 for the $1000 group. By the $10 grouping, we see that more than three-quarters of the $600 families and less than half of the $1000 families, report less than $10, while of the 14 families reporting more than $20, 3 only have incomes below $800, and 8 have incomes above $900.

The average by nationalities (Table 89, page 180) shows some variations that appear arbitrary. But the Americans spend more and the Italians less than the average, in every income-group. Some aberrations in the averages, as in individual cases, are due to the inclusion of the cost of washing-materials in cases where the woman takes in washing.

The sending of some articles to the laundry is reported by the majority of families. Table 90 (page 181) shows the details. Nearly half of the 151 families with incomes between $600 and $800 send some work to the laundry, although only 13 of them spend more than 10 cents a week. Two-thirds of the 94 families with incomes of $900 to $1100 report sending work to the laundry, and 16 of them pay more than 10 cents a week. The laundry finish is evidently a sign of a rising standard of living, for five-sixths of the 48 families with over $1100 a year send work to the laundry, and half of them pay more than 10 cents a week.

The nationalities differ widely in their dependence on the laundry. Only one-eighth of the 57 Italian families and only 5 of the 28 colored families pay for work done by this institution. Sixty-eight per cent. of the American families resort to it, and 22 per cent. of them pay over 10 cents a week. Eighty-seven per cent. of the Russians depend upon it, 15 per cent. paying over 10 cents a week. The work sent to the laundry is usually the collars and cuffs worn by the men and boys.

TABLE 79.—CLOTHING. AVERAGE ANNUAL EXPENDITURE AND PER CENT. OF TOTAL EXPENDITURE.—BY NATIONALITY AND INCOME.

NATIONALITY.	$600 TO $699			$700 TO $799			$800 TO $899			$900 TO $999			$1000 TO $1099		
	Number of Families.	Average Amount.	Per Cent.*	Number of Families.	Average Amount.	Per Cent.*	Number of Families.	Average Amount.	Per Cent.*	Number of Families.	Average Amount.	Per Cent.*	Number of Families.	Average Amount.	Per Cent.*
United States	11	$86.87	13.0	19	$112.95	14.8	13	$127.06	14.6	16	$143.26	15.0	8	$165.18	15.4
Teutonic	4	94.08	14.0	7	85.65	11.3	9	143.14	16.4	11	135.85	14.8	8	183.36	17.7
Irish	4	90.87	13.7	7	119.08	15.6	7	124.26	15.3	5	149.17	16.4	1	67.63	7.5
Colored	11	85.46	13.1	6	114.07	14.6	8	115.34	14.6	2	146.54	17.4	1	107.74	12.2
Bohemian	4	110.92	16.0	3	111.67	15.2	3	138.75	16.5	4	181.79	18.5	..	..	..
Russian	16	85.77	13.6	14	84.28	12.1	12	94.16	12.2	9	113.16	12.6	6	139.46	13.3
Austrian, etc.	6	62.48	10.4	9	86.43	12.2	9	108.68	13.2	7	130.87	14.4	1	177.30	18.1
Italian	16	74.02	11.2	14	89.14	12.7	12	86.28	11.5	9	94.43	11.6	6	140.84	15.7
Total	72	83.48	12.9	79	98.79	13.4	73	113.59	14.0	63	132.34	14.6	31	155.57	15.5

* Per cent. of expenditures for all purposes.

TABLE 80.—CLOTHING. NUMBER OF FAMILIES REPORTING GIFTS.
—BY NATIONALITY AND INCOME.

NATIONALITY.	$600 TO $699 Number of Families.		$700 TO $799 Number of Families.		$800 TO $899 Number of Families.		$900 TO $999 Number of Families.		$1000 TO $1099 Number of Families.		TOTAL. Number of Families.		
	Total.	Number Reporting Gifts.	Total.	Number Reporting Gifts.	Total.	Number Reporting Gifts.	Total.	Number Reporting Gifts.	Total.	Number Reporting Gifts.	Total.	Number Reporting Gifts.	Per Cent. of Families.
United States..	11	7	19	9	13	5	16	8	8	3	67	32	48
Teutonic......	4	4	7	3	9	3	11	1	8	2	39	13	33
Irish..........	4	2	7	2	7	4	5	2	1	1	24	11	46
Colored.......	11	7	6	2	8	4	2	1	1	1	28	15	54
Bohemian.....	4	2	3	1	3	..	4	..	..	..	14	3	21
Russian.......	16	..	14	..	12	1	9	2	6	..	57	3	5
Austrian, etc...	6	1	9	2	9	1	7	1	1	..	32	5	16
Italian........	16	2	14	2	12	1	9	..	6	..	57	5	9
Total.......	72	25	79	21	73	19	63	15	31	7	318	87	27

INCOME.	TOTAL NUMBER OF FAMILIES.	NUMBER REPORTING GIFTS.	PER CENT. REPORTING GIFTS.
$400 to $599..........	25	7	28
$600 to $799..........	151	46	30
$800 to $899..........	73	19	26
$900 to $1099..........	94	22	23
$1100 and over..........	48	6	13

TABLE 81.—CLOTHING. AVERAGES AND PER CENT. OF EXPENDITURE FOR EACH MEMBER OF THE FAMILY WITH AND WITHOUT GIFTS.—BY INCOME.

I. AVERAGES FOR ALL FAMILIES.

Income.	Total Expenditure for Clothing.			Expenditure for Father's Clothing.			Expenditure for Mother's Clothing.			Expenditure for Clothing of Each Boy.			Expenditure for Clothing of Each Girl.		
	Number of Families.	Average Expenditure.	Per Cent. of All Expenditure.	Number of Families.	Average Expenditure.	Per Cent. of Total Expenditure for Clothing.	Number of Families.	Average Expenditure.	Per Cent. of Total Expenditure for Clothing.	Number of Families.	Average Expenditure.	Per Cent. of Total Expenditure for Clothing.	Number of Families.	Average Expenditure.	Per Cent. of Total Expenditure for Clothing.
$600 to $699	72	$83.48	12.9	72	$28.10	33.6	72	$17.48	21.0	59	$10.68	12.8	63	$10.90	13.0
$700 to $799	79	98.79	13.4	79	34.19	34.6	79	20.23	20.5	65	12.98	13.2	68	12.23	12.4
$800 to $899	73	113.59	14.0	73	34.10	30.0	73	22.76	20.0	66	16.13	14.2	62	15.96	14.1
$900 to $999	63	132.34	14.6	62	40.36	30.5	62	27.71	21.3	56	19.29	14.6	57	16.86	12.8
$1000 to $1099	31	155.57	15.5	30	44.02	28.3	30	32.25	20.8	27	24.32	15.7	23	24.79	16.0

II. AVERAGES FOR FAMILIES WITHOUT GIFTS OF CLOTHING.

Income.	Total Expenditure for Clothing.			Expenditure for Father's Clothing.			Expenditure for Mother's Clothing.			Expenditure for Clothing of Each Boy.			Expenditure for Clothing of Each Girl.		
	Number of Families.	Average Expenditure.	Per Cent. of All Expenditure.	Number of Families.	Average Expenditure.	Per Cent. of Total Expenditure for Clothing.	Number of Families.	Average Expenditure.	Per Cent. of Total Expenditure for Clothing.	Number of Families.	Average Expenditure.	Per Cent. of Total Expenditure for Clothing.	Number of Families.	Average Expenditure.	Per Cent. of Total Expenditure for Clothing.
$600 to $699	47	$85.70	13.2	47	$30.53	35.6	47	$18.62	21.7	35	$10.75	12.5	41	$10.48	12.2
$700 to $799	58	102.79	14.0	57	36.28	35.0	57	22.49	21.9	48	13.68	13.3	51	12.17	11.9
$800 to $899	54	113.63	14.0	54	34.09	30.0	54	23.51	20.7	49	16.36	14.4	43	16.20	14.3
$900 to $999	48	135.67	15.4	47	41.92	30.8	47	28.89	21.3	43	20.63	15.2	43	17.21	12.7
$1000 to $1099	24	162.49	16.2	24	47.57	29.3	24	32.90	20.3	22	25.44	15.7	18	26.12	16.1

III. AVERAGES FOR FAMILIES RECEIVING GIFTS OF CLOTHING.

Income.	Total Expenditure for Clothing.			Expenditure for Father's Clothing.			Expenditure for Mother's Clothing.			Expenditure for Clothing of Each Boy.			Expenditure for Clothing of Each Girl.		
	Number of Families.	Average Expenditure.	Per Cent. of All Expenditure.	Number of Families.	Average Expenditure.	Per Cent. of Total Expenditure for Clothing.	Number of Families.	Average Expenditure.	Per Cent. of Total Expenditure for Clothing.	Number of Families.	Average Expenditure.	Per Cent. of Total Expenditure for Clothing.	Number of Families.	Average Expenditure.	Per Cent. of Total Expenditure for Clothing.
$600 to $699	25	$79.31	12.2	9	$16.97	21.4	8	$8.73	11.0	10	$8.48	10.7	10	$8.01	10.1
$700 to $799	21	86.99	11.8	10	24.67	28.4	11	11.98	13.8	7	6.66	7.7	9	9.35	10.7
$800 to $899	19	113.49	14.0	5	28.62	25.2	7	21.46	18.9	9	10.71	9.4	9	16.14	14.2
$900 to $999	15	122.06	13.4	8	27.42	22.4	7	15.21	12.5	5	9.98	8.2	7	12.74	10.5
$1000 to $1099	7	131.86	13.1	2	22.88	17.4	3	13.88	10.5	2	28.39	21.5	3	18.97	14.4

TABLE 82.—CLOTHING. AVERAGES AND PER CENT. OF EXPENDITURE FOR EACH MEMBER OF THE FAMILY: INCOMES UNDER $600 AND OVER $1100.—BY INCOME.

Income.	Total Expenditure for Clothing.			Expenditure for Father's Clothing.			Expenditure for Mother's Clothing.			Expenditure for Each Boy's Clothing.			Expenditure for Each Girl's Clothing.		
	Number of Families.	Average Expenditures.	Per Cent. of all Expenditures.	Number of Families.	Average Expenditure.	Per Cent. of Total Expenditure for Clothing.	Number of Families.	Average Expenditure.	Per Cent. of Total Expenditure for Clothing.	Number of Families.	Average Expenditure.	Per Cent. of Total Expenditure for Clothing.	Number of Families.	Average Expenditure.	Per Cent. of Total Expenditure for Clothing.
$400 to $499	8	$60.65	13.0	8	$16.30	27.0	8	$9.89	16.0	7	$11.11	18.0	7	$9.06	15.0
$500 to $599	17	67.95	12.4	17	25.26	37.0	17	14.81	22.0	12	9.54	14.0	14	7.88	12.0
$1100 to $1199	18	$163.80	14.9	18	$58.06	35.4	18	$38.49	23.5	16	$19.79	12.0	15	$18.13	11.0
$1200 to $1299	8	189.57	15.2	8	56.04	29.5	8	41.46	22.0	8	26.45	14.0	7	20.15	10.6
$1300 to $1399	8	180.48	13.7	8	52.35	29.0	8	41.81	23.0	7	25.42	14.0	7	28.05	15.5
$1500 to $1599	6	260.97	16.8	6	66.47	25.5	6	54.34	21.0	5	31.64	12.0	5	54.09	20.7

175

TABLE 83.—CLOTHING. AVERAGES AND PER CENT. OF EXPENDITURE FOR EACH MEMBER OF THE FAMILY, FOR FAMILIES WITHOUT GIFTS.—BY NATIONALITY.

INCOME $700 TO $799

NATIONALITY.	Total Expenditure for Clothing.		Father.			Mother.			Each Boy.			Each Girl.		
	Number of Families.	Average Amount.	Number of Families.	Average Amount.	Per Cent. of Total for Clothing.	Number of Families.	Average Amount.	Per Cent. of Total for Clothing.	Number of Families.	Average Amount.	Per Cent. of Total for Clothing.	Number of Families.	Average Amount.	Per Cent. of Total for Clothing.
United States	11	$131.40	10	$44.43	34	10	$29.10	22	10	$15.50	12	10	$15.25	12
Teutonic	4	95.81	3	42.44	44	3	26.18	28	3	10.93	11	2	13.46	14
Irish	5	125.05	5	43.81	35	5	24.99	20	3	20.26	16	4	16.40	13
Colored	4	113.35	4	32.99	35	4	28.62	25	3	16.21	14	4	11.59	10
Bohemian	2	125.48	2	30.93	24	2	18.18	14	2	16.82	13	2	16.27	13
Russian	14	84.28	14	27.97	33	14	18.01	21	13	11.20	13	13	11.25	13
Austrian, etc.	7	90.21	7	30.47	33	7	21.60	24	4	12.92	14	5	12.89	14
Italian	12	91.22	12	39.89	43	12	19.43	21	10	12.83	14	11	7.81	9
Total	59	102.79	57	36.98	36	57	22.49	22	48	13.68	13	51	12.17	12

INCOME $900 TO $999

NATIONALITY.	Total Expenditure for Clothing.		Father.			Mother.			Each Boy.			Each Girl.		
	Number of Families.	Average Amount.	Number of Families.	Average Amount.	Per Cent. of Total for Clothing.	Number of Families.	Average Amount.	Per Cent. of Total for Clothing.	Number of Families.	Average Amount.	Per Cent. of Total for Clothing.	Number of Families.	Average Amount.	Per Cent. of Total for Clothing.
United States	8	$158.12	8	$47.61	30	8	$28.35	18	8	$25.71	16	6	$18.24	11
Teutonic	10	136.20	9	44.15	32	9	33.63	24	9	23.07	17	8	22.21	16
Irish	3	161.80	3	47.50	30	3	39.33	24	3	21.82	13	3	19.77	12
Colored	1	147.75	1	35.75	24	1	21.20	14	1	17.17	12	1	17.43	12
Bohemian	4	181.80	4	35.80	20	4	27.94	16	3	26.47	15	4	28.54	16
Russian	7	121.36	7	35.81	29	7	28.69	23	7	22.03	18	7	13.23	11
Austrian, etc.	6	137.61	6	46.98	34	6	29.51	22	4	18.98	14	6	17.11	12
Italian	9	94.43	9	37.71	40	9	22.13	23	8	10.16	11	8	8.35	9
Total	48	135.67	47	41.92	31	47	28.89	21	43	20.63	15	43	17.21	13

TABLE 84.—UNDER-CLOTHED FAMILIES.—BY NATIONALITY AND INCOME.

NATIONALITY.	TOTAL NUMBER OF FAMILIES.	UNDER-CLOTHED. NUMBER OF FAMILIES.					
		$600 TO $699	$700 TO $799	$800 TO $899	$900 TO $999	$1000 TO $1099	Total.
United States	67	6	7	2	4	..	19
Teutonic	39	2	4	1	1	..	8
Irish	24	3	2	1	..	1	7
Colored	28	9	3	1	..	..	13
Bohemian	14	..	1	..	..	..	1
Russian	57	6	7	4	4	..	21
Austrian, etc.	32	5	6	4	3	..	18
Italian	57	14	11	10	4	..	39
Total	318	45	41	23	16	1	126

TABLE 85.—UNDER-CLOTHED FAMILIES. SOURCES OF INCOME.— BY INCOME AND NATIONALITY.

NATIONALITY.	$600 TO $699				$700 TO $799				$800 TO $899			
	Total Number of Families.	Number Under-clothed.	Income from: Father Only.	Income from: Other Sources.	Total Number of Families.	Number Under-clothed.	Income from: Father Only.	Income from: Other Sources.	Total Number of Families.	Number Under-clothed.	Income from: Father Only.	Income from: Other Sources.
United States	11	6	6	..	19	7	1	6	13	2	..	2
Teutonic	4	2	1	1	7	4	..	4	9	1	1	..
Irish	4	3	3	..	7	2	1	1	7	1	..	1
Colored	11	9	7	2	6	3	2	1	8	1	..	1
Bohemian	4	..	..	..	3	1	..	1	3	..	..	..
Russian	16	6	5	1	14	7	6	1	12	4	1	3
Austrian, etc.	6	5	5	..	9	6	2	4	9	4	..	4
Italian	16	14	7	7	14	11	7	4	12	10	3	7
Total	72	45	34	11	79	41	19	22	73	23	5	18

NATIONALITY.	$900 TO $999				$1000 TO $1099				TOTAL.					
	Total Number of Families.	Number Under-clothed.	Income from: Father Only.	Income from: Other Sources.	Total Number of Families.	Number Under-clothed.	Income from: Father Only.	Income from: Other Sources.	Number of Families.	Number Under-clothed.	Income from: Father Only. No.	Income from: Father Only. Per ct.	Income from: Other Sources. No.	Income from: Other Sources. Per ct.
United States	16	4	1	3	8	..	..	..	67	19	8	42	11	58
Teutonic	11	1	..	1	8	..	..	..	39	8	2	25	6	75
Irish	5	..	..	..	1	1	..	1	24	7	4	57	3	43
Colored	2	..	..	..	1	..	..	..	28	13	9	70	4	31
Bohemian	4	..	..	..	..	..	..	..	14	1	..	..	1	100
Russian	9	4	..	4	6	..	..	..	57	21	12	57	9	43
Austrian, etc.	7	3	1	2	1	..	..	..	32	18	8	44	10	55
Italian	9	4	3	1	6	..	..	..	57	39	20	51	19	49
Total	63	16	5	11	31	1	..	1	318	126	63	50	63	50

TABLE 86.—UNDER-CLOTHED FAMILIES. NUMBER REPORTING SURPLUS AND DEFICIT.—BY NATIONALITY AND INCOME.

NATIONALITY.	$600 TO $699				$700 TO $799				$800 TO $899			
	Number of Under-clothed Families.	Number Reporting:			Number Under-clothed Families.	Number Reporting:			Total Number of Under-clothed Families.	Number Reporting:		
		Balance within $25.00	Surplus.	Deficit.		Balance within $25.00	Surplus.	Deficit.		Balance within $25.00	Surplus.	Deficit.
United States....	6	3	2	1	7	4	1	2	2	..	1	1
Teutonic........	2	2	..	..	4	1	2	1	1	..	..	1
Irish............	3	2	..	1	2	1	1	..	1	..	1	..
Colored..........	9	5	2	2	3	1	1	1	1	..	1	..
Bohemian.......	..	..	..	..	1	1	..	..	..	..	..	..
Russian.........	6	1	3	2	7	1	6	..	4	..	4	..
Austrian, etc....	5	1	4	..	6	2	4	..	4	2	2	..
Italian..........	14	4	5	5	11	4	5	2	10	..	9	1
Total...........	45	18	16	11	41	15	20	6	23	2	18	3

NATIONALITY.	$900 TO $999				$1000 TO $1099				TOTAL.						
	Number of Under-clothed Families.	Number Reporting:			Number of Under-clothed Families.	Number Reporting:			Total Number of Under-clothed Families.	Families Reporting:					
		Balance within $25.00	Surplus.	Deficit.		Balance within $25.00	Surplus.	Deficit.		Balance within $25.00		Surplus.		Deficit.	
										Number.	Per Cent.	Number.	Per Cent.	Number.	Per Cent.
United States.	4	1	2	1	..	..	..	..	19	8	42	6	32	5	26
Teutonic......	1	1	..	..	..	..	..	..	8	4	50	2	25	2	25
Irish..........	..	..	..	..	1	..	1	..	7	3	43	3	43	1	14
Colored......	..	..	..	..	..	..	..	..	13	6	47	4	31	3	23
Bohemian....	..	..	..	..	..	..	..	..	1	1	100	..	..	..	..
Russian......	4	1	3	..	..	..	..	..	21	3	14	16	76	2	10
Austrian, etc.	3	1	2	..	..	..	..	..	18	6	33	12	66	..	..
Italian........	4	1	3	..	..	..	..	..	39	9	23	22	56	8	21
Total........	16	5	10	1	1		1	..	126	40	32	65	52	21	17

178

TABLE 87.—UNDER-CLOTHED FAMILIES. NUMBER AND PER CENT. REPORTING SURPLUS AND DEFICIT.—BY INCOME.

INCOME.	NUMBER OF FAMILIES.	NUMBER OF UNDER-CLOTHED.	REPORTING.					
			Balance within $25.00.		Surplus.		Deficit.	
			Number.	Per Cent.	Number.	Per Cent.	Number.	Per Cent.
$600 to $699.......	72	45	18	40	16	35	11	25
$700 to $799.......	79	41	15	37	20	48	6	15
$800 to $899.......	73	23	2	9	18	78	3	13
$900 to $999.......	63	16	5	31	10	63	1	6
$1000 to $1099.......	31	1	..	..	1	100	..	..
$600 to $799.......	151	86	33	38	36	42	17	20
$800 to $899.......	73	23	2	9	18	78	3	13
$900 to $1099.......	94	17	5	30	11	64	1	6
Total..............	318	126	40	32	65	52	21	17

TABLE 88.—WASHING. NUMBER AND PER CENT. OF FAMILIES REPORTING GIVEN AMOUNTS.—BY NATIONALITY AND INCOME.

INCOME.	NUMBER OF FAMILIES.	AVERAGE AMOUNT EXPENDED.	FAMILIES WITH EXPENDITURE OF:						LAUNDRY.					
			Under $10.		$10 to $20.		Over $20.		Families Reporting Expenditure		Families with Expenditure Weekly of:			
											10c. or less.		Over 10c.	
			Number.	Per Cent.	Number.	Per Cent.	Number.	Per Cent.	Number.	Per Cent.	Number.	Per Cent.	Number.	Per Cent.
$600 to $699..	72	$8.36	56	78	15	21	1	1	27	38	22	31	5	7
$700 to $799..	79	9.78	51	65	26	33	2	2	45	57	37	47	8	10
$800 to $899..	73	10.99	40	55	30	41	3	4	47	64	38	52	9	12
$900 to $999..	63	11.01	34	54	22	35	5	8	43	70	32	51	10	2
$1000 to $1099..	31	13.53	12	49	15	40	3	11	20	65	14	50	6	19
$400 to $599..	25	7.38	22	88	3	12	..	..	11	44	11	44	..	..
$600 to $799..	151	9.10	107	71	41	27	3	2	72	47	59	39	13	9
$800 to $899..	73	10.99	40	55	30	41	3	4	47	64	38	52	9	12
$900 to $1099..	94	11.84	46	49	37	39	8	8	63	67	46	49	16	17
$1100 and over..	48	20.24	12	25	22	46	13	28	40	83	16	33	24	50

TABLE 89.—WASHING. AVERAGE ANNUAL EXPENDITURE.—BY INCOME AND NATIONALITY.

NATIONALITY.	$600 TO $699.	$700 TO $799.	$800 TO $899.	$900 TO $999.	$1000 TO $1099.
United States........	$9.03	$10.82	$14.71	$12.17	$12.80
Teutonic............	6.62	13.18	11.95	7.11	17.03
Irish...............	4.49	7.28	8.62	6.52	17.68*
Colored............	9.50	9.25	12.67	11.70	13.00*
Bohemian..........	12.48	10.23	11.89	31.08	..
Russian............	9.26	8.99	10.47	9.00	10.88
Austrian, etc.	6.46	9.22	10.14	11.32	15.00*
Italian.............	7.32	9.21	7.58	8.05	11.54
Total............	8.36	9.78	10.99	11.01	13.53

* One case only

180

TABLE 90.—WASHING: LAUNDRY. NUMBER OF FAMILIES SPENDING GIVEN AMOUNTS.—BY NATIONALITY AND INCOME.

NATIONALITY.	$600 TO $699. Number of Families.				$700 TO $799. Number of Families.				$800 TO $899. Number of Families.			
	Total.	With Expenditure for Laundry.	With Weekly Expenditure of: 10c. or less.	Over 10c.	Total.	With Expenditure for Laundry.	With Weekly Expenditure of: 10c. or less.	Over 10c.	Total.	With Expenditure for Laundry.	With Weekly Expenditure of: 10c. or less.	Over 10c.
United States.......	11	4	2	2	19	11	9	2	13	11	8	3
Teutonic...........	4	3	3	..	7	3	1	2	9	8	6	2
Irish..............	4	..	..	..	7	3	3	..	7	5	4	1
Colored...........	11	2	1	1	6	1	1	..	8	1	..	1
Bohemian..........	4	2	2	..	3	3	3	..	3	3	3	..
Russian...........	16	11	10	1	14	14	12	2	12	10	8	2
Austrian, etc.......	6	3	3	..	9	7	6	1	9	9	9	..
Italian............	16	2	1	1	14	3	2	1	12	..	..	..
Total.............	72	27	22	5	79	45	37	8	73	47	38	9

NATIONALITY.	$900 TO $999. Number of Families.				$1000 TO $1099. Number of Families.				TOTAL.						
	Total.	With Expenditure for Laundry.	With Weekly Expenditure of: 10c. or less.	Over 10c.	Total.	With Expenditure for Laundry.	With Weekly Expenditure of: 10c. or less.	Over 10c.	Total Number of Families.	With Expenditure for Laundry. No.	Per Cent.	With Weekly Expenditure of 10c. or less. No.	Per Cent.	With Weekly Expenditure of over 10c. No.	Per Cent.
United States..	16	15	9	6	8	5	3	2	67	46	68.7	31	47	15	22
Teutonic......	11	5	5	..	8	6	6	..	39	25	64.1	21	54	4	10
Irish..........	5	3	2	1	1	1	1	..	24	12	50.0	10	42	2	8
Colored.......	2	1	1	..	1	..	..	..	28	5	17.8	3	11	2	7
Bohemian.....	4	4	2	2	..	..	..	..	14	12	85.7	10	71	2	14
Russian.......	9	9	8	..	6	6	3	3	57	50	87.7	41	72	8	15
Austrian, etc ..	7	5	4	1	1	1	..	1	32	25	78.1	22	69	3	9
Italian........	9	1	1	..	6	6	1	..	57	7	12.3	5	9	2	3
Total........	63	43	32	10	31	20	14	6	318	182	57.0	143	45	38	12

6. HEALTH.

Expenditures for the maintenance of health and the cure of disease are so intermittent in the history of any family that it is not possible to treat them like the regularly recurring expenditure for food and rent. The average of the expenditures of a large number of families on account of sickness must strike a point that marks the mean of what is spent neither by families where sickness prevails nor by families free from serious illness. Nevertheless the averages, including a considerable number of families of each kind, may serve as an indication of the degree to which expenditure for this purpose increases as income increases. As may be seen from Table 91 (page 186) the average expenditure for health ranges from $13.78 for the families with incomes between $600 and $700 to $23.30 for families with incomes between $900 and $1000. It falls to $14.80 in the $1000 group, and rises, on account of a few cases where the amount is very high, to $40.18 for the $1100 families (Table 15, page 70).

The percentage of total expenditure that is devoted to this purpose likewise fluctuates. It is 2.1 in the $600 group, 1.9 in the $700 group, 2.7 and 2.6 in the next two income-groups, but falls to 1.5 for the $1000 families. As between nationalities, it does not seem possible to make safe generalizations from the returns, by reason of the irregularities in the distribution of families with exceptional burdens of sickness to carry.

More light may perhaps be had by counting the number of families reporting certain significant details. (See Table 94, page 189.) Thirty-seven of the 318 families, or 11.6 per cent., report no expenditure on account of health. These cases are distributed pretty evenly among the income-groups, indicating that it was absence of sickness, rather than poverty that prevented the outlay. The only income-group where every family reports expenditure for this purpose is the $1100 group. The families not spending on this account are most numerous among the Americans, where 13 of the total 37 are found. No Bohemians, only 1 Italian family, and 2 Irish, are reported in the column of no expenditure.

Table 93 (page 188) shows more clearly how expenditure for

the cure of sickness increases as income increases. The table shows the number of families, by income and nationality, that report spending less than $10, from $10 to $20, and so on. It will be seen that the number of families reporting the smaller sums is greatest in the lower income-groups and vice versa. Of the 132 families with incomes between $600 and $800 that report expenditure for health 48.5 per cent. spend less than $10, as against 36.6 per cent. of the 82 families with incomes of from $900 to $1100 that report expenditure for health. On the other hand, expenditures of $75 and over are reported by 13.4 per cent. of the families in the upper income classes ($900 to $1099), and by but 3.8 per cent. of the families in the lower income-classes ($600 to $799).*

This disparity is not due to relative infrequency of serious illness among the poorer families. The third column of Table 94 (page 189) shows that such cases are to be found in just about the same frequency all along the line. The fourth column, "free medical aid," suggests that the dispensary and the free hospital take the place, to a certain extent, of medical aid paid for entirely by the family. The percentage of families reporting free medical assistance diminishes from 40 per cent. for the $600 families to 16 per cent. for the $1000 families.†

* The reports of the families with incomes below $600 and above $1100 show the following distribution of expenditures for health:

EXPENDITURE.	INCOME $400 TO $599. FAMILIES.	INCOME $1100 TO $1599. FAMILIES.
None	4	4
Under $10	10	14
$10 to $20	7	7
20 to 30	3	5
30 to 40	0	3
40 to 50	1	2
50 to 75		2
75 to 100		1
Over 100		3
	25	41

Of the three families spending more than $100 one reports paying $109, one $240, and one, with income of $1500, reports expenses of $600 for the mother in the hospital. Such expenditures are out of the question with the smaller incomes. One of these families with income of $1600 reports that the son, 20 years of age, a medical student, prescribes for the family.

† Little light is thrown by the schedules on the prevalence of the patent-medicine habit. One woman reported buying a 75-cent bottle of stomach medicine every

183

The reports regarding dentistry indicate a deplorable lack of attention to the teeth on the part of the large majority in all income-groups. Only 51 out of the 318 families, or 16 per cent., report paying for dentistry. The percentage of families that do pay the dentist increases, however, with increase of income. Only 1 in 9 of the $600 families reports this expenditure, as against 1 in 4 of the $1000 families. The details may be seen in the fifth column of Table 94 (page 189). The amount paid for dentistry varies from 50 cents for pulling a tooth, to $20 or more in exceptional cases.

An examination of the cases of serious illness shows how such an illness draws on the slender resources of the family.* An American family, for instance, in the $700 income-group, reports spending $41.60 for a child who did not live, and for the mother, who suffers from nervous prostration. In another case in the same income-group an expenditure of $41.00 is reported, with the statement that the mother had pleuropneumonia, following the birth of a child. These families spent 6 per cent. of their income, or three weeks' wages of the man, for relief in sickness. Items of $31.00, $24.50, $33.00, $53.00 must involve an even heavier burden on the families with from $600 to $700 that report them. In many cases where these expenditures on health-account are high, there is evi-

week, another reports buying a 25-cent bottle of Castoria every month. For the most part, however, the medicine is prescribed by a visiting physician or at the dispensary.

* The diseases reported include most of those prevalent in New York City. The enumeration of them would throw no special light on our present problem, for there seems to be no necessary connection between specific diseases and particular nationalities or income-groups, and the number of cases of any one disease must, with no more than 318 families, necessarily be small. Only 12 deaths are reported, but some were doubtless overlooked, since no point-blank question in the schedule relates to this point. Among the specifications most frequently reported are the following, the 318 families with incomes between $600 and $1100 being considered:

Pneumonia...13 cases
Accidents...13 "
Measles...11 "
Tuberculosis...................................... 7 "
Diphtheria.. 7 "
Typhoid fever..................................... 6 "
Nervous prostration............................... 6 "
Female disorders.................................. 6 "
Rheumatism.. 5 "

It is possible that tuberculosis was sometimes reported under another name.

dent curtailment of expenditure in other directions. An abnormally low expenditure for the man's clothing appears in one schedule, wherein it is stated also that the man was laid up in the hospital for several weeks. In other cases where doctor's bills are large, expenditures for amusement and recreation and for miscellaneous purposes disappear.

To judge from all these data, it seems that the liability to disease does not vary greatly in the different income-groups represented in our schedules, nor in different nationalities, but that the resources available for combatting disease are much more limited among families with only $700 or $800 to live on. These families are accordingly thrown upon dispensaries and other free medical assistance, or else their members are left to succumb to the attacks of disease without adequate medical aid. If the family undertakes to make better provision at its own charges, the result is a lowering of the standard of living at some other point. An income of less than $800 does not permit expenditures sufficient to care properly for the health of the family.

TABLE 91.—HEALTH. AVERAGE ANNUAL EXPENDITURE AND PER CENT. OF TOTAL EXPENDITURE.—BY NATIONALITY AND INCOME.

Nationality.	$600 to $699			$700 to $799			$800 to $899			$900 to $999			$1000 to $1099		
	Number of Families.	Average Amount.	Per Cent.*	Number of Families.	Average Amount.	Per Cent.*	Number of Families.	Average Amount.	Per Cent.*	Number of Families.	Average Amount.	Per Cent.*	Number of Families.	Average Amount.	Per Cent.*
United States	11	$11.09	1.6	19	$10.26	1.4	13	$8.53	1.0	16	$23.98	2.5	8	$13.55	1.3
Teutonic	4	15.33	2.3	7	7.51	1.0	9	30.30	3.5	11	22.02	2.4	8	7.72	0.7
Irish	4	17.05	2.6	7	20.16	2.6	7	19.41	2.4	5	9.53	1.0	1	21.00	2.3
Colored	11	7.95	1.2	6	5.02	0.6	8	15.91	2.0	2	13.25	1.6	1	1.00	0.1
Bohemian	4	9.50	1.4	3	12.53	1.7	3	18.40	2.2	4	37.41	3.8	..	..	..
Russian	16	14.38	2.3	14	26.52	3.8	12	27.18	3.5	9	27.21	3.0	6	32.92	3.1
Austrian, etc.	6	14.15	2.3	9	15.63	2.2	9	49.41	6.0	7	38.02	4.2	1	..	..
Italian	16	18.75	2.8	14	9.93	1.4	12	12.23	1.6	9	11.95	1.5	6	11.53	1.3
Total	72	13.78	2.1	79	14.02	1.9	73	22.19	2.7	63	23.30	2.6	31	14.80	1.5

* Per cent of expenditure for all purposes.

186

HEALTH

TABLE 92.—HEALTH. NUMBER OF FAMILIES REPORTING EXPEN-
DITURE OF GIVEN AMOUNTS.—BY INCOME AND
NATIONALITY.

(A) BY INCOME.

INCOME.	TOTAL NUMBER OF FAMILIES.	No Expenditure.	Under $10	$10 to $20	$20 to $30	$30 to $40	$40 to $50	$50 to $75	$75 to $100	Over $100
$600 to $699......	72	7	34	12	11	4	1	2	1	..
$700 to $799......	79*	11	30	20	8	4	3	..	1	1
$800 to $899......	73	7	28	20	5	4	1	4	1	3
$900 to $999......	63	7	16	16	10	4	2	3	4	1
$1000 to $1099......	31	5	14	5	3	..	1	3	..	..
Total...............	318*	37	122	73	37	16	8	12	7	5

(B) BY NATIONALITY.

NATIONALITY.	TOTAL NUMBER OF FAMILIES.	No Expenditure.	Under $10	$10 to $20	$20 to $30	$30 to $40	$40 to $50	$50 to $75	$75 to $100	Over $100
United States........	67*	13	27	13	4	3	3	1	1	1
Teutonic............	39	7	12	13	1	2	..	3	..	1
Irish...............	24	2	7	8	4	..	..	2	1	..
Colored.............	28	4	15	6	1	..	2	..	..	..
Bohemian...........	14	..	4	3	3	3	1	..	..	..
Russian.............	57	6	12	14	11	4	2	5	2	1
Austrian, etc.	32	4	11	6	4	3	..	..	2	2
Italian..............	57	1	34	10	9	1	..	1	1	..
Total...............	318*	37	122	73	37	16	8	12	7	5

* One case amount not specified.

TABLE 93.—HEALTH. PER CENT. OF FAMILIES REPORTING EXPENDITURE OF GIVEN AMOUNTS.—BY INCOME.

AMOUNT OF EXPENDITURE FOR HEALTH.	$600 TO $799			$800 TO $899			$900 TO $1099		
	Number of Families.	Per Cent. of all Families.	Per Cent. of Families Spending.	Number of Families.	Per Cent. of all Families.	Per Cent. of Families Spending.	Number of Families.	Per Cent. of all Families.	Per Cent. of Families Spending.
With no expenditure..	18	12.0	..	7	10.0	..	12	13.0	..
Under $10...........	64	42.4	48.5	28	37.4	42.4	30	31.9	36.6
$10 to $20..........	32	21.2	24.2	20	27.3	30.3	21	22.3	25.6
$20 to $30..........	19	12.6	14.4	5	6.8	7.6	13	13.8	15.8
$30 to $40..........	8	5.3	6.0	4	5.5	6.1	4	4.3	4.9
$40 to $50..........	4	2.6	3.0	1	1.4	1.5	3	3.2	3.7
$50 to $75..........	2	1.3	1.5	4	5.5	6.1	6	6.4	7.3
$75 to $100.........	2	1.3	1.5	1	1.4	1.5	4	4.3	4.9
Over $100...........	1	0.7	0.8	3	4.1	4.6	1	1.1	1.2
Under $30...........	115	76.2	87.1	53	72.6	80.3	64	68.0	78.0
$30 to $50..........	12	7.9	9.1	5	6.8	7.6	7	7.4	8.6
Over $50............	5	3.3	3.8	8	10.9	12.1	11	11.8	13.4

TABLE 94.—HEALTH. NUMBER OF FAMILIES REPORTING EXPEN-
DITURE, SERIOUS SICKNESS, FREE MEDICAL AID,
DENTISTRY.—BY NATIONALITY AND INCOME.

NATIONALITY.	$600 to $699.					$700 to $799.					$800 to $899.				
	Total Number of Families.	Families with no Expenditure for Health.	Cases of Serious Illness.	Free Medical Aid.	With Expenditure for Dentist.	Total Number of Families.	Families with no Expenditure for Health.	Cases of Serious Illness.	Free Medical Aid.	With Expenditure for Dentist.	Total Number of Families.	Families with no Expenditure for Health.	Cases of Serious Illness.	Free Medical Aid.	With Expenditure for Dentist.
United States	11	2	6	3	..	19	5	10	8	2	13	4	6	7	1
Teutonic	4	..	4	2	..	7	2	5	3	..	9	..	7	6	2
Irish	4	1	3	2	1	7	..	4	1	1	7	..	4	4	1
Colored	11	2	3	6	..	•6	2	1	3	..	8	..	5	5	2
Bohemian	4	..	3	2	1	3	..	2	2	..	3	..	2	1	..
Russian	16	1	9	8	3	14	1	12	7	3	12	1	8	5	4
Austrian, etc.	6	1	4	2	1	9	..	7	4	3	9	2	5	2	2
Italian	16	..	9	4	2	14	1	6	2	3	12	..	5	..	..
Total	72	7	41	29	8	79	11	47	30	12	73	7	42	30	12

NATIONALITY.	$900 to $999.					$1000 to $1099.					TOTAL.				
	Total Number of Families.	Families Without Expenditure for Health.	Cases of Serious Illness.	Free Medical Aid.	With Expenditure for Dentist.	Total Number of Families.	Families Without Expenditure for Health.	Cases of Serious Illness.	Free Medical Aid.	With Expenditure for Dentist.	Total Number of Families.	Families Without Expenditure for Health.	Cases of Serious Illness.	Free Medical Aid.	With Expenditure for Dentist.
United States	16	1	7	6	2	8	1	4	3	2	67	13	33	27	7
Teutonic	11	2	5	3	1	8	3	4	1	2	39	7	25	15	5
Irish	5	1	2	1	..	1	..	1	..	..	24	2	14	8	3
Colored	2	..	2	1	..	1	..	..	..	..	28	4	11	15	2
Bohemian	4	..	3	1	2	..	..	..	..	..	14	..	10	6	3
Russian	9	3	6	2	4	6	..	4	..	3	57	6	39	22	17
Austrian, etc.	7	..	5	2	2	1	1	..	..	..	32	4	21	13	8
Italian	9	..	4	..	1	6	..	2	1	..	57	1	26	7	6
Total	63	7	34	19	12	31	5	15	5	7	318	37	179	113	51

189

TABLE 95.—HEALTH. NUMBER AND PER CENT. OF FAMILIES RE-PORTING NO EXPENDITURE, SERIOUS SICKNESS, FREE MEDICAL AID, DENTISTRY.—BY INCOME.

INCOME.	NUMBER OF FAMILIES.	WITHOUT EXPENDITURE FOR HEALTH.		CASES OF SERIOUS ILLNESS.		FREE MEDICAL AID.		WITH EXPENDITURE FOR DENTIST.	
		Number.	Per Cent.	Number.	Per Cent.	Number.	Per Cent.	Number.	Per Cent.
$400 to $499.........	8	1	13	5	63	6	75	2	25
$500 to $599.........	17	3	18	9	53	7	41	2	12
$600 to $699.........	72	7	10	41	57	29	40	8	11
$700 to $799.........	79	11	14	47	59	30	38	12	15
$800 to $899.........	73	7	10	42	58	30	41	12	17
$900 to $999.........	63	7	11	34	54	19	30	12	19
$1000 to $1099.........	31	5	16	15	48	5	16	7	23
$1100 to $1199.........	18	..	..	9	50	3	16	6	33
$1200 to $1299.........	8	2	25	3	38	1	13	3	38
$1300 to $1399.........	8	2	25	5	63	1	13	..	..
$1400 and over.........	14	1	7	7	50	1	7	3	21
Total...............	391	46	11.8	217	55	132	34	67	16
$400 to $599.........	25	4	16	14	56	13	52	4	16
$600 to $799.........	151	18	12	88	58	59	39	20	13
$800 to $899.........	73	7	10	42	58	30	41	12	17
$990 to $1099.........	94	12	13	49	52	24	26	19	20
$1100 and over.........	48	5	10	24	50	6	13	12	25

7. INSURANCE.

A majority of the families included in our tables report expenditure for insurance of persons, and nearly half report insurance on property. (See Tables 96–99, pages 195–197). In exact figures, 191 out of the 318 families with incomes between $600 and $1100, or 60 per cent., pay for life-insurance, and 143, or 45 per cent., pay for insurance on property. The insurance on the lives

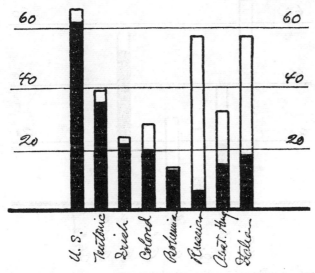

DIAGRAM 15.—Number of families carrying insurance on persons, in each nationality-group. (See Table 97.)

of persons is for the most part of the "industrial" type; that is, for a weekly payment of a fixed sum,—10 to 25 cents in most cases,—an amount, determined by the age of the insured, is paid to the family after death. The amount of the policy is usually about $100 for adults and $50 for children. The money received from the insurance company usually goes to pay the funeral expenses attendant on the death, so that it is more properly described as burial-insurance than as life-insurance. A limited number of families, as will be seen later (page 233), do carry a real life or endowment policy of $500 or even more. Some 56 cases are reported among the 318 families under consideration. In general, however, the insurance is not a provision for a rainy day, but a provision for meeting a single contingent expense; viz., the cost of burying the dead.

At the outset of the inquiry as to the average expenditure for insurance, we are met by a striking difference in the customs of the different nationalities in regard to insurance. (See Table 97,

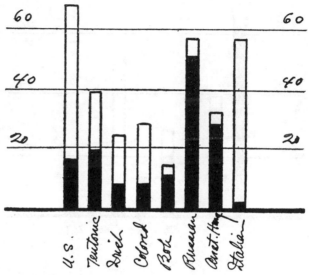

DIAGRAM 16.—Number of families carrying insurance on property in each nationality group. (See Table 97.)

page 196). Americans, the Germanic peoples, the Irish and the colored, insure almost every member of the family, but less frequently insure property. Of the 158 families of these nationalities, persons were insured in 139 cases, property in 51 cases. On the other hand, the Russians and Austro-Hungarians carry insurance as a rule on property, and as the exception on persons. Of the 89 Russian and Austro-Hungarian families, 79 carried insurance on property, and 21 on persons. In other words, in the first group personal insurance was carried by 88 per cent. of the families, insurance on property by 32 per cent.; in the second group personal insurance was carried by 24 per cent. of the families and insurance on property by 89 per cent. The Bohemians report in most cases insurance of both kinds; of 14 families, 13 report insurance on property, 11 insurance on persons. The Italians, on the contrary, report no insurance of any kind in the majority of cases. Of the 57 Italian families 18, or about one-third, carry insurance on persons; only 2 report insurance on property.

The lack of insurance on persons is compensated in a measure by membership in fraternal organizations. These societies usually give to members sick-benefits besides making provision for burial. The Russian and Austrian families are those most frequently reporting membership in these benefit societies, as appears from the table which follows:

NATIONALITY.	FAMILIES REPORTING MEMBERSHIP IN A BENEFIT SOCIETY.	FAMILIES REPORTING BOTH MEMBERSHIP AND INSURANCE ON PERSONS.
United States	7	6
Teutonic	8	8
Irish	1	1
Colored	3	3
Bohemian	8	8
Russian	26	4
Austrian	13	3
Italian	3	2
	69	35

These figures indicate that the benefit society is only a supplement to life insurance, save for the Russians and Austrians (the Jewish families), with whom it is a substitute.*

With these differences in national custom in mind we may look at the averages and percentages of expenditures for insurance (Table 96, page 195). For all nationalities combined, the average expenditure for insurance rises from $13.05, or 2 per cent. of total expenditure, for families in the $600 income-group, to $25.46, or 2.5 per cent. of total expenditure, for families in the $1000 group. For the American families the average is $25.26, or 3.8 per cent. in the $600 group, and $40.72, or 3.8 per cent. again in the $1000

---

* Among the Italians it is not infrequent for a group of relatives and friends to contribute $4 or $5 apiece for funeral expenses when a death occurs within their circle. This might be considered a form of fraternal insurance.

group. For the Russians, the averages for the $600 and $1000 families are $4.83 and $8.17 respectively, and the percentage of total expenditure 0.8 in both cases.

Variation in regard to insurance with rise of income appears in the data presented in Tables 97 and 98 (page 196). The number of families carrying insurance on persons and on property does not increase appreciably as the income increases, but the number of persons insured per family does increase, as may be seen in the following summary:

INCOME.	AVERAGE NUMBER OF PERSONS IN FAMILY.	AVERAGE NUMBER OF PERSONS INSURED.
$600 to $699	4.9	1.7
700 to 799	5.1	2.6
800 to 899	5.	2.2
900 to 999	5.1	2.5
1000 to 1099	5.	2.3

Separating the two groups of nationalities already distinguished, we find that in the first group (Americans, Teutonic nations, Irish, colored) out of 831 persons included in 158 families, 585 are insured, or an average of 3.7 persons per family. Among the Russians, Austrians and Italians, only 86 out of 711 persons included in 146 families are insured, or an average of 0.6 per family. Among the families of this second group it is usually the father only who is insured.

The question of the expensiveness of the insurance provided for the money paid in premiums lies beyond the scope of the present report.*

It is very evident from our data, however, that provision for the expenses of the last sickness and burial constitutes an essential part of the American standard of living, and that most families will go without many comforts in order to keep up their insurance. Even among the 25 poorest families, with incomes below $600, most of them over-crowded and under-fed, 6 report insurance on persons, while the American families with but from $600 to $700 to spend, contrive to pay $25 or $30 a year for insurance.

* See S. E. Forman's study of Industrial Insurance in the Bulletin of the United States Department of Labor, No. 67, Nov., 1906.

TABLE 96.—INSURANCE. AVERAGE ANNUAL EXPENDITURE AND PER CENT. OF TOTAL EXPENDITURE.—BY NATIONALITY AND INCOME.

Nationality.	$600 to $699			$700 to $799			$800 to $899			$900 to $999			$1000 to $1099		
	Number of Families.	Average Amount.	Per Cent.*	Number of Families.	Average Amount.	Per Cent.*	Number of Families.	Average Amount.	Per Cent.*	Number of Families.	Average Amount.	Per Cent.*	Number of Families.	Average Amount.	Per Cent.*
United States......	11	$25.26	3.8	19	$26.73	3.5	13	$24.86	2.9	16	$38.24	4.2	8	$40.72	3.8
Teutonic...........	4	31.02	4.6	7	36.67	4.5	9	25.33	2.9	11	31.52	3.4	8	43.97	4.3
Irish..............	4	36.00	5.4	7	24.18	3.1	7	23.37	2.9	5	41.83	4.6	1	..	..
Colored...........	11	19.59	3.3	6	27.02	3.4	8	23.31	3.0	2	25.06	2.9	1	20.80	2.3
Bohemian.........	4	6.73	1.0	3	19.03	2.5	3	17.97	2.1	4	28.40	2.9	..	..	..
Russian...........	16	4.83	0.8	14	3.28	0.5	12	6.99	0.9	9	5.92	0.6	6	8.17	0.8
Austrian, etc......	6	3.33	0.5	9	15.67	2.2	9	24.42	3.0	7	14.50	1.6	1	8.20	0.9
Italian............	16	3.38	0.5	14	7.24	1.0	12	2.31	0.3	9	.87	0.1	6	5.64	0.6
Total.............	72	13.05	2.0	79	18.24	2.5	73	17.62	2.2	63	23.71	2.6	31	25.46	2.5

* Per cent. of expenditure for all purposes.

195

TABLE 97.—INSURANCE. NUMBER OF FAMILIES CARRYING INSURANCE ON PERSONS AND ON PROPERTY.—BY NATIONALITY AND INCOME.

NATIONALITY.	TOTAL NUMBER OF FAMILIES.	NUMBER OF FAMILIES CARRYING INSURANCE.													
		$600 TO $699		$700 TO $799		$800 TO $899		$900 TO $999		$1000 TO $1099		Total.		Per Cent.	
		On Persons.	On Property.	On Persons.	On Property.	On Persons.	On Property.	On Persons.	On Property.	On Persons.	On Property.	On Persons.	On Property.	On Persons.	On Property.
United States....	67	11	4	17	1	11	5	16	5	7	1	62	16	92.6	23.9
Teutonic........	39	3	2	7	4	6	4	11	3	8	6	35	19	78.9	48.7
Irish............	24	4	1	7	2	7	4	4	1	..	..	22	8	73.4	26.7
Colored.........	28	11	5	6	2	..	1	2	..	1	..	20	8	71.5	28.6
Bohemian.......	14	3	2	3	2	3	3	4	4	..	..	13	11	72.9	78.6
Russian.........	57	2	13	..	13	2	10	1	9	1	6	6	51	10.5	89.5
Austrian, etc.....	32	..	5	5	8	5	8	4	6	1	1	15	28	46.8	77.5
Italian..........	57	4	1	8	1	3	..	1	..	2	..	18	2	31.6	3.5
Total..........	318	38	33	53	33	37	35	43	28	20	14	191	143	60.0	45.0

TABLE 98.—INSURANCE. AVERAGE NUMBER OF PERSONS INSURED.—BY NATIONALITY AND INCOME.

NATIONALITY.	TOTAL NUMBER OF FAMILIES.	AVERAGES OF NUMBER OF PERSONS IN FAMILY AND OF NUMBER OF PERSONS INSURED.											
		$600 to $699		$700 to $799		$800 to $899		$900 to $999		$1000 to $1099		Total.	
		Number in Family.	Number Insured.	Number in Family.	Number Insured.	Number in Family.	Number Insured.	Number in Family.	Number Insured.	Number in Family.	Number Insured.	Number in Family.	Number Insured.
United States....	67	5.0	3.2	5.3	3.9	5.0	3.2	5.2	4.3	5.4	4.7	5.2	3.9
Teutonic........	39	4.7	3.5	5.0	4.0	5.1	3.0	5.1	3.3	5.0	2.5	5.	3.2
Irish............	24	6.0	5.5	5.3	4.3	5.4	3.4	5.4	4.0	5.0	..	5.3	4.0
Colored.........	28	5.4	3.2	5.5	4.7	5.2	3.8	5.5	4.0	5.0	4.0	5.4	3.8
Bohemian.......	14	4.5	1.0	6.0	5.0	5.7	3.6	5.2	4.2	..	..	5.3	3.4
Russian.........	57	5.1	0.1	5.1	..	5.4	0.25	5.0	0.2	4.8	0.2	5.1	0.1
Austrian, etc.....	32	4.3	..	4.8	1.1	5.0	1.8	4.9	1.0	6.0	1.0	4.8	1.0
Italian..........	57	4.6	0.8	4.6	1.1	4.5	0.7	5.1	0.1	4.5	1.0	4.6	0.8
Total.........	318	4.9	1.7	5.1	2.6	5.0	2.2	5.1	2.5	5.0	2.3	5.0	2.3

TABLE 99.—INSURANCE. NUMBER AND PER CENT. OF FAMI-
LIES INSURED, AND AVERAGE NUMBER OF PERSONS
INSURED.—BY INCOME.

INCOME.	NUM-BER OF FAMI-LIES.	NUMBER OF FAMILIES INSURED.		PER CENT. OF FAMILIES INSURED.		AVERAGE NUMBER OF PERSONS.	
		On Persons.	On Property.	On Persons.	On Property	In Family.	Insured.
$400 to $499......	8	2	1	25.0	12.5	5.4	1.3
$500 to $599......	17	4	9	23.5	53.0	5.0	0.6
$600 to $699......	72	38	33	52.8	45.8	4.9	1.7
$700 to $799......	79	53	33	67.1	41.8	5.1	2.6
$800 to $899......	73	37	35	50.7	48.0	5.0	2.2
$900 to $999......	63	43	28	68.2	44.4	5.1	2.5
$100 to $1099......	31	20	14	64.6	45.1	5.0	2.3
$1100 to $1199......	18	4	11	22.2	61.0	5.0	2.7
$1200 to $1299......	8	2	5	25.0	62.5	5.4	2.1
$1300 to $1399......	8	2	4	25.0	50.0	4.9	3.3
$1400 and over	14	5	11	35.7	78.6	4.6	2.0
Total..............	391	210	184	53.7	47.1	5.0	2.2

8. SUNDRY MINOR ITEMS.

Under this head are grouped the items of the schedule not already considered; viz., Furniture, Dues and Contributions, Recreation and Amusement, Education and Reading, and Miscellaneous.   They represent expenditures for the satisfaction of what the economist calls "culture-wants"; that is, wants arising out of the desire for intellectual, social and aesthetic gratifications, as distinguished from wants connected with the mere prolongation of physical existence.   They include also some physical satisfactions, like tobacco and soda water, which are not indispensable to life.   Largely these headings include the cost of that which makes life worth living.

In considering these details, and especially in remarking on the small amount that the ordinary family has left for such expenditures, it must not be forgotten that much that satisfies the extra-physical wants can be had free of cost.   Public schools provide education for the children, the parks and playgrounds give opportunity for fresh air and recreation, the intercourse with kindred and neighbors gives social satisfaction, and the ever-varying pageant of street-life, sordid though it often is, gives constant novelty and diversion.   Nevertheless, there are important needs for which no gratuitous provision has been made, and the amount of expenditure for these purposes is an indication, so far as it goes, of the standard of culture attained, and of the opportunities for raising it.

Considering then, the expenditures for this group collectively (Table 100, page 199), it is instructive to note that they constitute but 7.3 per cent. of the total expenditures of the families with incomes between $600 and $700, and 11.4 per cent. of the expenditures of the families with between $1000 and $1100. The average amount spent is, for the lowest income-group, $47.55, and for the highest, $114.59.   The amount and the percentage increase constantly with each rise in the income-scale, showing that the desires for such satisfactions as we are considering always tend to push ahead of the means available for satisfying them, and that on the smallest incomes the margin left for them, after supplying a bare physical subsistence, is narrow enough.

TABLE 100.—SUNDRY MINOR ITEMS COLLECTIVELY. AVERAGE ANNUAL EXPENDITURE AND PER CENT. OF TOTAL EXPENDITURE.—BY NATIONALITY AND INCOME.

NATIONALITY.	$600 TO $699.			$700 TO $799.			$800 TO $899.			$900 TO $999.			$1000 TO $1099.		
	Number of Families.	Average Amount.	Per Cent.*	Number of Families.	Average Amount.	Per Cent.*	Number of Families.	Average Amount.	Per Cent.*	Number of Families.	Average Amount.	Per Cent.*	Number of Families.	Average Amount.	Per Cent.*
United States	11	$55.37	8.3	19	$51.36	6.7	13	$73.65	8.5	16	$88.91	9.4	8	$119.39	11.1
Teutonic	4	36.18	5.4	7	44.90	5.9	9	102.36	11.7	11	99.47	10.8	8	109.81	10.6
Irish	4	43.06	6.5	7	56.40	7.4	7	69.66	8.6	5	95.61	10.5	1	55.22	6.0
Colored	11	32.78	5.0	6	42.40	5.4	8	56.19	7.1	2	92.14	10.9	1	188.95	21.3
Bohemian	4	50.27	7.2	3	64.31	8.7	3	67.93	8.1	4	89.17	9.0	-	..	..
Russian	16	52.03	8.3	14	74.65	10.7	12	72.71	9.5	9	111.77	12.5	6	141.86	13.6
Austrian, etc.	6	48.34	8.0	9	63.51	8.9	9	87.18	10.6	7	85.67	9.5	1	62.48	6.4
Italian	16	50.86	7.7	14	72.36	10.3	12	60.92	8.2	9	58.74	7.2	6	93.46	10.5
Total	72	47.55	7.3	79	60.28	8.2	73	74.08	9.1	63	90.00	9.9	31	114.59	11.4

* Per cent. of expenditure for all purposes.

199

1. Furniture and Furnishings.—Table 101 (page 202) shows the average expenditure for furniture by income and nationality, and also the number of families reporting no expenditure for this purpose. The average amount, taking into account only the families that report this expenditure, is $6.22 for the $600 families, and $12.89 for the families with incomes of between $1000 and $1100. The increase is not very regular, however, counting by $100 stages. Yet the average expenditure of the 140 families with incomes between $600 and $800 is $7.56, and that of the 90 families with incomes of between $900 and $1100 is $13.20. The count of families spending given amounts (Tables 102 and 103, pages 203–204) shows more plainly than the table of averages the tendency to larger expenditures in the higher income-classes. Of the families in the $600 and $700 income-groups, 80 per cent. spend less than $10 for furniture. Of the families in the $900 and $1000 groups, 58 per cent. spend less than $10, and of the families with over $1100 a year only 35 per cent. spend less than $10, while 48 per cent. spend more than $20. The same table shows that of all the nationalities represented the Russians spend most liberally for furniture. Their average is the highest in each income-group, and the number of families reporting expenditures of $20 and more is likewise largest. The colored families report, as a rule, the least expenditure for furniture. As for the other nationalities, the variations between different families and income-groups within each nationality are quite as much in evidence as the differences between the different nationalities. It is obvious that expenditures for furniture must vary greatly, and that the averages will be affected by the accidental inclusion or exclusion, in a given group, of families that have had occasion to buy articles of considerable value.*

An effort was made to get an inventory of the furniture in each room of the apartment. On the basis of the returns the families were classified into groups according as the furniture described seemed to make meager, fairly comfortable or ample

* The purchase of furniture on the instalment plan was reported in a few instances, but too few to warrant generalization on this point. One family was paying a dollar a week on its furniture; another was paying $6 a month on a piano.

provision for the needs of the family. Where nothing beyond the barest supply of indispensable articles—beds and bedding, chairs, table—is reported, the outfit is designated "meager." Where some additional articles—rugs or oilcloth, mirrors,* easy-chairs—are reported, the furnishing is designated as "fair." Where there is an abundant supply both of necessary articles and of accessories, the designation "ample" is applied. Tables 103 and 104 (pages 204–205) show the number of families in each of these classes. It will be seen that the standard rises with the income. The percentage of "meager" falls from 54 for the $600 families to 13 for the $1000 group, and the percentage of "fair" increases from 46 in the $600 group to 74 in the $1000 group. Combining the $600 and $700 families and the $900 and $1000 groups, it is found that 52 per cent. of the families in the first double group are reported as having a meager equipment of furniture, and 3 per cent. as having ample. In the second double group 20 per cent. are reported meagerly equipped, and 14 per cent. as having ample furniture. The equipment of only 22 of the 318 families (with incomes between $600 and $1100) and of 32 of the whole 391 cases is graded as "ample," and of these cases 18 of the 22 and 28 of the 32 are found in families with more than $900 a year.

The possession of a piano may be considered as one sign of ample furnishing. The families that reported pianos were counted, and 18 altogether were found in the 391 families, 8 of them belonging to families having over $1100 a year. The distribution by incomes may be seen in the appended note.†

---

* Pier-glasses are much in demand by tenement-dwellers in many districts.

†Income.	Number of Pianos Reported.	Income.	Number of Pianos Reported.
$600 to $699	0	$1000 to $1099	2
$700 to $799	2	$1100 to $1199	1
$800 to $899	1	$1200 to $1299	1
$900 to $999	5	$1300 and over	6
		Total	18

TABLE 101.—FURNITURE. AVERAGE ANNUAL EXPENDITURE AND NUMBER OF FAMILIES REPORTING.—BY NATIONALITY AND INCOME.

Nationality.	$600 TO $699.			$700 TO $799.			$800 TO $899.			$900 TO $999.			$1000 TO $1099.			TOTAL.	
	Number of Families.		Average Amount.	Number of Families.		Average Amount.	Number of Families.		Average Amount.	Number of Families.		Average Amount.	Number of Families.		Average Amount.	Number of Families.	
	With Expenditure for Furniture.	Without Expenditure for Furniture.		With Expenditure for Furniture.	Without Expenditure for Furniture.		With Expenditure for Furniture.	Without Expenditure for Furniture.		With Expenditure for Furniture.	Without Expenditure for Furniture.		With Expenditure for Furniture.	Without Expenditure for Furniture.		With Expenditure for Furniture.	Without Expenditure for Furniture.
United States	9	2	$1.31	18	1	$6.52	13	..	$3.92	15	1	$11.53	8	..	$8.25	63	4
Teutonic	4	..	5.00	5	2	4.99	9	..	9.81	10	1	8.27	7	1	11.12	35	4
Irish	4	..	3.88	7	..	7.29	7	..	6.70	4	1	10.08	1	..	11.00	23	1
Colored	11	..	.89	4	2	.81	7	1	4.06	2	..	40.17	1	..	.75	25	3
Bohemian	4	..	11.52	3	..	7.68	3	..	8.43	4	..	13.60	..	..	..	14	..
Russian	16	..	12.79	13	1	17.86	11	1	15.94	9	..	24.26	6	..	24.92	55	..
Austrian, etc.	6	..	6.27	9	..	11.31	8	1	6.06	7	..	11.47	1	..	3.58	31	1
Italian	16	..	5.54	14	..	7.01	12	..	5.92	9	..	8.04	6	..	13.03	57	..
Total	70	2	..	73	6	..	70	3	..	60	3	..	30	1	..	303	15
Average of all families with expenditure for furniture	..	..	$6.22	..	..	$8.90	..	..	$7.64	..	..	$13.36	..	..	$12.89	..	..
Average of all families	..	..	6.05	..	..	8.22	..	..	7.33	..	..	12.73	..	..	12.48	..	..

TABLE 102.—FURNITURE. NUMBER OF FAMILIES REPORTING EXPENDITURE OF GIVEN AMOUNTS.—BY NATIONALITY AND INCOME.

NATIONALITY.	$600 TO $699.						$700 TO $799.						$800 TO $899.					
	Number of Families.	No Expenditure Reported.	Under $10.	$10 to $20.	$20 to $30.	Over $30	Number of Families.	No Expenditure Reported.	Under $10.	$10 to $20.	$20 to $30.	Over $30.	Number of Families.	No Expenditure Reported.	Under $10.	$10 to $20.	$20 to $30.	Over $30.
United States ...	11	2	9	..	..	..	19	1	15	2	..	1	13	..	12	1	..	..
Teutonic.........	4	..	3	1	..	..	7	2	5	..	..	..	9	..	5	3	1	..
Irish............	4	..	4	..	..	..	7	..	5	2	..	..	7	..	6	..	1	..
Colored..........	11	..	11	..	..	..	6	2	4	..	..	..	8	1	6	1	..	..
Bohemian	4	..	2	2	..	..	3	..	2	1	..	..	3	..	3	..	..	..
Russian	16	..	11	..	3	2	14	1	7	1	3	2	12	1	5	2	2	2
Austrian, etc	6	..	5	1	..	..	9	..	4	3	2	..	9	1	6	2	..	..
Italian..........	16	..	14	1	1	..	14	..	11	2	1	..	12	..	10	2	..	..
Total	72	2	59	5	4	2	79	6	53	11	6	3	73	3	53	11	4	2

NATIONALITY.	$900 TO $999.						$1000 TO $1099.						TOTAL.					
	Number of Families.	No Expenditure Reported.	Under $10.	$10 to $20.	$20 to $30.	Over $30.	Number of Families.	No Expenditure Reported.	Under $10.	$10 to $20.	$20 to $30.	Over $30.	Number of Families.	No Expenditure Reported.	Under $10.	$10 TO $20.	$20 to $30.	Over $30.
United States ...	16	1	9	5	..	1	8	..	6	1	1	..	67	4	51	9	1	2
Teutonic	11	1	7	3	..	..	8	1	4	2	1	..	39	4	24	9	2	..
Irish............	5	1	2	2	..	..	1	..	..	1	..	..	24	1	17	5	1	..
Colored	2	..	..	1	..	1	1	..	..	1	..	..	28	3	21	1	..	1
Bohemian	4	..	1	3	..	..	..	..	..	..	..	..	14	..	8	6	..	..
Russian	9	..	1	4	2	2	6	..	1	2	1	2	57	2	25	9	11	10
Austrian, etc	7	..	5	1	..	1	1	..	1	..	..	..	32	1	21	7	2	1
Italian..........	9	..	8	1	..	..	6	..	2	2	2	..	57	..	45	8	4	..
Total...........	63	3	33	20	2	5	31	1	14	9	5	2	318	15	212	54	21	14

TABLE 103.—FURNITURE. STANDARD, AND NUMBER OF FAMILIES REPORTING GIVEN AMOUNTS EXPENDED.—BY INCOME.

INCOME.	NUM-BER OF FAM-ILIES.	STANDARD.						ANNUAL EXPENDITURE.			
		Meager.		Fair.		Ample.		Under $10.		Over $20	
		Num-ber.	Per Cent.	Num-ber.	Per Cent.	Num-ber.	Per Cent.	Num-ber.	Per Cent.	Num-ber.	Per Cent.
$400 to $499......	8	7	88	1	12	..	..	8	100	..	..
$500 to $599......	17	13	76	4	24	..	..	14	82	2	12
$600 to $699......	72	39	54	33	46	..	..	61	85	6	8
$700 to $799......	79*	39	50	35	45	4	5	59	76	9	12
$800 to $899......	73	30	41	39	53	4	6	56	77	6	8
$900 to $999......	63	15	24	38	60	10	16	40	63	6	10
$1000 to $1099......	31	4	13	23	74	4	13	15	48	7	23
$1100 to $1199......	18	1	6	14	78	3	16	7	39	5	28
$1200 to $1299......	8†	..	..	4	67	2	33	4	50	4	50
$1300 to $1399......	8	..	..	6	75	2	25	3	38	4	50
$1400 and over......	14	..	..	11	79	3	21	3	21	10	71
Total..............	391	148	38	208	54	32	8	270	70	59	14
$400 to $599......	25	20	80	5	20	..	..	22	88	2	8
$600 to $799......	151*	78	52	68	45	4	3	120	80	15	10
$800 to $899......	73	30	41	39	53	4	6	56	77	6	8
$900 to $1099......	94	19	20	61	65	14	15	55	58	13	14
$1100 and over*.....	48†	1	2	35	76	10	22	17	35	23	48

* Standard not reported in 1 case.
† Standard not reported in 2 cases.

TABLE 104.—FURNITURE. STANDARD, AND NUMBER OF FAMILIES REPORTING.—BY NATIONALITY AND INCOME.

NATIONALITY.	$600 TO $699.				$700 TO $799.				$800 TO $899.			
	Number of Families.	Meager.	Fair.	Ample.	Number of Families.	Meager.	Fair.	Ample.	Number of Families.	Meager.	Fair.	Ample.
United States	11	1	10	..	19	6	11	2	13	2	10	1
Teutonic	4	1	3	..	7	2	5	..	9	1	7	1
Irish	4	2	2	..	7	3	4	..	7	1	5	1
Colored	11	6	5	..	6	3	1	2	8	..	7	1
Bohemian	4	3	1	..	3	3	..	..	3	3	..	..
Russian	16	10	6	..	14	8	6	..	12	7	5	..
Austrian, etc.	6	4	2	..	9	5	4	..	9	6	3	..
Italian	16	12	4	..	13*	9	4	..	12	10	2	..
Total	72	39	33	..	78	39	35	4	73	30	39	4

NATIONALITY.	$900 TO $999.				$1000 TO $1099.				TOTAL.						
	Number of Families.	Meager.	Fair.	Ample.	Number of Families.	Meager.	Fair.	Ample.	Number of Families.	Meager.		Fair.		Ample.	
										Number.	Per cent.	Number.	Per cent.	Number.	Per cent.
United States	16	..	12	4	8	1	6	1	67	10	15	49	73	8	12
Teutonic	11	3	8	..	8	..	5	3	39	7	18	28	72	4	10
Irish	5	..	5	..	1	..	1	..	24	6	25	17	71	1	4
Colored	2	..	1	1	1	1	..	..	28	10	36	14	50	4	14
Bohemian	4	2	2	..	..	..	..	..	14	11	79	3	21	..	..
Russian	9	1	5	3	6	..	6	..	57	26	46	28	49	3	5
Austrian, etc.	7	6	..	1	1	1	..	..	32	22	69	9	28	1	3
Italian	9	3	5	1	6	1	5	..	56*	35	62	20	36	1	2
Total	63	15	38	10	31	4	23	4	317*	127	40	168	53	22	7

* Standard not reported in 1 case.

205

2. TAXES, DUES, AND CONTRIBUTIONS.—Under this head are grouped expenditures for the support of labor organizations, churches, and other religious societies, social and benefit societies, and also gifts of friendship and charity. Of such gifts the entries are few and far between. Taxes for the support of the government are not reported, save in the case of 6 house-owning families, which, by reason of this departure from type, were not included in the number tabulated. Tables 105 and 106 (pages 208–209) show the principal items as returned on the schedules of the 318 families with incomes between $600 and $1100.

No expenditures at all under this general head are reported from 62 families. Of these, 35, or more than half, are in the lowest 2 income-groups, and only 14, or one-quarter of the whole, in the $900 and $1000 groups. By nationalities, the Italians furnish the largest number of families without expenditure for social organizations, 25 of all the 57 Italian families, or 44 per cent., spending nothing. Fifteen of the 67 American families make the same return, and only 4 of the 57 Russian, and 2 of the 32 Austrian.

The average expenditure included in the table is that of families reporting such expenditure. It varies among the nationalities in a manner corresponding to the distribution of the families reporting no expenditure, the Russians and Austrians returning a high average, the Italians and colored a low average amount. The 13 Bohemian families show the highest average, and report spending for a greater variety of purposes than most of the other nationalities, but the number of families is small. By income-groups the average amount increases with each advance in the scale, rising from $10.96 in the $600 group to $18.65 in the $1000 group. This latter sum would permit the payment of 10 cents a week to the church, 50 cents a month to the labor union, and the same amount to a lodge.

Looking now at the principal social organizations for whose advantages the laborer pays, we find that 83 families, or 26 per cent., report contributions to labor unions; 175, or 55 per cent., contribute to religious organizations, and 126, or 40 per cent., to lodges and similar organizations. Membership in the unions seems to be about as frequent in the lower income-groups as in the higher. Combining, however, the $600 and $700 incomes and comparing them with the combined $900 and $1000 groups, it appears that

25 per cent. of the families in the lower groups belong to unions, and 32 per cent. of the families in the higher income-groups. Twenty-five per cent. of the American families, 23 per cent. of the Italians, 35 per cent. of the Russians and 18 per cent. of the colored contribute to the unions. These differences may be due to accident in the selection of families reporting, and too much stress is not to be laid upon them.

For the support of religious organizations, the families with higher incomes more often report expenditure than those with lower incomes. Forty-eight per cent. of the families having incomes of $600 to $800 report such expenditure, as against 61 per cent. of the families with incomes between $900 and $1100.* A comparison of nationalities shows that seven-eighths of the Irish pay something for this purpose, while five-eighths of the Teutonic and American families, two-thirds of the Russians and Bohemians, more than half of the Austrians, less than half of the colored families, and only one-fourth of the Italians report payments for this object. To lodges, 38 per cent. of the families with incomes between $600 and $800 contribute, while 45 per cent. of families with incomes between $900 and $1100 spend for this purpose. A smaller proportion of the Irish and colored families report paying lodge dues than of the other nationalities. Twelve of the 14 Bohemian families report such payments, 31 of the 57 Russian, and 20 of the 67 American families. Under this head are included societies paying sick and death-benefits. So far as could be distinguished from the returns, 69 of the families included in the 126 that supported lodges belonged to benefit societies. A sharp difference between nationalities appears at this point, the American, Teutonic, Irish and colored families in only 19 cases reporting payment for benefit societies, while 50 families in the other 4 nationalities report such expenditure. It has already been pointed out (page 192) that insurance of persons is favored by these groups of nationalities in exactly the converse proportion.

---

* The amount of payment for religious organizations differs greatly among different families as well as between different nationalities. Ten cents a Sunday is a common contribution for attendants at Protestant and Roman Catholic churches. Many Jewish families report for the year only $2 or $3, given for the services at the annual festivals. In many cases the fraternal societies are related to some religious organization. One schedule reports the woman as saying, "The church has more money than we; this is why we don't go to church."

TABLE 105.—TAXES, DUES AND CONTRIBUTIONS. NUMBER OF FAMILIES REPORTING EXPENDITURE FOR GIVEN PURPOSES.—BY NATIONALITY AND INCOME.

NATIONALITY.	$600 TO $699.						$700 TO $799.						$800 TO $899.					
	Average Expenditure.	Total.	With no Expenditure.	Labor Union.	Religion.	Lodge, etc.	Average Expenditure.	Total.	With no Expenditure.	Labor Union.	Religion.	Lodge, etc.	Average Expenditure.	Total.	With no Expenditure.	Labor Union.	Religion.	Lodge, etc.
United States ...	$11.24	11	2	5	5	3	$9.51	19	4	5	11	6	$8.83	13	2	2	10	4
Teutonic	5.27	4	2	..	2	1	9.73	7	2	..	3	2	13.28	9	1	1	8	2
Irish	10.90	4	1	1	3	..	15.02	7	1	2	5	1	18.79	7	..	2	7	2
Colored	4.22	11	3	2	3	4	9.32	6	1	2	2	2	6.80	8	3	1	4	1
Bohemian	20.86	4	1	2	3	2	19.63	3	..	1	1	3	28.97	3	..	..	3	3
Russian	13.33	16	3	3	11	7	10.04	14	1	4	7	6	16.42	12	..	6	6	7
Austrian, etc.....	17.29	6	1	1	3	4	11.88	9	..	3	4	6	15.25	9	1	1	5	6
Italian	7.75	16	7	3	6	5	9.29	14	6	3	4	4	4.80	12	6	3	2	2
Total	10.96	72	20	17	36	26	11.10	79	15	20	37	30	13.39	73	13	16	45	27

NATIONALITY.	$900 TO $999.						$1000 TO $1099.						TOTAL.					
	Average Expenditure.	Total.	With no Expenditure.	Labor Union.	Religion.	Lodge, etc.	Average Expenditure.	Total.	With no Expenditure.	Labor Union.	Religion.	Lodge, etc.	Average Expenditure.	Total.	With no Expenditure.	Labor Union.	Religion.	Lodge, etc.
United States ..	$13.11	16	5	3	10	3	$18.84	8	2	2	5	4	$11.51	67	15	17	41	20
Teutonic	18.91	11	1	4	6	5	19.29	8	..	3	5	5	15.41	39	6	8	24	15
Irish	13.79	5	..	2	5	..	5.20	1	..	..	1	..	14.93	24	2	7	21	3
Colored	5.30	2	..	..	1	2	19.80	1	..	..	1	1	6.89	28	7	5	11	10
Bohemian	33.85	4	..	2	3	4	..						26.45	14	1	5	10	12
Russian	18.50	9	..	3	6	7	18.67	6	..	5	6	4	15.30	57	4	21	36	31
Austrian, etc....	20.75	7	..	2	5	3	26.00	1	..	..	1	1	15.55	32	2	7	18	20
Italian	10.08	9	4	1	2	1	13.30	6	2	3	..	3	8.64	57	25	13	14	15
Total	16.78	63	10	17	38	25	18.65	31	4	13	19	18	13.58	318	62	83	175	126

TABLE 106.—TAXES, DUES AND CONTRIBUTIONS. NUMBER AND PER CENT. OF FAMILIES REPORTING EXPENDITURE FOR GIVEN PURPOSES.—BY INCOME.

INCOME.	NUMBER OF FAMILIES.	WITHOUT EXPENDITURE FOR TAXES, ETC.		WITH EXPENDITURE FOR:					
				Labor Unions.		Religion.		Lodge, etc.	
		Number.	Per Cent.	Number.	Per Cent.	Number.	Per Cent.	Number.	Per Cent.
$600 to $699	72	20	28	17	24	36	50	26	36
$700 to $799	79	15	19	20	25	37	47	30	38
$800 to $899	73	13	18	16	22	45	62	27	37
$900 to $999	63	10	16	17	27	38	60	25	40
$1000 to $1099	31	4	13	13	42	19	61	18	58
$400 to $599	25	5	20	4	16	11	44	7	28
$600 to $799	151	35	23	37	25	73	48	57	38
$800 to $899	73	13	18	16	22	45	62	27	37
$900 to $1099	94	14	15	30	32	57	61	42	45
$1100 and over	48	1	2	14	29	33	69	28	58

3. RECREATION AND AMUSEMENT.—The way in which expenditure for purposes beyond subsistence-wants is restricted
by poverty appears very plainly in the table showing average
expenditures for recreation and amusement (Table 107, page 212).
The average for the $600 families is $3.79; for the $800 families
$8.44, for the $1000 families $14.76, and if we look at the families
with incomes between $1100 and $1600 we find an average of
$22.29. A comparison of the averages by nationalities (Table
108, page 213) shows that a larger expenditure for amusement and
recreation prevails among the nationalities that have adopted most
completely the American standard. The Italians, however, show
an average above the general average in every income-group save
one.

The families reporting no expenditure for recreation number
32, more than half of them among the families in the lowest 2 income-groups, only 4 in the highest 2. One-third of them are
among the Russians, one-half among the Russians and Austrians.
Those who report no money-expenditure make remarks like
the following: "Never go any place at all except to the woman's
parents, who live across the way." "The only recreation is the
display of their furniture." "In the evening they sit in front
of the house." Twelve of these 32 families report the use of
parks or some other form of recreation involving no expense, but
in 20 cases no mention is made of any form of recreation.*

Three forms of recreation specified in Table 108 (page 213) are:
the use of parks, excursions, and theaters. The use of parks was
not made a direct question in the schedule, as were the other forms,
but they are mentioned in the answers to the general question as to the forms of amusement and recreation enjoyed by
the family. In this connection they are specified in 102 of the
318 schedules, somewhat more often in the families with the lower
incomes. Excursions, involving at least the cost of car-fare, for
visits to parks or to friends, are reported in 237 of the 318 cases,
or 74.5 per cent. Thirty-four per cent., or 109 families, report
expenditure for the theater. A comparison of the number of

---

* The transference of an old-world tradition appears in the following note in
an Italian schedule: "The daughter has better chance at marriage by staying
away from public amusements."

families reporting expenditures for theaters and excursions in the upper and lower income-groups is instructive. Twenty-five per cent. of the $600 and $700 families spend for theaters, 66 per cent. for excursions. Of the $900 and $1000 families, 51 per cent. spend for theaters and 87 per cent. for excursions. By nationalities, theaters seem to be best patronized by Americans, the Teutonic families, and the Italians, and the expenditure for excursions is likewise most frequent among these same nationalities.

The amount of expenditure varies greatly in individual cases. One family puts down $1 weekly for theater-going, out of an income of about $900. Others report 5 or 10 cents occasionally for the "five-cent theater" or moving-picture exhibition. Excursions range from visits to the parks to a three months' visit with a sister in the country for mother and children. Very seldom is mention made of a stated vacation for the principal wage-earner. Outings provided by the fresh-air charities are specified in a few cases, and visits to Coney Island or Fort George by the whole family once or twice a summer are not infrequently mentioned. Expenditure for dances, although entered separately in the schedule, is very seldom reported. One family reports spending $14 for phonograph records, and the phonograph appears in perhaps 4 other cases. The voluntary societies, mentioned in the preceding section, often furnish means of recreation, such as social gatherings, picnics and excursions, and expenditure for recreation is sometimes not differentiated from dues and payments to the society.

4. EDUCATION AND READING.—(See Tables 109–111, pages 216–218.) The public school furnishes free the means of giving the children a formal education, and the free libraries provide reading matter. But additional instruction (e. g., in music) is often desired, and the newspapers cost a cent apiece. With these items are grouped expenditures for postage and stationery, and incidental expenditures for children at school. The total amount reported under this heading is less than that under any other of the group-heads of the schedule, and increases with income on the average less than many other items. The average for the $600 families reporting expenditure under this head is $5.56; for the $1000 families the average amount is $8.54.

TABLE 107.—RECREATION AND AMUSEMENT. NUMBER AND PER CENT. OF FAMILIES REPORTING, AND AVERAGE ANNUAL EXPENDITURE.—BY INCOME.

INCOME.	NUMBER OF FAMILIES.	WITHOUT EXPENDITURE FOR RECREATION.		FORM OF RECREATION REPORTED.						AVERAGE AMOUNT EXPENDED.*
				Parks.		Excursions.		Theaters.		
		Number.	Per Cent.	Number.	Per Cent.	Number.	Per Cent.	Number.	Per Cent.	
$600 to $699	72	7	10	21	29	44	61	15	21	$3.79
$700 to $799	79	12	15	26	33	55	70	23	29	7.07
$800 to $899	73	9	12	26	36	56	77	23	32	8.44
$900 to $999	63	3	5	22	35	55	87	29	46	11.71
$1000 to $1099	31	1	3	7	23	27	87	19	61	14.76
$400 to $599	25	7	28	7	28	11	44	4	16	$2.72
$600 to $799	151	19	12	47	31	99	66	38	25	5.42
$800 to $899	73	9	12	26	36	56	77	23	32	8.44
$900 to $1099	94	4	4	29	31	82	87	48	51	12.73
$1100 and over	48	1	2	14	29	38	79	33	69	22.29†

* Average for families spending.
† Average of 41 families with incomes between $1100 and $1599.

TABLE 108.—RECREATION AND AMUSEMENT. NUMBER OF FAM-
ILIES REPORTING VARIOUS KINDS.—BY NATIONALITY
AND INCOME.

NATIONALITY.	$600 to $699						$700 to $799						$800 to $899					
	Average Amount.	Number of Families.		Form of Recreation.			Average Amount.	Number of Families.		Form of Recreation.			Average Amount.	Number of Families.		Form of Recreation.		
		Total.	With no Expenditure.	Parks.	Excursions.	Theaters.		Total.	With no Expenditure.	Parks.	Excursions.	Theaters.		Total.	With no Expenditure.	Parks.	Excursions.	Theaters
United States...	$3.32	11	..	3	10	4	$7.54	19	4	5	11	7	$9.01	13	1	4	13	4
Teutonic.......	6.35	4	..	3	4	..	7.71	7	2	1	3	..	11.73	9	..	7	9	5
Irish..........	4.62	4	..	..	3	1	7.17	7	..	1	7	2	7.48	7	..	..	5	2
Colored........	3.00	11	..	..	5	1	2.56	6	..	..	4	1	2.14	8	1	..	3	..
Bohemian.......	2.87	4	..	3	4	1	6.83	3	..	2	3	1	4.00	3	..	2	3	..
Russian........	3.25	16	5	7	7	2	8.12	14	4	9	8	3	4.61	12	3	7	9	4
Austrian, etc....	2.18	6	1	3	2	2	3.96	9	..	7	7	1	7.87	9	3	6	4	2
Italian.........	4.98	16	1	2	9	4	9.92	14	2	1	12	8	14.42	12	1	..	10	6
Total..........	3.79	72	7	21	44	15	7.07	79	12	26	55	23	8.44	73	9	26	56	23

NATIONALITY.	$900 to $999						$1000 to $1099						Total.					
	Average Amount.	Number of Families.		Form of Recreation.			Average Amount.	Number of Families.		Form of Recreation.			Average Amount.	Number of Families.		Form of Recreation		
		Total.	With no Expenditure.	Parks.	Excursions.	Theaters.		Total.	With no Expenditure.	Parks.	Excursions.	Theaters.		Total.	With no Expenditure.	Parks.	Excursions.	Theaters.
United States...	$15.48	16	..	6	15	7	$16.40	8	1	2	6	5	$9.54	67	6	20	55	27
Teutonic.......	14.83	11	..	2	9	5	15.52	8	..	2	7	6	12.35	39	2	15	32	16
Irish..........	10.78	5	..	..	5	4	2.00	1	..	..	1	..	7.38	24	..	1	21	9
Colored........	2.50	2	..	1	2	..	5.00	1	..	..	1	..	2.72	28	1	1	15	2
Bohemian.......	11.00	4	..	3	4	2	..						6.29	14	..	10	14	4
Russian........	6.09	9	1	3	7	4	11.12	6	..	1	6	4	6.23	57	13	27	37	17
Austrian, etc....	7.31	7	2	7	4	4	2.00	1	..	1	1	1	5.37	32	6	24	18	10
Italian.........	10.72	9	..	..	9	3	21.34	6	..	1	5	3	10.88	57	4	4	45	24
Total..........	11.71	63	3	22	55	29	14.76	31	1	7	27	19	8.41	318	32	102	237	109

213

By nationalities the highest average amounts are found among the English-speaking people, the lowest among the Italians. Some expenditure for education and reading is reported in all but 24 of the 318 cases. In 19 cases, however, less than 75 cents is reported. Both classes are included in the column "with no expenditure" in the table, making 43 cases in all. Of these 43 cases, 28 are in families with less than $800 a year, 5 only in families with $900 or over. Twenty-one of them are Italian families, and only 2 occur among the 130 families of American, Teutonic, and Irish descent. All of the 24 Irish families report something spent for reading. (Table 110, page 217.)

Almost all of the money spent under this general head goes for newspapers. One or two 1-cent dailies 6 days in the week, and 5 cents weekly for a Sunday paper, amounts to between $5 and $8 a year, according to the number of one-cent papers purchased. In a few cases (printers or barbers), newspapers are obtained without cost. What kind of newspapers are read may be seen in Table 111 (page 218), from which it appears that the "Journal" and "World" are far in the lead with readers of English; that there are some in all of the foreign-speaking nationalities that read the papers printed in English; and that among the Russians, Austrians and Italians a majority of the people buy papers printed in their native tongues. Of the 158 families of the first 4 nationalities on our list, 78 mention the "Journal" or "American," 59 the "World," and 16 all other newspapers. In 25 cases, however, the name of the paper bought is not stated. There are 160 families in the group comprising Bohemians, Russians, Austrians and Italians. Twenty-six of these name the "Journal," 16 the "World," and none any other paper in English. Ninety-one, or 57 per cent., buy papers in the foreign languages, and 30 cases are reported in which newspapers are bought, but no names of papers are given.*

* The following list shows the papers mentioned, outside of the "Journal" and "World," with the number of families reporting each paper:

Press	5
Sun	2
Times	2
Herald	3
Eagle	2
St. Andrew's Cross	1
The Worker	1
Carried forward	16

Newspapers are less frequently omitted by families with $900 and $1000 than by those with lower incomes. Ninety-three per cent. of all families in the 2 highest income-groups have newspapers, as against 79 per cent. in the 2 lowest income-groups. By nationalities, practically every family in the first 3 nationality-groups has newspapers, while 21 of the 57 Italian families go without, and 13 of the 89 Russian and Austrian families.

As an indication of interest in reading, questions were put as to whether there were books in the house, and whether use was made of the public library. The answers to these questions are tabulated in Tables 109 and 110 (pages 216, 217), and show that books were reported in 97 of the 318 families, or 30.5 per cent., and that use of the library was reported in 68 cases, or 21.4 per cent. The figures, as far as they go, indicate a somewhat greater use of books by the families with larger incomes. The books most frequently named were novels and religious books.*

Brought forward	16
Eternal Progress	1
Munsey's Argosy	2
Ladies' Home Journal	1
Standard Union	2
Herald	9
Journal (German)	3
Volkszeitung	1
Staatszeitung	2
Tageblatt	7
Morgen	1
Wahrheit	11
Amerikaner	3
Vorwärts	21
New Yorker Liste	5
Amerika Echo	2
Freedom (Hungarian)	1
Slovak American	1
Italo Amerikano	3
Progresso	5
Heraldo	8
Bollettino dela Sera	8
Telegrapho	6
Total	119

Only 3 families, all Americans, mention monthly magazines.

* Outside of the items tabulated, some interesting details appeared in the schedules. One Jewish family, recently arrived, was paying a Rabbi $3 a month for teaching two children. Twenty-five cents was entered, in one schedule, as paid for writing a letter. The entries for postage and stationery are seldom more than a few cents. One schedule reports, "In 3 years 1 letter, 3 cents."

TABLE 109.—EDUCATION AND READING. AVERAGE ANNUAL EXPENDITURE AND PER CENT. OF FAMILIES REPORTING USE OF NEWSPAPERS, BOOKS, PUBLIC LIBRARY.—BY INCOME.

INCOME.	NUMBER OF FAMILIES.	FAMILIES SPENDING LESS THAN 75 CENTS.		FAMILIES REPORTING:						AVERAGE AMOUNT EXPENDED.*
				Newspapers.		Books at Home.		Use of Library.		
		Number.	Per Cent.	Number.	Per Cent.	Number.	Per Cent.	Number.	Per Cent.	
$600 to $699....	72	17	24	53	74	20	28	15	21	$5.56
$700 to $799....	79	11	14	66	84	21	27	11	14	4.93
$800 to $899....	73	10	14	60	82	27	37	14	19	7.66
$900 to $999....	63	4	6	57	90	16	25	18	29	6.70
$1000 to $1099....	31	1	3	30	97	13	42	10	32	8.54
$400 to $599....	25	5	20	18	72	10	40	4	16	3.64
$600 to $799....	151	28	11	119	79	41	27	26	17	4.69
$800 to $899....	73	10	14	60	82	27	37	14	19	7.66
$900 to $1099....	94	5	5	87	93	29	31	28	30	7.08
$1100 and over....	48	..	..	45	94	27	56	14	29	10.33†

* Average of families spending.
† Average of 41 families with incomes between $1100 and $1599.

216

TABLE 110.—EDUCATION AND READING. AVERAGE ANNUAL EXPENDITURE, AND NUMBER OF FAMILIES REPORTING USE OF NEWSPAPERS, BOOKS, PUBLIC LIBRARY.—BY NATIONALITY AND INCOME.

NATIONALITY.	$600 to $699						$700 to $799						$800 to $899					
	Average Amount.	Number of Families.		Number Reporting.			Average Amount.	Number of Families.		Number Reporting.			Average Amount.	Number of Families.		Number Reporting.		
		Total.	With no Expenditure.*	Newspapers.	Books.	Use of Library.		Total.	With no Expenditure.*	Newspapers.	Books.	Use of Library.		Total.	With no Expenditure.*	Newspapers.	Books.	Use of Library.
United States...	$6.13	11	..	11	1	2	$5.80	19	..	18	4	5	$8.81	13	..	13	5	5
Teutonic.......	7.33	4	..	4	1	1	5.29	7	1	7	1	1	8.09	9	..	9	3	3
Irish..........	8.16	4	..	4	..	..	6.01	7	..	6	..	..	11.95	7	..	7	3	3
Colored........	5.43	11	3	6	4	3	7.36	6	..	6	4	..	5.49	8	1	6	2	..
Bohemian......	6.39	4	2	2	3	1	6.57	3	..	3	..	1	5.62	3	..	2	..	1
Russian........	5.43	16	3	13	5	3	4.12	14	2	10	5	3	6.55	12	1	10	4	..
Austrian, etc....	5.85	6	3	4	1	2	3.16	9	2	8	..	1	10.03	9	1	8	5	2
Italian.........	3.27	16	6	9	5	3	3.08	14	6	8	7	..	2.74	12	7	5	5	..
Total.........	5.56	72	17	53	20	15	4.93	79	11	66	21	11	7.66	73	10	60	27	14

NATIONALITY.	$900 to $999						$1000 to $1099						Total.					
	Average Amount.	Number of Families.		Number Reporting.			Average Amount.	Number of Families.		Number Reporting.			Average Amount.	Number of Families.		Number Reporting.		
		Total.	With no Expenditure.*	Newspapers.	Books.	Use of Library.		Total.	With no Expenditure.*	Newspapers.	Books.	Use of Library.		Total.	With no Expenditure.*	Newspapers.	Books.	Use of Library.
United States...	$7.82	16	..	16	4	4	$11.53	8	1	7	2	3	$7.85	67	1	65	16	19
Teutonic.......	7.34	11	..	11	2	1	10.98	8	..	8	4	4	8.10	39	1	39	11	10
Irish..........	5.55	5	..	4	1	..	6.22	1	..	1	..	1	8.01	24	..	22	4	4
Colored........	3.74	2	..	1	..	..	3.60	1	..	1	1	..	5.94	28	4	20	11	3
Bohemian......	5.98	4	1	3	3	2	..	..	..	..	..	..	6.14	14	3	10	6	5
Russian........	5.91	9	..	9	3	5	7.22	6	..	6	1	1	6.14	57	6	48	18	12
Austrian, etc....	7.82	7	1	6	1	4	6.90	1	..	1	1	1	7.61	32	7	27	8	10
Italian.........	5.48	9	2	7	2	2	4.62	6	..	6	4	..	4.37	57	21	35	23	5
Total.........	6.70	63	4	57	16	18	8.54	31	1	30	13	10	6.98	318	43	266	97	68

* Including cases with expenditure less than 75 cents.

217

TABLE 111.—EDUCATION AND READING. NUMBER OF FAMILIES REPORTING PURCHASE OF GIVEN NEWS-PAPERS.—BY NATIONALITY.

Nationality.	Number of Families.	Number of Families Reporting News-papers.	"Journal" and "American."	"World."	Other U.S. Papers.	Magazines.	Papers in Foreign Languages.	Not Specified.	Total.
United States.....	67	65	38	29	11	3	..	8	89
Teutonic........	39	39	20	13	2	..	7	11	53
Irish...........	24	22	13	8	1	..	..	4	26
Colored........	28	20	7	9	2	..	..	2	20
Bohemian......	14	10	3	3	2	..	6	2	16
Russian.......	57	48	8	2	..	..	37	13	60
Austrian, etc......	32	27	8	5	..	..	18	8	39
Italian........	57	35	7	6	..	..	30	7	50
Total.........	318	266	104	75	18	3	98	55	353

5. MISCELLANEOUS EXPENDITURES.—Under this head are included items not easily classified under any of the preceding heads. Here fall expenditures for tobacco, for alcoholic drinks away from home, for barber's services; the spending money not otherwise accounted for, funeral expenses, the cost of moving, and a variety of other charges.

The expenditures for these miscellaneous items are an expression of the individuality of the members of the family. The range for such expression is very restricted on the narrow incomes, but increases with increase of resources. The expenditures chosen out of those included in this group are also an index of the character and experiences of the members of the family. An excessive drink-bill tells its own story; an entry of $50 for repayment of debts suggests a happier state of affairs.

A comparison of the averages of the amounts included under miscellaneous expenditures for the different income-groups shows a marked increase with increase of income (Table 112, page 224). The averages for the 5 income-groups between $600 and $1100 are $25.47, $32.38, $41.31, $45.51, $63.31. The average for the 150 families with incomes between $600 and $800 is $27.09; for the 94 families with incomes between $900 and $1100 is $51.38, or nearly twice as much as for the poorer families. Tables 113 and 114 (pages 224–225) show the number of families spending sums within given limits, in each income-group. The preponderance of entries of the lower sums for the smaller incomes is as striking as the frequency of the larger sums on the higher incomes. Table 114 (page 225) shows that only 1* of the 25 families with less than $600 a year spends over $30 for miscellanies, that 61 per cent. of the families with from $600 to $800 a year do not exceed this limit, and that only 36 per cent. of the families with from $900 to $1100 a year fall below it. Of the 48 families with $1100 a year and more, only 8, or 16.7 per cent., spend less than $30 for miscellaneous items, and 58 per cent. report more than $50.

The different nationalities show little difference in the total amount charged to the account of miscellaneous expenditures. A few large entries for certain families bring up the averages

---

* This family, under-fed and in poor health, reports $66.40 for spending money, probably for intoxicants.

in a few cases, but Table 115 (page 226) shows a general correspondence in the number of families spending given amounts. Even more striking is Table 116, showing these data for the two groups of nationalities; the first group comprising Americans, the Teutonic nations, Irish and colored; the second, Bohemians, Russians, Austrians and Italians. It appears that almost exactly the same number is to be found spending less than $30, from $30 to $50, and over $50.

It will not be without importance to consider some of these items separately. The details included under the title "miscellaneous" are sometimes concealed under the general head of "spending money." The schedule asked for a return of spending-money for the different members of the family, and in some cases this was entered at large as 50 cents or $1 a week, without further explanation. In other words there was obvious duplication with other entries, as for tobacco and car-fare. In the sheets showing details for each family, these duplications have been eliminated and nothing is charged to spending-money which is elsewhere charged to tobacco, car-fare or other stated objects of expenditure. In many families the mother is the cashier and receives her husband's wage week by week, allowing him out of it a fixed sum, say $1 or $2, for his pocket-money. Out of this he pays for car-fare, lunches, tobacco, and what not. To the children small sums are given from time to time, but seldom as a regular amount every week. Under the general head of spending money are sometimes included expenditures for questionable purposes, such as an excessive amount for drink, or for gambling. No attempt has been made to draw the line in such cases.

Expenditures reported for tobacco are shown in Tables 117 and 118 (pages 227–228). The average amounts expended increase from $9.40 for the $600 incomes, to $16.16 for incomes between $1000 and $1100. This would mean a little under 20 cents a week in the first case, and something over 30 cents a week in the second case. The Russians and Austrians report a relatively high expenditure for this purpose, although a larger proportion of cases with no expenditure for tobacco is reported from these nationalities than from any others. The use of tobacco is reported in all but 63 of the 318 families with incomes between $600 and $1100. In 8 cases it is reported as received without cost, either as a gift, or in connection with employment in the tobacco trades. Its use is so general that it must be included as forming part of the established standard of living.

The returns in regard to alcoholic drinks away from home are so incomplete as to warrant small inference from them. In certain cases the details are given with completeness, as stated in another connection (page 133). But more often the expenditure for drink has been hidden under "spending money," or "meals away from home," or in one or two obvious instances omitted entirely, leaving an apparent surplus quite irreconcilable with the meager provision reported for the necessities of life. The amount actually reported for drinks away from home may safely be considered as not exaggerated. It has been included in the table concerning alcoholic drinks at home (page 149). A few exceptionally large entries for drinks away from home are $200 in the $800 group of Americans, $233.60 for one $1000 American family. No sums so large as these are reported by the families of other nationalities. For the Italians the returns give something under this head for three-fourths of the families. The amounts are usually not large. In a few cases occurs an entry of from $30 to $40, or about 10 cents a day. Illustrations for the temperance lecturer may be found in the report of one woman that she bought heavy cups so the drunken husband might not break them, and in the entry under "playthings for children" that the only expenditure was on one occasion when the father was drunk and bought a 5-cent toy for each child.

For the services of the barber something is reported from the great majority of families. The children's hair is often cut at home. One case of co-operative hair-cutting is reported—"The neighbors cut the father's hair." But for the most part the barber is patronized for this service, and in the majority of cases for shaving also. A count of the cases shows that in 176 of the 318 cases, or 55 per cent., there is resort to the barber for shaving at least once a week. The cost is usually 10 cents, in some cases 5; or for hair-cut and shave together, 25 cents. The distribution of the 176 families by income and nationality may be seen in the footnote.*

The amount of expenditure for funerals is reported in only 12 cases. The amounts range from $30 to $50 for the funeral of a child, to $130 for the funeral of an adult. In 8 of the 12 cases expenditures are reported of from $30 to $50; in the other 4 cases the amounts are $65, $78, $120, $130. The details of these expenditures are not given. In one case it is stated that $40 out of the $65 spent was given by relatives.

For moving, expenditures vary. Three dollars, $5 and $7 are common entries under this head, but the entries are too few to warrant tabulation.

Expenditures for candy, ice cream and soda water are reported in a number of schedules. A dollar a week in the summer is perhaps the maximum entry. Another family reports $18.20 for the year for this purpose. The pennies of the children that go for these luxuries are more often entered under the head of spending money for children.

It remains only to notice a few single cases where a large entry among the miscellaneous items sheds some light on the gen-

---

*FAMILIES REPORTING EXPENDITURE FOR SHAVING AT THE BARBER'S.

	By Nationality.				By Income.		
	Total Number of Families.	With Expenditure for Shaving.			Total Number of Families.	With Expenditure for Shaving.	
		Number.	Per Cent.			Number.	Per Cent.
United States....	67	38	57	$600 to $699....	72	31	43
Teutonic........	39	19	49	$700 to $799....	79	41	52
Irish...........	24	12	50	$800 to $899....	73	39	53
Colored.........	28	7	25	$900 to $999....	63	44	70
Bohemian.......	14	10	71	$1000 to $1099....	31	21	68
Russian.........	57	43	75				
Austrian........	32	25	78		318	176	55
Italian..........	57	22	39				
	318	176	55				

eral conditions of work and life. One milk-driver receives an allowance, in addition to regular wages, of $2 a week from his employer, which he is expected to spend among the small dealers to whom he delivers milk. Another milk-driver is required to deposit $200 with his employer as surety for his honesty. One man, earning $1300 a year, paid $48 for a watch and chain for his wife; one gas-fitter, with an income of $1600, was obliged to make good the loss of $250 worth of materials stolen from a building where he had been employed. In most of the cases, however, where the amount spent for miscellanies reaches $75 or more, it is accounted for under the vague term "spending money", or under the items of tobacco and drink.

TABLE 112.—MISCELLANEOUS EXPENDITURES. AVERAGE ANNUAL
EXPENDITURE OF ALL FAMILIES.—BY INCOME
AND NATIONALITY.

NATIONALITY.	$600 TO $699		$700 TO $799		$800 TO $899		$900 TO $999		$1000 TO $1099	
	Number of Families.	Average Expenditure.	Number of Families.	Average Expenditure.	Number of Families.	Average Expenditure.	Number of Families.	Average Expenditure.	Number of Families.	Average Expenditure.
United States .	11	$35.65	19	$26.02	13	$45.12	16	$45.77	8	$72.55
Teutonic	4	14.66	7	23.59	9	60.93	11	52.59	8	54.29
Irish.........	4	18.23	7	23.06	7	24.73	5	57.42	1	30.80
Colored	11	21.87	6	24.17	8	41.02	2	40.43	1	159.80
Bohemian	4	13.85	3	23.60	3	20.91	4	24.74	..	..
Russian	16	20.77	14	37.98	12	32.21	9	57.70	6	76.59
Austrian, etc..	6	22.92	9	33.19	9	52.96	7	43.44	1	24.00
Italian	16	34.04	14	49.34	12	37.77	9	29.53	6	45.60
Average......	72	25.47	79	32.38	73	41.31	63	45.51	31	63.31

TABLE 113.—MISCELLANEOUS EXPENDITURES. NUMBER AND
PER CENT. OF FAMILIES REPORTING EXPENDITURE
OF GIVEN AMOUNTS.—BY INCOME.

INCOME.	NUMBER OF FAMILIES.	FAMILIES WITH EXPENDITURE OF:					
		Under $30		$30 to $50		Over $50	
		Number.	Per Cent.	Number.	Per Cent.	Number.	Per Cent.
$600 to $699......	72	50	69.5	15	20.8	7	9.7
$700 to $799......	79	42	53.2	22	27.8	15	19.0
$800 to $899......	73	37	49.5	19	26.0	17	24.5
$900 to $999......	63	24	38.1	21	33.3	18	28.6
$1000 to $1099......	31	10	32.2	6	19.3	15	48.5
Total, $600 to $1099	318	163	51.1	83	26.2	72	22.7
$400 to $599......	25	24	96.0	..	..	1	4.0
$600 to $799......	151	92	60.9	37	24.5	22	14.6
$800 to $899......	73	37	49.5	19	26.0	17	24.5
$900 to $1099......	94	34	36.2	27	28.7	33	35.1
$1100 and over.....	48	8	16.7	12	25.0	28	58.3

TABLE 114.—MISCELLANEOUS EXPENDITURES. NUMBER OF FAMILIES REPORTING EXPENDITURE OF GIVEN AMOUNTS.—BY INCOME.

INCOME.	TOTAL NUMBER OF FAMILIES.	EXPENDITURE.										
		Under $10	$10 to $20	$20 to $30	$30 to $40	$40 to $50	$50 to $60	$60 to $70	$70 to $80	$80 to $90	$90 to $100	Over $100
$400 to $499	8	4	2	1	..	..	..	..	1	..	..	..
$500 to $599	17	5	9	3	..	..	..	..	..	..	..	..
Total, $400 to $599	25	9	11	4	..	..	..	..	1	..	..	..
$600 to $699	72	11	18	21	8	7	2	3	1	1	..	..
$700 to $799	79	8	20	14	13	9	6	5	1	..	1	2
$800 to $899	73	6	15	16	8	11	8	2	1	1	..	5
$900 to $999	63	1	10	13	13	8	4	3	2	2	2	5
$1000 to $1099	31	..	4	6	5	1	1	..	5	2	2	5
Total, $600 to $1099	318	26	67	70	47	36	21	13	10	6	5	17
$1100 to $1199	18	..	2	1	4	2	2	..	2	1	1	3
$1200 to $ 299	8	1	..	..	1	1	..	..	2	..	..	3
$1300 to $1399	8	..	..	1	..	1	..	2	..	..	..	4
$1400 to $1499	1	..	..	..	..	..	1	..	..	..	..	..
$1500 to $1599	6	1	..	..	1	1	1	..	..	..	1	1
$1600 and over	7	1	..	1	1	..	1	..	..	..	..	3
Total, $1100 and over	48	3	2	3	7	5	5	2	4	1	2	14

TABLE 115.—MISCELLANEOUS EXPENDITURES. NUMBER OF FAMILIES REPORTING EXPENDITURE OF GIVEN AMOUNTS.—BY NATIONALITY.

NATIONALITY.	Total Number of Families.	EXPENDITURE.										
		Under $10.	$10 to $20.	$20 to $30.	$30 to $40.	$40 to $50.	$50 to $60.	$60 to $70.	$70 to $80.	$80 to $90.	$90 to $100.	Over $100.
United States	67	6	16	9	11	7	8	4	..	1	2	3
Teutonic	39	2	9	7	8	3	3	..	1	..	1	5
Irish	24	3	5	9	2	2	..	1	..	..	1	1
Colored	28	4	5	7	5	3	..	1	1	1	..	1
Bohemian	14	3	5	1	4	1	..	..	..	..	..	..
Russian	57	2	15	15	3	5	4	3	6	2	..	2
Austrian, etc.	32	3	4	11	3	4	1	2	..	1	1	2
Italian	57	3	8	11	11	11	5	2	2	1	..	3
Total	318	26	67	70	47	36	21	13	10	6	5	17

TABLE 116.—MISCELLANEOUS EXPENDITURES. NUMBER OF FAMILIES SPENDING GIVEN AMOUNTS.—BY NATIONALITY-GROUPS AND INCOME.

INCOME.	Total Number of Families.		Under $30.		$30 to $50.		Over $50.	
	Group I.*	Group II.†	Group I.	Group II.	Group I.	Group II.	Group I.	Group II.
$600 to $699	30	42	22	28	4	11	4	3
$700 to $799	39	40	24	18	11	11	4	11
$800 to $899	37	36	20	17	9	10	8	9
$900 to $999	34	29	11	13	12	9	11	7
$1000 to $1099	18	13	5	5	5	1	8	7
Total	158	160	82	81	41	42	35	37

* Group I includes Americans, Teutonic nations, Irish, and colored.
† Group II includes Bohemians, Russians, Austrians, etc., and Italians.

TABLE 117.—TOBACCO. AVERAGE EXPENDITURE OF ALL FAMILIES.—BY INCOME.

INCOME.	NUMBER OF FAMILIES.	REPORTING NO EXPENDITURE.		AVERAGE AMOUNT.
		Number.	Per Cent.	
$600 to $699	72	20	27	$9.40
$700 to $799	79	17	22	10.81
$800 to $899	73	15	21	11.52
$900 to $999	63	13	21	11.63
$1000 to $1099	31	6	19	16.16
$400 to $599	25	7	28	$6.48
$600 to $799	151	37	24	9.74
$800 to $899	73	15	21	11.52
$900 to $1099	94	19	20	13.15
$1100 and over	48	18	37	14.85*

* Average of expenditures reported by 26 families reporting; incomes, $1100 to $1599.

TABLE 118.—TOBACCO. AVERAGE EXPENDITURE OF ALL FAMI-LIES.—BY NATIONALITY AND INCOME.

NATIONALITY.	$600 TO $699. Number of Families. Total.	With no Expenditure.	Average Amount.	$700 TO $799. Number of Families. Total.	With no Expenditure.	Average Amount.	$800 TO $899. Number of Families. Total.	With no Expenditure.	Average Amount.
United States	11	2	$ 8.21	19	5	$11.31	13	3	$10.74
Teutonic	4	..	5.25	7	3	10.78	9	1	11.05
Irish	4	2	5.06	7	2	6.64	7	1	8.27
Colored	11	3	8.12	6	2	9.10	8	1	12.21
Bohemian	4	2	5.65	3	..	6.07	3	1	7.80
Russian	16	7	8.66	14	5	16.09	12	2	12.65
Austrian, etc.	6	2	13.00	9	..	13.36	9	3	17.06
Italian	16	2	11.25	14	..	8.29	12	3	10.33
Total	72	20	9.40	79	17	10.81	73	15	11.52

NATIONALITY.	$900 TO $999. Number of Families. Total.	With no Expenditure.	Average Amount.	$1000 TO $1099. Number of Families. Total.	With no Expenditure.	Average Amount.	TOTAL. Number of Families. Total.	With no Expenditure.	Average Amount.
United States	16	1	$10.09	8	1	$24.03	67	12	$10.16
Teutonic	11	3	15.29	8	2	10.53	39	9	11.29
Irish	5	1	12.42	1	..	13.00	24	6	8.65
Colored	2	..	5.20	1	..	7.80	28	6	9.32
Bohemian	4	3	10.40	..	..	..	14	6	6.94
Russian	9	1	13.10	6	2	14.07	57	17	13.25
Austrian, etc.	7	1	13.84	1	..	5.20	32	6	13.95
Italian	9	3	8.28	6	1	18.08	57	9	10.55
Total	63	13	11.63	31	6	16.16	318	71	10.98

IV. Relation of Income to Expenditure

Having considered the elements of the subsistence that our families provide, it remains to consider the question how far they are able to provide this subsistence out of the incomes that they have. If a family is able to make both ends meet out of its income, it seems a fair inference that it is able to maintain such standard of living as is represented by its expenditures. Still more probable is this if the family has a surplus of income over expenditures. This is not to say that the standard maintained is normal or adequate, however. It may be so low that in the course of a few years, if not sooner, the physique and morale of the family must deteriorate, or the effects may be apparent only in the gradual deterioration of a whole group of the population in the course of one or two generations. This deterioration may be going on at the same time that individual families are living as best they can within their incomes. The comparison of income with expenditure has therefore been deferred until after the examination of the main items of expenditure in the several income-groups.

In comparing the income and expenditure of the families included in our tables, three classes have been made: families with an even balance, those showing a surplus, and those reporting a deficiency. In view of the probabilities of error in the estimates which the figures represent, a margin of $25 has been allowed, and all cases where the difference either way between income and expenditure does not exceed this sum, are counted as having neither surplus nor deficiency. Tables 119 and 120 (pages 235–236) show the results of this enumeration. Of the 318 families that have incomes between $600 and $1100, 116 show an even balance within $25, 116 show a surplus, and 86 show a deficiency. Of the 25 families with incomes under $600, 13 came out even within $25, 5 show a surplus of more than $25, and 7 show a deficiency. Among the 48 families with incomes of $1100 and above, 15 come out within the $25 limit, 22 report a surplus, and 11 a deficiency. This comparison shows that there are extravagant families and economical families on whatever income. It suggests also, what figures already presented substantiate, that the families that

229

make both ends meet on less than $600 are living far below the normal standard.

Examining by income-groups the returns for the 318 families with incomes between $600 and $1100, we find that the percentage of those reporting deficiency tends to diminish with increase of income, but with a movement in the opposite direction for the $800 groups. The table of averages shows no such interruption,* so that the amount of the deficiency must be smaller in the families with incomes of $800 and $900, even if the number of families reporting deficiency increases. The table indicates that a comfortable margin of income over expenditure is first possible with an income between $800 and $900.

If the column · showing the number of families reporting a surplus be examined, it will be found that the percentage here increases from 28 in the $600 group to 42 in the $1000 group. The $800 families, which report the largest percentage of families with deficit, report also the largest percentage of families with a surplus, 48 per cent., and the smallest percentage (22) of families with balance within $25. An examination of the tabulation by nationalities furnishes an explanation of these variations. In the $800 income-group, only 3 families of our second nationality-group (Bohemians, Russians, Austrians, Italians) report a deficit, or 8 per cent., while of the 37 families in the first nationality-group (Americans, Teutonic nations, Irish, colored) 19, or 50 per cent., report a deficit. The standard set by the nations of Southern Europe can be attained on $800 much more certainly than the American standard.†

The figures for the various nationalities taken by income-groups and as a whole tend to confirm the inference that has been made regarding the difference between the American standard and that of the natives of Southern Europe. Only 32 of the 86 families

* Income Groups.		Average Total Income.	Average Total Expenditure.
$600 to	$699	$650.17	$650.57
700 to	799	748.83	735.98
800 to	899	846.26	811.88
900 to	999	942.03	906.70
1,000 to	1,099	1,044.48	1,009.57

† It appears further that these 37 families of the first group contain an exceptional proportion of families with high equivalents in demand for food.

reporting a deficiency are in the 4 nationalities representing Southern Europe, although these 4 comprise a full half of the 318 families under discussion. Further, of these 32 families only 11 are found in the 3 income-groups above $800. If we look at the families reporting a surplus, we find that more than 50 per cent. of all Russian, Austrian, and Italian families report a surplus as against only 23 per cent. of the American and Teutonic families. Even on incomes between $600 and $800, among the combined Russian, Austrian and Italian families, a surplus is reported by 39 per cent. of the families in the $600 group and by 49 per cent. in the $700 group, as compared with 17 per cent. of the combined nationalities of the first group (American, Teutonic, Irish, colored) in the $600 group, and 21 per cent. in the $700 group.

Taking all incomes together, the largest percentage of families with deficit is found among the colored people (43 per cent.); the next largest (37 per cent.) is reported by the American families; the largest percentage with surplus is 58, which falls to the Italians; next come the Russians, with 51 per cent.; while the lowest percentage, as has already been stated, is found among the American and Teutonic families.

The economic disadvantage of the family not drawing upon other sources of income than the father's earnings appears in a comparison of the standing, as regards surplus and deficit, of the families of this sort and families with a composite income. This may be found in Tables 121–123 (pages 237–239). In every income-group from $500 up to $1100, the percentage of families reporting a deficit is larger among the families supported only by the father than in the other class; the percentage reporting surplus is smaller in the greater number of income-groups, and for these families as a whole, than for the families with composite income.

A survey of the various nationalities represented in the tables shows the same tendency in favor of the families with composite income (Tables 121 and 122, pages 237–238). For the 67 American families, 45 per cent. of those supported by the father alone report a deficit, and 26 per cent. of the families with composite income. The percentage of families reporting a surplus is the same for both classes, namely, 22 per cent., but the percentage of families with even balance is 52 for the families with composite income and but 33 for families supported by the father alone. Among the Irish and Russians only is there an exception. However, there are only 7 Irish families altogether with composite income. Even in the Russian families those with composite income show a larger percentage with surplus than the families supported by the father alone.

Considered from the view-point of the content of a standard of living, this tendency indicates that where the families are compelled to resort to the supplementary sources of income, they are either content with a lower standard of comforts than families of the other class, or are able to attain it at a lower expense. Put in another form, it appears that many families send their children to work at an early age, and cramp their housing accommodations by taking lodgers, in order to lay up money, rather than to maintain a given standard of living in their current expenditures. This interpretation is supported by corroborative details in a large number of the individual schedules for families with composite income, especially those of the families of foreign birth.

The under-fed, under-clothed, and over-crowded families (Tables 124–126, pages 240–242), as has already been shown, make a better showing in keeping expenditures within income than do the families as a whole. This indicates that on the lower incomes, where most of these cases with sub-normal standard are found, an even balance or a surplus can be attained only by curtailing expenditures for necessaries below the point of meeting the requirements of healthy existence. This inference is further substantiated by noting the location, by income-classes, of the families that are reported as below the minimum standards assumed. Table 124 (page 240) shows that two-thirds of the 33 families, both under-fed and under-clothed, have incomes under $800; two-thirds (29 out of 45) of the families both under-fed and over-crowded, and two-thirds (56 out of 81) of the families under-clothed and over-crowded are likewise in the same income-classes. Fourteen of the 20 families below standard in all three respects are in the $600 and $700 income-groups, 5 are in the $800 group, and only 1 among the families with incomes above $900.

Table 127 (page 243) shows the returns made as to savings, and as to insurance that is comparable with saving; that is, where the policy, whether an ordinary life policy, or one of the endowment type, is for a sum that represents something more than burial expenses. The table shows the number of families reporting that they had savings in one form or another, and the number reporting an insurance policy of $500 or over, the limit of $500 being arbitrarily assumed as marking something more than the ordinary industrial or burial insurance. It should be remembered that not all families reporting a surplus of income over expenditure admitted possessing savings or investments in any form; hence the numbers in the table doubtless are under-statements. At the same time, there is no reason to suppose that the concealment of savings and investment would be more frequent in one income-group than in another.

Taking the figures as they stand, savings are reported by 15 per cent. of the $600 families, 20 per cent. of the $700 families, 38 per cent. of those with incomes between $800 and $900, 23 per cent. of those in the $900 group, and 45 per cent. of the $1000 families. Insurance of $500 or more is reported in about the same proportion of families in each income-group, and by 56, or 18 per cent., of the 318 families under consideration.* These figures, so far as they go, show that saving is relatively infrequent until the $800 line is reached.†

The converse of savings is borrowing (Table 128, page 244). Here, too, the reports cannot be assumed to be inclusive of all actual cases among our families. It is safe to assume that borrowing did occur in every case where it is reported. Pawning is reported in about half of the cases of borrowing. Only 42 of the 318 families admit borrowing, and 23 pawning. Inasmuch as the amount borrowed is not in every case stated, it is not possible always to distinguish between small sums borrowed in anticipation of pay-day, and loans of considerable sums to meet a serious deficiency of income, or provide for an extraordinary emergency.

* By nationalities, the American families report savings in the smallest number of cases (save the Irish), and the largest number of cases of life insurance. The Italians report the largest proportion of families with savings (29 out of 57), but no insurance for as much as $500. About one-third of the Russian and of the Teutonic families report savings.

† The savings are not always invested in savings banks. Several families reported buying lots in Long Island or New Jersey; one or two reported making additions to business capital.

Taking the figures for what they are worth, nearly half of the cases of borrowing reported (20 out of 42) are in the $600 income-group; one-quarter are in the $700 group.   The pawning reported is likewise nearly half of it in the $600 families.   This corroborates the suggestion already made, that the task of making both ends meet is too severe to be successfully accomplished in ordinary circumstances, on all incomes under $800, without a lowering of the standard of living below the normal demands of health, working efficiency, and social decency.*

* The question, "In case of retrenchment, what expenditures are curtailed?" while not eliciting all that was hoped for, brought out some suggestive answers. In one case it is reported that "In case of retrenchment they live principally on bread and coffee or tea, curtailing all other expenses for food." In other cases clothing, amusements, and certain articles of food are mentioned.   More eloquent than these answers are the pages of the books that show the severest struggle with poverty,—the absence of entries for newspapers, society dues, recreation in any form. The meager diet is epitomized in this quotation: "I believe we can eat more, but it has to be sufficient." Another family buys cracked eggs: "They are much cheaper, about one cent each." Economy in dress is well represented by the statement regarding the expenditures for hats of a woman married some ten years, "One hat, bought long before she knew him."

TABLE 119.—SURPLUS AND DEFICIT. NUMBER OF FAMILIES REPORTING.—BY NATIONALITY AND INCOME.

Nationality.	Total Number of Families.	$600 to $699 Balance within $25.00.	$600 to $699 Surplus.	$600 to $699 Deficit.	$700 to $799 Balance within $25.00.	$700 to $799 Surplus.	$700 to $799 Deficit.	$800 to $899 Balance within $25.00.	$800 to $899 Surplus.	$800 to $899 Deficit.	$900 to $999 Balance within $25.00.	$900 to $999 Surplus.	$900 to $999 Deficit.	$1000 to $1099 Balance within $25.00.	$1000 to $1099 Surplus.	$1000 to $1099 Deficit.	Total Balance within $25. Number.	Total Balance within $25. Per Cent.	Total Surplus. Number.	Total Surplus. Per Cent.	Total Deficit. Number.	Total Deficit. Per Cent.
United States	67	6	3	2	10	3	6	3	4	6	3	5	8	5	..	3	27	40	15	23	25	37
Teutonic	39	4	..	..	3	3	1	4	1	4	6	3	2	4	2	2	21	54	9	23	9	23
Irish	24	2	1	1	3	1	3	..	3	4	4	1	..	..	1	..	9	38	7	29	8	33
Colored	28	5	1	5	3	1	2	..	3	5	1	1	..	..	1	..	9	32	7	25	12	43
Bohemian	14	2	..	2	3	..	..	3	..	..	4	..	..	..	..	..	12	86	..	..	2	14
Russian	57	5	6	5	2	8	4	1	10	1	3	3	3	..	2	4	11	19	29	51	17	30
Austrian, etc.	32	2	4	..	4	4	1	4	4	1	3	3	1	..	1	..	13	41	16	50	3	9
Italian	57	5	5	6	5	6	3	1	10	1	3	6	..	..	6	..	14	25	33	58	10	17
Total	318	31	20	21	33	26	20	16	35	22	27	22	14	9	13	9	116	36.5	116	36.5	86	27

TABLE 120.—SURPLUS AND DEFICIT. NUMBER OF FAMILIES REPORTING.—BY INCOME.

Income.	Number of Families.	Balance within $25.00		Surplus.		Deficit.	
		Number.	Per Cent.	Number.	Per Cent.	Number.	Per Cent.
$400 to $499	8	5	63	..	..	3	37
$500 to $599	17	8	47	5	29	4	24
$600 to $699	72	31	43	20	28	21	29
$700 to $799	79	33	42	26	33	20	25
$800 to $899	73	16	22	35	48	22	30
$900 to $999	63	27	43	22	35	14	22
$1000 to $1099	31	9	29	13	42	9	29
$1100 to $1199	18	8	44	7	39	3	17
$1200 to $1299	8	3	38	2	25	3	38
$1300 to $1399	8	1	12	4	50	3	38
$1400 and over	14	3	22	9	64	2	14
Total	391	144	37	143	36	104	27

TABLE 121.—SURPLUS AND DEFICIT. NUMBER OF FAMILIES REPORTING INCOME FROM EARNINGS OF FATHER ONLY.—BY NATIONALITY AND INCOME.

NATIONALITY.	Total Number of Families.	$600 to $699			$700 to $799			$800 to $899			$900 to $999			$1000 to $1099			TOTAL.					
		Balance within $25.	Surplus.	Deficit.	Balance within $25.	Surplus.	Deficit.	Balance within $25.	Surplus.	Deficit.	Balance within $25.	Surplus.	Deficit.	Balance within $25.	Surplus.	Deficit.	Balance within $25. Number.	Balance within $25. Per Cent.	Surplus. Number.	Surplus. Per Cent.	Deficit. Number.	Deficit. Per Cent.
United States	40	5	3	2	5	2	4	2	2	3	:	2	7	1	:	2	13	33	9	22	18	45
Teutonic	20	5	:	:	:	2	:	2	:	3	4	2	2	:	1	2	8	40	5	25	7	35
Irish	17	2	1	1	2	1	2	:	2	1	4	1	:	:	:	:	8	47	5	30	4	23
Colored	12	3	1	5	2	:	1	:	:	:	:	:	:	:	:	:	5	42	1	8	6	50
Bohemian	3	1	:	:	2	:	:	:	:	:	:	:	:	:	:	:	3	100	:	:	:	:
Russian	21	5	4	2	:	3	3	:	2	:	1	1	:	:	:	:	6	29	10	48	5	23
Austrian, etc.	7	:	1	:	:	2	:	:	1	:	3	:	:	:	:	:	3	47	4	57	:	:
Italian	29	2	2	4	3	5	1	:	3	1	:	6	:	:	2	:	5	17	18	62	6	21
Total	149	20	12	14	14	15	11	4	10	8	12	12	9	1	3	4	51	34	52	35	46	31

TABLE 122.—SURPLUS AND DEFICIT. NUMBER OF FAMILIES REPORTING COMPOSITE INCOME.—BY NATIONALITY AND INCOME.

Nationality.	Total Number of Families.	$600 to $699 Balance within $25.	$600 to $699 Surplus.	$600 to $699 Deficit.	$700 to $799 Balance within $25.	$700 to $799 Surplus.	$700 to $799 Deficit.	$800 to $899 Balance within $25.	$800 to $899 Surplus.	$800 to $899 Deficit.	$900 to $999 Balance within $25.	$900 to $999 Surplus.	$900 to $999 Deficit.	$1000 to $1099 Balance within $25.	$1000 to $1099 Surplus.	$1000 to $1099 Deficit.	Total Balance within $25. Number.	Total Balance within $25. Per Cent.	Total Surplus. Number.	Total Surplus. Per Cent.	Total Deficit. Number.	Total Deficit. Per Cent.
United States	27	1	..	..	5	1	2	1	2	3	3	3	1	4	..	1	14	52	6	22	7	26
Teutonic	19	2	..	..	3	1	1	2	1	1	2	1	..	4	1	..	13	68	4	21	2	11
Irish	7	..	..	..	1	..	1	..	1	3	..	..	..	..	1	..	1	14	2	29	4	57
Colored	16	2	..	..	1	1	1	..	3	5	1	1	..	..	1	..	4	25	6	37.5	6	37.5
Bohemian	11	1	..	2	1	..	..	3	..	..	4	..	..	..	..	..	9	82	..	..	2	18
Russian	36	..	2	3	2	5	1	1	8	1	2	2	3	..	2	4	5	14	19	53	12	33
Austrian, etc.	25	2	3	..	4	2	1	4	3	1	..	3	1	..	1	..	10	40	12	48	3	12
Italian	28	3	3	2	2	1	2	1	7	..	3	..	..	..	4	..	9	32	15	54	4	14
Total	169	11	8	7	19	11	9	12	25	14	15	10	5	8	10	5	65	38	64	38	40	24

TABLE 123.—SURPLUS AND DEFICIT. NUMBER AND PER CENT. OF FAMILIES REPORTING.—BY SOURCES OF INCOME AND INCOME-GROUP.

INCOME.	TOTAL NUMBER OF FAMILIES.	FAMILIES SUPPORTED BY FATHER ALONE.							FAMILIES HAVING COMPOSITE INCOME.						
		Number of Families.	Balance within $25.00		Surplus.		Deficit.		Number of Families.	Balance within $25.00		Surplus.		Deficit.	
			Number.	Per Cent.	Number.	Per Cent.	Number.	Per Cent.		Number.	Per Cent.	Number.	Per Cent.	Number.	Per Cent.
$400 to $499	8	6	5	83	..	..	1	17	2	2	100	..	..	..	..
$500 to $599	17	14	6	43	4	28.5	4	28.5	3	2	67	1	33	..	..
$600 to $699	72	46	20	43	12	26	14	31	26	11	42	8	31	7	27
$700 to $799	79	40	14	35	15	38	11	27	39	19	49	11	28	9	23
$800 to $899	73	22	4	19	10	45	8	36	51	12	24	25	49	14	27
$900 to $999	63	33	12	36	12	36	9	28	30	15	50	10	33	5	17
$1000 to $1099	31	8	1	12	3	38	4	50	23	8	35	10	43	5	22
$1100 to $1199	18	7	3	42	2	29	2	29	11	5	45.5	5	45.5	1	9
$1200 to $1299	8	4	2	50	1	25	1	25	4	1	25	1	25	2	50
$1300 to $1399	8	2	..	..	2	100	..	..	6	1	17	2	33	3	50
$1400 and over	14	3	1	33	1	33	1	33	11	2	18	8	73	1	9
Total.........	391	185	68	37	62	33	55	30	206	78	38	81	39	47	23
$400 to $599	25	20	11	55	4	20	5	25	5	4	80	1	20	..	..
$600 to $1099	318	149	51	34	52	35	46	31	169	65	38	64	38	40	24
$1100 and over	48	16	6	37.5	6	37.5	4	25	32	9	28	16	50	7	22

239

TABLE 124.—NUMBER OF FAMILIES BELOW STANDARD AS REGARDS BOTH FOOD AND CLOTHING, BOTH FOOD AND SHELTER, OR BOTH SHELTER AND CLOTHING.—BY NATIONALITY AND INCOME.

NATIONALITY.	$600 to $699					$700 to $799					$800 to $899				
	Total Number of Families.	Number Under-fed and Under-clothed.	Number Under-fed and Over-crowded.	Number Under-clothed and Over-crowded.	Number Under-fed, Under-clothed, and Over-crowded.	Total Number of Families.	Number Under-fed and Under-clothed.	Number Under-fed and Over-crowded.	Number Under-clothed and Over-crowded.	Number Under-fed, Under-clothed, and Over-crowded.	Total Number of Families.	Number Under-fed and Under-clothed.	Number Under-fed and Over-crowded.	Number Under-clothed and Over-crowded.	Number Under-fed, Under-clothed, and Over-crowded.
United States..	11	3	2	3	2	19	1	2	3	..	13	..	..	..	..
Teutonic......	4	..	1	..	..	7	3	1	..	..	9	..	..	1	..
Irish..........	4	1	2	3	1	7	..	..	2	..	7	..	..	1	..
Colored........	11	2	1	6	..	6	..	2	2	..	8	1	1	..	..
Bohemian.....	4	..	1	..	..	3	..	1	1	..	3	..	1	..	..
Russian........	16	4	3	2	1	14	5	6	7	5	12	3	6	4	3
Austrian, etc...	6	1	2	2	1	9	2	3	5	2	9	3	3	3	2
Italian.........	16	2	2	12	..	14	..	..	8	..	12	..	..	9	..
Total.........	72	13	14	28	7	79	11	15	28	7	73	7	11	18	5

NATIONALITY.	$900 to $999					$1000 to $1099					TOTAL.				
	Total Number of Families.	Number Under-fed and Under-clothed.	Number Under-fed and Over-crowded.	Number Under-clothed and Over-crowded.	Number Under-fed, Under-clothed, and Over-crowded.	Total Number of Families.	Number Under-fed and Under-clothed.	Number Under-fed and Over-crowded.	Number Under-clothed and Over-crowded.	Number Under-fed, Under-clothed, and Over-crowded.	Total Number of Families.	Number Under-fed and Under-clothed.	Number Under-fed and Over-crowded.	Number Under-clothed and Over-crowded.	Number Under-fed, Under-clothed, and Over-crowded.
United States..	16	..	..	1	..	8	..	..	..	..	67	4	4	7	2
Teutonic... ..	11	..	..	..	..	8	..	..	..	..	39	3	2	1	..
Irish..........	5	..	..	..	..	1	..	..	..	..	24	1	2	6	1
Colored........	2	..	..	..	..	1	..	1	..	..	28	3	5	8	..
Bohemian.....	4	..	1	..	..	..	..	..	..	..	14	..	4	1	..
Russian.......	9	2	3	1	1	6	..	..	..	..	57	14	18	14	10
Austrian, etc ..	7	..	..	3	..	1	..	..	..	..	32	6	8	13	5
Italian.........	9	..	..	2	..	6	..	..	..	..	57	2	2	31	2
Total.........	63	2	4	7	1	31	..	1	..	..	318	33	45	81	20

TABLE 125.—FAMILIES UNDER-FED, UNDER-CLOTHED, AND OVER-CROWDED. NUMBER AND PERCENTAGES.—BY INCOME.

INCOME.	NUMBER OF FAMILIES.	UNDER-FED.		UNDER-CLOTHED.		OVER-CROWDED.		UNDER-FED AND UNDER-CLOTHED.		UNDER-FED AND OVER-CROWDED.		UNDER-CLOTHED AND OVER-CROWDED.	
		Number.	Per Cent.	Number.	Per Cent.	Number.	Per Cent.	Number.	Per Cent.	Number.	Per Cent.	Number.	Per Cent.
$400 to $499	8	8	100	7	88	5	63	7	88	5	63	4	50
$500 to $599	17	11	65	15	88	12	71	10	59	8	47	9	53
$600 to $699	72	24	33	45	63	41	57	13	18	14	19	28	39
$700 to $799	79	24	30	41	52	46	58	11	14	15	19	28	35
$800 to $899	73	16	22	23	32	39	53	7	10	11	15	18	25
$900 to $999	63	5	8	16	25	25	40	2	3	4	6	7	11
$1000 to $1099	31	3	10	1	3	9	30	..	..	1	3	..	..
$1100 to $1199	18	..	..	3	6	10	21	..	..	..	..	..	..
$1200 to $1299	8	..	..	..	..	..	..	..	..	..	..	..	..
$1300 to $1399	8	..	..	..	..	..	..	..	..	..	..	..	..
$1400 and over	14	..	..	..	..	..	..	..	..	..	..	..	..
Total.........	391	..	..	..	..	..	..	..	..	..	..	..	..
$400 to $599	25	19	76	22	88	17	68	17	68	13	52	13	52
$600 to $799	151	48	32	86	57	87	58	24	16	29	19	56	37
$800 to $899	73	16	22	23	32	39	53	7	10	11	15	18	25
$900 to $1099	94	8	9	17	18	34	36	2	2	5	5	7	7
$1100 and over	48	..	..	3	6	10	21	..	..	..	..	..	..

TABLE 126.—FAMILIES UNDER-FED, UNDER-CLOTHED, AND OVER-CROWDED. NUMBER AND PERCENTAGES.—BY INCOME AND SOURCES OF INCOME.

Income.	Number of Families.	Number Under-fed.	Under-fed with Income.				Number of Under-clothed.	Under-clothed with Income.				Number of Over-crowded.	Over-crowded with Income.			
			From Father only.		From other Sources.			From Father only.		From other Sources.			From Father only.		From other Sources.	
			Number.	Per Cent.	Number.	Per Cent.		Number.	Per Cent.	Number.	Per Cent.		Number.	Per Cent.	Number.	Per Cent.
$600 to $699	72	24	15	63	9	37	45	34	76	11	24	41	24	59	17	41
$700 to $799	79	24	11	46	13	54	41	19	46	22	54	46	20	43	26	57
$800 to $899	73	16	3	19	13	81	23	5	22	18	78	39	11	28	28	72
$900 to $999	63	5	1	20	4	80	16	5	31	11	69	25	9	36	16	64
$1000 to $1099	31	3	..	..	3	100	1	..	..	1	100	9	2	22	7	78
$600 to $799	151	48	26	54	22	46	86	53	62	33	38	87	44	51	43	49
$800 to $899	73	16	3	19	13	81	23	5	22	18	78	39	11	28	28	72
$900 to $1099	94	8	1	12	7	88	17	5	30	12	70	34	11	30	23	70

242

TABLE 127.—SAVINGS AND INSURANCE.* NUMBER OF FAMILIES REPORTING.—BY NATIONALITY AND INCOME.

NATIONALITY.	Number of Families.	$600 to $699.		$700 to $799.		$800 to $899.		$900 to $999.		$1000 to $1099.		TOTAL.	
		Savings.	Insurance.	Savings.	Insurance.	Savings.	Insurance.	Savings.	Insurance.	Savings.	Insurance.	Savings.	Insurance.
United States	67	1	5	2	6	2†	3	..	7	..	2	5	23
Teutonic	39	..	2	..	..	6†	..	3†	2	5†	4	14	8
Irish	24	..	1	..	8	1	2	..	2	..	..	1	7
Colored	28	2*	3	1	1	2	2	1	1	..	..	6	7
Bohemian	14	4†	..	..	..	..	..	..	..	..	..	..	..
Russian	57	1	1	5	..	4	2	4	..	2	..	19	3
Austrian, etc.	32	2	1	1	3	3	3	3	1	1	..	9	8
Italian	57	..	..	7*	..	10*	..	4	..	6	..	29	..
Total	318	10	13	16	12	28	12	15	13	14	6	83	56
Per cent. of all families	..	15	16.4	20.3	15.1	38.4	16.4	23.8	20.8	45.1	19.04	26.1	17.6

* Drew on savings, 2.   † Drew on savings, 2.   ‡ Drew on savings, 3.

NATIONALITY.	Number of Families.	$400 to $499.		$500 to $599.		$1100 to $1199.		$1200 to $1299.		$1300 to $1399.		$1400 to $1499.		$1500 to $1599.		$1600 and Over.		TOTAL.	
		Savings.	Insurance.	Savings.	Insurance.	Savings.	Insurance.	Savings.	Insurance.	Savings.	Insurance.	Savings.	Insurance.	Savings.	Insurance.	Savings.	Insurance.	Savings.	Insurance.
All nationalities	73	..	..	1	..	8	3	1	3	3	3	1	..	1	3	5	3	..	..

* Insurance on persons to amount of $500 or over.

243

TABLE 128.—BORROWING AND PAWNING. NUMBER OF FAMILIES REPORTING.—BY NATIONALITY AND INCOME.

Nationality.	Number of Families.	$600 to $699 Borrowed.	$600 to $699 Pawned.	$700 to $799 Borrowed.	$700 to $799 Pawned.	$800 to $899 Borrowed.	$800 to $899 Pawned.	$900 to $999 Borrowed.	$900 to $999 Pawned.	$1000 to $1099 Borrowed.	$1000 to $1099 Pawned.	Total Borrowed.	Total Pawned.
United States.	67	2	:	6	1	:	:	:	:	:	:	8	1
Teutonic.	39	1	:	:	:	:	:	:	1	:	:	1	1
Irish.	24	2	1	3	:	2	2	:	:	:	:	7	3
Colored.	28	:	:	:	:	:	1	:	:	:	:	:	1
Bohemian.	14	2	1	:	:	:	:	:	:	:	:	2	1
Russian.	57	4	1	2	1	2	1	1	:	4	3	13	6
Austrian, etc.	32	:	:	:	:	1	1	1	1	:	:	2	2
Italian.	57	9	8	:	:	:	:	:	:	:	:	9	8
Total	318	20	11	11	2	5	5	2	2	4	3	42	23

Nationality.	Number of Families.	$400 to $499 Borrowed.	$400 to $499 Pawned.	$500 to $599 Borrowed.	$500 to $599 Pawned.	$1100 to $1199 Borrowed.	$1100 to $1199 Pawned.	$1200 to $1299 Borrowed.	$1200 to $1299 Pawned.	$1300 to $1399 Borrowed.	$1300 to $1399 Pawned.	$1400 to $1499 Borrowed.	$1400 to $1499 Pawned.	$1500 to $1599 Borrowed.	$1500 to $1599 Pawned.	$1600 and Over. Borrowed.	$1600 and Over. Pawned.
All nationalities	73	3	4	5	2	1	3	..	..	..	..	..	..	..	..	..	..

Conclusions

1. It seems safe to conclude from all the data that we have been considering, that an income under $800 is not enough to permit the maintenance of a normal standard. A survey of the detail of expenditure for each item in the budget shows some manifest deficiency for almost every family in the $600 and $700 groups. The housing average shows scarcely more than 3 rooms for 5 persons. Three-fifths of the families have less than 4 rooms and more than 1½ persons to a room. Fuel is gathered on the street by half of the $600 families and by more than one-third of the $700 families. One-third of the $600 families are not able to afford gas. One-third of the $600 families are within the 22-cent minimum limit for food, and 30 per cent. of the $700 families spend 22 cents or under. In the same way the average expenditure for clothing in neither of these groups reaches $100, and 30 per cent. of the families are in receipt of gifts to eke out the supplies of clothing. In sickness the dispensary is the main dependence of these families, each of whom spends less than $10 annually in the average, on account of health, and only 1 family in 10 in the $600 group, and 1 in 6 of the $700 group, spends anything for the care of the teeth. The returns as to the furnishing of the houses show that in the $600 and $700 groups adequate furnishing is scarcely attained as the rule, and it is difficult to see how it could be kept up with the average expenditure reported for this purpose. In regard to membership in organizations, such as labor unions and churches, $1100 does not permit generous co-operation, and the families in the lower income-groups are seen to be represented in smaller proportion in these organizations than are the families in higher income-groups. Recreation and education are reduced to their lowest terms, save in so far as they may be had without expense. Items included under the head of miscellaneous expenditures represent, to a certain extent, the modest comforts above physical necessities, and the average of $25 or $30 puts a pretty narrow limit to what may be enjoyed in this category. As to provision for the future, industrial or burial insurance is one of the necessities that the poorest families provide, and the returns show cases where some-

245

thing is saved out of a $700 income, but the savings are at the expense of essentials of the present, as is seen in the number of under-fed families reporting a surplus at the end of the year.

2. On the other hand, an income of $900 or over probably permits the maintenance of a normal standard, at least so far as the physical man is concerned.

An examination of the items of the budget shows that the families having from $900 to $1000 a year are able, in general, to get food enough to keep soul and body together, and clothing and shelter enough to meet the most urgent demands of decency. Sixty-eight per cent. of the $900 families have 4 rooms or more, the average number of rooms being 3.75. The average expenditure for fuel allows comfortable provision; one-quarter of the families report gathering wood on the streets. Only 1 family in 6, in Manhattan only 1 in 15, is without gas. The average expenditure for food is a trifle over $400, enough to provide adequate nourishment, and only 5 families out of 63, or 1 in 12, report less than the minimum of 22 cents per man per day. As to clothing, gifts are reported still in one-fourth of the cases, but the average amount expended is between $130 and $140, and 3 families out of every 4 spend more than $100. Dispensaries and free hospitals are not for the $900 and $1000 families the main dependence in cases of illness. The expenditures for furniture indicate that the existing outfit is fairly well maintained and the equipment as it stands is reported fairly comfortable in the case of three-fourths of the $900 families, and of seven-eighths in the $1000 group. Participation in the benefits of labor unions or religious and fraternal organizations becomes possible to the majority of the families, and some margin is available for the pursuit of amusements and recreation, the purchase of books and papers, and the indulgence of personal tastes outside of the indispensable necessities of existence.

3. Whether an income between $800 and $900 can be made to suffice is a question to which our data do not warrant a dogmatic answer. In some respects the $800 families make no better showing than those with incomes of between $700 and $800, for instance, in regard to insurance, free fuel, and kerosene. Even as to food, there is a large percentage of under-fed families in this group, and the average expenditure is only $25 above that of the

income-group below. In regard to housing, distinctly better conditions prevail and the limit of the tolerable is perhaps reached by half of the families in this group. In regard to clothing also, conditions are better than with the $700 families, but in view of the fact that one-third of the 73 $800 families spend less than $100 for clothing, it seems an open question whether a normal standard is maintained in the group as a whole. The same query arises regarding expenditures for social obligations, amusements, and miscellaneous purposes. It is important to notice that in this income-group the cases of families below our assumed standards for food, clothing, and housing are largely in the second (South-European) group of nationalities. Anticipating the paragraph which follows, it seems probable that on $800 to $900 the standards prevailing among Bohemians, Russians, Austrians, and Italians may be maintained, but that it is the exception rather than the rule when the more expensive standards of the Americans and kindred nationalities are maintained on this amount.

4. A comparison of the families by nationalities shows that at almost every point a lower standard of expenditures prevails among the Bohemians, Austrians, Russians, and Italians than among the Americans, Teutons, and Irish. The families of the former group on incomes above $700 or $800 begin to save and show a surplus, and the sum total of expenditures above this point does not, as a rule, increase in proportion to increase of income. The families of the other group, on the contrary, do not reach the saturation point, so to speak, below an income of $900 or $1000. Expenditures in these families increase all along the line with increase of income, and the point where saving is preferred to immediate satisfaction is scarcely reached at $1100.

5. In the interpretation of the results of such an investigation as ours, certain serious difficulties arise. We have assumed that a normal standard of living exists, and that it can be maintained by a given family only by the expenditure of a certain minimum income. That is, when a family falls below the normal standard, the primary explanation is to be sought in a low income, or if ultimate causes are sought, in the reasons, personal or social, why this income is so small. It may be said, however, that the failure to maintain a normal standard may be due to

causes quite outside of the capacity of the individual bread-winner, or of the economic forces that determine the rate of wages. Two of these outside considerations are the presence of too many mouths to be fed and the inability to make a wise use of the money earned. Over-population on the one hand, improvidence, extravagance, and vice on the other, are alleged to explain why so many families make so poor a showing on $600 or $700 a year.

With reference to the proposition that the falling short of a normal standard is to be referred to the increase of numbers, without a corresponding increase of resources, it is, perhaps, sufficient to point out that however such a tendency might operate in its influence on wages, considered with regard to the whole mass of the wage-earners, it cannot properly be adduced to account for the failure of a family of only normal size to make out a decent living on its income. Not only is the average size of all the families in the United States not far from 5 persons, but the prevailing average must be near that point if the population of the country is to hold its own in numbers, apart from immigration. Our investigation has included only families of 4, 5, and 6 persons, almost exactly 5 on the average, so that a failure to keep up to the standard on the part of a family of only normal size cannot be attributed to the presence of too many members in it, unless we are willing to set a standard so high that the population at large must be diminished in order to reach it.*

In regard to the second point, that the maintenance of the standard depends more upon the wise use of the family income than upon the mere amount received, the schedules returned in this investigation afford much evidence in its support. But they also furnish evidence that there are limits to what can be done by thrift and economy. In Manhattan decent, sanitary, adequate housing cannot be had under $12 to $14 a month—in many parts of the island more is required. A family cannot be brought up in health and strength for work on bread and tea, even if these can be supplied for a dollar a week. Coal will burn up, coats and shoes will wear out, notwithstanding all that mending can do.

* The average number of persons per family, for the families included in this investigation is almost exactly 5 in each income-group. The details are given in Table 6A (page 53).

Further, to bring expenditures down to the exact requirements of an ideal economy, even supposing that all that is claimed could hereby be saved, is not within the ability of the ordinary wage-earner's wife. She cannot spend hours in bargain-hunting, in experimenting with new food-combinations, in making and mending garments. She has not, and cannot be expected to have, the training and ability to do all these things, even if she had the time. She has to take the methods of housekeeping that are traditional in her environment and apply them as skilfully and intelligently as her native and acquired powers of mind and body permit. What the exceptional woman might do cannot be made the measure of what the average woman may be expected to do, and if the morale and efficiency of the population are to be kept up, provision must be made for what the woman of average capacity must have to keep her family up to the prevailing standard. Only when education in a better economy is widely diffused, will it be possible to maintain the existing standards of physique and character on a lower absolute income.

One form of bad management of the family income is an excessive expenditure for indulgences like tobacco and drink. Where over-indulgence results in lowered earning-power, such expenditure reacts to lower the standard by diminishing income. Where this extreme result is not reached, expenditures of more fundamental importance are often curtailed. Instances of this sort were not wanting in the schedules received, and have been alluded to in another connection. But the number of cases in which the failure to come up to the normal standard could be attributed to over-indulgence was not large enough to warrant us in making this a comprehensive explanation. As has often been remarked, poverty is a cause of drink, as truly as drink is a cause of poverty.

In summary, therefore, the results of our investigation indicate that, while the personal factor does operate in the case of every family, both as regards the habits of the father and the managing ability of the mother, the limits within which it may affect the actual sum total of material comforts that make up the living of the family are set by social forces. These social forces find expression, on the one side, in the income which the family receives—that is, in the rate of wages received by the father and others who are at work; on the other side, they are expressed in the prices that have to be paid to get housing, food, and the other means of subsistence. The actual standard that prevails is set primarily, therefore, by the wages paid and the prices charged. Into the discussion of the causes that underlie these phenomena it is no part of our task to enter. This investigation has aimed only to show wherein the actual content of the standard (what things, and how many, are had) varies as the two jaws of the vise, wages and prices, contract and relax; and to show how the possibilities of human well-being are modified in consequence of the movement of the external forces that set the economic limits of the standard of living.

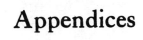

Appendices

APPENDIX I

Report of the Committee on Standard of Living

Seventh New York State Conference of Charities and
Correction.   Held at Rochester, November 13, 1906

By Frank Tucker, *Chairman*

The progress of social thought in this country has been closely
related to the National and State Conferences of Charities and
Correction.   It is true that the history of the National Conference
begins with the problem of the charitable and correctional institutions of the State; it is true that our various State Conferences
are largely given over to discussion of the administrative and
financial problems of institutions and activities dealing with the
wrecked, the broken, the deficient, and those offending law;
but ever increasingly has there developed a desire to get at causes
of poverty and crime, to know the reasons for industrial inefficiency,
physical infirmities, lack of character, and subnormal mental
capacity.   We know the amount of the bill we have to pay;
we want to know why it is so big and why it rolls up in the face
of what we call "prosperous times."

The future historian of social work will, I am sure, record two
addresses as distinguishing the recent Philadelphia session of the
National Conference.

In the Presidential address of Dr. Devine we find the spirit
of this Conference, which seeks expression in to-night's session,
summed up in the following passage:

"If I have rightly conceived the dominant idea of the modern
philanthropy, it is embodied in a determination to seek out and
strike effectively at those organized forces of evil, at those particular causes of dependence and intolerable living conditions which

are beyond the control of the individuals whom they injure and whom they too often destroy."

In Dr. Frankel's address, as Chairman of the Section on Needy Families, we find a new statement of the causes of poverty, and in the discussion of those causes we realize he is really setting up the elements of a standard of living which cannot be violated without the social unit becoming a social deficit.

Dr. Frankel says: "Stripped of all verbiage and reduced to their elements, we find that all existing poverty and pauperism are attributable and may be attributed to one of three major causes; for the sake of clearness, however, we shall define four causes:

"1. Ignorance.
"2. Industrial Inefficiency.
"3. Exploitation of Labor.
"4. Defects in governmental supervision of the welfare of citizens."

To discuss satisfactorily the "standard of living" it is obvious that we must first endeavor to define the phrase in such terms as to permit it to convey a common meaning to all who use it. If such a definition can be evolved, the obvious next step is to agree upon the essentials of a standard of living which shall mean, for each individual, existence as a happy and independent member of society. Accepting these essentials as founded upon experience and embodying the best thought of social economists, it should not be difficult to measure them in terms of dollars and cents for given social units in definite localities. And, again, having such schedules setting forth in terms of dollars and cents the cost of the essentials of a standard of living which will permit a given social unit in a definite locality to exist in a happy, healthy, and independent manner, it should not be impossible to compare such schedules of cost with the known standards of compensation in the same localities. And by such comparisons alone shall we know the extent to which labor is exploited; and if exploited, we are led to inquire how the deficiency is made up. We shall be led to inquire the price that society pays when the work of women and children is necessary to supplement the wages of the father. We shall be led to inquire the price that society pays when a portion of it is housed below the standard, is fed below the standard, is clothed, is warmed, has its rest and pleasures, is protected against sickness and accident, below the standard, because that portion is ignorant through lack of education, because it is incapable through lack of education, because its services are exploited for the selfish purpose of others, or because of the unenlightened attitude of some who conscientiously (perhaps) maintain that labor is a commodity to be paid for according to supply and demand, without regard to the essentials of a normal standard of living and the cost of those essentials.

And, again, having such schedules setting forth in terms of dollars and cents the cost of the essentials of a normal standard of living, have we not found a measure by which the "adequate relief" of our modern theory method of aiding dependent families may be measured?

In short, it seems apparent that until the essentials of a normal standard of living are set up and accepted, and until investigation discloses the cost of such essentials in definite localities for given social units, society cannot determine:

Whether labor in that community is exploited or adequately compensated.

How inadequate compensation of the natural wage-earner is supplemented and at what cost to the well-being of the family.

Whether our educational systems are effective in preparing boys and girls for the problems of our modern life.

Whether the standards by which our material relief for dependent families is measured are really "adequate" or not.

Nor, in the absence of this knowledge, can labor in its various subdivisions intelligently move from one locality to another.

Offhand it seems a simple thing to define the phrase "standard of living," but when the attempt is made, terms that define are found to be elusive, and the natural inclination is to seek a definition by describing the essential elements of a normal standard of living. In the hope that it will stand the test of analysis and as offering a basis for our discussion the following definition is put forth:

A standard of living is a measurement of life expressed in a daily routine which is determined by income and the conditions under which it is earned, economic and social environment and capacity for distributing the income.

A normal standard of living is one which permits each individual of a social unit to exist as a healthy human being, morally, mentally, and physically.

A normal standard of living requires as essential elements in the daily routine of life:

    I. Government—for control of common acts, needs, and property.

    II. Compensation for labor—that there may be secured for the family:

    1. Education.

    2. Shelter.

    3. Food.

    4. Clothing.

    5. Fuel.

    6. Light.

    7. Furniture and Household Furnishings.

    8. Transportation.

    9. Recreation.

    10. Provision for sickness and accident, dental, surgical, and other care necessary for the establishment and preservation of sound health.

    11. Savings.

    12. Insurance.

    13. Burial (through Insurance or Savings).

It should not be difficult to bring about a general acceptance of the essentials. The list given above is generally accepted by those who have written recently on this subject. It is varied but slightly by a group of social workers who have prepared budgets for given social units which will be referred to later.

At this point two questions naturally arise:

Has the cost of these essentials been determined?

Can the cost be reasonably determined?

To the first question I answer that so far as I know the present-day writers on social economics have assumed certain round sums as the cost of living; as, for instance, Dr. Devine in his "Principles of Relief" says:

"Recognizing the tentative character of such an estimate, it may be worth while to record the opinion that in New York City, where rentals and provisions are, perhaps, more expensive than in any other large city, for an average family of five persons the minimum income on which it is practicable to remain self-supporting, and to maintain any approach to a decent standard of living, is $600 a year."

Professor Albion W. Small is quoted as saying in a lecture: "No man can live, bring up a family, and enjoy the ordinary human happiness on a wage of less than $1000 a year."

Mr. John Mitchell estimates the minimum wage that will maintain a workingman and his family according to the "American standard" as $600 a year.

Nor have I been able to find any government tables which are based on given units and definite localities.

The estimate of Dr. Devine has a value in that it is for a given social unit in a definite locality, but it is insufficient in that it does not set up a standard of essentials and the total is not reached by a detailed estimate of the cost of each element—and he frankly says so. Professor Small's estimate is without value; it is a sweeping generalization dealing with no unit, measured by economic conditions in no locality, and without educational effect because it is refuted by the experience of many men in many places. While Mr. Mitchell's estimate in its explanation conveys a more definite picture than Professor Small's, it is of doubtful value because it is a generalization, and the processes by which it is arrived at are not set out for our judgment as to their soundness.

Only those estimates of the cost of a normal standard of living are sound which are based on a given social unit and on the cost of the essential elements of that standard in a given community, and at a given time.

Can these costs be determined in such a way as to make society believe that they are well founded?

To this question I answer, Yes, I believe they can. And my belief is the result of a careful experiment to test the possibility of just such an effort. About three months ago five social workers came together in New York by accident, and the above question was asked. The essential elements of a normal standard of living were agreed upon—the list is set out in the earlier part of this paper. The social unit was fixed as a man and his wife and three children under earning age. The cost of each essential was calculated in reasonable detail and with more than an average knowledge of economic conditions. The total when cast made each man and woman at that meeting look at his neighbor and wonder if there was anything wrong with the figures. That total was $931, which meant a compensation of $3.10 per day for 300 working days for the natural bread-winner of that family.

If those figures were sound, it meant hard thinking for some people in that great city. But were they sound? To test them this question was put to two groups of the ablest social workers among dependent families in New York—women familiar with the necessary quantities, qualities, and costs of the essentials; women whose daily work it is to deal with them.

"What items other than the following enter into a family budget?

"1, Rent; 2, food and drink; 3, clothing and shoes; 4, light and fuel; 5, provision for sickness and accident, dental, surgical, and other care necessary for establishment and preservation of sound health; 6, insurance; 7, recreation; 8, furniture and furnishings; 9, car-fares; 10, savings; 11, spending money and incidentals.

"Would you eliminate any of these items as unnecessary? Will you make up a budget which will show the cost of living for a family of a man and his wife and three children, the children being under earning age, it being assumed that the family is housed, fed, clothed, etc., in such a way as to preserve health, mind, and character, and permit the man to be a self-respecting citizen, and the children to grow up as such? It should also be assumed that both man and woman have average character and average capacity for management. To sum up, what ought it to cost a normal family of this size to live in a normal way under the conditions that prevail in New York at the present time?"

One group consisting of six sent in a combined estimate which was the result of their joint deliberations; the other group sent in individual estimates.

The estimate of the first group was $942 a year.

The individual estimates of the second group of ten showed three divisions.   In division one there was:

1 Estimate...............................$1,449
1   "   1,403
1   "   1,394

In division two there was:

1 Estimate...............................$1,078
1   "   986
1   "   901
1   "   900
1   "   879

In division three there were:

2 Estimates............................. $768

In both estimates of division three no allowance was made for medical services, furniture and furnishings, savings, or insurance. Had these items been included these estimates would have been in the second division, a fair average of which is $950.

It will be noticed that the estimates in division one are entirely consistent, and an examination of the details of cost shows a higher ideal of life than that contemplated by the problem to be answered.

The reasonable establishment by these estimates of $950 a year as the cost of the essentials of a normal standard of living for the social unit of a man and his wife and three children in New York City points the way for investigations and estimates in other communities by a body whose findings would carry weight in each community in which it worked.

But assuming that the essential elements of a normal standard are accepted; their cost for different social units in definite localities known; how can this knowledge affect standards of compensation, adequate compensation being necessary to the maintenance of the standard? and what basis has society for interfering between employer and employee in a matter which is personal to them?

Let us answer the last question first. It is fundamental that society has a right to protect itself against the acts of its individual members detrimental to the general welfare. Poverty is detrimental to the general welfare. Therefore, society, which pays the bill for poverty, has the right to say whether poverty that is preventable shall continue to exist. And if a cause of preventable poverty is the exploitation of labor, as Dr. Frankel says it is, then it is the duty of society to investigate and determine the facts; it is the right of society to say to the employer, "You are not obliged to employ this man or woman, but if you do you must pay him a living wage for a given day's work and you must permit him to work under proper conditions."

Society has been quick to enact laws for the protection of physical property and dumb animals, but against the destruction of human beings by all the *subtle causes growing out of a subnormal standard of living* there is little or no protection as yet. The cause is not difficult to find; we hold human life too cheap and we pay the bill for its destruction by *subtle causes* too indirectly.

At the same time society has the right to say, and does say, to the employee, "You must live in a way that is not detrimental to the general good."

Before this audience one may predict, without being thought a visionary, that some of us may live to see a new court created to try new social crimes which will be recognized as growing out of violations of an established standard of living.

And now let us consider how knowledge of the cost of a normal standard of living can affect standards of compensation. In the first place, how are standards of compensation set up? (Having in mind people of moderate earning capacity.)

1. By obligation on the part of the employer, when organization on the part of labor is powerful enough to command the rate and supply.
2. By mutual agreement on the part of employer and employees when there is an intelligent conception by both of the rights of each.
3. By thought and consideration on the part of intelligent employers who consider the welfare of their employees as well as their own interests.
4. By payment of what they call "going wages" on the part of thoughtless but not necessarily selfish employers. (These

"going wages" have usually been going for twenty-five years or more and may originally have had some logical basis in the conditions that prevailed at the time of their establishment.)

5. By exploitation on the part of employer; the needs of the employee being used to reduce the compensation to the minimum.

With that portion of labor compensated by the first three methods named we need not concern ourselves. It usually commands a sufficient wage to maintain a normal standard at least.

For that body of labor whose destinies are controlled by thoughtless employers there would be new hope if upon their standards of compensation could be fixed the light of authoritative statement of what is necessary to a normal standard of living and what these essentials cost. To-day the wages of hundreds of thousands of porters, cleaners, drivers, delivery-men, clerks, and others are fixed by employers on the basis of what they have been in the habit of paying, regardless of the cost of living or any other interest of the employee; and to-day the *working conditions* of hundreds of thousands are fixed by thoughtless employers without regard to the happiness or well-being of the employees. And I regret to say that among this group of offending employers may be found the managers of some of our charitable institutions and activities, although in the past few years there has been great improvement in this direction.

Individual cases illustrating the above situation have multiplied in my own experience; they might be cited here, but time forbids.

For the thoughtless employer there must be an educational campaign based on knowledge; public opinion can only be formed when facts are produced. All our life of to-day is too much affected by attitudes of mind which originate in precedents and axiomatic sayings based on facts of years ago.

For the selfish exploiter of the dire needs of men and women there is nothing but the stern arm of the law. But law cannot be intelligently enacted unless there is knowledge of the conditions that demand it. Law fixing a minimum daily wage must be based on knowledge of the requisites of a normal standard of living and their cost in definite localities. We have decreed in many places the physical and moral conditions under which labor may be performed, and we have decreed those conditions in order that the lives of men and women may be prolonged. We have decreed in many places the physical and moral conditions under which men and women may live. And why stop short and not say that in that mutual relation of men and women we call labor, there shall be paid by one to another at least sufficient to maintain a family according to an established normal standard?

For the intelligence of employer and competence of employed, society is responsible through its educational systems. For the exploitation of one by the other it is responsible through its legislation. For intelligent action in both directions we must have facts, and facts can only be obtained by investigation by those who are competent and fair seekers for truth.

APPENDIX II

Report of the Special Committee on Standard of Living*

Eighth New York State Conference of Charities and Correction. Held at Albany, November 12 to 14, 1907

By Lee K. Frankel, *Chairman*

To the Members of the Conference:

The Committee on Standard of Living was appointed pursuant to a resolution adopted by the seventh New York State Conference of Charities and Correction, which reads as follows:

Resolved, that the President of this Conference be authorized to appoint a Committee of not less than eight nor more than sixteen to report to this Conference what constitutes the essentials of a normal standard of living, and the cost of such a standard of living for a definite social unit at this time, in the cities and towns of this State; and further

Resolved, that the raising of special funds to defray the expenses of this Committee be referred to the Executive Committee with power.

Acting upon this resolution, the Committee held its first meeting on January 21, 1907. At this meeting it was reported that the Executive Committee had made an appropriation of $300 for the work of the Committee, and that when the usual appeal for funds to meet the expense of the Conference was sent out in the spring, a special request was to be included for money to meet the expenses of the Committee on Standard of Living.

Under these conditions, the Committee decided to attempt to obtain the necessary information regarding the cost of living

---

* The figures here given correspond with those in the Secretary's final report, which differ in many details, though not fundamentally, from the results of the preliminary computations.

through voluntary effort. The Committee was fortunate in securing the services of Professor Robert C. Chapin, of Beloit College, as secretary, until September, when his college duties required his return. It is in order at this time to extend to Professor Chapin the sincere thanks of the Committee for the conscientious and painstaking services which he has rendered.

THE SCHEDULE

At this meeting, a sub-committee was appointed to prepare a schedule of questions for the Committee's use. The schedule as finally adopted was purposely made very comprehensive so as to include every possible item of income and disbursement of a family's budget, and to express at the same time the Committee's conception of the essentials of a normal standard of living. A copy of the schedule is printed in Appendix III, following this report (page 283). In general, the schedule brings out the sources of the family income, showing not only the earnings of the members of the family of working age, but likewise the income derived from boarders, lodgers and other sources. The disbursement account was subdivided into twelve general headings, as follows: Housing; car-fare; fuel and light; furniture; insurance; food; clothing; health; taxes, dues and contributions; recreation and amusements; education and reading, and miscellaneous.

HOUSING. Under this heading are included questions to ascertain the type of dwelling occupied by the family; the rent paid and the rent of similar dwellings in the neighborhood; the size of the rooms and the number of rooms having direct access to the outer air; the size of the yard; the distance from the place of business of the working members of the family, and the distance from the school attended by the children. It was deemed important to determine whether the family had a private bathroom and a private toilet.

FUEL AND LIGHT. No special explanation of this subdivision is necessary. The questions in the schedule sought to bring out the kind and methods of fuel and light used.

FOOD. The food schedule was very carefully itemized, to bring out in detail the cost of the actual food purchases, and to show the quantities used during a week, from which the amount spent per annum could be estimated. The subdivisions as arranged in the schedule brought out, furthermore, the amounts of animal and of vegetable food. The classification adopted was based largely upon the reports of the United States Commissioner of Labor, upon investigations made by the Bureau of Agriculture, and upon studies made by Professors Atwater and Chittenden. The units adopted in these various reports have been adopted by the Committee. We have taken as a unit, for the purpose of this inquiry, an adult man. Compared with him an adult woman consumes .8 as much food; a child of twelve consumes .7; a child of ten to eleven consumes .6; a child of two to five consumes .4, etc. All calculations with respect to the cost of food have been based on these units instead of upon the actual number of individuals comprising the family. Meals taken away from home by the father or other wage-earners have been considered separately and have not been added to the general food budget. The effort has been made to determine from the families' statements whether the food provided was wholesome and sufficient. Naturally a wide margin of opinion must be allowed here since the opinions of investigators are at variance. Again, the questions under this heading brought out the components of the meals partaken of by the family. To determine with some degree of accuracy and to limit as largely as possible the personal equation regarding the amount and sufficiency of food, 100 schedules were submitted for examination to Dr. Frank P. Underhill, assistant professor of Physiological Chemistry in Yale University. Dr. Underhill analyzed these schedules to determine their food values, in terms of proteids, fats, carbo-hydrates and calories. The calculations were based on the amounts of food materials bought, and not on the amounts eaten, which necessarily could not be determined. No allowance was made for waste. Results of scientific value could not be obtained in this manner, and emphasis is laid on the fact that there has been no intention of drawing any conclusions, the bases of which would necessitate exactness. All that was hoped for from the investigation, was the determination in a general way whether the families were buying food of the amount and kind to keep them in bodily health and vigor.

265

On the basis of the cost of food in New York City, May, 1907, as shown by the schedules, Dr. Underhill estimates that in general, when less than 22 cents per man per day is spent for food, the nourishment derived is insufficient; when more than 22 cents per man per day is expended, the family is well nourished. The latter statement does not hold so well as the former. Of interest is the relatively large quantities of fat bought by both classes, which in Dr. Underhill's opinion is uneconomical both financially and physiologically. While the failure of some of the families to live well is due to injudicious buying, the majority of failures do not appear to be due to this cause, but to the inability to purchase food in sufficient amount and variety at less than 22 cents per man per day. This amount will allow of the purchase of food containing proteids, fats and carbo-hydrates, to produce a fuel value approximating 3000 calories. The Committee is not in a position to set up a minimum standard of fuel value. Various authorities who have written on this subject give minimums ranging from 2500 to 7000 calories. For the purpose of this report, it is sufficient to state that the standard mentioned by the Committee is approximately the minimum given by those who have investigated the subject.

INSURANCE. It is interesting to note that nearly all families carry insurance to a greater or less extent. Practically all of the insurance is in the so-called "industrial companies," for which a proportionately high premium is paid. The carrying of insurance, however, is no indication that the family necessarily has means for a proper standard of living; in many instances insurance is carried at the expense of food and clothing. Insurance is largely of the burial order, and the amount received from the insurance companies at death is expended for the payment of the burial charges.

SAVINGS. Probably of all the replies received in answer to the questions in the schedule, those under savings are the least satisfactory. Where in many instances no difficulty was experienced in obtaining requisite information regarding the other subdivisions of the schedule, there was hesitancy or in some instances even misstatement regarding the amount of savings. The Committee is of the opinion that in a number of instances where no savings were given, judging from the schedule returns there must have been distinct savings for which no accounting is made.   On the other hand, as appears later on in the report, many families are ashamed to mention the fact that they have borrowed money or sought the pawn shops to obtain necessary means to live.   That such must have been so, however, is likewise indicated by the schedules where the disbursements are in excess of the receipts, and where the entire situation of the family shows there must have been sources of income other than those actually admitted.

CLOTHING.   What has been said for the food schedule holds likewise for the clothing schedule.   Every possible expenditure for clothing for the father, mother and children in the family has here been included, together with any expenditures for repairs, laundry, washing materials, new materials, and for garments made at home.   Of extreme importance was the ascertaining of information regarding the amount of clothing which families received as gifts from friends, employers, relatives, benevolent organizations, churches, and other sources.   It does not seem to be infrequent, judging from the schedules, for families to purchase clothing at second hand.

HEALTH.   Under this heading have been included disbursements for physicians, dentists, oculists, nurses, surgical appliances, medicines, hospital charges, dispensary charges, spectacles and eye-glasses.   The questions under this heading also show the amount of free medical attendance that has been received, particularly from dispensaries and hospitals.   It may be said here that many have omitted to mention gratuitous treatment of this kind.

FURNITURE AND FURNISHINGS.   The replies under this heading show expenditures made for various articles of household equipment of the family.   In some instances a much higher standard of equipment was shown than would be warranted by the family income for the year.   The explanation of this is obvious.   In many cases, the family had at some previous period, at the time the equipment was provided, a larger earning ability.   Instances are in evidence where furniture was sold to meet living expenses. Much of the furniture, such as washstands, ice boxes, beds, mirrors, and sewing machines, is bought on the instalment plan.

Taxes, Dues and Contributions. Under this heading have been included all disbursements made on account of labor unions, fraternal orders, benefit societies, lodges, and religious and social organizations.

Recreation and Amusement. The questions under this subdivision were framed to bring out not only the amount of expenditure of the family for recreation and amusement, but to determine the manner in which the family takes its relaxation. The replies show expenditures for theater, dances, excursions and pleasure trips, for toys and other playthings for the children, and other amusements of all kinds.

Car-fares. This subdivision includes car-fares of the wage-earners to and from work, for children to and from school, and disbursements on this account for visits, recreation, etc.

Education and Reading. Under this heading are grouped the expenses of children at school, and disbursements for newspapers, periodicals, books, postage and stationery. The replies received also brought out the kind and titles of the newspapers, periodicals and books read by the family, and the extent to which public libraries were made use of.

Miscellaneous Expenditures. Under this heading have been grouped all expenses not readily classifiable under any of the above subdivisions. Among other disbursements there are funeral expenses, legal expenses, expenses for moving, interest on debt, expenditures for tobacco, liquor, barber, and the personal expenditures of the various members of the family.

Under date of May 27, 1907, the chairman of the Committee reported to the Executive Committee that the effort to obtain information from volunteers had met with only indifferent success. The schedule which the Committee had prepared had been distributed throughout the city and state, among settlement and charity workers, secretaries of labor unions, college students, etc., but the returns at the time of the meeting of the Executive Committee were comparatively meagre. The Executive Committee thereupon appropriated $200 additional for the purposes of the Committee, and authorized the Committee to receive money directly from any source whatever for the prosecution of its work. Sufficient funds were obtained from private sources to enable the Committee, in June, to begin more active work, the results of which are appended below.

METHOD OF INVESTIGATION. Three thousand schedules were printed. Of these over 400 were distributed to volunteers engaged in social work, particularly to residents in the various settlements and church houses, to agents of charitable and relief agencies, to students at the universities, and to others. Of these, 57 were returned. In the belief that highly valuable information could be obtained from representatives of the trades unions, a list of the secretaries and officers of these organizations in New York City was obtained through Mr. Robinson, the local president of the Federation of Labor. To each of these officers a schedule was sent, together with a letter of instruction and advice, which was subsequently followed up by other letters. A total of 690 of these schedules was thus distributed: 34 of them have been returned. Since June, practically all of the replies to the schedules of Greater New York have been obtained by paid investigators.

In obtaining replies to questions in the schedules, the effort was made to limit the inquiry to a family of five individuals, composed of husband, wife and three children under working age, with an income over $600 and under $1000. As can readily be understood this was not always possible.

At an early stage of the investigation, it was seen that an income of $1000 was ample to meet the demands of the normal family of 5. Similarly, it was shown that an income of less than $600 was insufficient to keep up a proper standard of living for the same social unit. The facts on which these conclusions were based will be developed later in the report.

Careful instructions were given to the enumerators in regard to the inquiries to be made on the questions in the schedules. For certain elements of the schedule, such as rent, number of rooms, income, etc., it was possible to get fairly exact replies. Inquiries with reference to cost of food, cost of clothing, and other essentials had, to a certain extent, to be averaged. Wherever possible, the individual interviewed,—and in nearly all instances this individual was the mother of the family,—was requested to keep an itemized statement of her disbursements for a period of one week, and upon the statement which she presented the estimate for the year's disbursements was made. Where such statement could not be secured, it was found possible in a number of instances to make use of the expense book which the housewife kept with the grocer, butcher, etc. Where both of these methods failed, it was necessary for the investigator to carefully go over each item in the schedule with the individual interviewed and to endeavor to obtain as accurate a statement as possible. Naturally there are inherent errors in such a procedure. In many instances there was a tendency to exaggeration. On the other hand, it can safely be said that certain items, particularly those showing savings and expenditures for liquor, were under-estimated. While the replies for this reason are not scientifically exact, they nevertheless indicate, with sufficient accuracy, the general character and amounts of the disbursements made by the families who were interviewed, and bring out enough salient features upon which to base a judgment as to the cost of living at the present time.

The Committee, however, does not feel that the investigation which has been made is more than a preliminary one, and for this reason its findings are but the interpretation of the facts presented in the schedules. The number of schedules returned, while larger than in any similar investigation made heretofore, is still too small to postulate definite conclusions. So many factors enter into the question of the cost of living, such as thrift, economy, ability of the housekeeper to utilize most advantageously the purchases made, that the amount on which one family may live with some degree of comfort and decency will be found inadequate for another family which is improvident and shiftless.

RESULTS

The Committee has received a total of 728 schedules. Of these it was found necessary to discard 139, as the information contained therein was either inaccurate or incomplete. Of the balance of the schedules, 503 were obtained in Greater New York, 86 in the towns and cities outside of Greater New York. Of those for Greater New York it has been deemed unnecessary for the purposes of this inquiry to go very carefully into 185 schedules in which the income was below $600 or above $1100, or where the number in the family deviated very largely from the unit of inquiry; in other words, where the number in the family was below 4 or above 7. The schedules showing incomes from $300 to $600 were at once eliminated, as the analyses of the most important items of the budget, such as food, rent and clothing, indicated that the families were maintaining an exceptionally low standard of living, and were not independent of outside assistance.

As a matter of fact, 17 schedules of families showing incomes between $500 and $600 were examined. The average rental of these 17 families was $141 per annum. Disbursements for food averaged 20 cents per man per day or 2 cents less than Dr. Underhill's minimum. The family spent $68 per annum for clothing. The disbursements for the other essentials of the budget were proportionately so low that a more detailed study of the group was deemed unnecessary. Of the 318 families remaining,

72 have incomes between $600 and $700,
79 have incomes between $700 and $800,
73 have incomes between $800 and $900,
63 have incomes between $900 and $1000,
31 have incomes between $1000 and $1100.

The appended tables show the distribution of these families according to nationality and residence:

TABLE I.

NATIONALITY.	TOTAL.	INCOME.				
		$600 to $699	$700 to $799	$800 to $899	$900 to $999	$1000 to $1099
United States	67	11	19	13	16	8
Teutonic	39	4	7	9	11	8
Irish	24	4	7	7	5	1
Colored	28	11	6	8	2	1
Bohemian	14	4	3	3	4	..
Russian	57	16	14	12	9	6
Austrian, etc.	32	6	9	9	7	1
Italian	57	16	14	12	9	6
Total	318	72	79	73	63	31

TABLE II.

Income.	Manhattan.	Brooklyn.	Bronx.	Queens.	Total.
$600 to $699.............	52	15	5	0	72
$700 to $799.............	63	14	2	0	79
$800 to $899.............	58	9	5	1	73
$900 to $999.............	45	10	2	6	63
$1000 to $1099.............	25	4	1	1	31
Total....................	243	52	15	8	318

THE FAMILY BUDGET

For the immediate purpose of this report, the inquiry has been confined to 224 schedules of families ranging in income between $600 and $900, for reasons that will appear below. The occupations of the wage-earners are shown in Tables 3–6 (pages 46–52) of the final report. The average incomes and disbursements of these three groups are shown in the following table:

TABLE III.

	Group I. $600 to $699	Group II. $700 to $799	Group III. $800 to $899
	Average Income. $650	Average Income. $748	Average Income. $846
Rent................................	$154	$161	$168
Car-fare............................	11	10	16
Fuel and light......................	38	37	41
Furniture...........................	6	8	7
Insurance...........................	13	18	18
Food................................	279	314	341
Meals eaten away from home.........	11	22	18
Clothing............................	83	99	114
Health..............................	14	14	22
Taxes, dues and contributions.......	8	9	11
Recreation and amusement...........	3	6	7
Education...........................	5	5	7
Miscellaneous.......................	25	32	41
Total...............................	$650	$735	$811

272

GROUP I.—$600 TO $700.

This group included 72 families, of which 52 are in the Borough of Manhattan, 15 in the Borough of Brooklyn, and 5 in the Borough of the Bronx. The 72 families show an average income of $650, and an average disbursement of $650. For the purpose of this report, the Committee has endeavored to interpret these figures in connection with all other replies presented in the schedules. The limitations of time and space will not permit of the presentation of statistical tables. These the Committee hopes will be published at length in book form.

The income of these 72 families is derived from various sources. In many instances the employment of the father is irregular and must be supplemented. In 7 families the mother adds to the income and in 3 families children help in the family support. Seventeen families keep 23 lodgers, of whom a few take meals with the family.

The question naturally arises,—"Do these 72 families showing incomes varying from $600 to $700 and who have an average income of $650 maintain a standard of living sufficient to preserve physical and mental efficiency?" The Committee is of the opinion that the figures speak for themselves. Without attempting at great length to show the facts by statistics, it appears from a careful study of this group that the average family of five persons pays $13 per month for rent. For this they are able to obtain, in the Borough of Manhattan, from 2 to 3 rooms, depending upon the section in which they live. Rents seem to be highest on the upper West Side, in central Manhattan, and on the lower East Side. Occasionally on the upper East Side and in other sections of the city, it is possible to find cheaper rentals than the one given. Such a family has no bath and only 1 family in 10 has a toilet within the apartment. The rooms are apt to be low and comparatively small, and one room is usually dark; i. e., has no window to the outer air, or no window at all. Kerosene is used for lighting, and coal for cooking and heating. Every other family uses wood which the father brings home with him or which the children collect on the streets. In some homes, gas is used for cooking in summer. The cost of fuel and light averages in this group, $38 per annum.

The furniture equipment of such a family is in most instances meagre.   If there are three rooms, the so-called parlor is a combined parlor, sitting-room and bed-room.   As a rule, it contains a table, a bed and a few chairs.   Occasionally a rocking-chair or a sofa is found.   In the corner there is a sewing-machine; on the walls a few cheap pictures, family portraits and the like.   Cheap ornaments are found here and there.   In some few instances the floor is covered with a cheap carpet.   The second room, which is a combination dining-room and kitchen, has a table covered with oil-cloth, a few chairs, a stove, and kitchen utensils which hang on the walls, owing to the lack of a cupboard.   Frequently an ice-box is found.   The third room, which is a bed-room, contains an iron folding bed, chair and trunk.   Clothes hang on the wall; seldom is there a bureau.   The washing of the family is done at the sink in the kitchen, there being no wash-stands or wash-bowls in the bed-rooms.   In one case only was a piano found.   The disbursements per annum for furniture average $6, for which the housewife declares she can purchase only the necessary things.   These include dishes, table, linens, beds, chairs, kitchen utensils, and supplies for cleaning.   If more than this is required, for example, mirrors, sewing-machines, etc., resort must be made to instalment purchases.

The value of the furniture is indicated by the cost of moving, which varies from $3 to $5, and but rarely does it pay to have the furniture insured against fire.   Most of the disbursements for insurance, which averages $13 per annum, are for so-called life or burial insurance.

The food disbursement for such a family approximates $270 per annum, for five individuals or 3.3 units.   This is $82 per annum per unit or 22½ cents per man per day.   For breakfast the family has rolls and coffee; sometimes bread with butter; occasionally eggs or oatmeal.   The nature of the meal varies with the nationality of the family.   Some families are satisfied with herring or a piece of sliced salmon for breakfast.   The father or wage-earner is usually not home for lunch.   This, however, means an additional expense to the family of $11 for lunches eaten away from home.   The other members of the family make their lunch out of food left over from the preceding evening,—for example cold meat, potatoes, occasionally coffee or tea; or else are satisfied with bread and milk, crackers and milk, eggs, bread and tea; or bread and onions.   Occasionally the family have a full meal (so-called) at mid-day, but in this case they have no supper; if they are hungry in the evening, they eat bread.   In nearly all these families the important meal of the day is in the evening, when the entire family is present.   The menu consists of meat, potatoes, occasionally soup, coffee or beer.   On Sunday the family allows itself greater latitude for dinner; a roast is served and cake as dessert about once a month.   Many families, however, make no difference between Sundays and other days. The above menus apply largely to native families.   Russian and Austrian Jewish families have special dinners on Friday evenings or on Saturday, using fish and fowl.   The Italian lives chiefly on macaroni, fish or meat, lentils and beans.   Food is bought daily in all these families in small quantities; dry food, such as potatoes, flour, tea, coffee and sugar, is generally bought in quantities to last a week.   Chicken and fish are purchased in exceptional cases only.   The same is true of fresh fruits.   There is little variety in the food used.   Guests are seldom to be found at the table; in fact, this question frequently brought forth the reply, "We are glad to have enough to eat for ourselves."   Only on holidays and on special celebrations are relatives invited.   Twenty per cent. of the food disbursements is for bread and similar forms of food; 6.2 per cent. of the total disbursement for food is for liquor used in the home.

The family clothes itself at a cost of $84 per annum.   Of this amount approximately $28 is disbursed for the clothing of the father, $18 for the clothing of the mother, and $28 for the clothing of the three children.   Ten dollars a year must be expended for washing materials, laundry supplies and for repairs.

The question whether a family of 5 can purchase sufficient clothing for their needs on $80 per annum is difficult to answer. There can be no doubt that clothes can be worn and are worn even when they become exceedingly shabby and torn.   A partial answer to this question is shown by the schedules.   Of the 72 families, 25 admitted receiving gifts of clothing from relatives, employers, private individuals, churches and charitable organizations.   This happens more frequently among native-born families than among foreign-born families. The latter apparently make greater use of the second-hand clothing stores. Under all circumstances, the ability to get along on $80 per annum assumes a large amount of thrift and economy on the part of the housewife, and the skill constantly to repair the clothing which is purchased. If more clothing than the above is desired, it must be purchased on the instalment plan, or by cutting down the other important items in the budget, particularly that of food.

The budget permits a disbursement of $14 for the preservation of the health of the family,—or rather sickness requires this disbursement. The money expended is almost wholly paid for physicians and medicines in cases of acute and chronic illness. Almost none of it goes for care of the teeth; only 8 families (11 per cent.) out of the 72 reporting the use of the dentist, whom they pay in instalments. Twenty-nine families out of the 72 (40 per cent.) make use of free dispensaries. Twelve families report using free hospitals. Where illness becomes chronic and covers a long period of time the family almost invariably runs into debt.

Eight dollars is spent annually by this family for taxes and contributions. It can safely be said that this average has largely been raised by the Catholic families, whose contributions to churches are far in excess of those of any other religious denomination. Either the father or the mother belongs to a political organization, to a labor union, or to some religious body.

Depending upon the location in which the family lives, the amount spent for car-fare varies. Where the car-fare item is low, and the father lives near his place of work, it frequently happens that the saving in car-fare is used for rental. Practically all of the car-fare is used by the wage-earner in going to and from his place of work. Very little remains for recreation, or for excursions to the country. The $3 that the family may spend for recreation permits of almost no diversion. Occasionally in the summer-time the family goes to Coney Island, to Fort George, to the beaches around the city, or listens to the gramophone on the Bowery, 14th Street, and other places where this form of amusement is to be found. Two families out of the 72 visited the theatre; many of the families spend part of their Sundays in the parks.

For educational purposes the family spends $5 per annum,

276

most of which is used for the daily newspaper. The children spend for school supplies 50 cents per annum, and postage and stationery may run up to 25 or 50 cents a year. There is practically no expenditure for books. Seventeen families report the use of public libraries.

This leaves a total of $25 per annum for miscellaneous expenditures, including moving, payment of debts, etc. Of this, the larger amount is spent for personal expenses of the father, such as tobacco, liquor, barber and spending money. Expenditures for funerals are given in comparatively few instances, the assumption being that insurance money is used for this purpose.

To summarize, a family having an income of $650 per annum spends 24 per cent. of its income for rent, 45 per cent. for food, or 85 per cent. of its income for four items, food, rent, clothing, fuel and light. Only 2.5 per cent. is spent for education, recreation, and dues to societies; the other 12.5 per cent. is for health, insurance, furniture, car-fare, meals away from home, and miscellaneous. The family is unable to make any provision against accident or to lay by anything for a rainy day. As a matter of fact, the schedules show that the families are unable to live within this income under the conditions shown above. Twenty of the 72 families admit being in debt, the money being borrowed for food and rent. Not rarely do they visit the pawnshop. Ten of these families claim to have small savings varying from $5 to $25 per annum. A study of these 10 families, however, shows that the savings are due to exceptionally favorable conditions. Most of them have less than 5 persons in the family. The children are very young and hence consume less food and require less clothing; the conditions of health are better than in the average family, and the income of the father is above the average of $650. In addition, in most instances, the father has steady work and an income which lasts throughout the year. These families likewise show a high degree of thrift and economy. The amount spent for food and clothing is comparatively low, and they receive gifts of various kinds. Rentals, likewise, are lower than the average, and all in all these families may be considered as variations rather than as normal types.

The Committee is of the opinion that an income between $600

and $700 per annum is insufficient for a family of 5 to maintain a
proper standard of living in the Borough of Manhattan. Leaving
aside the exceptions, it is apparent that on an income of $600 to
$700 many families in Manhattan have a fierce struggle for ex-
istence. The maximum of food purchases approximates the minimum set up by authorities on this subject. The narrowest margin
is allowed for other essentials. No provision can be made for
accident or emergency. If either of these occur, the family runs
into debt. Were it not for the charity of friends, relatives, employers or philanthropic organizations, the expenditure of the
family would be, and frequently is, larger than the income.

Such a family literally lives a hand-to-mouth existence, with
neither opportunity nor means for enjoyment or recreation. It can
make no provision for repairs to equipment. The health of its
members cannot be safeguarded from its own resources. The
housing accommodations barely prevent over-crowding. *It requires
no citation of elaborate statistics to bring convincing proof that $600 to
$700 is wholly inadequate to maintain a proper standard of living,
and no self-respecting family should be asked or expected to live on
such an income.*

GROUP II.—$700 TO $800.

Of primary interest in this group is the fact that the 79 families
in the group, having 5 to the family, manage to live within their
incomes—the disbursement being practically the same as the income. A difference of $85 in the average expenditures of this and
the preceding group is readily accounted for,—$45 more being
spent in the second group for food and $16 more for clothing, the
two together making over 70 per cent. of the additional disbursement. The balance of $24 is fairly distributed among the other
items of the budget. There is a difference of $2 per annum for
health and an additional disbursement of $2 per annum for furni-
ture, $1 for taxes, $3 for recreation, $7 for miscellaneous expendi-
tures, $7 for housing and $11 for meals taken away from home.
It is of particular interest to note that there is practically no increase in the expenditure for rent. The housing conditions remain
the same,—if anything, if the housing conditions may be assumed
to have been bad in the preceding group, they are somewhat accen-

278

tuated in this group by the fact that a larger number of the families, to obtain the above income, keep lodgers and boarders. In the first group, 24 per cent. of the families increased their income through this means; in the present group 26 families out of the 79, or 33 per cent., keep lodgers or boarders, being 1 family out of every 3. In the food budget, the $45 additional permits a larger amount of animal food and a better quality of food, the per capita per day having risen to 25 cents or 9 per cent. There is a decrease in the number of families who receive free gifts of clothing, 35 per cent. in the first group receiving gifts from various sources and 27 per cent. in the present group. There is similarly a reduction from 40 per cent. to 38 per cent. in the number of families who receive free dispensary treatment. Only 8 families report using free hospitals. Only 35 per cent. use free wood. The family spends proportionately more per annum for medical services. More families make use of dentists in this group. All in all there is a tendency toward improvement in condition, and were it not for the fact that housing conditions have not improved, it might be assumed that the family is beginning to reach the point where a fairly decent standard of living is being maintained.

The Committee believes that with an income of between $700 and $800 a family can barely support itself, provided that it is subject to no extraordinary expenditures by reason of sickness, death or other untoward circumstances. Such a family can live without charitable assistance through exceptional management and in the absence of emergencies.

GROUP III.—$800 TO $900.

This group at once shows a marked variation from the preceding groups, particularly from the first group. Not only is the family apparently able to live on its income, but it can save on its income. The average income in the group being $846 and the average disbursement $811. It is true that 12 families in this group claim to be in debt. The indebtedness, however, is lower than in the preceding groups, and the causes of indebtedness are personal to the families and not characteristic of the group. Twenty-one families actually show savings in the schedules,—these savings running from $50 to $100. Even in those schedules where no actual savings are shown, the schedules indicate that the families have not used their entire incomes. Only in cases of chronic illness have the families spent their entire income and shown indebtedness. In one instance, for example, the family shows a disbursement of over $200 for physicians and medicines. This, however, is exceptional. There is an increase in disbursements over the previous group of $76 per annum, of which 50 per cent. goes for food and clothing; 10 per cent. for rent; 15 per cent. for miscellaneous, and 25 per cent. for other items. In practically the same proportion there is an increase in disbursements for rent, the increase averaging 60 cents per month.

The average, however, does not tell the full story, either for this or for the preceding groups. Of families paying $120 or less per annum ($10 per month), there are:

> In $600 to $700 group...14 families, or 19 per cent.
> In $700 to $800 group...17 families, or 21 per cent.
> In $800 to $900 group... 8 families, or 11 per cent.

Of families paying $228 or over per annum there are:

> In $600 to $700 group... 1 family, or 1.4 per cent.
> In $700 to $800 group... 7 families or 9 per cent.
> In $800 to $900 group...10 families or 14 per cent.

Of families paying $168 or over per annum (for which 4 rooms can usually be obtained) there are:

> In $600 to $700 group...21 families, or 29 per cent.
> In $700 to $800 group...33 families, or 42 per cent.
> In $800 to $900 group...37 families, or 51 per cent.

There are more baths, and particularly more toilets, in the apartments. The rooms are larger and have more light. The families in this group keep a proportionately larger number of lodgers than in the other group. Of 73 families, 25, or 34 per cent., keep 49 lodgers. In all these groups, lodgers are necessarily kept to meet additional expenditures. The keeping of lodgers is not primarily a question of standard of living, but rather one of wages. If these families had sufficient income from their wage-earners so as not to be compelled to take in lodgers, the housing accommodations which could be obtained for the rentals paid by this group would be sufficiently ample and hygienic for a family of normal size. The amount that is now disbursed for food (27 cents per day) and for clothing appears to be adequate. All along the line there is the opportunity for larger disbursements, and in the miscellaneous group considerable latitude is allowed, the average being $41, to which can be added the $35 surplus in case of necessity. It may be mentioned in this connection that the amount of gifts in clothing, free dispensaries, etc., is materially decreased. More provision is made for health and for replenishing the furniture equipment. Of most importance, however, is the statement made above that there is an indication of actual saving by the families here discussed. These families seem to be able to provide themselves with the food which they require, with the clothing which they require, and to live under conditions which they consider fairly decent. They have opportunities for recreation and for amusement which are fairly normal, and apparently these families are typical of hundreds, if not thousands, of wage-earners and small tradesmen of the middle class who are self-respecting and self-supporting. *In view of all these facts, the Committee is of the opinion that it is fairly conservative in its estimate that $825 is sufficient for the average family of 5 individuals, comprising the father, mother and 3 children under 14 years of age to maintain a fairly proper standard of living in the Borough of Manhattan.* The extent to which this amount would be changed in the other boroughs of Greater New York would be measured largely by the item of rent, and not by the other items in the budget. This item may vary from $15 to $30 per annum in the Borough of Brooklyn; probably a similar amount in the Borough of the Bronx. In the Borough of Queens, from the very few schedules which have been obtained, the Committee, while it does not draw any conclusions, is of the impression that the rent item would be even lower.

NATIONALITIES

A word should be said on the subject from the standpoint of the nationalities of the families investigated. The schedules show that in native and Irish families the greater the income, the greater the disbursements for so-called necessities. In other foreign-born families, particularly Italian, Austrian and Russian, the tendency is to save even if a lower standard must be maintained, the ratio of disbursements not keeping pace with the increase of income. It is among the foreign-born that one finds most of the lodgers and boarders, and where most of the working mothers and children are to be found; all this, of course, for the purpose of increasing income and corresponding savings.

In conclusion it should be repeated that the inferences drawn are based on the facts as presented in the schedules. The Committee believes that they have a distinct practical and social value and they are submitted to the Conference in this belief.

APPENDIX III

The Schedule

INSTRUCTIONS TO INVESTIGATORS

The object of the Committee, in this investigation, is to find out both the cost and the elements of a normal standard of living. Its success depends absolutely upon the patience, tact and accuracy of those who gather the information from families of their acquaintance.

1. The families selected should be those with which the visitor has already established friendly relations. The schedule is to be filled out by the visitor, not by the members of the family. Several visits may be necessary to secure all the information desired.

2. Each family should be a representative family: (a) self-supporting; (b) comprising father, mother, 2 to 5 children under 16, and preferably no other members; (c) of average earning power and economy. Where practicable, the selection of two or more families in the same occupation will facilitate comparisons.

3. The answers to the questions should be filled out as exactly and fully as possible. It is essential to know, not only the cost of the articles purchased, but also what the family gets for what it pays—what things, how many, how good. Hence the questions are drawn out in detail, not in order to increase labor, but to save it.

4. Families should be assured that the information will be regarded as confidential, and informed of the purpose for which it is sought. The names of the families are not to appear on the schedules.

5. The details of expenditure, especially for food and clothing, should be derived from accounts kept by the housekeeper already, or which she may be induced to keep for a few weeks for the purposes of this investigation. Where this proves impracticable, it

may be necessary to fall back on estimates as to details and totals, obtained by careful inquiry. The first method is greatly to be preferred, and will have an added value if the original accounts can be filed with the schedule. Where the second method is used, the process by which the estimates were reached should be stated on the schedule.

6. Duplications should be avoided. An examination of the schedule as a whole will show the place designed for each item. Lunches and car-fares, for example, are specified separately, and should not be included under spending-money.

The secretary will be pleased to give additional explanations in answer to inquiries. It is requested that the accompanying schedule be returned within thirty days of the time when it is received.

When completed, this schedule should be returned to the Secretary of the Special Committee on the Standard of Living appointed by the New York State Conference of Charities and Correction, Robert C. Chapin, 105 East 22d Street, New York City.

FAMILY REPORT ON STANDARD OF LIVING

NEW YORK CITY, BOROUGH .... SCHEDULE NO. ....

RESIDENCE OF FAMILY, NO. .... STREET

REPORTED BY .... OF ....
(P. O. ADDRESS)

DATA GATHERED BETWEEN ...., AND.................................

1. BIRTHPLACE OF FATHER? .... OF HIS PARENTS? ....

2. BIRTHPLACE OF MOTHER? .... OF HER PARENTS? ....

3. IF FOREIGN-BORN, YEARS SPENT IN THE U.S. BY FATHER? .... BY MOTHER? ....

4. COMPOSITION, OCCUPATION and EARNINGS of the FAMILY

MEMBERS	AGE	SEX	OCCUPATION	HOURS EMPLOYED PER WEEK	DAYS UNEMPLOYED PER YEAR	EARNINGS	
						WEEKLY MAXIMUM	ACTUAL TOTAL PER YEAR
						$	$
FATHER							
MOTHER							
OLDEST CHILD							
2ND CHILD							
3RD CHILD							
4TH CHILD							
5TH CHILD							

TOTAL INCOME FROM WAGES FOR THE YEAR .... $

5. OTHERS LIVING WITH FAMILY	NUMBER		AMOUNT PAID	
	MALE	FEMALE	WEEKLY	YEARLY
RELATIVES (SPECIFY RELATIONSHIP)			$	$
....				
....				
LODGERS				
BOARDERS				
TABLE BOARDERS				

INCOME FROM LODGERS, BOARDERS ETC. FOR YEAR ....

INCOME FROM OTHER SOURCES FOR YEAR (SPECIFY SOURCES)

....

....

TOTAL PAID BY LODGERS ETC FOR YEAR $

INCOME FROM ALL SOURCES FOR THE YEAR $

B. WHERE MORE SPACE IS NEEDED USE BLANK PAGES

DESCRIPTION of the FAMILY

(CHARACTERIZE FATHER, MOTHER AND CHILDREN WITH REFERENCE TO PHYSICAL, MENTAL AND MORAL TRAITS; NOTE ANY INHERITED DEFECTS, ANY MARKED ABILITY)

6. PHYSICAL CONDITION

FATHER ......

MOTHER ......

CHILDREN ......

7. MENTAL CONDITION and CAPACITY

FATHER ......

MOTHER ......

CHILDREN ......

8. ARE CHILDREN NORMAL IN PHYSIQUE, MIND AND HABITS? ......

9. HABITS OF FATHER, SO FAR AS ASCERTAINABLE. ......

10. CAPACITY OF MOTHER AS EXPRESSED BY CONDITION OF ROOMS, FURNISHINGS, CLOTHING, USE OF FOOD SUPPLIES, AND GENERAL APPEARANCE OF HOME ......

11. IN CASE OF RETRENCHMENT, WHAT EXPENDITURES ARE CURTAILED OR ELIMINATED? ......

12. WHAT ARTICLES, IF ANY, ARE BOUGHT ON THE INSTALMENT-PLAN? ......

13. WHAT, IF ANY, WITH TRADING-STAMPS? ......

14. ARE HOUSEHOLD GOODS EVER MORTGAGED? ......

IS PERSONAL PROPERTY EVER PAWNED? ......

IS MONEY EVER BORROWED ON PERSONAL CREDIT ① FROM FRIENDS? ......

② FROM MONEYLENDERS? ......

15. FOR WHAT PURPOSE IS THE MONEY BORROWED IN ANY OF THESE WAYS USED? ......

HOUSING

1. TYPE OF HOUSE – (TENEMENT, DETACHED DWELLING ETC.) _____

2. IS DWELLING RENTED OR OWNED? _____

3. IF RENTED, ANNUAL RENT PAID? $ _____

4 A. IF OWNED; ESTIMATED VALUE? $ _____

   B. ANNUAL RENT OF LIKE HOUSES NEAR? $ _____

   C. IS IT MORTGAGED? _____ FOR HOW MUCH? $ _____

   D. ANNUAL INTEREST PAID $ _____

5. IF RENTED; DOES RENT INCLUDE WATER? _____ LIGHT? _____
   JANITOR SERVICE? _____
_____

6. IS IT A CORNER-BUILDING? _____ A REAR TENEMENT? _____
_____

7. ON WHICH FLOOR? _____

8. SIZE OF YARD? _____

9. HOW IS YARD USED? _____
_____

10. WHAT USE DOES FAMILY MAKE OF ROOF? _____
_____

11. NUMBER OF ROOMS OCCUPIED, EXCLUSIVE OF BATH-ROOM? _____

12. IS THERE A BATHROOM? _____

13A. IS THERE A TOILET? _____

   B. IS IT LOCATED IN APARTMENT, IN HALL, OR IN YARD? _____

14. HOW MANY STORE-CLOSETS? _____

15. HOW ARE ROOMS HEATED? _____ HOW LIGHTED AT NIGHT? _____

16. HOW IS WATER OBTAINED? _____

17 WHAT FACILITIES FOR WASHING AND DRYING CLOTHES? _____
_____

18. STATE OF REPAIR OF WOODWORK AND WALLS? _____
_____

19 WHERE IS COAL STORED? _____
_____

20. * DESIGNATION of ROOMS	SIZE IN FEET			NUMBER OF WINDOWS	DIRECT ACCESS TO OUTSIDE AIR (YES OR NO)
	WIDTH	LENGTH	HEIGHT		
1					
2					
3					
4					
5					
6					
7					
* NAMES USED BY FAMILY					

21A. TIME AND DISTANCE FROM HOUSE TO PLACE WHERE FATHER REPORTS FOR WORK?

B. TIME AND DISTANCE TO PLACE WHERE ANY OTHER WORKING MEMBER REPORTS?

C. TIME AND DISTANCE TO SCHOOL ATTENDED BY CHILDREN?

22. ARE ROOMS USED FOR OTHER THAN DWELLING PURPOSES?

IF SO, FOR WHAT PURPOSES?

23. HOW LONG HAS FAMILY BEEN IN PRESENT DWELLING?

24. HAS RENT BEEN INCREASED WITHIN TWO YEARS?

HOW MUCH INCREASE?

FUEL AND LIGHT

ARTICLES	BOUGHT BY TON OR BUSHEL?	PRICE PER UNIT	YEARLY	
			QUANTITY USED	TOTAL PAID
COAL				$
COKE				
WOOD				
CANDLES				
KEROSENE				
MATCHES				
GAS				
TOTAL EXPENDITURE FOR FUEL AND LIGHT FOR YEAR				$

2. WHAT FUEL, IF ANY, IS GATHERED FREE OF COST?

3. IS GAS USED FOR COOKING?

4. IS GAS USED FOR LIGHTING?

5. NUMBER OF BURNERS? HOW MANY USUALLY BURNED ALL THE EVENING?

6. IS A SLOT-METER USED?

7. WHERE IS COAL BOUGHT?

ARTICLES	WEEKLY			YEARLY AMOUNT PAID	REMARKS
	QUANTITY	PRICE $	AMT PAID $	$	
BAKER'S					
LOAVES OF BREAD					
ROLLS					
PIES					
CAKE					
CRACKERS					
OTHER GOODS					
FLOUR					
CEREALS					
BEEF					
FRESH					
SALT					
CANNED					
PORK					
FRESH					
SALT					
HAM, BACON ETC.					
SAUSAGE					
READY COOKED MEATS					
MUTTON, LAMB, VEAL ETC.					
POULTRY					
FISH					
FRESH					
CANNED					
SALT, DRIED					
OYSTERS, CLAMS, LOBSTERS					
LARD					
OLEOMARGARINE					
BUTTER					
CHEESE					

ARTICLES	WEEKLY			YEARLY AMT. PAID	REMARKS
	QUANTITY	PRICE	AM'T PAID		
EGGS					
MILK					
LOOSE MILK QTS.					
BOTTLES					
CONDENSED, CANS					
DO. LOOSE					
BUTTERMILK					
POTATOES LB. Q.T. BUSHEL					
TURNIPS					
ONIONS					
CARROTS					
FRESH VEGETABLES					
DRIED BEANS					
DO. PEAS					
CANNED GOODS					
VEGETABLES					
FRUITS					
JAMS, JELLIES ETC.					
FRUITS					
FRESH					
DRIED					
NUTS					
TEA					
COFFE					
COCOA					
SUGAR					
MOLASSES, SYRUP					

ARTICLES	WEEKLY			YEARLY AMT. PAID	REMARKS
	QUANTITY	PRICE	AMT. PAID		
LIQUORS (USED AT TABLE)					
BEER					
ALE					
WINE					
WHISKEY					
GIN					
OTHER DISTILLED LIQUORS					
PICKLES					
SPICES					
ICE LBS USED......WEEKS					
WATER (IF NOT PAID BY LANDLORD)					

MEALS AWAY FROM HOME	WHAT MEALS	NUMBER PER WEEK	PROVIDED FROM HOUSE (YES OR NO)	BOUGHT OUTSIDE	
				COST PER WEEK	COST PER YEAR
FATHER				$	$
MOTHER					
CHILDREN AT WORK					
CHILDREN AT SCHOOL					
					$

TOTAL COST OF MEALS BOUGHT AWAY FROM HOME

TOTAL ANNUAL EXPENDITURE FOR FOOD $...

IS FOOD PROVIDED WHOLESOME?.......................SUFFICIENT?.................

STATE ANY EVIDENCE OF INADEQUACY IN KIND OR AMOUNT...............................

....

....

IN HOW SMALL QUANTITIES AND HOW FREQUENTLY IS FOOD BOUGHT?.......................

....

....

....

....

....

4. WHERE ARE FOOD-SUPPLIES PURCHASED? (UNDERLINE) AT GROCERS' AND BUTCHERS' SHOPS, MARKETS, DELICATESSEN-STORES, OR STREET-VENDERS. ....

5. ARE PREPARED BREAKFAST-FOODS USED?.............. HOW MUCH?.........................

6. WHAT FACILITIES FOR KEEPING PROVISIONS AND COOKED FOOD?...................................

7A. WHAT IS ORDINARILY SERVED FOR BREAKFAST?...................................
....

B. FOR THE NOON MEAL?...................................
....

C. FOR THE EVENING MEAL?...................................
....

D. FOR SUNDAYS DINNER?...................................
....

8. AT WHAT MEALS DOES THE FAMILY SIT DOWN TOGETHER?...................................
....

9. HOW FREQUENTLY ARE GUESTS PRESENT AT MEALS?...................................
....

INSURANCE

FOR INSURANCE OF	KIND OF INSURANCE	AMOUNT CARRIED	AMOUNT PAID PER WEEK	PER YEAR
FATHER		$		
MOTHER				
1ST CHILD				
2ND CHILD				
3RD CHILD				
4TH CHILD				
5TH CHILD				

SAVINGS

WHICH MEMBERS OF THE FAMILY HAVE A SAVINGS BANK ACC'T?...

....

WHAT WAS ADDED TO IT DURING YEAR? $.................

WHAT WAS DRAWN FROM IT DURING YEAR? $.................

TOTAL FOR INSURANCE OF PERSONS

IS FURNITURE INSURED?...................

FOR HOW MUCH? $............... ANNUAL PREMIUM).........

IS HOUSE INSURED?...................

FOR HOW MUCH? $............... ANNUAL PREMIUM).........

$

TOTAL FOR INSURANCE OF PERSONS AND PROPERTY

CLOTHING (EXPENDITURES FOR THE YEAR)

1. FOR FATHER

ARTICLES	NUMBER	TOTAL COST	REMARKS
HATS, CAPS		$	
OVERCOATS			
SUITS			
EXTRA PANTALOONS			
OVERALLS			
WORKING-SHIRTS			
DRESS-SHIRTS			
COLLARS			
CUFFS			
TIES			
HANDKERCHIEFS			
NIGHT-SHIRTS			
UNDERWEAR-SUMMER			
DO. -WINTER			
STOCKINGS			
SHOES-NEW			
DO. -REPAIRS			
RUBBERS			
GLOVES, MITTENS			
JEWELRY			
SUNDRIES			

TOTAL COST $

2. FOR ...... BOYS

ARTICLES	NUMBER	TOTAL COST	REMARKS
HATS, CAPS		$	
OVERCOATS			
SUITS			
EXTRA TROUSERS			
OVERALLS			
SHIRTS			
WAISTS			
COLLARS			
CUFFS			
TIES			
HANDKERCHIEFS			
NIGHT-SHIRTS			
UNDERWEAR-SUMMER			
DO. -WINTER			
STOCKINGS			
SHOES-NEW			
DO. -REPAIRS			
RUBBERS			
GLOVES, MITTENS			
JEWELRY			
SUNDRIES			

TOTAL COST $

9

CLOTHING (EXPENDITURES FOR YEAR)

3. FOR MOTHER

ARTICLES	NUMBER	TOTAL COST	REMARKS
HATS, BONNETS		$	
CLOAKS, FURS			
DRESSES - OF WASH-GOODS			
DO. OF WOOLEN			
WAISTS			
PETTICOATS			
LINEN, ETC.			
UNDERWEAR - SUMMER			
DO. - WINTER			
NIGHT - DRESSES			
RIBBONS, ETC.			
HANDKERCHIEFS			
GLOVES, MITTENS			
APRONS			
STOCKINGS			
SHOES - NEW			
DO. - REPAIRS			
RUBBERS			
JEWELRY			
SUNDRIES			
TOTAL COST		$	

4. FOR .... GIRLS

ARTICLES	NUMBER	TOTAL COST	REMARKS
HATS		$	
CLOAKS, FURS			
DRESSES - OF WASH-GOODS			
DO. OF WOOLEN			
WAISTS			
PETTICOATS			
LINEN, ETC.			
UNDERWEAR - SUMMER			
DO. - WINTER			
NIGHT - DRESSES			
RIBBONS, ETC.			
HANDKERCHIEFS			
GLOVES, MITTENS			
APRONS			
STOCKINGS			
SHOES - NEW			
DO. - REPAIRS			
RUBBERS			
JEWELRY			
SUNDRIES			
TOTAL COST		$	

EXPENDITURES FOR THE YEAR FOR:		7. SUMMARY	
5. MATERIALS FOR HOME-MADE GARMENTS	$	EXPENDITURES FOR CLOTHING	
MATERIALS FOR MENDING CLOTHES		FATHER'S CLOTHING	$
LABOR FOR MAKING AND MENDING		BOYS' CLOTHING	
TOTAL FOR MAKING AND MENDING		MOTHER'S CLOTHING	
6. WASHING MATERIALS (SOAP, STARCH ETC.)	$	GIRLS' CLOTHING	
LABOR FOR WASHING		FOR MAKING AND MENDING	
FOR WORK SENT TO THE LAUNDRY		FOR WASHING AND LAUNDRY	
TOTAL FOR WASHING AND LAUNDRY	$	TOTAL	$

8. WHAT GARMENTS FOR MEMBERS OF THE FAMILY ARE MADE IN THE HOME? ....

....

9. WHAT GARMENTS ARE RE-MADE AND MENDED? ....

10. WHERE IS CLOTHING BOUGHT? ....

11. WHAT ARTICLES, IF ANY, ARE BOUGHT AT SECOND-HAND? ....

12. TO WHAT EXTENT ARE GIFTS OF CLOTHING RECEIVED? ....

13. TO WHAT EXTENT ARE SUCH GIFTS MADE? ....

14. GENERAL APPEARANCE OF DRESS OF MEMBERS OF THE FAMILY. ....

....

HEALTH

EXPENDITURES FOR THE YEAR FOR:			AMT. BROT. FWD. $
PHYSICIAN	$	MEDICINES PRESCRIBED BY PHYSICIAN	$
DENTIST		OTHER MEDICINES	
OCULIST		HOSPITAL CHARGES	
NURSE		DISPENSARY CHARGES	
SURGICAL APPLIANCES		SPECTACLES, EYE-GLASSES	
	AMT. FWD. $		$

1. TOTAL EXPENDITURE ON ACCOUNT OF HEALTH FOR THE YEAR

2. WHAT CASES OF SERIOUS ILLNESS OR ACCIDENT HAVE OCCURED DURING THE YEAR? ....

....

....

3. WHAT FREE MEDICAL ATTENDANCE HAS BEEN RECEIVED? ....

....

FURNITURE AND FURNISHINGS

1. EXPENDITURES FOR THE YEAR FOR:	$		AM'T FWD.	$
FLOOR-COVERINGS		PICTURES, CURTAINS, ORNAMENTS		
CHAIRS, TABLES		PIANO, OTHER MUSICAL INSTRUM'TS		
OTHER WOODEN FURNITURE		BEDS, BEDDING, BED-LINEN		
DISHES AND TABLE-WARE		KITCHEN UTENSILS		
TABLE-LINEN, TOWELS		STOVES: REFRIGERATOR		
SUPPLIES FOR SWEEPING AND CLEANING		OTHER		
AMT FWD.	$	TOTAL EXPENDITURES FOR FURNITURE AND FURNISHINGS		$

2 PRESENT EQUIPMENT;

(Enumerate the principal articles in each room, designating the rooms as parlor kitchen etc. and state the kind of furniture (eg. folding bed, lace curtains), and present condition)

1st ROOM _ _ _ _ _ _ _ _ _ _ _ _ _ _ _ _ _ _

_ _

2nd. ROOM _ _ _ _ _ _ _ _ _ _ _ _ _ _ _ _ _

_ _

3rd. ROOM _ _ _ _ _ _ _ _ _ _ _ _ _ _ _ _ _

_ _

4th. ROOM _ _ _ _ _ _ _ _ _ _ _ _ _ _ _ _ _

_ _

5th ROOM _ _ _ _ _ _ _ _ _ _ _ _ _ _ _ _ _

_ _

6th. ROOM _ _ _ _ _ _ _ _ _ _ _ _ _ _ _ _ _

_ _

7th. ROOM _ _ _ _ _ _ _ _ _ _ _ _ _ _ _ _ _

_ _

3 WHAT IS THE STANDARD OF TASTE AND ECONOMY REPRESENTED BY THE FURNITURE AND FURNISHINGS? _ _ _ _ _ _ _ _ _ _ _ _ _ _ _

_ _

4 IS ANY FURNITURE BOUGHT AT SECOND-HAND? _ _ _ _ _ _ _ _ _

_ _

TAXES, DUES and CONTRIBUTIONS

1. WHAT MEMBERS OF THE FAMILY BELONG TO LABOR-UNIONS? ....

2. AMOUNT PAID TO LABOR-UNIONS	PER WEEK	PER YEAR		$
	$	$	3. AMOUNT PAID IN TAXES FOR THE YEAR	
BY FATHER			4. AMOUNT IN GIFTS OF FRIENDSHIP (OUTSIDE OF THE FAMILY)	
BY			5. AMOUNT PAID IN GIFTS OF CHARITY	
BY			6. AMOUNT PAID TO CHURCH OR OTHER RELIGIOUS ORGAN-	
TOTAL PAID TO LABOR-UNIONS FOR		$	IZATIONS FOR THE YEAR .. .. ⌐	

7. WHAT MEMBERS OF THE FAMILY BELONG TO A LODGE OR OTHER SOCIAL ORGANIZATION? .....

....

....

..................................— 8. AMOUNT PAID TO SUCH SOCITIES PER YEAR

(2) AMOUNT PAID TO LABOR-UNIONS FOR THE YEAR — $

TOTAL EXPENDITURES FOR TAXES, DUES AND CONTRIBUTIONS

RECREATION and AMUSEMENTS

IN WHAT WAYS DO ADULT MEMBERS OF THE FAMILY SEEK AMUSEMENT AND RECREATION? ......

....

....

....

....

.... $

2. EXPENDITURES FOR THE YEAR FOR THE THEATRE

3. EXPENDITURES FOR THE YEAR FOR DANCES

4. FOR EXCURSIONS AND PLEASURE-TRIPS (EXCLUDING CAR-FARES)

5. FOR TOYS AND PLAYTHINGS

6. FOR OTHER FORMS OF AMUSEMENTS (STATE THE PURPOSES) ....

.... $

....

TOTAL EXPENDITURES FOR RECREATION AND AMUSEMENTS $

CAR-FARES

AMOUNT PAID FOR CAR-FARES OF FATHER TO AND FROM PLACE OF WORK	$
FOR CAR-FARES OF OTHER WAGE-EARNERS TO AND FROM PLACE OF WORK	
FOR CAR-FARES OF CHILDREN TO AND FROM SCHOOL	
FOR CAR-FARES OF MOTHER	
CAR-FARES FOR VISITING, RECREATION, ETC.	
TOTAL EXPENDITURES FOR CAR-FARES FOR THE YEAR	$

EDUCATION AND READING

	$
SCHOOL EXPENSES OF CHILDREN FOR THE YEAR (EXCLUSIVE OF CAR-FARES)	
NEWSPAPERS AND PERIODICALS	
BOOKS	
POSTAGE AND STATIONERY	
TOTAL EXPENDITURE FOR EDUCATION AND READING	$

WHAT NEWSPAPERS AND PERIODICALS ARE .... BOUGHT? ..... _

_ _

_ _

WHAT BOOKS DOES THE FAMILY HAVE? _ _ _ . . .

_ _

_ _

IS PUBLIC LIBRARY USED? _

BY WHICH MEMBERS OF FAMILY? _

_ _

MISCELLANEOUS EXPENDITURES

		AMT FWD. $ _ _ _ _ _ _ _ _
CONTINGENT EXPENSES. (FOR THE YEAR)		EXPENDITURE FOR YEAR FOR BARBER
FUNERAL EXPENSES	$	FOR OTHER PERSONAL SERVICE
LEGAL EXPENSES		SPENDING MONEY (NOT OTHERWISE SPECIFIED)
EXPENSES OF MOVING		FATHER PER WEEK $ PER YEAR $
INTEREST ON DEBTS		MOTHER DO. $ DO. $
REPAYMENT OF DEBTS		CHILDREN AT WORK DO. $ DO. $
EXPENDITURE FOR YEAR FOR:		CHILDREN AT SCHOOL DO. $ DO. $
TOBACCO		TOOLS
BEER, WHISKEY, ETC (DRUNK AWAY FROM HOME)		INCIDENTALS
ICE-CREAM		_ _
CANDY AND SODA-WATER		
EXPENDITURES FOR RECREATION AND AMUSEMENTS AMT FWD.		TOTAL MISCELLANEOUS EXPENDITURES $

SUMMARY of ANNUAL EXPENDITURES

	$
HOUSING	
FUEL AND LIGHT	
FOOD	
INSURANCE	
CLOTHING	
HEALTH	
FURNITURE AND FURNISHINGS	
TAXES, DUES AND CONTRIBUTIONS	
RECREATION AND AMUSEMENTS	
CAR-FARES	
EDUCATION AND READING	
MISCELLANEOUS	
TOTAL	$

REMARKS

WHEN FILLED OUT, SEND THIS SCHEDULE TO THE SECRETARY OF THE COMMITTEE ON STANDARD OF LIVING OF THE N.Y. STATE CONFERENCE OF CHARITIES AND CORRECTIONS, ROBERT C CHAPIN,

Report from Nine Cities and Towns Outside of Greater New York

Returns were received in the summer of 1907 from ten cities and towns in the state outside of Greater New York, including in all 86 schedules. Grateful mention should be made of the willingness and efficiency of those who co-operated with the Committee in gathering the information.* The schedules from Buffalo, Syracuse and Richfield Springs were gathered by paid investigators; in the other cities and towns by volunteers.

The more exhaustive investigation into the standard of living in Buffalo made by Mr. Howard, in 1908 (see Appendix V, page 307) renders unnecessary, in the present connection, the consideration of the 30 Buffalo schedules of 1907. Three of the remaining 56 schedules were rejected because of incompleteness, and the data from the remainder have been tabulated. The returns utilized include schedules from nine localities, as follows:

Syracuse	19
Rochester	7
Victor	2
Honeoye Falls	2
Richfield Springs	10
Elmira	6
Albany	3
Whitehall	3
Maryland	1
	—
	53

By income, the distribution appears in the following table:

* The thanks of the Committee are due especially to Mr. John R. Howard, Jr., Buffalo, Mrs. Lewis Bigelow, Rochester, Professor E. L. Earp, Syracuse, Miss Anna B. Pratt, Elmira, Miss Alida Lattimore, Whitehall, Mr. Robert W. Hill and Mr. Arthur W. Towne, Albany.

	TOTAL	$300 TO $399	$400 TO $499	$500 TO $599	$600 TO $699	$700 TO $799	$800 TO $899	$900 TO $999	$1000 TO $1099	$1100 TO $1199	$1200 TO $1299	$1300 AND OVER
Syracuse	19	..	..	1	3	1	3	2	1	4	3	1
Richfield Springs	10	..	..	2	3	3	1	1	..	..	..	..
Rochester	7	..	..	1	2	1	..	..	..	1	1	1
Victor	2	..	..	..	1	..	..	..	..	..	1	..
Honeoye Falls	2	..	..	..	1	..	..	..	..	..	1	..
Elmira	6	..	1	..	..	2	1	..	1	..	..	1
Albany	3	..	..	..	..	..	2	..	1	..	..	..
Whitehall	3	..	..	..	..	1	1	..	1	..	..	..
Maryland	1	1	..	..	..	..	..	..	..	..	..	..
Total	53	1	1	4	10	8	8	3	4	5	6	3

In view of the small number of schedules obtained, it has been deemed advisable to include not only those of families with incomes well above $1000, but also those of families with less than 4 and more than 6 members. This wide range, however, together with the small number of schedules, makes difficult any very exact comparison of the returns from the different localities. Nevertheless these returns have a distinct value, and it is hoped that the publication of them may suggest the value of a more comprehensive study of local conditions in each locality.

The occupations of these 53 families are typical of the communities in which they live. Factory-operatives predominate in the manufacturing centers, with employees in the building-trades, clerks, laborers and railway employees. In the smaller places are clerks, printers, artisans and laborers.

For the purpose of exhibiting some of the resemblances and differences, so far as they appear in the schedules received, Tables 129-130 (pages 305-306) have been prepared. In several cases, where only one family could be taken, it is not safe to assume that this family, or the averages for 3 or 5 families, are typical, and too much should not be inferred from these tables. They do at least show what is possible in a given case, and the selection has been made so as to include a wide variety of circumstances. Rochester and Syracuse are manufacturing cities, Victor is a suburban outpost of Rochester, Richfield Springs a country town of 3000 inhabitants. For these localities, comparison of the families with incomes of from $600 to $700 has been possible, and the figures for the New York City families of the same income-group are reproduced for comparison. Elmira and Albany are cities of a different type, and Whitehall is a small manufacturing city in a locality where fuel is dear. The one schedule from the town of Maryland gives the budget of a farm laborer, who occupies a 4-room house at the nominal rent of $2 a month.

The salient feature of these schedules from outside New York City is the lower cost of housing. This appears in two forms: in the lower rental charges, and in the large proportion of house-owners among wage-earners. The proportion of income spent for rent is less, the smaller the city. In New York rent absorbs 24 per cent. of the expenditure of a family with an income between $600 and $700. In Syracuse and Rochester it takes less than 20 per cent., in Richfield Springs 14 per cent. (in 2 cases out of 3), in Victor 14 per cent.

In the second place, the number of house-owners reported is suggestive. In Rochester and its suburbs 8 of the 11 families own houses, or are buying them on the instalment plan. Two of the Rochester families averaged in the $600 column are paying for houses of their own. One of these, an Italian family of 5 persons, occupies 3 rooms and rents the rest of the house for $132, paying $48 a year for interest on a mortgage of $600. An English shoe-maker, with a family of 4 and a total income of $680, is paying for his house in instalments of $200 a year. Clothing is the only item in his budget that seems to suffer in consequence, although the food-expenditure is at the rate of 24 cents per man per day. Altogether, 15 of the 53 families are reported as owning their houses.*

In the tables two Whitehall families are entered, one owning and one renting its dwelling. The house-owning family has a money income of $780, as against $884 for the house-renting family. But the charge of $120 for rent in the budget of the latter family consumes the difference, and leaves the expenditure for the remaining items nearly the same for the two families.

* Out of 642 schedules received from Greater New York, only 6 were of house-owning families; 4 of these were from Brooklyn, 2 from Manhattan, and in all but 1 case the family income was over $1000.

The principal exception is in the matter of taxes, where the house-owning family pays $45 as against $12 for the other family. In the schedules of house-owning families in other cities the taxes appear as a larger item than for the house-renters, and the surplus otherwise seems to be expended among the various items according to no fixed rule.*

Not only is the cost of housing less in the cities outside of New York, but the accommodations enjoyed are better. Detached houses are the rule, with no question of access to light and air. The number of rooms is 3 in only 1 case of the 53 (Rochester); only 6 report 4 rooms, and 7 and 8 rooms are of frequent occurrence. In cities with water service a private toilet is the rule, and a bath-room is frequently reported. For $8 a month in the smaller towns of the State and $10 or $11 in the cities like Syracuse, better accommodations can be secured than for $15 in Manhattan.

In the smaller places there is opportunity to raise vegetables and fruit in a garden, and this is noted in many of the schedules. Eggs and poultry are also raised in many instances at home. The calculation of food-expenditures per man per day, on the cash basis, needs supplementing in these cases. The large size of some of the families reported, especially in Syracuse, explains in part the low allowance for food per man per day.

In regard to clothing the averages and percentages as tabulated point to a larger expenditure for this purpose outside of New York City than within it. It would be interesting to pursue the subject further, especially with regard to Rochester. Rochester is, like New York, a center of the garment-trades, and the 3 families there with incomes between $600 and $700 report a lower average expenditure for clothing than the average of the 72 with the same income in New York City. With this exception, the figures point to a higher cost of clothing in the state at large than in New York City.

A comparison of the expenditures for the various items of the budget in the several localities may be facilitated by the tables of averages and percentages on pages 305 and 306. In many in-

---

* In the tabulation of the Syracuse schedules an amount equal to the rental value of the house owned is added to the total income, and the same amount is entered under "Housing" and included in the total of expenditures.

stances the variations indicate merely the taste and habit of a single family rather than a social standard. It would be hazardous on the basis of so small a number of cases to make an estimate of the sum required to maintain a normal standard in each community. It would certainly fall below the amount needed in New York City, but the exact measure of the difference requires a larger induction of cases.

TABLE 129.—NINE CITIES AND TOWNS OF NEW YORK STATE. PER CENT. OF TOTAL ANNUAL EXPENDITURE REPORTED FOR THE SEVERAL PRINCIPAL ITEMS OF THE BUDGET.

	NEW YORK.	ROCHESTER.	VICTOR.	RICHFIELD SPRINGS.	SYRACUSE.	ELMIRA.	ALBANY.	WHITE HALL. (House-owner.)	WHITE HALL. (Renter.)	MARYLAND.
	72 Families. Income $600 to $700. Various.* 4.9.†	3 Families.‡ Income $580 to $680. Various.* 4.5.†	1 Family U.S.* 5.†	3 Families.‡ Income $600 to $700. U.S.* 5.†	5 Families.‡ Income $589 to $700. Various.* 5.9.†	3 Families.‡ Income $750 to $810. Various.* 7.7.†	1 Family U.S.* 4.†	1 Family U.S.* 5.†	1 Family U.S.* 3.†	1 Family U.S.* 6.†
Total income	$650.17	$627.66	$600.00	$624.00	$628.40	$769.12	$815.00	$780.00	$884.00	$380.00
Total expenditure	650.57	636.41	595.41	571.82	2654.94	795.68	804.82	803.65	894.42	356.36
	Per Cent.	Per Cent.	Per Cent.	Per Cent.	Per Cent.	Per Cent.	Per Cent.	Per Cent.	Per Cent.	Per Cent.
Housing	23.6	19.9	14.1	18.2	19.7	10.3	12.0	..	13.4	6.8
Car-fares	1.7	1.6	..		0.2	0.2	0.6	..	..	..
Fuel and light	5.8	6.5	6.8	4.5	6.9	6.6	4.9	9.3	9.6	4.4
Food	44.6	42.0	34.6	46.5	34.0	53.3	57.3	51.0	43.5	51.3
Clothing	12.9	11.4	27.3	21.2	20.4	15.1	13.3	17.9	17.5	19.9
Insurance	2.0	1.9	..		5.5	1.8	0.7	10.6	9.2	1.4
Health	2.1	2.7	1.7	3.7	2.5	2.2	3.3	1.0	0.9	1.4
Furniture	1.0	8.3	2.5	1.0	3.0	4.3	1.4	0.1	0.5	1.4
Taxes, dues, etc	1.2	2.8	0.3	1.3	1.1	0.6	.6	5.6	1.3	..
Recreation and amusement	0.5	0.6	5.5	1.0	0.5	0.3	1.5	0.4	1.6	1.4
Education and reading	0.7	0.7	1.7	0.5	0.9	1.0	0.6	3.2	0.4	1.8
Miscellaneous	3.9	1.6	5.5	2.1	4.9	4.3	3.8	0.9	2.1	10.2

* Nationality.   † Average number of persons in family.   ‡ Average.

20

305

TABLE 130.—NINE CITIES AND TOWNS OF NEW YORK STATE. AVERAGE AMOUNT OF EXPENDITURE FOR THE SEVERAL PRINCIPAL ITEMS OF THE BUDGET.

	NEW YORK.	ROCHESTER.	VICTOR.	RICHFIELD SPRINGS.	SYRACUSE.	ELMIRA.	ALBANY.	WHITE-HALL. (House-owner.)	WHITE-HALL. (Renter.)	MARY-LAND.
	72 Families. Income $600 to $700. Various.* 4.9.†	3 Families.‡ Income $580 to $680. Various.* 4.5.†	1 Family U. S.* 5.†	3 Families.‡ Income $600 to $700. U. S.* 5.†	5 Families.‡ Income $580 to $700. Various.* 5.9.†	3 Families.‡ Income $750 to $810. Various.* 7.7.†	1 Family U. S.* 4.†	1 Family U. S.* 5.†	1 Family U. S.* 3.†	1 Family U. S.* 6.†
Total income..........	$650.17	$627.66	$600.00	$624.00	$628.40	$769.12	$815.00	$780.00	$884.00	$380.00
Total expenditure......	650.57	636.41	595.45	571.82	645.94	795.68	804.82	803.65	894.42	356.36
Housing.............	153.59	126.90	84.00	104.00	127.20	81.66	96.00	..	120.00	24.00
Car-fares...........	11.31	10.33	..	..	1.12	1.53	5.00	..	5.00	..
Fuel and light.......	37.31	43.10	40.50	25.77	45.04	52.25	38.90	74.98	85.94	15.75
Food................	290.10	267.29	207.00	265.90	220.01	426.12	462.97	409.09	388.44	183.36
Clothing............	83.48	80.16	162.95	121.52	132.46	119.55	166.45	144.18	155.95	71.25
Insurance...........	13.05	12.05	10.00	..	35.72	14.13	6.00	85.40	82.33	5.00
Health..............	13.78	7.16	15.00	21.68	16.10	17.73	26.50	8.00	8.00	5.00
Furniture...........	6.05	52.80	2.00	5.72	19.44	34.00	11.00	1.16	4.70	5.00
Taxes, dues, etc.....	7.90	18.30	31.00	7.60	7.60	4.61	5.00	45.00	12.00	..
Recreation and amusement.....	3.42	3.92	10.00	5.67	3.72	2.53	12.00	3.00	14.06	5.00
Education and reading.....	4.71	4.96	33.00	1.96	5.94	7.60	5.00	25.60	4.00	6.00
Miscellaneous........	25.47	10.33	33.00	12.00	31.57	33.94	30.00	7.24	19.00	36.00

* Nationality.   † Average number of persons in family.   ‡ Average.

APPENDIX V

Report on the Standard of Living among Workingmen's Families in Buffalo, New York

By John R. Howard, Jr.

The investigation of the cost of living in Buffalo, undertaken on behalf of the Committee on Standard of Living of the New York State Conference of Charities and Correction, was limited to 100 families. This was done partly because the amount of the appropriation and the brief time allowed (three summer months) admitted of no more extensive study; and partly in the belief that 100 families, selected with care and interviewed by a few experienced investigators, would yield more accurate results than a larger number selected at random and interviewed by untrained volunteers. Miss Emma O. Lundberg, Master of Arts in the University of Wisconsin, who was chosen to execute the work, gathered her own facts from 51 of the 100 families; while 30 of the families of foreign birth were interviewed by three women peculiarly qualified by experience and nationality for work in this field, and the other 19 by social workers, men and women, most of whom had the advantage of long-standing acquaintance with the families they selected for the study.

After careful consideration of the study that had previously been made in New York City, the investigators in Buffalo came to the conclusion that the single standard adopted in the New York investigation would not be satisfactory for all nationalities. It was believed, for instance, that the Poles, of whom there are about 95,000 in the city, and the Italians, of whom there are about 20,000, would show, and would require, a lower standard of life than the other, more Americanized peoples. It was therefore determined to select 50 families of various nationalities, 25 Polish, and 25 Italian, believing that while the numbers were not sufficient accurately to define standards of life for families of these three types, they would at least indicate prevailing differences, and taken together form an adequate ground for comparison with the standard set up for New York by the Committee last year.

It was suggested that the investigation be limited to families with incomes not exceeding $500, the supposed maximum wage of the average day laborer, in order to discover what the ordinary workingman was able to provide for his family; but it was concluded that the investigation must include incomes large enough to provide the essentials of a proper standard of living, in order to learn the cost of such essentials. Accordingly, the investigation was limited to families with incomes not exceeding $700, a sum generally considered ample in Buffalo.

THE SCHEDULE.—The procedure with respect to filling out schedules for these families was similar to that followed in New York. The schedules were identical. It is not necessary, therefore, again to describe the questions asked under the several headings with regard to housing, fuel and light, furniture, insurance, food, clothing, taxes, dues and contributions, recreation and amusements, education and reading, and miscellaneous.

NATIONALITIES.—As has already been indicated, 25 of the 100 families were Italians and 25 Polish. Of the other 50 families, 19 were Americans, 13 Germans, 5 Irish, 3 Scotch, 2 English, 2 Canadians, 2 Swedish, 1 colored, 1 Dutch, 1 Austrian, and 1 Roumanian.

OCCUPATIONS.—Among those selected were 42 laborers, 8 carpenters, 3 paperhangers, 3 moulders, 3 painters, 3 watchmen, 3 hackmen, 2 delivery men, 2 tailors, 2 gardeners, and 1 each of twenty-seven other occupations.

INCOME.

The average income of the 100 families was $600, and the average disbursement $632. This discrepancy, however, seems to have been due more to the hard times than to permanent inability to make ends meet. The largest part of it occurs in the Polish families, who have no idea how their money goes, and so are at a loss to know how to meet the emergency when earnings are curtailed.

In 29 per cent. of the 100 families the mother's earnings added to the income, the number of cases being pretty evenly distributed among the races, with one exception. The exception was, as might be supposed, in the Italian families, where only one mother was reported as adding to the income, and she by work in the country during the summer. There would undoubtedly have been more cases reported of this kind of labor had the investigation not been made in the summer, for hundreds of the low-wage Italians move to the canning districts with the spring.

Six per cent. of the families have lodgers and 31 per cent. have incomes from children's earnings and other sources. It is in the Polish families that the man's earnings are most frequently supplemented, as indicated by the fact that the average income of the Polish families is $604, while the average wage of a Polish man is $422.

EXPENDITURES.

In discussing the various expenditures of these families, comparison will be made with the 72 families of the $600 to $700 group in the New York study, the average disbursement of that group being $650, while the average disbursement of the Buffalo families is $632.

It should be noted that the New York family averages 5 persons, and the Buffalo family 6. This in itself may indicate a less severe struggle for existence in Buffalo than in New York, though it may also be due to a difference in selection of cases.

HOUSING.

The average amount paid for rent by the Buffalo family of 6 is $8.00 a month. For this, 4 rooms are obtained, with an average of 1½ windows to a room, each opening upon the outer air. The New York family of 5 persons pays $13 a month for 3 rooms, one of which is without access to the outer air. In the Buffalo investigation 7 dark rooms only were found, 2 of them alcoves of rooms with outside windows. In addition to this, half of the families live in one- or two-family, detached, frame houses with air-space on four sides, and the other half live, for the most part, in houses to which the name tenement-houses is applied only because there are three or more families in them. The typical Buffalo house is a two-story, detached frame house, having a grass plot in front and a yard behind. Almost any residence street on the east side of Buffalo is wider, greener, and quieter than the finest residence streets in Manhattan, but clean air is lacking. Buffalo is a smoky city.

There is over-crowding in Buffalo, but, outside of a few large tenement-houses, the crowding occurs within detached houses surrounded by ample air-space. Over-crowding under such conditions may be a serious evil if health laws are not wise and health officers vigilant, but in Buffalo the laws are good, and they are well enforced. There are, however, among the 50 Polish and Italian families of this study, 13 families averaging 5 persons who live in 2 rooms, 2 of these families having 7 persons; and there are 12 families averaging 6 persons who live in 3 rooms, one a family of 9, and three others numbering 7 persons each.

FURNITURE.

The annual expenditure for furniture is $7.00, $1.00 more than in New York. When it is considered that this sum, amounting to 13½ cents a week, provides for all furniture and household and kitchen utensils, it is seen to be little enough. All large purchases must be made on the instalment plan, but there was very little of this last year because of the hard times, even those with normal earnings seeming to hold back for fear of coming to want.

INSURANCE.

Twenty dollars is the average amount spent for insurance, as against $13 in New York; and in Buffalo, as in New York, this is chiefly for life insurance, only 13 of the families having property insured. Sixty-five per cent. of the 100 families were insured: of the Italian families, only 28 per cent., of the Polish families, 84 per cent., and of the other 50 families, 74 per cent.

310

FOOD.

In discussing the food item, it should be pointed out that the average Buffalo family is 3.8 units, figuring an adult man as the unit, and the mother and children in proportion thereto, while the average New York family of the group under consideration is 3.3 units.

In the New York investigation 100 schedules were submitted to Dr. Frank P. Underhill, assistant professor of Physiological Chemistry at Yale, to determine the nutritive values of the food actually bought by these families, and to calculate from such figures what expenditure was necessary to maintain physical efficiency. Dr. Underhill estimated that families that spent less than 22 cents per man per day were insufficiently nourished, and that those who spent 22 cents or more per man per day were sufficiently nourished. (See Appendix VI, page 322.)

In like manner, 50 of the Buffalo food schedules were submitted to Dr. Underhill for analysis (see page 324). The item "liquor used at table," however, which was included in the New York schedules analyzed, was omitted. From this study it appears that 21 cents per man per day is the minimum for Buffalo; but when the item "liqour used at table" is included, it brings the standard up to the 22 cents estimated for New York. Because of some misunderstanding with respect to this standard, the fact must be emphasized that it is not an *a priori* standard based upon the cost of food bought in assumed quantities and variety, but a figure based upon the actual food bought by representative families. The analysis showed that of the 50 Buffalo schedules submitted, 80 per cent. of those showing an expenditure of 21 cents or more per man per day were sufficiently nourished, and 83 per cent. of those showing an expenditure of less than 21 cents per man per day were insufficiently nourished.

The average disbursement for food in Buffalo is $299, compared with $279 in New York; but, as we have seen, the New York families average 3.3 units, while the Buffalo families average 3.8. The actual expenditure per man per day is $21\frac{1}{2}$ cents in Buffalo, and 23 cents in New York, comparing always with the $600 to $700 group in New York. These figures include liquor at table, so that the average Buffalo family spends one-half cent less than the standard of 22 cents, and the average New York family spends 1 cent more than the standard.*

The meals correspond very nearly to those of the New York families. The meals in the Polish families are not unlike those of the other nationalities in Buffalo, except that a breakfast of coffee and bread only is more common, meat is oftener served at lunch, and a chicken for Sunday dinner is not infrequent. The Italians have macaroni once or twice a day, beer every day, and a greater variety of food than the other nationalities. It may be of interest to note, here, that 10 of the 50 schedules submitted to Dr. Underhill were of Polish families, and 10 Italian, and that the tables show that the same minimum of 22 cents per man per day holds even more decidedly for these nationalities. Pertinent to this subject is Dr. Underhill's statement to the effect that "no definite relation appears to exist between the purchase of a preponderance of animal or vegetable food and an ability to live at a low figure." In spite, then, of the apparent variety of the Italians' food, it is interesting to note that they average but 20½ cents per man per day, and so are probably undernourished; and, further, that 1½ cents of this amount goes for beer, so that 19 cents is the amount spent for nutritive food, or an amount 2 cents below the minimum set by Dr. Underhill. The expense per man per day of the Poles is 21½ cents with liquor, which is one-half cent below minimum, and 20 cents without liquor, which is 1 cent below minimum. The expense per man per day for the other 50 families is 22 cents, which equals the minimum; and because they spend less for liquor at table, their expense without this item is 21½ cents, or one-half cent above the minimum. The New York families spend 6.2 per cent. of the total disbursement for food for liquor used in the home, which reduces their actual expenditure for nutritive food to 21½ cents per man per day, as in Buffalo.

* The number of cents per man per day is here calculated as in the report of Dr. Frankel, page 265, by dividing the average annual expenditure for food by the average number of "units," and this annual average per unit by 365. For Table 64, page 141, calculation was made for each family, as explained on page 126, and the results averaged by income and nationality. The variations in the results obtained by the two methods are due to the difference in treating meals away from home.

CLOTHING.

The Buffalo family spends for clothing $117, or 18½ per cent. of the total expenditure, where the New York family spends $83, or 13 per cent. of the total. In Buffalo $10.50 of this goes for washing; in New York $8.50. One-third of the families receive gifts of clothing in both cities.

HEALTH.

The average amount spent for health in Buffalo is $15. This shows an average expenditure of $1.00 more than was shown in New York, but there was less use of free dispensaries, probably because they are not so available in Buffalo. Twelve of the families reported having had free medical aid; only 4 had employed a dentist.

CAR-FARE.

Fifteen dollars is the average sum spent for car-fare, nearly all by the man going to and from work. This item is $4.00 higher than for New York, probably because of the greater distances of the homes from the places of work.

TAXES, DUES, AND CONTRIBUTIONS.

To religious organizations, labor unions, and lodges about $8.00 is contributed. This is the same as in New York; but in New York 28 per cent. of the families spent nothing for these purposes, while in Buffalo but 20 per cent. reported no expenditures under this head.

RECREATION.

Four dollars is spent for recreation and amusement, 14 per cent. more than in New York. Twenty-five of the families reported taking excursions, 21 attendance at the theaters, and 39 the use of the parks; but the amount of such recreation that can be enjoyed by a family of 6 on an expenditure of $4.00 per year may be easily reckoned.

EDUCATION AND READING.

The Buffalo family spends $6.00 for education and reading, mostly for newspapers; the New York family, $5.00. The expenditures of the Poles bring up the average of this item because of their parochial-school tax. Sixty-eight families buy newspapers, 35 have books in their homes, and 38 make use of the public library.

MISCELLANEOUS.

For miscellaneous expenditures, including all spending money and incidentals, the average amount is $12. Most of this goes for tobacco and shaving for the man. In the New York group this item is $25, of which $10 is spent for tobacco alone.

SUMMARY.

To summarize the results and comparisons, the average expenditures (by percentages) are:

	BUFFALO.	NEW YORK.
Rent	15 per cent.	23½ per cent.
Food	47 " "	44½ " "
Clothing	18½ " "	13 " "
Fuel and Light	6 " "	6 " "
Total	86½ per cent.	87 per cent.
Car-fare, Insurance and Health	8 per cent.	6 per cent.
Sundries	5½ " "	7 " "
Total	100 per cent.	100 per cent.

From a study of the New York report and the Buffalo schedules, it appears that the only item of real difference in the respective schedules is rent. The high rentals in New York render it impossible for families in that city to spend as much upon the other items as families of the same income in Buffalo. The excess on food expenditure in Buffalo is due entirely to the larger sized family. The greater expenditure for clothing may be explained partly by the additional member in the family, but is undoubtedly due mainly, as are the larger expenditures for the remaining items, to the fact that there is a greater surplus available, owing to the lower cost of housing.

If all the items but rent, then, be practically the same, or if there is no fundamental reason why they should not be the same for the same sized family in New York and Buffalo, what is to prevent our transposing the standard proposed for New York to Buffalo, simply by modifying this one item? The New York report (page 279) reads: "With an income of between $700 and $800 a family can barely support itself, provided that it is subject to no extraordinary expenditures by reason of sickness, death, or other untoward circumstances. Such a family can live without charitable assistance through exceptional management and in the absence of emergencies." But the difference in rent between the Buffalo families ($96) and the New York families with an income of $700 to $800 ($161) is $65; so by substituting $635 to $735 for $700 to $800 in the above statement, we arrive at an analogous standard for Buffalo. Again, the New York report (page 281) reads: "It is a fairly conservative estimate that $825 is sufficient for the average family of 5 individuals, comprising father, mother, and 3 children under fourteen years of age, to maintain a fairly proper standard of living in the Borough of Manhattan." The difference between the Buffalo rent ($96) and that of the $800 to $900 group in New York ($168) is $72, so the standard of $825 proposed for New York becomes approximately $755 in Buffalo, because of the difference in rent. This standard seems to be as necessary for Poles and Italians as for the other nationalities.

This New York standard of $825 is, as stated above, based upon the average expenditure of the $800 to $900 group (Table III, page 272), namely $811, the surplus being allowed for emergencies. The New York report says of this group (page 281) that all its main items of expense seem to provide for a normal standard. Examination of the Buffalo families leads to the belief that the items of expense as shown for this group in New York, with one exception, would provide in Buffalo what should be called a *minimum* standard. The one exception is the item of food. For this item the amount of $359 appears. Eighteen dollars of this is for meals away from home, an item that does not appear in the Buffalo budgets, and the remaining $341 provides an allowance of 27 cents per day per unit. That is 5 cents per day per unit, or $64 a year, more than the minimum set by Dr. Underhill. Dr. Underhill demonstrates that a large proportion of the families spending 22 cents per day per unit or more (in Buffalo 80 per cent.) were, as far as could be determined, sufficiently nourished. The minimum was purposely set at a figure that made the chances greatly in favor of this condition. Dr. Underhill himself says of this minimum: "The task of deciding whether a person is receiving sufficient food is not easy, owing to the many standards upheld by the various schools of nutrition. However, if the average standard generally accepted be adopted, there need be no hesitation in the acceptance of the condition of *sufficient* nourishment." Therefore, in determining a minimum standard for Buffalo, a sum upon which a family of 5 can maintain physical efficiency, which surely demands a "fairly proper standard of living," it seems fair to adhere to Dr. Underhill's minimum of 22 cents per day per unit for food. To do this we must subtract from the standard of $755 already proposed, $18 for the meals away from home, and $64 for the lower food allowance, and so obtain a standard for Buffalo approximating $675.

In estimating a minimum standard, the item of rent is readily determined. The $800 to $900 group in New York spends $168 for rent, which is $72 more than the Buffalo families spend. They obtain for this 3½ rooms, one of which is dark, while the Buffalo families have 4 rooms, all opening on the outer air. Under present conditions the New York standard of housing cannot be raised nor the Buffalo standard lowered, for New York tenement-houses do not permit of the one, nor the Buffalo detached houses of the other. In the matter of clothing, the studies reveal important facts bearing on a possible minimum. But who can say that an average family of five needs this amount or that? And if there is difficulty in determining the item of clothing, what is to be said of such items as health, insurance, education, or amusements? Does any one who believes recreation to be an essential part of the cost of a proper standard of living really think that $6.00 covers the need for a family of 5 for a year? The man who agrees to $6.00 will probably agree also to $10. How are we to decide which is right? What process of reasoning is actually applied to the items outside of food, rent, and clothing, in basing a standard of living upon the expenditures shown by 400 families? Is there any actual measuring of the efficacy of the average disbursements? There is not; and the method is an *a priori* method, modified possibly by the facts shown, but in a very vague way that by no means establishes the standard on empirical grounds.

These remarks are not offered as a criticism of the New York investigation. The New York committee very distinctly says that it "does not feel that the investigation which has been made is more than a preliminary one, and for this reason its findings are but the interpretation of the facts presented in the schedules"; that "the number of schedules returned, while larger than in any similar investigation made heretofore, is still too small to postulate definite conclusions." But there is need of insisting on the very general and unfinal nature of such reports as that of this year and last, because the standard set for New York by the committee has been widely received as a definite standard to be accepted without further inquiry. The figures of the New York committee have even been incorporated in the most recent book on economics, from a trusted university department, having been accepted there as a standard for the average American city! Times have changed, when academic scholars accept as established standards the tentative conclusions of a small number of social workers; but if this change has come, it is all the more important for us to be accurate in method and conservative in statement.

In conclusion, if there can be no agreement as to the accuracy of the standards proposed for New York and Buffalo, all will agree that one point has been established without question, namely, that the average wage of unskilled labor in these two cities is far below the income necessary to provide what any one of us could call a minimum standard of living. Such a conclusion, together with a knowledge of the methods and results of these studies, emphasizes the importance of a more thorough investigation of the whole subject, extending over a far larger number of families, and through a period of at least twelve months.

TABLE 131.—ONE HUNDRED BUFFALO FAMILIES. EXPENDITURES FOR PRINCIPAL ITEMS OF THE BUDGET. AVERAGES AND PERCENTAGES.—BY NATIONALITY.

	25 Families, Italian.		25 Families, Polish.		50 Families Various.		Total, 100 Families. All Nationalities.	
Total income..........	$578.08		$603.59		$609.91		$600.37	
Total expenditure.....	$564.77		$678.18		$643.43		$632.45	
	Average.	Per cent.*	Average.	Per cent.*	Average.	Per cent.*	Average.	Per cent.*
Housing.............	$88.52	15.7	$90.24	13.3	$102.18	15.8	$95.78	15.1
Fuel and light........	29.88	5.3	38.66	5.7	39.10	6.	36.93	5.8
Furniture............	5.93	1.	5.10	.7	8.15	1.4	6.83	1.
Insurance............	4.52	.8	26.94	4.	23.37	3.6	19.58	3.1
Food................	265.23	47.	335.23	49.4	298.16	46.3	299.20	47.
Clothing.............	127.85	22.6	114.91	17.	112.59	17.5	117.23	18.5
Health..............	8.86	1.5	15.70	2.3	17.63	2.7	14.96	2.3
Car-fare.............	13.56	2.4	19.81	3.	11.98	1.8	14.83	2.3
Recreation and amusements.............	4.63	.8	4.90	.7	3.03	.4	3.90	.6
Education and reading	2.50	.4	8.58	1.2	6.72	1.	6.13	.9
Taxes, dues, and contributions..........	5.52	.9	9.30	1.3	8.11	1.4	7.76	1.2
Miscellaneous........	7.14	1.2	7.87	1.1	15.60	2.4	11.55	1.8
Number of units......	3.5		4.3		3.7		3.8	
Food expenditure per day per unit........	20½c.		21½c.		22c.		21½c.	
Number of rooms.....	3.3		3.8		4.7		4.1	
Percentage of families with lodgers........	4%		12%		4%		6%	
Percentage reporting purchase of newspaper..............	48%		76%		74%		68%	
Percentage reporting use of public library	36%		48%		34%		38%	

* Percentage of total expenditure.

APPENDIX VI

Report on Nutrition Investigation

From Data Collected by the Special Committee on Standard of Living

By FRANK P. UNDERHILL, PH.D.

ASSISTANT PROFESSOR OF PHYSIOLOGICAL CHEMISTRY, SHEFFIELD LABORATORY OF PHYSIOLOGICAL CHEMISTRY, YALE UNIVERSITY

NEW YORK CITY, 1907

The present investigation was primarily undertaken with a view to ascertaining the cost of living in New York City among various representative classes of people. Subsequently there arose the query whether some indication might be obtained concerning the nutritive condition of these classes of people as judged from the quantities and kinds of food materials bought. In the following pages this subject is discussed.

In any determination of the nutritive condition of man several methods of procedure are open to the investigator. To the one desiring exact data the estimation and analysis of the body ingesta and egesta are essential. On the other hand, where merely the amount and kind of food consumed is desired, a determination of the amount of food consumed is computed by the difference between the food bought and the waste. The food values may be ascertained by actual analysis of food samples or may be calculated from tables issued by the U. S. Dept. of Agriculture (Bulletin 28, Revised Edition, 1899). Many such metabolism experiments have been carried out in recent years by the department named.

In the present investigation the method employed has been to calculate the food values of food materials bought by the various classes of people for a period of a week. The data obtained were collected from grocery and meat books of the family, from account books kept by the housewife, and finally from estimations by the family of the various staple articles bought. It is at once apparent that from such data results of any scientific value cannot be

319

obtained, and emphasis is laid upon the fact that there has been no intention of drawing any conclusions the basis of which would necessitate exactness. The most that can be hoped for from such an investigation is merely the determination, in a most general way, whether the various classes are buying food of the amount and kind to keep them in bodily health and vigor. Even the question of waste cannot be entered into, although this item is probably small, judging from dietary studies made in the same city by Atwater and Woods (Bulletin 46, U. S. Dept. of Agriculture). The results presented here then are calculated upon the food *bought*, and the values given were computed from analyses of food materials made by the U. S. Dept. of Agriculture (Bulletin 28, Revised Edition) upon the materials as purchased.

One hundred representative families, preferably those with two or more children, and with various earning powers, have been chosen from among the various nationalities (Italians, Bohemians, Negroes, Russians, Austrians, Hungarians, Americans, English, Dutch, Germans, Irish, and Swedes) in New York City. The amount of food (and the various components comprising that food) bought by the family, together with the cost, has been reduced to terms of per man per day, upon the assumption that women and children eat less than a man. This reduction has been made possible by the employment of standard factors adopted by the U. S. Dept. of Agriculture (see Bulletin 46, page 6).

The question whether a person is eating sufficient food is a difficult one. According to the so-called dietary standards, a man of 70 kilos body-weight at moderate muscular work needs 125 grams protein and enough of fats and carbo-hydrates to furnish 3000 to 3500 calories per day. Other standards call for 118 grams protein and 2800 calories. Indeed, the older standards vary from 100 to 150 grams protein with a fuel value of from 2500 to 7000, the variations depending upon body-weight, habit, and occupation. It is evident that a man engaged in strenuous muscular work needs more energy-yielding food than one whose labor calls for less muscular activity. Opinions vary somewhat with regard to the relative amounts of fat and carbo-hydrate that should be eaten to supply this energy. To sum up the question, the consensus of opinion is in favor of a preponderance of carbo-hydrate material. Fat has twice the potential energy of carbo-hydrate, but for two reasons it is unwise to obtain the greater proportion of energy from that source. In the first place, fat costs more than carbo-hydrate; and, secondly, it is uneconomical from a physiological standpoint, inasmuch as it is very difficult of digestion when compared with carbo-hydrate. For a man of average weight, performing moderate muscular work, from 50 to 60 grams of fat and from 400 to 500 grams of carbo-hydrate are not far from the right proportions from the viewpoint of physiological economy.

The amount of protein necessary is a question upon which there exist two opinions. In the first place, the data given above are derived from observations made upon man concerning the actual quantities he is in the *habit* of eating, not how much he really *needs*. Within recent years the extensive experiments of Chittenden have shown that the protein intake may be diminished by half that usually considered necessary, with a greatly decreased calorific value, and man still maintain health and vigor and perform his accustomed duties. Some of the difficulties of deciding the query whether a man is eating sufficient are at once obvious from the above considerations, and to attempt to do so in more than a most general way is to open the way for criticism, and justly. Accordingly, when in the present discussion the data obtained have been divided into two classes, representing (1) families well nourished, and (2) those poorly nourished, it has been done by comparison with the older dietary standards having a range for protein from 100 to 150 grams, of fat from 50 to 70 grams, of carbo-hydrate from 350 to 600 grams, and a fuel value of from 2500 to 7000 calories. The division cannot be hard and fast, especially when the figures given represent materials *purchased*, not necessarily eaten; and account must also be taken of the digestibility—or, better, availability—of the foods, together with another important factor, namely, absorbability. Inasmuch as the calculations presented have been made upon the materials as purchased, not ready to eat, consideration as to waste, etc., is unnecessary.

Comparison between the amounts spent for food by well

nourished and poorly nourished families indicates that in general when less than 22 cents per man per day is spent for food the nourishment derived is insufficient, and when more than 22 cents per man per day is expended the family is well nourished. But the latter statement does not hold so well as the former. Another point of interest is the relatively large quantities of fat bought by both classes, which is uneconomical both financially and physiologically.

Classified according to nationality, it has been found that of the Italian families (19) represented, 89 per cent. are listed in the class of those well nourished; of the Bohemian (5), 40 per cent.; of the negroes (5), 60 per cent.; of the Russian (19), 33 per cent.; of the American (25), 57 per cent.; of the Irish (9), 77 per cent.; of German (6), 86 per cent.; while Austrian (2), Hungarian (1), English (3), Dutch (1), and Swedish (2) were all well nourished. The Italians and Dutch obtained their protein largely from the vegetable kingdom. The Bohemians, Negroes, Americans, English, Irish, and Swedes obtained their protein about equally from animal and vegetable sources. The Russians, Austrians, Hungarians, and Germans preferred protein from the animal kingdom. To a greater extent than the other nationalities, the Italians obtained their energy from the vegetable kingdom.

The explanation of the failure of some of the above classes of people to live well is not so much a question of ability to purchase nourishing food at the price given (22 cents per man per day) as of injudicious buying. For example, 3 pounds of butter per week at 30 cents per pound is extravagance when this amount represents 13 per cent. of the total spent for food. The item of beer, wine, pickles, etc., used at table is also a factor of considerable importance in this connection. For instance, to cite a specific case, in one family, out of a total of $6.17 spent for food, $1.83 was expended for beer, wine, and pickles—about 30 per cent. On the other hand, the majority of failures does not appear to be due to the above causes, but to an inability to purchase food at less than 22 cents in sufficient amount and variety; and in nutrition, variety of food plays almost as important a rôle as does sufficiency.

The following schedules are printed as an illustration of the method employed in the calculation of nutritive values:

SCHEDULE NO. 1.

MEALS

```
1 man.................................................21
1 woman (21 × 0.8).................................17
1 child (21 × 0.5)................................10
2 children (21 × 0.4)............................17
```
                                                    65

Equivalent to 1 man for 22 days.

FOOD.

4 lbs. beef..................at $0.48	12 lbs. bread..................at $0.60
4 " salt....................." .28	4 " rolls....................." .35
1 lb. ham....................." .16	1 lb. crackers................." .10
1 " chicken................." .14	1 " flour....................." .05
1 " fish......................" .05	2 lbs. rolled oats............." .10
1 " butter..................." .27	5 " potatoes................." .16
3 lbs. eggs..................." .25	1 lb. onions................." .05
14 " milk..................." .70	½ " string beans..........." .05
1 lb. milk (cond.)........." .10	½ " dried peas............." .05
	2 lbs. canned tomatoes......." .08
$2.43	1 lb. apples................." .05
	1 " tea....................." .18
	3½ lbs. sugar................." .17
	¼ lb. molasses............." .03
	" beer, pickles..........." .30

$2.32

SCHEDULE No. 2.

KIND OF FOOD.	WEIGHTS AND FUEL VALUE PER MAN PER DAY.					COST.
	Food Material (Grams).	Protein. (Grams).	Fat (Grams).	Carbo-hydrates (Grams).	Fuel Value. (Calories.)	
Beef, veal, mutton......	158	32	16	..	221	..
Pork, ham, bacon, etc. ..	20	3	10	..	108	..
Poultry.................	20	3	2	..	34	..
Fish, etc...............	20	1	..	..	8	..
Eggs....................	64	8	6	..	90	..
Butter, lard............	20	..	17	..	158	..
Cheese..................	..	..	..	..	..	..
Milk....................	313	12	14	11	272	..
Total animal food	615	59	65	1	891	$0.11
Bread, cake, etc........	337	30	7	185	940	..
Flour, cereals..........	60	8	3	41	232	..
Vegetables..............	180	5	..	26	134	..
Fruits..................	20	..	..	2	10	..
Tea, coffee, etc.	..	..	..	..	..	..
Sugar, molasses........	74	..	..	72	297	..
Liquors.................	..	..	..	..	..	..
Total vegetable food....	671	43	10	326	1613	$0.10
Total food.............	1286	102	75	337	2504	$0.21

BUFFALO, 1908

In the course of an investigation similar to that carried on in New York City to determine the cost of living in the city of Buffalo among several representative classes of people, the question arose here also as to the nutritive condition of the subjects judged by the quantity and kind of food bought. Estimations of the cost and quantity of food bought for a period of a year have been collected. From 50 such schedules an endeavor has been made to divide the families thus represented into those receiving sufficient nutriment and those whose nourishment is insufficient.

As in the report on the cases selected in New York City, the conclusions herein drawn should not be regarded as exact; their purpose is merely to serve as an indication of nutritive condition. Nevertheless, in a very general way, the data submitted may be accepted as being not far from the true condition. The results were computed from the food *bought*, and the values were calculated from the analyses of food materials made by the U. S. Dept. of Agriculture (Bull. 28, Revised 1899) upon the materials as purchased.

Fifty typical families, containing two or more children, were selected for observation, of which number thirty fall into a group designated "General," with reference to nationality. The remaining twenty were equally divided between Italian and Polish families. The amount of food (and the components of that food) bought by the family, together with the cost, have been reduced to terms of one man per day, according to the standard factors adopted by the U. S. Dept. of Agriculture (Bull. 46, page 6).

The task of deciding whether a person is receiving sufficient food is not easy, owing to the many standards upheld by the various schools of nutrition. However, if the average standard generally accepted is adopted, there need be no hesitation in the acceptance of the condition of *sufficient* nourishment. A person at moderate muscular work, according to this standard, consumes 100 to 125 grams protein, 50 to 70 grams fat, 350 to 600 grams carbo-hydrate, with fuel value ranging from 3000 to 7000 calories per day. Taking these figures as a criterion, the results obtained in the present investigation may be divided into two groups: (1) representing families buying sufficient food, (2) representing families buying insufficient food.

A general analysis of the data obtained follows.

It was found that in general, when less than 21 cents is spent for food per man per day, the nourishment derived is insufficient, and in general when more than this sum is spent the family is well nourished. This relation between food value and cost holds equally well for all three classes of families represented.

Reduced to terms of percentage, of those families spending 21 cents or more for food per man per day, 75 per cent. received sufficient nourishment; and with this sum 25 per cent. had insufficient food. Of those families who spent less than 21 cents per man per day for food, 16 per cent. were well fed, 84 per cent. were not. In the same group of those who spent 22 cents or more per man per day, 85 per cent. were well nourished and 15 per cent. bought food insufficient for health, vigor, and work.

Turning to the Italian group, 86 per cent. of those spending 21 cents or more for food per man per day were well nourished, and 14 per cent. were not. No family spending less than 21 cents per man per day was well nourished.

Of the Polish families, 86 per cent. were well nourished when 21 cents or more were spent and 14 per cent. were poorly nourished. Thirty-three per cent. of those well nourished spent less than 21 cents per man per day.

The conditions existing in the Italian and Polish families give to these groups a rather large advantage over the "general" group. In the "general" group of those spending 21 cents or more per man per day 75 per cent. were well nourished, while under similar conditions the Italian and Polish groups contained 86 per cent.

The general conclusion may therefore be drawn that for 21 cents per man per day sufficient nourishment may be bought in the city of Buffalo to keep a man in bodily health and vigor at moderate muscular work.

No definite relation appears to exist between the purchase of a preponderance of animal or vegetable food and an ability to live at a low figure.

APPENDIX VII

A Workingman's Budget.—F. Le Play*

TRANSLATED BY LOUISE CHARVET

A Type-setter of Brussels, Belgium, Working by the Day
under the System of Indeterminate Engagements

FROM INFORMATION GATHERED ON THE SPOT, IN NOVEMBER, 1857,
BY M. J. DAUBY

PRELIMINARY STATEMENTS

Defining the Condition of the Different Members of the Family.
Description of the Place, of the Industrial Organization,
and of the Family.

1. LAND, INDUSTRY, AND POPULATION.

The family of the type-setter lives in Louvain, in the commune
of St. Jean-ten-Noode, one of the most important suburbs of Brussels. This commune, situated for the most part in a valley, extends around the capital, from the Leopold district to the river
Senne, a distance of one and a half miles.

During the past few years the commune of St. Jean-ten-Noode
has had a remarkable growth. Its population was 1340 in 1826,
5000 in 1836, 14,850 in 1846, 17,700 in 1856. To-day it has a
population of more than 18,000, in spite of the loss of a district
comprising about 350 acres which was annexed to Brussels, and
which forms now the Leopold district, with 5000 inhabitants.

The commune now covers 250 acres; it has 35 streets, and 27
courts or alleys inhabited mostly by the working class. There
are 2600 houses constructed of stone. In October, 1846, when
the census was taken, St. Jean-ten-Noode had 120 vacant houses
and 2283 houses that were occupied. The 2283 houses had 13,517
rooms occupied by 3782 families. Of this number, 808 families

* " Les Ouvriers Européens." Vol. V, ch. III, p. 103.

had one room each, 983 had two rooms each, and 1991 had three rooms and more.

The family of the workman who is the subject of this monograph lives in a court in the eastern part of the town. This court is remarkable for being well-kept, and is inhabited by an exceptionally good class of people. On the left side are large gardens with villas. The houses on the right side are inhabited by well-to-do workmen, upper-class clerks, and men of independent means.

The economic activities of St. Jean-ten-Noode are at the same time agricultural, industrial, and commercial. It has several important printing establishments, and about one hundred of the employees have their homes there. Brussels with its suburbs includes among its inhabitants about 700 printers, 500 of whom are compositors and 200 pressmen.

Almost all of them belong to societies whose objects are the maintenance of wages, mutual benefits, and the promotion of thrift. The principle of a standard invariable wage has been in force for a long time. However, some changes have lately been made. There are both piece-workers and day workers. The latter generally have steadier work and better pay. Although the relation between employer and employee is based on the system of indeterminate engagements, it is not uncommon to find workmen employed for many years by the same master. The workman described here has been with the same employer for seventeen years.

2. COMPOSITION OF THE FAMILY.

The family consists of husband, wife, and four children, viz.:

John Francis D., head of the family, married for
    15 years, born at Brussels....................34 years old
Katherine B., his wife, born at Brussels........35 " "
Henry Octavius D., their first son, born at Brus-
    sels.....................................14 " "
Armand Constant D., second son, born at Brus-
    sels.....................................12 " "
Adolphe Joseph D., third son, born at Brussels. 10½ " "
Antoinette Constance D., their daughter, born at
    St. Jean-ten-Noode...................... 1 year old

327

The father and mother and one of the brothers of the workman are still living. The father is a shoemaker in the same town. Though 65 years of age, he is in perfect health and is able almost entirely to support himself and his wife, who is thrifty. The brother is a type-setter and is employed in the same shop as the workman. He lives with his parents, whom he helps a little. The wife's father has been dead ten years; her mother lives in Louvain with one of her sons. The mother has an income from a house which her children agreed to leave to her. The wife has another brother and two sisters, who are all married and who support themselves.

3. RELIGION AND MORAL HABITS.

Our workman and his wife were born of Catholic parents. He had very little religious instruction, because as he began to work at 9 years of age, it was difficult for him to find time to learn the catechism. The hard school of adversity and of work inculcated moral and religious feelings which he never lost. Every Sunday he goes to church with his sons, who consider it a real punishment when they cannot accompany him. In fine weather they take a short walk after the service. The father takes this occasion to impress his children with the greatness of the works of the Creator, telling them to think of Him in all their actions. At the same time he develops their minds and their morals, and often takes pleasure in testing the good results of his instruction.

The morning and evening meals always begin with a silent prayer and the sign of the cross. Before the dinner, which they take all together, the children by turns say the prayer aloud. Not one would willingly give up his turn, but when one is absent and the usual order is interrupted, it is a pleasant sight to see how anxious the others are to take his place. The wife seldom takes any part in this. Since the birth of the last child, she has been almost entirely absorbed in her household cares, and very rarely attends religious services. She leaves to her husband the moral training of her sons, which she considers herself incapable of undertaking.

Our workman is inclined to be irritable. However, he values the esteem of his employer and his fellow-workmen; he is anxious to have the reputation of an intelligent, industrious, and honest man. It is by pursuing incessantly this purpose and by his hard work that he has been able to obtain a good position, which he tries every day to improve.

He went to school only between the ages of 7 and 9 years. However, because of the demands of his profession and owing to his perseverance, he has acquired a good education. He devotes his spare time to the study of literary, economic, and social matters. He has written on these subjects several little works which have been well received. In a scientific and literary competition at Bruges in 1853, he won a silver-gilt medal and was elected corresponding member of a scientific society. The report that he wrote on that occasion received the honor of being printed. In 1856 he won another medal at the exhibition of domestic economy at Brussels for the manuscript of a book written especially for the working classes, in which he gives advice on the principal points which concern the physical and the moral welfare of the workman under the three-fold aspect of his life—in society, in the shop, and in the family. This work received the approbation of several eminent persons, who gave our workman much encouragement.

He occupies a high position among his companions. On several occasions, when the interests of the firm were at stake, he has been chosen to represent it, together with others of his colleagues. He has also taken an active part in the founding of the associations of which he is a member.

The three boys go to the public school of St. Jean-ten-Noode. The two oldest are clever, the youngest is less gifted. As to the wife, she has no education to speak of; but she atones for this lack by a great deal of common sense, and by incessant devotion to her family duties.

The husband and wife lead a regular life, in perfect accord, and avoid all discussions which might have a bad influence on the children. A few years ago, difficulties connected with the household management, together with his extreme youth, nearly started the husband on a downward path. But he was not slow in recovering his better self, when he had perceived how detrimental his conduct was to the physical and moral welfare of the family.

4. PHYSICAL TRAITS AND CARE OF THE HEALTH.

Our workman is rather tall, 5 feet 10 inches, and has a sanguine and nervous temperament. Although he enjoys good health, his constitution is not strong, and for this reason, he was exempted from military service. Except for some children's diseases, such as measles and scarlet fever, he has had only one serious illness, typhus fever, which a few months after his marriage proved almost fatal. After this illness, he decided to join a mutual benefit society, of which he has been a member for nearly 14 years, without having received pecuniary assistance except for 14 days.

The wife is of medium height, 5 feet 4 inches, has a good constitution, and a phlegmatic yet cheerful temperament. At the time of her marriage she showed a tendency to pulmonary tuberculosis, which developed two years later and made her an invalid for nine months. The birth of a child served to restore her health and to enable her again to devote herself to the cares of her household, which had seriously suffered on account of her sickness. Since then she has had no serious sickness except for an affliction of the eyes which lasted a few weeks. On the whole, however, her health is not very satisfactory. It seems as if the material cares were not sufficiently counterbalanced by intellectual and moral interests.

The oldest child has had the various infantile diseases. Like his father, he had an attack of typhus fever complicated by a miliary fever, which did away with the most alarming symptoms of the first disease. Since his recovery his eyes have been weak and he has had quinsy. He is now recovering from the last effects of his illness. For five or six years the second child had uninterruptedly sickness after sickness. These were of such serious character that his life was despaired of twenty times. He was almost totally blind for five months; at four years of age he had hardly recovered from a severe attack of measles when he broke his leg. Now he is perfectly well. The last boy has a robust constitution. He has also had measles and typhoid fever, both very severely. His temperament is like his mother's; he has little ability, but an honest and obliging disposition. The daughter, who is only one year old, has always been well. During the first years of his married life our workman was under considerable expense for medical service. However, as the members of the family have been in better health since that time, the yearly medical expense can be estimated at about 20 francs, or 300 francs for the past fifteen years, including the monthly dues to the workman's association. According to an agreement with the physician of the association, since 1858, our workman, like the other members of the association, has received medical service for six francs a year, medicines not included.

5. STANDING OF THE FAMILY.

Independently of the easy circumstances which a high salary and industrious habits have assured the family, our workman has attained a distinguished position in his firm. His ability and good conduct soon induced his employer to give him the management of the workshops as well as the clerical work, which is rather complicated because of the numerous details involved in the special line of work.

Before the Belgian Revolution of 1830, his parents as a result of hard work were in easy circumstances. But an exaggerated patriotism induced our workman's father perhaps too fully to perform the military duties instituted at that time. As a result the family was impoverished, so that at the age of 9 our workman was obliged to leave the school for the shop in order to help the household, which at 14 years of age he supported almost entirely.

The wife comes from an honorable family whose interests had been greatly injured by the unwise management of her father and by many domestic troubles. Several members of the family have good positions as notaries, doctors, and merchants. Our workman is the only one in his family who has kept in touch with any of them. Though obliged to depend entirely on his work, and in spite of the hard times he has gone through, he has never asked aid either from charitable institutions or from private individuals. This fact, of which he is justly very proud, has greatly helped him to retain his independence. On the part of our workman, who is gifted with fine moral qualities, the difference of condition between employers and employees creates neither hate nor envy, which is not the case with many other type-setters of Brussels.

MEANS OF SUBSISTENCE OF THE FAMILY

6. PROPERTY.

(Furniture and Clothes not Included.)

Real Estate..0.00 fr.

The family does not own any real estate, and has no income from the dwelling which is a part of the inheritance left by the wife's father. This house is what remains from a former prosperous time and the widow has the exclusive use of it until her death.

Money...51.71 fr.

This sum, deposited in the Savings Bank, at 3% interest, represents wages paid for clerical work. It was originally 100 francs, and was increased to 160 francs, interest included. Several family expenses, such as those caused by the first communion of two of the children, obliged our workman to break into it several times. On the other hand, the hard times which have oppressed the laboring classes for several years, especially the high price of food, have not yet made it possible for him to make good the amount.

Special equipment for work and industry................ 66 fr.

Tools.—Two iron composing sticks, 10 fr.; 2 wooden composing sticks, 1 fr.; printers' tweezers, 2.25 fr.; 1 copy holder, 1 fr.; 1 knife, 0.50 fr.; total, 14.75 fr.
Special Books and Office Supplies Necessary for the Correction of Proofs at Home and for Book-keeping.—1 dictionary of the French Academy with supplement (bound), 40 fr.; 1 Flemish-French dictionary, 5 fr.; 1 grammar, 0.75 fr.; 1 French Latin grammar, 2 fr.; 1 table of French verbs, 0.50 fr.; ink-wells, pens, penholders, pencils, ruler and paper, 3 fr.; total, 51.25 fr.

Total value of property...........................117.71 fr.

7. SUBSIDIARY CONTRIBUTIONS TO REAL INCOME.

The only assistance received by the family is the free tuition given in the city school attended by the three boys up to last August. At that time the oldest, having won the highest prize, had to leave, according to the rules of the school. The other two stayed the rest of the year. Had they been in a private school, the cost would have been 4 francs a month for each child; that is, 88 francs for the two children for the school year of 11 months, and 28 francs for the oldest child for seven months—in all, 116 francs. To that must be added 15 francs, the cost of the tuition for the oldest boy, who for 3 months attended the Academy of Fine Arts.

In the course of the year 1857 the Government gave our workman 300 francs to help him publish a book written for the working class. Nearly the whole amount of this subsidy, granted in exchange for 500 copies of this work, served to pay the publishing expenses. Under the head of subventions may be mentioned books given from time to time to our workman by his employer and by the authors, as well as some pieces of bric-à-brac presented by his fellow-workmen on his patron saint's day. These may be found in the list of the pieces of furniture under Section 10. Their annual value amounts to 20 or 25 francs.

8. WORK AND INDUSTRY.

The Type-setter's Work.—The work is done by the hour in the shop, as well as at home, for an employer. It consists of type-setting, paging, proof-reading, book-keeping, and the management of the shop where the type-setters work. He is paid half a franc an hour and works on an average of eleven hours a day. When business is not pressing, he finishes work on Monday at 4 P. M., and he works regularly a few hours at home on Sunday. The shop is closed on Sunday and holidays, except three or four times a year when there is a rush of business. Wages are paid very regularly every fortnight on Saturday evening, and pay-day is never an occasion for unnecessary expense.

The Wife's Work.—The wife devotes all her time to household duties, sewing, repairing and washing the family linen. She excels in all kinds of sewing. Before her marriage she was a dress-maker and was at the head of the last dressmaking establishment in which she worked. In the first years of her married life she worked for several customers, but for the last ten years household cares have kept her busy. She is active and industrious, and her

333

home is pointed to as a model of cleanliness, in spite of the work inevitably occasioned by children.

The Children's Work.—The oldest son has just become an apprentice in the shop where his father works; he earns ten francs a month. The other children do no work.

Industries Pursued by the Family.—The workman has the management of the printing shop. In case of pressure, he supplements his wages by reading proof at home, which may add about 6.50 francs a fortnight to his income. The wife's chief work is the sewing and washing of the family linen and clothes.

MODE OF LIVING OF THE FAMILY

9. FOOD AND MEALS.

The family take three meals a day: in the morning, at noon, and in the evening. During the summer the husband has a second breakfast in the shop and a luncheon at half past four every day. The breakfast consists invariably of coffee with or without milk and bread and butter. The bread is of the first quality. The dinner consists of meat soup or vegetable soup, potatoes or other vegetables according to the season, boiled or roasted beef or veal. From time to time, poultry, rabbit, or dressed pork takes the place of other meat. Dinner is often followed by a dessert of fruit: nuts, cherries, apples, pears, apricots, grapes (from their own vines), and always by a cup of coffee. On Friday, instead of meat, fish (cod, herrings, eels) or eggs are served. In the summer, salads of different sorts are the main food.

When the children return from school, they have a luncheon of coffee and bread with the mother. The husband's luncheon consists of bread, meat or cheese, and beer.

The supper taken on our workman's return from the shop consists of cold meat or Holland cheese with bread and butter and beer, or more often coffee, which is the favorite drink of the family. They live well and lack nothing so far as food is concerned. However, except on New Year's Day, or on some great occasion, no wine or liquor is drunk and beer is drunk but rarely. Away

334

from home, our workman drinks beer in moderate quantity, for example, on Sunday or in some of the meetings of the societies of which he is a member.

The family do not buy food on credit as most workmen do, and in consequence they buy more cheaply.

10. HOUSE, FURNITURE, AND CLOTHING.

The family have lived for four years in a little dwelling, one of the walls of which is covered with a vine about 13 yards in length.

This house consists of four rooms, two of which are on the first floor and two on the second floor, of a cellar, a garret, and a yard with an area of about 900 sq. ft. The rooms on the first floor are about 9 ft. high, those on the next floor are 6 ft. 10 in. high. The average height of the garret with slanting roof is about 7 ft. and that of the cellar about 6 ft. 3 in.

Though the rooms are rather small, the dwelling is comfortable, and the workman is willing to make all the sacrifices compatible with his position to preserve what he calls "his luxury and quiet," for he has occupied many lodgings composed of sometimes one large room and sometimes several rooms where he has experienced all sorts of discomforts.

The rent is 18 francs a month or 216 francs a year; the owner pays the taxes. A well, used by several families of the neighborhood, is near the house and furnishes very pure water. There is no cistern, but rain-water is caught in large tubs.

Except for some articles given to our workman by his comrades on his patron saint's day, the furniture is very simple, but it is well cared for. It may be valued as follows:

Furniture...904.50 fr.

I. Beds and Bedding.—2 bedsteads, beechwood, slats and crossbars of oak, 35 fr.; 1 mattress, woolen, 25 fr.; 1 mattress, seaweed, 14 fr.; 3 mattresses, straw, 21 fr.; 1 bolster, feathers, 8 fr.; 3 pillows, 8 fr.; 1 blanket, woolen, 15 fr.; 3 blankets, cotton, 18 fr.; 1 cradle with bedding, 15 fr.; total, 159 fr.

II. Living-room Furniture (ground-floor).—1 bureau, elm, 18 fr.; 1 table with oil cloth and cover, 10.50 fr.; 1 clock, gilded frame, 48 fr.; 2 vases, china, with artificial flowers, 20 fr.; 2 large frames with colored pictures, 20 fr.; 4 small frames, with portraits, 8 fr.; 1 frame, reward won by workman, 5 fr.; 1 small mirror, 3 fr.; 2 medallions, plaster, religious subjects, 2 fr.; 2 statuettes, Saxon china, 9 fr.; 1 St. Joseph, imitation alabaster, 2 fr.; 6 chairs, cherry, 20 fr.; 1 arm-chair, beech,

8 fr.; 1 jardiniere, with natural flowers, 10 fr.; 1 screen, 1 fr.; 3 framed medals, 1 silver gilt, 2 bronze, 30 fr.; total, 214.50 fr.

III. Kitchen Furniture.—1 large cupboard, white wood, 8 fr.; 1 table, beech, 5 fr.; 5 chairs and 1 armchair, beech, straw-bottomed, 18 fr.; 1 child's chair, 5 fr.; 1 kitchen stove, with pipe, 14 fr.; 1 statuette (Gutenberg), 4 fr.; 1 bird cage, 2 fr.; total, 56 fr.

IV. Workroom Furniture.—1 large desk, with bookshelf, 28 fr.; 2 tables, beech, 6 fr.; 1 cupboard, elm, 3 fr.; 1 small cupboard, cherry, 5 fr.; 1 small stove, with pipe, 7 fr.; 4 chairs, beech, straw-bottomed, 8 fr.; 1 mirror, 1.50 fr.; total, 58.50 fr.

V. Bedroom and Attic Furniture.—1 small table, beech, 3 fr.; 2 chairs, beech, straw-bottomed, 4 fr.; 1 picture of Christ in frame, 2 fr.; 1 crucifix and several religious pictures, near children's bed, 1.50 fr.; several pieces of old furniture not in use, 6 fr.; total, 16.50 fr.

VI. Books.—Our workman owns a small library composed of about 300 books and pamphlets. Some of these, which he helped to print or of which he read the proof, he owes to the generosity of his employer, or of the authors. Others, among which are several scientific and literary works, he bought for himself. The remaining 25 volumes are classical works given as school prizes to the children. Approximate value, 400 fr.

Utensils.—In sufficient quantity and well cared for.....235.25 fr.

I. For the Fire.—2 fire shovels, 1 fr.; 2 fire hooks, 1.50 fr.; 1 grate, 1 fr.; 2 coal scuttles, 2 fr.; 1 charcoal basket, .25 fr.; total, 5.75 fr.

II. For the Table and the Preparation of Food.—1 glass carafe and 6 tumblers, 10 fr.; 1 coffee set and 1 tea set, china, 25 fr.; 1 liquor set on tin stand, 15 fr.; 1 pint bottle in fine gilded ware, 5 fr.; 6 plates, 6 fr.; 15 plates, common white earthenware, 4.50 fr.; 2 china bowls, 2.50 fr.; 6 bowls, white earthenware, 1 fr.; 1 salad bowl, 1 pepper box and 6 glasses, 2 fr.; 1 pot, earthenware, 1.50 fr; 1 butter dish and 2 earthenware egg-cups, 1.50 fr.; 5 vases, varnished, earthenware, 2.50 fr.; 1 water jug, 1 fr.; 6 spoons, 6 forks and 1 ladle, silver-plated, 25 fr.; 1 ladle, tin, 1.25 fr.; knives, spoons and forks, 5 fr.; pots and bottles, 4 fr.; 3 pails, zinc, 11 fr., 1 saucepan, wrought iron, 5 fr.; 1 frying pan, wrought iron, 1.25 fr.; 1 kettle and 1 copper teakettle, 12 fr.; 1 coffee pot and 1 tin teakettle, 5 fr.; 1 coffee mill, 3 fr.; 1 strainer, tin, 1 fr.; 1 market basket, tin, 3 fr.; 1 basket, tin, 2.50 fr.; 1 basket, wicker, 1 fr.; 2 vegetable baskets, 2 fr.; other small articles, 1.50 fr.; total, 161 fr.

III. For Cleaning Purposes.—2 big brushes and 2 brooms, 5 fr.; 1 clothes brush and 2 shoe brushes, 2 fr.; 2 flatirons, 2 fr.; 2 water jugs, 1.50 fr.; 1 wash basin, earthenware, 2 fr.; 3 razors, with accessories, 4.50 fr.; 1 shaving mirror, 1.50 fr.; total, 18.50 fr.

IV. For Various Uses.—1 astral lamp, 20 fr.; 1 lamp, copper, 5 fr.; 2 candlesticks, copper, 5 fr.; 1 large barrel for catching rain-water, 6 fr.; 2 small barrels, 7 fr.; 3 clothes pegs, 2 fr.; 1 tailor's goose, with accessories, 3 fr.; 1 pair snuffers and 1 extinguisher, 1 fr.; small articles, 1 fr.; total, 50 fr.

Household linen (in good order, but meager supply) ....81 fr.

Linen.—2 sheets, linen, 12 fr.; 6 sheets, cotton, 21 fr.; 12 sheets, small, for children, 12 fr.; 2 napkins, 5 fr.; 5 window curtains, muslin, 15 fr.; 4 window curtains, cotton, 4 fr.; 12 hand towels, 8 fr.; 4 hand towels, hemp, 2fr.; 6 dusters and dish cloths, 2 fr.; total, 81 fr.

Clothing ....730 fr.

(Parents' clothing is very simple; though small in quantity, is in good condition.)

Man's Clothing (317.50 fr.). Of the style worn by the middle class.

I. Sunday Clothes.—1 overcoat, blue cloth, 65 fr.; 1 frock coat, black cloth,

30 fr.; 1 vest, black satin, 12 fr.; 1 pair trousers, black cloth, 18 fr.; 1 silk hat, 12 fr.; 1 scarf, black satin, 8 fr.; 1 pair boots, 15 fr.; total, 160 fr.

II. Everyday Clothes.—1 overcoat, black cloth, 25 fr.; 1 coat, black cloth, 15 fr.; 1 pair trousers, woolen, 13 fr.; 1 pair trousers, woolen, 13 fr.; 1 pair trousers, cotton, 3 fr.; 2 waistcoats, woolen, with sleeves, 8 fr.; 2 work blouses, blue linen, 9 fr.; 6 shirts, cotton (2 of good quality), 18 fr.; 3 neckties, cotton and linen, 1.50 fr.; 1 necktie, merino, 2 fr.; 2 pairs knit drawers, cotton, 4 fr.; 2 knit undershirts, cotton, 4 fr.; 2 pairs stockings, woolen, 4 fr.; 4 pairs stockings, cotton, 6 fr.; 1 pair boots, 10 fr.; 1 pair slippers, 5 fr.; 1 cap, 2 fr.; small articles, 3 fr.; total, 132.50 fr.

III. Jewelry.—1 watch, silver, 25 fr.

Wife's Clothing (171.50 fr.). Like that of her class.

I. Sunday Clothes.—1 dress, brown woolen, 16 fr.; 1 shawl, woolen, 15 fr.; 1 dress skirt, muslin, 8.50 fr.; 1 waist, black silk, 6 fr.; 1 apron, black silk, 5 fr.; 1 cloak, black silk, 6 fr.; 1 bonnet, trimmed, 6 fr.; 1 skirt, white dimity, 4 fr.; 3 chemisettes, fine quality, 5 fr.; 6 handkerchiefs, fine linen, 4 fr.; 2 pairs under-sleeves, embroidered muslin, 4 fr.; 3 pairs stockings, white, 5.50 fr.; 1 pair shoes, 5 fr.; total, 90 fr.

II. Everyday Clothes.—1 skirt, wool and cotton, 8 fr.; 1 skirt, black merino, 2 fr.; 1 cloak, cotton goods, 3 fr.; 2 jackets, cotton, 5 fr.; 2 aprons, cotton, 3 fr.; 1 apron, blue linen, 2 fr.; 1 cap, black tulle, 3.50 fr.; 4 night caps, 4 fr.; 6 chemises, cotton, 15 fr.; 1 pair stockings, black woolen, 3 fr.; 2 pairs stockings, cotton, 4 fr.; 3 neckerchiefs, 3 fr.; 2 pairs gloves, 2.50 fr.; 1 pair shoes, 5 fr.; 1 pair slippers, 2.50 fr.; total, 65.50 fr.

III. Jewelry.—1 gold ring, 7 fr.; 1 pin, gold enameled, 6 fr.; 1 pair earrings, 3 fr.; total, 16 fr.

Children's Clothing (241.00 fr.). Well taken care of.

I. Clothes of the Three Boys.—2 blouses, black velvet, 20 fr.; 1 blouse, black merino, 6 fr.; 6 blouses, cotton, 18 fr.; 2 coats, black cloth, 18 fr.; 2 coats, black merino, 10 fr.; 3 pairs trousers, cloth, 18 fr.; 3 pairs trousers, cotton, 7 fr.; 3 waistcoats, woolen, 6 fr.; 6 caps, cloth, 9 fr.; 9 shirts, cotton, 17 fr.; 6 pairs stockings, 6 fr.; 6 collars, white percale, 3 fr.; 3 neckties, cotton, 2 fr.; 9 handkerchiefs, cotton, 4.50 fr.; 3 scarfs, woolen, 3 fr.; 3 night caps, 1.50 fr.; 6 pairs of boots and shoes, 25 fr.; total, 174 fr.

II. Girl's Clothes.—1 coat, quilted black silk, 6 fr.; 5 dresses, woolen, 20 fr.; 6 slips, white dimity, 6 fr.; 6 chemises, white cotton, 4 fr.; 5 aprons, white muslin, 5 fr.; 2 hats, silk, 8 fr.; 3 caps, trimmed, 4 fr.; 6 caps, white percale, 3 fr.; 3 caps, muslin, 3 fr.; 4 neckerchiefs, 2 fr.; 2 pairs stockings, woolen, 2 fr.; 4 pairs stockings, cotton, 2.50 fr.; 1 pair shoes, cloth, 1.50 fr.; total, 67 fr.

NOTE.—A great part of the children's clothing is made from the parents' cast-off clothing, and is generally made by the wife.

Total value of furniture and clothing ....1,950.75 fr.

11. RECREATION.

For some years the husband and wife have been perfectly contented with such family recreations as might be within their means. In the summer they go regularly to the country on Sundays and holidays. Sometimes they visit one of the towns situated on the railroad in the neighborhood of Brussels, such as Vilvorde, Baitsfort, and Ruisbrank. It is a great pleasure to the children to return by train. In winter the family generally stays at home on Sundays; except the father, who goes in the evening to play dominoes with some of his friends who live in a neighboring suburb and who are at least twice as old as he. Sometimes he takes his family to the opera, vaudeville, or circus; but more often to musical entertainments arranged by members of his firm, in a hall rented for that purpose. These are real family gatherings, where all licentious songs are strictly forbidden. At these meetings there are also readings on subjects of general interest to the working classes in Belgium, especially to the type-setters, but political subjects are always forbidden.

The family derives some pleasure, also, from its intercourse with relatives. Each family event, such as a birth, a marriage, or a patron saint's day, is occasion for an informal dinner party, when the sincerest cordiality reigns. As a rule, our workman goes each year to Louvain at the time of the annual fair, to visit his wife's relatives. Sometimes he is accompanied by his wife or one of the children. Two or three of these relatives return the visit in September, at the time of the national holiday, which is celebrated with a certain amount of pomp at Brussels.

Among recreations, and in addition to the annual banquet which most of the type-setters attend, must be mentioned a dinner given yearly by our workman to his friends, on the occasion of his patron saint's day (St. Joseph). This dinner is given in return for a present made him by his friends. But his greatest pleasure is derived from study, to which he would willingly devote all his spare time, were it not for the demands of health, and his family's need of diversion. It is with the greatest difficulty that he can be torn from his literary work for any kind of pleasure. By such inclination, rather than by habits of thrift, does he resemble the middle class.

HISTORY OF THE FAMILY

12. PRINCIPAL EVENTS IN THE LIFE OF THE FAMILY.

Our workman was born at Brussels in 1824. His father, who was a bootmaker, had many workmen under him and did a good business. He was in easy circumstances, owing chiefly to hard work, but this condition was greatly changed by the Belgian Revolution of 1830, which took away the majority of his customers, and obliged him to perform civic duties, to which he sacrificed personal interests. Two years later his family was reduced to a state of great poverty. In 1833 they were in such want that the son, then only 9 years of age, was obliged suddenly to leave school, where he had learned only the rudiments of reading and writing, and to work as an apprentice in one of the city book stores. Here he ran errands, and later made newspaper wrappers. After fifteen months of stubborn work, he succeeded in acquiring a fairly good elementary education; but the small wages he earned (7 francs a month) induced his mother to seek more lucrative employment for him. A new daily paper had just been established in Brussels; by it he was engaged as an apprentice at type-setting and at gathering the sheets as they came from the press. On account of his double duties he was obliged to work eighteen hours a day, interrupted only by the running of errands. Even in winter he had to be in the shop from 5 A. M. to 11 P. M. And on Sunday this murderous work, for which he received five francs a week, was not interrupted. At the end of a year, finding no improvement in his position, he decided to make a change, in spite of having acquired but little skill in type-setting. He was not successful at first, but after a second change he entered a shop in which he was able to perfect himself in the business. After fifteen months be went back to his first employer on a salary of fifteen francs a week, working eight and a half hours a day.

He visited successively several shops, to perfect his business knowledge, and finally, in 1840, he entered the printing establishment where he is at present.

The struggles that he had to make during the hard times that we have just mentioned so seriously weakened his constitution that he was exempted from military service. After several disputes with his parents, occasioned by his relations with his future wife, at nineteen years of age he married, with no other resources than the sum of one hundred francs, which his employer kindly advanced him, and which served to buy furniture and indispensable household articles. Unfortunately, the young couple suffered from several attacks of sickness, in their early married life.

The confinements of the wife, together with her inexperience, caused her to live beyond her means, and without her husband's knowledge she was soon in a whirlpool of debt. A thousand petty domestic annoyances almost separated the young couple, but the husband did not lose courage. Fully aware of the danger of his position, he changed his manner of living, and forbade all unnecessary expense. At the end of three years he saw his efforts crowned with success: his debts paid, his furniture increased, and the general welfare of his family greatly augmented. A radical change in the wife's manner of living, and a courageous effort on her part to join her husband in his undertaking, saved the family which had been so severely tried. To-day they are contented and happy.

Catherine B. was born in Brussels in 1822. Her father, a locksmith by profession, and a master tradesman, carried on his business at home. He had a talent for invention, which he used with doubtful advantage to a family of twelve children. He had besides a passion for fishing, to which he often devoted his working time. He soon found himself therefore in a critical position. As a result Catherine was entrusted with the care of the younger children, to the detriment of her education. Later she was taught dressmaking, so that she might help the family in a more efficacious manner. As her wages were habitually taken for family use, she had no savings when she married, and as a dowry only a few articles of small value.

To sum up: thanks to the good conduct and perseverance of the husband and wife, thanks also to their watchful care over their children, the position of the family is a comparatively happy one.

13. PRACTICES AND INSTITUTIONS INSURING THE PHYSICAL AND MORAL WELFARE OF THE FAMILY.

The family described in this monograph is assured of a certain degree of well-being, because of the remarkably good qualities which our workman possesses. However, these traits are not those which, under a régime of industrial liberty, would enable him to rise to the position of employer. Although being, as we have seen, in sufficiently easy circumstances to lay aside a part of his income without curtailing necessary expenses, he shows no tendency to save. From this very lack of foresight one must conclude that he feels himself destined to remain always in the position of workman, and that he never thinks of attaining a more secure or more independent position.

For fourteen years he has been a member of the Type-setters' Mutual Aid Society, which, in return for a monthly due of 1.50 fr., assures to its members, in case of sickness, pecuniary aid, medicine, and medical attendance. He is also a member of another society, which has the double aim of maintaining salaries and of providing assistance in case of enforced idleness. These societies can give relief in emergencies, and can assure the peace of mind on the part of the workman necessary for prosecuting studies on social economy. However, they ought not to release him from the efforts that a higher degree of foresight would demand; for the family would be left without resources, were it to lose its head.

Since the abolition of the old manufacturing corporations, which crowded into the cities, workmen are often forced to face a condition of destitution. Even those who honestly perform the duties of their position are never free from danger unless they submit rigorously to the privations which foresight demands. The causes of the great change which has come about in this respect, in the position of the working classes, are often pointed out in this work. For Belgium a summary is to be found farther on.

The history of our workman, given in the present monograph, proves the accuracy of this picture. Born of a family of artisans who had reached a position of well-being through their work, but were suddenly ruined by the Revolution of 1830, he found himself from early childhood in a condition of total destitution. Endowed with excellent qualities, which would permit him to occupy an honorable position in the bourgeois class, he has no inclination whatever to provide for the future. He spends his entire salary in obtaining material comforts for himself and his family, together with mental and moral recreations. It is true that, in the present state of urban communities, the ruin of the father's business does not always bring ruin to the rising generation, as happened in the family here described; but it brings the loss of an assured future. This lack of security is especially striking in the social constitution of Belgium, and in the other countries which are continually upset by the compulsory division of estates. This hard servitude imposed by the law and perpetuated by the apparent interest of the state treasury, and by the interested zeal of numerous public officers in each generation, destroys the homes and shops created by the work and fortitude of heads of families. In this incessant work of destruction, that which has remained for a time, thanks to the wisdom of individuals, is soon destroyed by the universal subjection of the family.

14. BUDGET OF ANNUAL RECEIPTS.

Sources of Income.	Approximate Value of Various Assets. Value of Property.	Receipts.	Amount of Receipts. Value of Goods Received in Kind.	Receipts in Money.
	Francs.		*Francs.*	*Francs.*
Section I. **Property Owned by the Family.**		**Section I.** **Revenues from Property.**		
1. Real estate. (The family owns no property of this nature.)		1. Revenue from real estate. (The family enjoys no revenue from this source.)		
2. Personal property. Special working equipment Equipment required in type-setting and proofreading....	66.00	2. Revenue from personal property. Interest (5 per cent.) on the value of the working equipment.	3.30	..
Money: Deposited in Savings Bank......	51.71	Interest (3 per cent.) on money deposited in Savings Bank	..	1.55
3. Insurance. Mutual Benefit Society, 300 members; capital, 7000 fr.; share....	23.33	3. Insurance. Value of the claim, equal to the annual contribution........24.50 fr.	..	..
Society for insurance against unemployment, 300 members; capital, 10,000 fr.; share....	33.33	Value of the claim, equal to the annual contribution..... 8.00 fr.	..	..
		(As these amounts balance equal sums expended by the family, both are omitted.)		
Total value of property....	174.37	Total revenue from property....	3.30	1.55
Section II. **Subsidiary Contributions to Real Income.**		**Section II.** **Proceeds of Value of Subsidiary Contributions.**		
1. Property received in usufruct. (The family receives no property in usufruct.)		1. Proceeds from property received in usufruct. (The family receives no income from this source.)		
2. The right to use neighboring property. (The family enjoys no privileges of this nature.)		2. Benefits from right to use neighboring property. (The family receives no benefits of this nature.)		
3. Grants of goods and of service. Provision for education....		3. Goods and services granted. Free instruction for the children in the city school....	116.00	..
		Free attendance at the Academy of Fine Arts, for the oldest boy....	15.00	..
		Total profits from subsidiary contributions	131.00	..

	SOURCES OF INCOME (continued).						RECEIPTS (continued).		
	QUANTITY OF WORK DONE.			AMOUNT OF DAILY WAGES.				AMOUNT OF RECEIPTS.	
DESCRIPTION OF WORK AND TIME EMPLOYED.	Father.	Mother.	Oldest Boy.	Father.	Mother.	Oldest Boy.	SECTION III. Wages.	Value of Goods in Kind.	Receipts in Money.
	Days.	*Days.*	*Days.*	*Francs.*	*Francs.*	*Francs*		*Francs.*	*Francs.*
SECTION III. **Work Done by the Family.** Work done by the day for employer:									
Regular work; type-setting (11 hour day)	333.3	..	..	4.50	..	..	Total wages, according to the number of days' work	..	1499.85
Extra work: proofreading and writing	23.1	..	..	4.50	..	..	Total wages for this work....	..	103.95
Apprentice work by the month (10.00 fr.) for employer	..	..	90	..	..	0.33	Total wages for this work....	..	30.00
Housework; purchase and preparation of food; care of the children; care of the dwelling	..	220	..	..	..	..	(Wages cannot be calculated.)		
Making and mending the family clothing and household linen	..	50	..	..	1.10	..	Total wages that an employe would receive for performing the same work.....	55.00	..
Washing clothing and linen	..	43	..	..	1.00	..	Total wages that an employe would receive.....	43.00	..
Total days employed	356.4	313	90	..	..	..	Total earnings of family....	98.00	1,633.80

SECTION IV.
Industries Undertaken by the Family.
(On their own account.)

Employment connected with the typographical work performed for employer.....

Supervisory work in the composition room.....

SECTION IV.
Profits from Family Industries.

	Average Daily Wage.
	Francs.
Average wage of ordinary type-setter, in 333.3 days	4.50
Additional wage allowed for this work	0.50
Average daily wage	5.00

Independent enterprises of the family

		Value of Goods in Kind.	Receipts in Money.
Proofreading and bookkeeping (16 A)	Returns yielded by this work ...	..	166.55
Making of clothing and household linen (16 B)	Expense avoided by this work....	70.50	61.55
Washing and mending of linen (16 C)	Expense avoided by this work....	58.25	..
	Total quasi-returns from these industries.....	128.75	228.20

NOTE.—Besides the receipts shown in the above account, the industries yield a profit of 60.06 fr., which is reinvested in the same enterprises. This amount. and the expenditures which balance it, have been omitted from both budgets.

	Value of Goods in Kind.	Receipts in Money.
Total receipts for the year (balancing the expenditures) . (2224.60 fr.)	361.05	1863.55

15. BUDGET OF ANNUAL EXPENDITURES.

Expenditures for Commodities and Services.	Quantity and Cost of Food Materials.		Amounts Expended.	
	Quantities Consumed.	Cost per Kilogram.	Value of Materials Consumed in Kind.	Expenditures in Money.
Section I. *Expenditures for Food.* I. Food consumed at home. (By the workman, his wife, and their four children, during 365 days.)	*Kilograms.*	*Francs.*	*Francs.*	*Francs.*
Cereals:				
Bread, loaves of 1 k., first quality (white bread)...........................	836.0	0.390	..	326.04
Rolls, for soup, weighing 0.120 k. each, and costing 0.05 fr., 100...................	12.0	0.417	..	5.00
Fancy rolls, for special celebrations, weighing 0.100 k. each, and costing 0.05 fr., 50.	5.0	0.500	..	2.50
Wheat flour, first quality, for cooking and pastry..............................	12.0	0.700	..	8.40
Rice, for soup and various dishes.........	12.0	1.000	..	12.00
Vermicelli and semolina.................	8.0	0.960	..	7.68
Macaroni	5.0	0.960	..	4.80
Total quantity and average cost......	890.0	0.412		
Fats:				
Butter for cooking.......................	54.8	3.000	..	164.40
Beef and pork tallow, extracted at home, used for cooking......................	2.0	2.000	..	4.00
Total quantity and average cost......	56.8	2.965		
Milk-foods and eggs:				
Skim milk for coffee and porridge........	10.0	0.250	..	2.50
White cheese...........................	26.0	0.400	..	10.40
Brussels cheese, called *Letekecs*...........	11.0	2.000	..	22.00
Holland cheese.........................	10.0	2.160	..	21.60
Eggs, used for various dishes, 380 @ 0.06 fr.	22.0	1.036	..	22.80
Total quantity and average cost......	79.0	1.004		
Meats and fish:				
Beef, 52 k. @ 1.20 fr. (deducting 1 k. for fat)	52.0	1.200	..	62.40
Veal....................................	56.0	1.200	..	67.20
Pork, 6 k. @ 1.80 fr. (deducting 1 k. for fat)	16.0	2.025	..	32.40
Poultry: 6 chickens.....................	6.0	1.500	..	9.00
Game: 12 rabbits........................	18.0	1.000	..	18.00
Fish: stockfish, cod, eel, and herring.......	26.0	0.800	..	20.80
Total quantity and average cost......	174.0	1.206		

EXPENDITURES FOR COMMODITIES AND SERVICES.	QUANTITY AND COST OF FOOD MATERIALS.		AMOUNTS EXPENDED.	
	Quantities Consumed.	Cost per Kilogram.	Value of Materials Consumed in Kind.	Expenditures in Money.
	Kilograms.	*Francs.*	*Francs.*	*Francs.*
Vegetables and fruits:				
Potatoes, white and sweet................	400.0	0.100	..	40.00
Dried vegetables: white beans............	10.0	0.500	..	5.00
Fresh vegetables for cooking: French beans, 12 k. @ 0.450 fr., 5.40 fr.; green peas, 20 k. @ 0.480 fr., 9.60 fr.; cauliflower, 5 k. @ 0.400 fr., 2.00 fr.; red cabbage and kale 30 k. @ 0.150 fr., 4.50 fr.; asparagus, 6 k. @ 0.400 fr., 2.40 fr.; chicory, 5 k. @ 0.150 fr., 4.50 fr.; sorrel, 1 k. @ 0.200 fr., 0.20 fr..................................	79.0	0.315	..	24.85
Root vegetables: carrots, 30 k. @ 0.350 fr., 10.50 fr.; beets, 6 k. @ 0.360 fr., 2.16 fr.; turnips, 4.50 k. @ 0.250 fr., 1.12 fr.; salsify, 1 k. @ 0.240 fr., 0.24 fr.........	41.5	0.337	..	14.02
Savory vegetables: onions, 25 k. @ 0.400 fr., 10.00 fr.; shallot, 1 k. @ 1.050 fr., 1.05 fr.	26.0	0.425	..	11.05
Salad vegetables.........................	51.0	0.380	..	19.38
Cucumbers: gherkins	0.5	1.000	..	0.50
Fruits: cherries, 18 k. @ 0.220 fr., 3.96 fr.; apples, used chiefly for apple stew, 130 k. @ 0.440 fr., 57.07 fr.; pears, 26 k.@ 0.600 fr., 15.60 fr.; strawberries, 4.4 k. @ 0.700 fr., 3.08 fr.; currants, 1.5 k. @ 0.750 fr., 1.12 fr.; peaches and apricots, 2 k. @ 2.90 fr., 5.80 fr.; nuts, 9 k. @ 0.300 fr., 2.70 fr.; raisins, from own grape-vines, 5.5 k. @ 1.00 fr., 5.50 fr......	196.4	0.483	..	94.83
Total quantity and average cost......	804.4	0.261		
Condiments and beverages:				
White salt..............................	20.0	0.300	..	6.00
Pepper, cloves and nutmeg...............	0.9	2.000	..	1.80
Vinegar for salad and cooking............	20.0	0.200	..	4.00
Sugars: white, 20 k.@ 1.50 fr., 30.00 fr.; syrup, 9 k. @ 1.18 fr., 10.62 fr.........	29.0	1.400	..	40.62
Aromatic drinks: coffee, purchased in the bean, roasted, not ground, 21 k. @ 2.75 fr., 57.75 fr.; chicory, 8 k. @ 0.35 fr., 2.80 fr..................................	29.0	2.088	..	60.55
Total quantity and average cost......	98.9	1.142		

EXPENDITURES FOR COMMODITIES AND SERVICES.	QUANTITY AND COST OF FOOD MATERIALS.		AMOUNTS EXPENDED.	
	Quantities Consumed.	Cost per Kilogram.	Value of Materials Consumed in Kind.	Expenditures in Money.
	Kilograms.	Francs.	Francs.	Francs.
Fermented drinks:				
Beer (Faro) purchased by the litre..........	25.0	0.240	..	6.00
Wine...................................	1.0	1.000	..	1.00
Total quantity and average cost......	26.0	0.270		
II. Food prepared and eaten away from home.				
Meals taken occasionally at restaurants by the workman and his family				21.00
Drinks: Beer, especially for the father......	..	..	..	22.84
Total expenditure for food...........	..	..	..	1197.36

EXPENDITURES FOR COMMODITIES AND SERVICES.	AMOUNTS EXPENDED.	
	Value of Materials Consumed in Kind.	Expenditures in Money.
SECTION II. *Expenditures for Housing.*	Francs.	Francs.
Dwelling house:		
Rent of the house occupied by the family (18.00 fr. per month), with deduction of the value of the raisins produced by a vine (15, Section I).....................	..	210.50
Repairs and maintenance...........................	..	18.00
Furniture:		
Maintenance, and mending of chairs.................	..	10.00
Fuel:		
Pit coal, 2000 k. @ 24 fr. per 1000 k.	..	48.00
Charcoal and wood................................	..	8.00
Light:		
Candles, 24 k. @ 1.66 fr., 39.84 fr.; oil, 4 lit. @ 1.05 fr., 4.20 fr.; night-lights, 3 boxes @ 0.18 fr., 0.54 fr.; matches, 26 boxes @ 0.05 fr., 1.30 fr.; large matches, 1.50 fr...	..	47.38
Total expenditure for housing....................		341.88

EXPENDITURES FOR COMMODITIES AND SERVICES.	AMOUNTS EXPENDED.	
	Value of Materials Consumed in Kind.	Expenditures in Money.
	Francs.	*Francs.*

SECTION III.

Expenditures for Clothing.

Clothing:

Of the father; cost of materials purchased and home-labor (16 E) .... **20.00** | **62.25**

Of the mother; cost of materials purchased and home-labor (16 E) .... **..** | **..**

Of the children; cost of materials purchased and home-labor (16 E) .... **..** | **..**

Repair of household linen and clothing (16 B)........ **8.50** | **0.25**

Washing:

Washing of household linen and clothing (16 C)........ **101.25** | **49.50**

Total expenditure for clothing.................... **226.75** | **214.00**

SECTION IV.

Expenditures for Education, for Recreation, and for Health.

Religion:

Annual expenses: sittings in church.................... **..** | **5.12**

Education of the children:

School expenses paid by the city, 116.00 fr.; free attendance in the courses of the Academy of Fine Arts for the oldest boy, for 3 months at 5.00 fr. per month, 15.00 fr.; books, stationery, pens, pencils, ink, 12.50 fr.. **131.00** | **12.50**

For charitable assistance:

Relief to fellow-workmen, or to their widows and orphans, various contributions, 8.00 fr.; subscription to the Mutual Benefit Society, for the widows and orphans of deceased members, 4.50 fr. (See Sec. V).. **..** | **8.00**

Recreation:

Dinner given by the workman on his patron saint's day, 28.00 fr.; annual banquet of the Association, 5.50 fr.; expenses for excursions, 10.00 fr.; theatre, 6.00 fr.; tobacco and cigars for the workman, 12.60 fr.; binding of books, 9.09 fr................................. **..** | **71.19**

Health:

Services of physician, 8.00 fr.; medicine, 5.50 fr.; subscription to Mutual Benefit Society, contributions and assessments, 20.00 fr (See Section V)............... **..** | **13.50**

Total expenditure for culture, recreation, and health. **131.00** | **110.31**

348

EXPENDITURES FOR COMMODITIES AND SERVICES.	AMOUNTS EXPENDED.	
	Value of Materials Consumed in Kind.	Expenditures in Money.
	Francs.	*Francs.*
SECTION V.		
Expenditures for the Family Industries, for Interest on Debts, for Taxes, and Insurance.		
For industries:		
Interest on the value of the type-setter's working equipment..	3.30	..
NOTE.—The other expenses connected with the industries amount to.............................262.01 fr.	..	..
They are offset by the returns from these industries:		
Namely, money and materials used for household needs, or considered as part of the savings and placed under that title in the present budget............201.95 fr.		
Money reinvested in the industries (14, Section IV), which cannot, therefore, figure among the household expenses....... 60.06 fr. 262.01 fr.		
Interest on debts:		
(The family has no debts, nor any goods in pawn.)		
Taxes:		
(The family pays no direct tax.)		
Insurance, to safeguard the physical and moral welfare of the family:		
Contribution of the workman to the Typographers' Mutual Benefit Society, 12 months at 1.50 fr., 18.00 fr.; fines for absence from meetings, 2.00 fr.; contribution for relief of widows of deceased members, 4.50 fr. (These expenditures, and the receipts which balance them, are omitted from the budget.)	..	..
Contribution of the workman to the association for the maintenance of wages, 12 months @ 0.50 fr., 6.00 fr.; fines for absence from meetings, o. (Expenditures omitted, as are receipts which balance them.)		
Total expenditures for industries, for interest on debts, for taxes and insurance.............................	3.30	..
Annual savings:		
The family accumulated no savings; all earnings went to promote their present well-being.		
Total annual expenditure (balancing the income) (2,224.60 fr.)	..	..
	361.05	1863.55

16. ACCOUNTS APPENDED TO THE BUDGET.

	Value.	
	In Kind.	In Money.
I. ACCOUNT OF EARNINGS FROM WORK CARRIED ON BY THE FAMILY ON ITS OWN ACCOUNT.	*Francs.*	*Francs.*
A. CORRECTION OF PROOF.		
Receipts.		
Compensation paid by employer....................	..	171.06
Expenditures.		
Candles, 2.3 kilo at 1.66 fr...........................	..	3.81
Paper, pens, and ink................................	..	1.75
Labor of man, 23.1 days, at 4.50 fr..................	..	103.95
Profits from the industry...........................	..	61.55
Total	..	171.06
B. MAKING AND REPAIRING GARMENTS OF THE FAMILY.		
Receipts.		
Amount that would be paid for these purposes.........	125.50	5.00
Expenditures.		
Cost of cloth and sewing materials..................	..	5.00
Labor of mother, 50 days at 1.10 fr..................	55.00	..
Quasi-gain resulting from this work................	70.50	..
Total.....................................	125.50	5.00
C. WASHING. *Receipts.*		
Amount that would be paid for this purpose.........	101.25	49.50
Expenditures.		
Soft soap, 24.96 fr.; hard soap, 6.00 fr.; bluing, 10.40 fr...	..	..
Starch, 1.30 fr.; sal-soda, when rain-water is lacking, 3.84 fr...	..	46.50
Coal for ironing....................................	..	3.00
Labor of woman, 43 days at 1.00 fr..................	43.00	..
Quasi-gain resulting from this work................	58.25	..
	101.25	49.50
D. SUMMARY OF THE ABOVE (A-C).		
Total Receipts.		
Labor and materials used upon clothing [including washing].......................................	226.75	54.50
Money received and expended in connection with operation..	..	60.06
Money received and applied to family expenditures..	..	111.00
Total...	226.75	225.56

	VALUE.	
	In Kind.	In Money.
Total Expenditures.	*Francs.*	*Francs.*
Wages chargeable to these operations...............	98.00	103.95
Money expenditures requiring reimbursement from the profits of these industries.....................	..	60.06
Total expenditures ....(262.01 fr.)	98.00	164.01
Total gain resulting from supplementary activities...............................(190.30 fr.)	128.75	61.55
	226.75	225.56

II. ACCOUNT OF SUBSIDIARY CONTRIBUTIONS TO REAL INCOME.
(Omitted for this family because included in the budget itself.)

	PURCHASE PRICE.		
III. SUNDRY ACCOUNTS.	*Francs.*		
E. ACCOUNT OF ANNUAL EXPENDITURES FOR CLOTHING.			
1. *Clothing of Man.*			
Sunday-clothes:			
1 blue overcoat, velvet collar........	68.00	..	4.00
1 black coat.......................	40.00	..	4.00
1 waistcoat, black satin.............	12.00	..	2.00
1 pair black pantaloons.............	20.00	..	2.00
1 silk hat..........................	13.50	..	1.50
1 scarf, black satin.................	10.00	..	1.00
1 pair boots.......................	16.00	..	8.00
Working-clothes (some worn on Sunday, while new):			
1 winter-overcoat, green cloth.......	66.00	..	3.00
1 black coat.......................	30.00	..	2.00
1 pair pantaloons, woolen..........	13.50	2.50	2.00
1 pair pantaloons, cotton...........	6.00	2.00	1.00
2 woolen jackets	9.00	1.50	3.00
2 work-blouses, blue...............	10.50	1.50	2.00
6 shirts, white cotton (including 2 fine shirts)......................	22.50	6.00	3.00
3 cravats, cotton and woolen........	2.00	1.50	0.50
1 cravat, black merino.............	3.00	0.50	0.50
2 pair drawers, cotton.............	4.50	1.00	2.00
2 undershirts, cotton...............	5.00	1.00	1.50
4 pair stockings, cotton............	6.00	1.50	1.50
2 pair stockings, woolen............	4.50	1.00	2.00
1 pair slippers.....................	5.50	..	5.50
1 pair boots, often repaired.........	15.00	..	7.50
1 cap..............................	2.75	..	2.75
Total......................	385.25	20.00	62.25

	PURCHASE PRICE.	VALUE.	
		In Kind.	In Money.
2. *Clothing of Woman.*	*Francs.*	*Francs.*	*Francs.*
Sunday-clothes:			
1 dress, brown woolen.............	20.00	1.00	1.50
1 shawl, woolen....................	18.00	..	3.00
1 skirt, muslin.....................	10.50	1.50	2.00
1 waist, black silk.................	10.50	1.00	2.50
1 apron, black silk.................	6.00	0.50	0.50
1 cloak, black silk.................	12.25	0.50	1.25
1 bonnet, trimmed.................	6.00	..	3.00
1 skirt, dimity.....................	5.00	1.00	1.50
3 chemisettes, embroidered.........	6.00	1.50	1.50
6 handkerchiefs, Scotch linen.......	5.00	0.50	0.50
3 pair stockings, cotton............	6.00	1.00	1.00
2 pair undersleeves, embroidered muslin.........................	5.00	0.50	0.50
1 pair shoes......................	5.00	..	2.50
Working-clothes:			
1 skirt, cotton and wool mixture....	9.00	1.50	3.00
1 skirt, black merino..............	9.00	0.50	1.00
2 jackets, colored cotton...........	6.00	0.50	2.50
1 wrapper, cotton.................	5.00	0.25	0.75
2 aprons, cotton...................	4.00	0.50	1.50
1 apron, blue stuff................	2.50	1.00	1.50
1 bonnet, white tulle, silk ribbons...	5.00	2.00	3.00
4 caps, white cotton, trimmed with lace............................	6.00	1.75	2.25
6 chemises, cotton.................	18.00	3.00	3.00
Handkerchiefs, gloves and stockings	17.50	2.50	6.25
Foot-wear, 1 pair shoes, 1 pair slippers..........................	9.00	..	4.50
Total.....................	206.25	22.50	50.50
3. *Clothing of Children.*			
Clothing for Sunday and working-days....		74.50	51.50

Following the details of the budget are descriptions of institutions and discussions of the family-type represented by the given family. In the present instance the titles of the remaining sections, grouped under the general head "Elements of the Social Constitution," are as follows:

17. Successive stages of stability and instability (of the family relation) in Belgium.

18. Mutual benefit societies of the typographers of Brussels.

19. Increase of wages of type-setters in 1857.

20. Banquets or annual reunions of typographers.

APPENDIX VIII

Partial Bibliography of Works on the Standard of Living

By ROBERT C. CHAPIN, PH.D.

This bibliography is not exhaustive, and includes only general works on the standard of living and workingmen's budgets

I. BIBLIOGRAPHY AND CRITICISM

Bauer, Stephan: Article "Konsumtionsbudget" in Conrad's Handwörterbuch der Staatswissenschaften. (II. Auflage, V: 316–333.)

A succinct critical account of the methods and results of the successive attempts to study workingmen's budgets, with bibliographical references.

Bücher, Karl: Haushaltungsrechnungen oder Wirtschaftsrechnungen. Zeitschrift für die gesamte Staatswissenschaft. 1906. S. 686, ff.

Introduces a ten-years' household account.

Cheysson et Toqué: Les Budgets Compares des cent Monographies de Families. Bulletin de l'Institut Internationale de Statistique, VI, p. I (1891).

Contains a description and defense of Le Play's method, a bibliography, and a synopsis of 100 budgets gathered by Le Play and members of his school.

Engel, Ernst: Lebenskosten Belgischer Arbeiterfamilien. Bulletin de l'Institut Internationale de Statistique, IX: (1895) p. l.

Engel discusses in the opening sections the problem of method in the light of his own labors of 40 years. His proposed "quet" is here described.

Higgs, Henry: Workingmen's Budgets. Journal of the Royal Statistical Society, 1893; pp. 255–285.

Contains, besides the discussion of method, specimen budgets extracted from Davies, Eden, Le Play and more recent sources.

Landolt, Carl (Karl): Directions Sur la Manière de dresser les Budgets d'Ouvriers Industrielles et d'Artisans. Bulletin de l'Institut Internationale de Statistique, VI: 289 ff. (1891). Bibliographie, pp. 301–304.

A severe critic of Le Play and an advocate of the account-book method.

Landolt, Karl: Mode und Technik der Haushaltsstatistik. Freiburg, 1894.

Le Play, Frédéric: La Methode Sociale. Les Ouvriers Européens. Vol. I, of the definitive edition. Paris, 1879.

Contains Le Play's charming description of his own purpose and method.

Lexis, Wilhelm: Die Haushaltungsbudget. In Schönberg's Handbuch der Politischen Oekonomie, I, 814–816.

Mayo-Smith, Richmond: Statistics and Economics, Chapter II. New York, 1897.

Discusses methods and sociological significance of statistics of family consumption, with bibliographical note.

Price, L. L.: Article "Comfort, Standard of," in Palgrave's Dictionary of Political Economy. I, 387. London, 1890.

Traces briefly the discussion of the standard of comfort by the British economists.

United States Bureau of Labor: Third Special Report. (Revised, 1902.) Index of reports issued by Bureaus of Labor Statistics in the United States.

Contains references to all investigations into cost of living carried on by the state labor bureaus down to 1902.

2. ESTIMATES AND INVESTIGATIONS PRIOR TO THE NINETEENTH CENTURY

Petty, Sir William: Political Arithmetic, Chapter VII. Written 1671–76, published 1690.
Political Anatomy of Ireland, Chapter XI. Written 1672, published 1691.

Vanderlint, Jacob: Money Answers All Things. 1734.
Inquiry into the Melancholy Circumstances of Great Britain, circa 1735; p. 29.

Thierry: Monuments inedits de l'Histoire du Tiers Etat. I. Series T. IV, p. 545. (Contains budget of a weaver of Abbeville, 1764.)

Smith, Adam: Wealth of Nations. 1776.

Part I, Chapter VIII, contains an exposition of the advantage to the community of a rising standard of living among the laboring classes.

Davies, David : The Case of the Laborers in Husbandry, stated and considered in three parts. Part I: A view of their distressed condition. Part II: The principal causes of their growing distress and number and of the consequent increase of the poor-rate. Part III: Means of relief proposed, with an appendix containing a collection of accounts, showing the earnings and expenses of labouring families, in different parts of the kingdom. Bath and London, 1795.

Eden, Sir Frederick Morton : The State of the Poor. Three volumes, London, 1797.

Fifty-four family budgets are grouped in the appendix (Vol. III), but others are scattered through the text of Volumes II and III.

References to other eighteenth-century estimates are appended to the article of Bauer, already referred to.

3. WORKS OF MORE RECENT TIMES

Berlin : Statistisches Jahrbuch der Stadt Berlin.

Successive volumes contain synopses of budget-investigations as follows:
    1879. Jahrgang 7; S. 137.   15 budgets, secured by schedule-inquiry.
    1880. Jahrgang 8; S. 164.   2 budgets, from account-books.
    1901. Jahrgang 27; S. 269.   142 budgets, from schedule-inquiry.
    1903. Jahrgang 28; S. 200.   908 budgets, from schedule-inquiry.
The detailed report of the last investigation was published separately under the title which follows:

Berliner Statistik : Heft 3. Lohnermittlungen und Haushaltungsrechnungen der minder bemittelten Bevölkerung im Jahre 1903. Statistisches Amt der Stadt Berlin, 1904.

Blanqui, A. J. : Les Classes Ouvrières en France pendant l'année 1848, p. 736. (Budget of a family in Lille.)

Booth, Charles : Life and Labor of the People in London. London, 1889–1892.

Vol. I, Part V and VI. Vol. IX, Part III, Chapter 13. The budgets of 30 families are given in Vol. I, pp. 136–139.

Bosanquet, Mrs. Bernard : (Helen Dandy.) The Standard of Life and other Studies. London, 1898.

A discussion of the conception of the standard of living and its relation to wages.

Devine, Edward T.: Principles of Relief. New York, 1905. Chapter III, The Standard of Living.

Ducpétiaux, Edouard: Budgets Économiques des Classes Ouvrières en Belgique. Bulletin de la Commission Centrale de la Statistique (Belgium), Vol. VI (1855): 261–440.

Economic Club, London: Family Budgets: Being the Income and Expenses of Twenty-eight British Households, 1891–94. London, 1896.

Charles Booth, Ernest Aves, Henry Higgs, were the committee of the Club in charge of the inquiry.

Emminghaus: Zum Kapital der Haushaltskosten. Jahrbücher für National-ökonomie und Statistik, Nov., 1904, S. 650–661.

The household accounts of a German official covering the period 1862–1903.

Engel, Ernst: Productions-und Konsumtionsverhältnisse des Königreichs Sachsen. Zeitschrift des Statistischen Bureaus des Königlichen Sächsischen Ministeriums des Innern, 1857, S. 153 ff. (Reprinted also in the Bulletin de l'Institut Internationale de Statistique, Vol. IX. 1895.)

This is the epoch-making work of Engel, who continued to work upon the general subject until his death in 1896. The titles of his contributions to the statistical journals may be found in detail in the German bibliographies. The "Lebenskosten" contains the summing up of his life-work in this field. The three shorter books named below are among the most significant of his minor works.

Engel, Ernst: Lebenskosten Belgischer Arbeiterfamilien. Bulletin de l'Institut Internationale de Statistique, IX: (1895) p. I.
Der Preis der Arbeit. Berlin, 1866.
Das Rechnungsbuch der Hausfrau. Berlin, 1882.
Der Werth des Menschen. Berlin, 1883.

Forman, S. E.: Conditions of Living Among the Poor. Bulletin of the United States Bureau of Labor, No. 64, May, 1906.

Expenditures in detail for 5 weeks for 19 families in the District of Columbia.

Cost of Industrial Insurance in the District of Columbia. Bulletin No. 67, United States Bureau of Labor, Nov., 1906.

Gerloff, Wilhelm: Verbrauch und Verbrauchsbelastung kleiner und mittlerer Einkommen in Deutschland. Jahrbücher für National-ökonomie und Statistik, 3te Folge, Band 35, S. 1 und 145.

A study of the tendency of indirect taxes to bear most heavily on families with small incomes. Recent German studies of family budgets are cited, in addition to the Berlin inquiry of 1904, as follows:
Berichte der bayrischen Fabrik-und Gewerbeinspektoren, 1900–1905.

Haushaltungsrechnungen Nürnberger Lohnarbeiter. Arbeitersekretariat Nurnberg, 1901.

Haushaltungsrechnungen. Hamburgischer Volksschullehrer, Hamburg, 1906.

Der Haushalt der Postassistenten. Deutsche Postzeitung, 1903.

Fuchs. Die Verhältnisse der Industriearbeiter in 17 Landgemeinden bei Karlsruhe, 1904.

Fuchs. Sociale Lage der Pforzheimer Bijouteriearbeiter. Karlsruhe, 1901.

Haushaltungsrechnungen zweier Fabrikarbeiter. J. H. Salomon, Altona, 1906.

Abelsdorf. Beiträge zur Socialstatistik deutscher Buchdrucker, 1897.

Feuerstein. Lohn und Haushalt der Uhrenfabrikarbeiter der bädischen Schwarzwald, 1905.

Enquete zur Verbreitung der Kunftigen Handelsverträge von der Schweizerischen Bauernsekretariat, 1902.

Goodyear, Caroline: Household Budgets of the Poor. "Charities and the Commons," May 5, 1906, pp. 191-197.

Gould, E. R. L.: Social Condition of Labor. Johns Hopkins University Studies, vol. xi, No. 1. Baltimore, 1893.

A comparison of family budgets of workers in coal, iron, and steel in the United States and in Europe, based on the sixth and seventh annual reports of the United States Bureau of Labor.

Great Britain, Board of Trade: British and Foreign Trade and Industry, 1903, Series 1. 209–258. Consumption of Food and Cost of Living. (Cd. 1761.)

Contains (1) estimates regarding quantity and cost of food for a typical family; (2) itemized returns of expenditures for food from 286 urban families.

Great Britain Board of Trade: Memoranda on British and foreign trade and industrial conditions, 1904, Series 2. (Cd. 2337.)

Embraces deductions from reports received from 1800 families with reference to weekly expenditure for food and for housing together with calculations of the variations in cost of all the principal items of household expenditures since 1880.

Great Britain, Board of Trade: Cost of Living of the Working Classes. Report of an enquiry into working-class rents, housing, and retail prices, with the standard rates of wages in the principal industrial towns of the United Kingdom. London, 1908. (Cd. 3864.)

Compares by index-numbers rents in 89 towns with rents in London, with data regarding cost of food and fuel.

Great Britain, Board of Trade: Cost of Living in German Towns. London, 1908. (Cd. 4032.)

A comparison of housing and retail prices of food and fuel in 33 German towns with conditions in the United Kingdom. The total number of family reports obtained is 5,046.

Herzfeld, Elsa G. : Family Monographs, New York, 1905.

Twenty-four families on the West Side of New York City are studied, primarily from the sociological rather than the economic point of view.

Hirschberg, E. : Die Sociale Lage der arbeitenden Klassen in Berlin, 1896. (13 budgets.)

Knauer : Budgets Ouvriers en Frankfort, 1890.

Landolt, Karl : Dix Menages Ouvriers Balois, 1891.

The two foregoing exemplify the account-book method.

Le Play, Frédéric : Les Ouvriers Européens. Paris, 1855–1879.

Contains in 5 volumes monographs descriptive of 57 families, in many countries· The work of Le Play is the authoritative exemplification of the intensive method. His followers continued the series in ten volumes of additional monographs, entitled, "Les Ouvriers des Deux Mondes."

More, Louise Bolard : Wage-Earners' Budgets. A Study of Standards and Cost of Living in New York City. New York, 1907.

A study of 200 family budgets, obtained in the South-western section of New York.

Patten, S. N. : The New Basis of Civilization. New York, 1907.

A suggestive interpretation of the meaning of an ample standard of living in its effect upon the welfare of mankind.

Pelloutier, Fernand et Maurice : La Vie Ouvrière en France. Paris, 1900.

Chapter VI contains ten representative budgets.

Richards, Ellen H. : The Cost of Living. New York, 1899.

Suggestions as to economy in expenditures, especially for families with incomes between $1500 and $2500.

Rowntree, B. Seebohm : Poverty, a Study of Town Life. London, 1901.

A study of the city of York. Chapter III deals with the standard of life of various income-classes; Chapter VI with housing; Chapter VII with health; Chapter VIII contains analyses of 18 family budgets with discussion of dietary standard.

Ryan, John A. : A Living Wage; its Ethical and Economic Aspects. New York, 1906.

A vindication of the right to a living wage, with an estimate of its actual content.

Shadwell, Arthur : Industrial Efficiency; a Comparative Study of Industrial Life in England, Germany and America. London, 1906.

In Vol. II, Chapter XI treats of Housing; XII, of Cost of Living; XIII, of Social Conditions.

Sherwell and Million: Report of Edinburgh Charity Organization Society on the Physical Condition of Fourteen Hundred School Children. Edinburgh, 1906.

Reports of 1389 children from 781 families. Complete budgets of the families are not given, but interesting data as to habits, income, housing, etc., are included.

Wörishofer, F.: Die Sociale Lage der Fabrikarbeiter in Mannheim. Karlsruhe, 1891. Part VII includes a tabulation of 28 family budgets, and discussion of nutrition.

4. PUBLICATIONS OF THE NATIONAL AND STATE GOVERNMENTS IN THE UNITED STATES

United States Bureau of Labor: Sixth annual report, 1890. Cost of Production: Iron, Steel, Coal.

Compilation of returns from 3260 families in these industries, including 770 families in Europe, engaged in the same occupations.

Seventh annual report, 1891. Cost of Production: the Textiles and Glass (with returns from 5284 families).
Eighth Special report, 1895. The Housing of the Working People.
Ninth Special report, 1897. The Italians in Chicago.

Pages 44–50, food-expenditures of 742 families.

Eighteenth annual report, 1903. Cost of Living and Retail Prices of Food.

Returns from 25,440 families in all occupations in 33 states. The data regarding prices have been continued for each succeeding year in the Bulletins of the Department, Nos. 54, 59, 65, 71, 77.

United States Bureau of Labor Bulletins.

The movement of wages and prices, following the lines of the work done by the Bureau for the Aldrich Report, is given at intervals, covering the period from 1890 to 1907 inclusive, in Bulletins Nos. 59, 65, 71, 77. No. 53 contains a summary of the Eighteenth Annual Report of the Bureau on Cost of Living. Nos. 64 and 67 contain the studies of Mr. Forman, already referred to. Other investigations more or less germane to the standard of living may be found in the list of titles of leading articles for the whole series, printed at the end of each number of the Bulletin.

United States Bureau of Statistics: Industrial Education and Industrial Conditions in Germany. Special Consular Reports, Vol. 33, 1905, pp. 220–229. Cost of Living.

The budgets of five Prussian and five Saxon families.

United States Senate Reports: First Session, Fifty-Second Congress; Vol. VI (The "Aldrich Report").

Contains discussion and summary of twelve studies of family budgets in the United States (Part I, xl–lv), and details of 232 budgets collected for use in the weighing of averages to be used in the body of the report (Part II, 2040–2096).

Young, Edward : Labor in Europe and America. United States Bureau of Statistics, 1875.

Includes reports of family budgets designed to show differences in cost of living between Europe and America.

REPORTS OF STATE LABOR BUREAUS

The complete list of reports of the State Bureaus that contain material bearing upon our subject will be found in the index issued by the United States Bureau of Labor, already referred to (Third Special Report, revised 1902). Among the more valuable are the following, which are arranged by States and the dates of the year of publication:

Connecticut, 1885.
  1888, pp. 87–135.

Reports from 102 families made out by members of the family.

Illinois, 1884.
Iowa, 1884–85, pp. 246–259.

Budgets of School-teachers. 1888-89.

Kansas, 1886.
  1887.

Massachusetts, 1875.

The first investigation of family budgets published by Carroll D. Wright, including 397 families.

  1881.
  1884.
  1901, pp. 239–314.
  1904, pp. 81–130. The Cost of High Prices.

New Jersey, 1899.
  1900.

New York, 1892.

Maryland, 1906.

Ohio, 1893.

Wisconsin, 1885–86.

Washington, 1905–06.

Index

Index

363

pendix IV (p. 303); families reporting gifts, 163–164, Appendix II (pp. 275–276); estimate of clothing required and its cost, 165–167, Appendix II (pp. 275–276); under-clad families, 167–169, Diagrams 13–14 (pp. 167–168); expense for washing, 170–171, Appendix II (p. 275).—Tables 15–16, 79–90 (pp. 70–74, 172–181)

Colored families—
Sources of income, 59; housing and rent, 76, 77, 79, 81; fuel and light, 115; food-expenditure in relation to rent, 123; under-fed families among, 128; reliance on baker, 132; meals away from home, 132; clothing, 163, 168; carrying insurance, 191–194, Diagrams 15–16 (pp. 191–192); low expenditure for furniture, 200; taxes, dues, and contributions, 206, 207; reporting surplus and deficit, 230, 231; conclusions on standards of, 247. See also Tables under the various headings

Committee on Standard of Living—
Formation and membership of, vii, Appendix II (p. 263)

Compensation
Standards of, Appendix I (pp. 254, 255, 260–261)

Conclusions as to results of the New York City investigation, 245–250, Appendix II (p. 263 ff.)

Consuming-power. See Dietary requirements; Food-consumption; Unit of Consumption

Contributions. See Taxes, Dues, and Contributions

Cost of living—
Objects of inquiries into, vii, 3, 4, 5, 20–21, Appendices I (pp. 253–262), II (p. 263); investigations of, see Standard of Living Investigations

Cost of the New York investigation. See Expenses

Court suggested, to try new social crimes, Appendix I (p. 260)

"Culture-wants," 198

Davies, David—
Investigations by, 6, 7, 21; "Case of the Laborers in Husbandry," 6

Deficit. See Surplus and Deficit

Dentistry, 184, 245, Appendix II (pp. 276, 279).—Tables 94–95 (pp. 189–190). See also Health

Devine, Dr. Edward T.—
Member Committee on Standard of Living, vii, viii; note from Presidential address at National Conference, 1906, Appendix I (p. 253); estimate on cost of living, Appendix I (pp. 256–257)

Dietary requirements, 15, 15 (notes), 16, 16 (note), 18–19; Dr. Underhill's analysis of, Appendix VI (pp. 319–325). See also Food; Engel; Atwater; Underhill; U. S. Bureau of Labor, etc.

Difficulties of the investigation, 30–31; Appendix II (pp. 269–270)

Drescher, Wm.
Member Committee on Standard of Living, vii

Ducpétiaux, Edouard—
Belgian investigations conducted by, 9, 11, 12, 13; "Budgets Économiques," 11; his "normal family," 14

Dues. See Taxes, Dues and Contributions

Earnings, of father and others—
Amounts and relative proportions of, 54–60, Diagrams 4–5 (pp. 54, 56); relation of occupations to, 55–56; from lodgers, 58–59; source of, with respect to surplus and deficit, 231, Appendix II (p. 264); of families in Buffalo, Appendix V (p. 309).—Tables 3–6, 7–14, 121–123 (pp. 46–52, 61–67, 237–239). See also Income, sources of

Earp, Professor E. L., Appendix IV (p. 300, note)

24

POVERTY, U. S. A.

THE HISTORICAL RECORD

An Arno Press/New York Times Collection

Adams, Grace. **Workers on Relief.** 1939.

The Almshouse Experience: Collected Reports. 1821-1827.

Armstrong, Louise V. **We Too Are The People.** 1938.

Bloodworth, Jessie A. and Elizabeth J. Greenwood.
The Personal Side. 1939.

Brunner, Edmund de S. and Irving Lorge.
**Rural Trends in Depression Years: A Survey of
Village-Centered Agricultural Communities, 1930-1936.**
1937.

Calkins, Raymond.
**Substitutes for the Saloon: An Investigation Originally
made for The Committee of Fifty.** 1919.

Cavan, Ruth Shonle and Katherine Howland Ranck.
**The Family and the Depression: A Study of
One Hundred Chicago Families.** 1938.

Chapin, Robert Coit.
**The Standard of Living Among Workingmen's Families
in New York City.** 1909.

**The Charitable Impulse in Eighteenth Century America:
Collected Papers.** 1711-1797.

Children's Aid Society.
Children's Aid Society Annual Reports, 1-10.
February 1854-February 1863.

Conference on the Care of Dependent Children.
**Proceedings of the Conference on the Care
of Dependent Children.** 1909.

Conyngton, Mary.
How to Help: A Manual of Practical Charity. 1909.

Devine, Edward T. **Misery and its Causes.** 1909.

Devine, Edward T. **Principles of Relief.** 1904.

Dix, Dorothea L.
On Behalf of the Insane Poor: Selected Reports. 1843-1852.

Douglas, Paul H.
**Social Security in the United States: An Analysis and
Appraisal of the Federal Social Security Act.** 1936.

Farm Tenancy: Black and White. Two Reports. 1935, 1937.

Feder, Leah Hannah.
**Unemployment Relief in Periods of Depression:
A Study of Measures Adopted in Certain American
Cities, 1857 through 1922.** 1936.

Folks, Homer.
**The Care of Destitute, Neglected, and
Delinquent Children.** 1900.

Guardians of the Poor.
**A Compilation of the Poor Laws of the State of
Pennsylvania from the Year 1700 to 1788, Inclusive.** 1788.

Hart, Hastings, H.
Preventive Treatment of Neglected Children.
(Correction and Prevention, Vol. 4) 1910.

Herring, Harriet L.
**Welfare Work in Mill Villages: The Story of Extra-Mill
Activities in North Carolina.** 1929.

The Jacksonians on the Poor: Collected Pamphlets.
1822-1844.

Karpf, Maurice J.
Jewish Community Organization in the United States.
1938.

Kellor, Frances A.
Out of Work: A Study of Unemployment. 1915.

Kirkpatrick, Ellis Lore.
The Farmer's Standard of Living. 1929.

Komarovsky, Mirra.
The Unemployed Man and His Family: The Effect of Unemployment Upon the Status of the Man in Fifty-Nine Families. 1940.

Leupp, Francis E. **The Indian and His Problem.** 1910.

Lowell, Josephine Shaw.
Public Relief and Private Charity. 1884.

More, Louise Bolard.
Wage Earners' Budgets: A Study of Standards and Cost of Living in New York City. 1907.

New York Association for Improving the Condition of the Poor.
AICP First Annual Reports Investigating Poverty. 1845-1853.

O'Grady, John.
Catholic Charities in the United States: History and Problems. 1930.

Raper, Arthur F.
Preface to Peasantry: A Tale of Two Black Belt Counties. 1936.

Raper, Arthur F. **Tenants of The Almighty.** 1943.

Richmond, Mary E.
What is Social Case Work? An Introductory Description. 1922.

Riis, Jacob A. **The Children of the Poor.** 1892.

Rural Poor in the Great Depression: Three Studies. 1938.

Sedgwick, Theodore.
Public and Private Economy: Part I. 1836.

Smith, Reginald Heber. **Justice and the Poor.** 1919.

Sutherland, Edwin H. and Harvey J. Locke.
Twenty Thousand Homeless Men: A Study of Unemployed Men in the Chicago Shelters. 1936.

Tuckerman, Joseph.
On the Elevation of the Poor: A Selection From His Reports as Minister at Large in Boston. 1874.

Warner, Amos G. **American Charities.** 1894.

Watson, Frank Dekker.
The Charity Organization Movement in the United States: A Study in American Philanthropy. 1922.

Woods, Robert A., et al. **The Poor in Great Cities.** 1895.